FOR
THE SOUL
OF THE
PEOPLE

FOR
THE SOUL
OF THE
PEOPLE

*Prostestant Protest
Against Hitler*

Victoria Barnett

New York   Oxford
OXFORD UNIVERSITY PRESS
1992

Oxford University Press

Oxford   New York   Toronto
Delhi   Bombay   Calcutta   Madras   Karachi
Kuala Lumpur   Singapore   Hong Kong   Tokyo
Nairobi   Dar es Salaam   Cape Town
Melbourne   Auckland

and associated companies in
Berlin   Ibadan

Published by Oxford University Press, Inc.
200 Madison Avenue, New York, New York 10016

Oxford is a registered trademark of Oxford University Press

Library of Congress Cataloging–in–Publication Data
Barnett, Victoria.
For the soul of the people : Protestant protest against Hitler /
by Victoria Barnett.
p.   cm.   Includes bibliographical references and index.
ISBN   0–19–505306–0
1. Bekennende Kirche.   2. Church and state—Germany—
History—1933–1945.   3. Germany—Church history—1933–1945
I. Title.
BX4844.55.A4B37   1992   280'.4'094309043—dc20   91–31024

1 3 5 7 9 8 6 4 2

Printed in the United States of America
on acid-free paper

For Ruth McGinnis,
and for Ulrich
sine qua non

Acknowledgments

PORTIONS OF THIS BOOK originally appeared in a slightly different form in *Christianity and Crisis, The Christian Century, The Witness,* and the news bulletins of Religious News Service.

During my work on this book, I have been fortunate to recieve encouragement and support from a number of people. To some individuals, I would like to express particularly deep thanks: to Gerald Renner and Gerry Fitzgerald, both of whom were formerly at Religious News Service and who showed interest in the early stages of this book; Daniel Conklin, at that time at Diakonisches Werk in Stuttgart, also offered early support. I am very grateful for the travel grant that Diakonisches Werk gave me during 1981–1982, which enabled me to travel throughout Germany to conduct many of these interviews. Helga Tönges at the Evangelisches Zentralarchiv in Berlin was immeasurably helpful, as were Dr. Hans Steinberg and his successor, Dr. Bernd Hey, at the Landeskirchliches Archiv in Westphalia. Dr. Wolfgang Kätzner at the Zentralarchiv in Bethel offered assistance in tracking down some hard-to-find information, and Dr. Anneliese Hochmuth in Bethel was also helpful in discussing the effects of the Nazi era in Bethel. The Berlin Document Center replied to my queries promptly and helpfully, as did the photographic archives that supplied the illustrations for this book.

Several people were instrumental in commenting on the manuscript. Lore Tornow and the late Ruth Moser not only helped correct the German transcriptions of my interviews but offered considerable insight into their contents. Doris Bergen took an unconscionable amount of time out from her own doctoral research to read and comment on the early chapters. My correspondence and conversations with Robert McAfee Brown, Dorthee Sölle, Fulbert Steffensky, and James Breeden were invaluable. I hope only that the new ideas and insights they gave me have enriched this book as much as they enriched the process of writing it. My special gratitude goes to Robert McAfee Brown, who, despite his busy schedule, read and commented on the entire manuscript and was incredibly supportive throughout the writing of the book.

I am principally indebted, of course, to the people I interviewed for this book — to their openness, their hospitality, and their interest and support in what I was trying to do. If I have managed to convey a sense of what happened in Germany in this century, it is due to them. Here, particular thanks must go to the late Kurt Scharf and to Liselotte Lawerenz and Ilse Härter, who not only agreed to be interviewed but offered assistance in tracking down additional information and documentation. The late Brigitte Gollwitzer was also helpful in answering my queries about obscure historical facts.

My thanks go as well to the numerous other people who helped briefly, in one way or another, during the writing of this book, and to my family, who did not help with the manuscript, but offered unlimited moral support, which was just as important.

And finally, I express my gratitude to Cynthia Read at Oxford University Press, for being so supportive, and more patient than any editor should have to be.

Bielefeld, Germany V.B.
June 1992

Contents

FOR
THE SOUL
OF THE
PEOPLE

Introduction

IN MAY 1945, a convoy of eight privately owned cars left the city of Breslau for Hannover, 550 kilometers to the northwest. The cars, driven by German Red Cross workers, were filled with cartons of Red Cross records and whatever personal belongings could be fit in. Like thousands of Germans in the spring and early summer of 1945, the workers were fleeing the Soviet army.[1]

In the early days after World War II, such journeys often were made on foot. Refugees piled wheelbarrows with clothes, dishes, and family valuables; children perched on top of these possessions or were carried. When the refugees spotted soldiers or military vehicles, they hid in deserted farmhouses, bushes, or the woods. Tales had spread of Russian soldiers summarily executing any German suspected of being a Nazi, of soldiers gang-raping German women and girls, and of their stealing watches, jewelry, and whatever treasures the refugees had. Centuries of enmity between the Germans and the peoples of Eastern Europe had hardened into hatred after the German army marched east in 1939, committing the very atrocities that German refugees now feared at the hands of Russian soldiers.

Although the region around Breslau had been taken by the Soviet army in the final months of the war, Breslau itself was not surrendered until May 6. To evade the Soviet army, the Red Cross workers took a circuitous route toward the Czechoslovakian border and then back north through German Saxony. They traveled several weeks; north of Dresden, they were stopped by U.S. soldiers. The cars were searched, the boxes of records examined. The members of the convoy had to present their papers. A few were taken into a makeshift office for questioning.

One of them was a petite 51-year-old woman named Stefanie von Mackensen. In Hannover, she hoped to trace her husband and two daughters, with whom she had lost contact in the chaotic last months of the war. She was anxious and uncertain. So were the people with whom she was traveling. Having abandoned most of their belongings, already feeling the burden of their pasts, and uncertain of their immediate future, they panicked when the soldiers stopped them. One man informed on Stefanie von Mackensen. She had indeed worked for the Red Cross, he told a U.S. soldier, but she was not an ordinary refugee. Her husband was a nephew of General August von Mackensen, a highly decorated World War I hero and early supporter of Hitler. Her husband had been a government official, and both he and his wife had been members of the Nazi party.

Stefanie von Mackensen was led into a barracks and questioned by two pleasant

3

young officers. Yes, she told them, she had been in the Nazi party, and her husband had been vice president of Pomerania—a post he had held before the Nazis came to power in 1933—until 1938. But she insisted that she had grown disenchanted with Nazism and that the Nazi party had brought proceedings against her and her husband in 1938.

Then she asked them, "Do you know what's happened to Martin Niemöller? We worked together."

The officers looked at each other. They called in a superior officer. "Look," they told him, "here's someone who knows Niemöller." They turned back to Stefanie von Mackensen. "But you admitted you were in the Nazi party."

"Yes," she replied. "I was in the party. But I was also on the governing council of the Confessing Church."

The officers talked a long time among themselves. Finally, she heard one of them say, "Whoever was in the Confessing Church can't be an enemy of ours." Stefanie von Mackensen rejoined the others in her car. A GI filled their gas tank, wishing them luck, and they drove on to Hannover.

The U.S. officers were understandably taken aback by her story, although everything she had told them was true. Some Protestants publicly opposed Nazi attempts to create an "Aryan" church in the first months of the Third Reich. In 1934, these Protestants gathered in the town of Barmen and issued the Barmen Declaration of Faith, which stated that the freedom given each human being through Christ was above the dictates of political totalitarianism. This declaration—that Christian faith must remain independent of Nazi ideology—was the foundation of the Confessing Church.

The Confessing Church's initial battle was with the "German Christians," a group of Protestants sympathetic to Nazism. But it was inevitable that Confessing Christians would come into conflict with the Nazi system. For that reason, the Confessing Church's witness had implications for all Germans. The Nazis recognized this early. The infamous Wittenberg "brown synod" in September 1933 was so named because many church delegates attended wearing the brown-shirted SA (the storm troopers, the Nazi party militia) uniform. There, Ludwig Müller, the "German Christian" Reich bishop, threw down the gauntlet to his church opponents. "The old has come to an end," he proclaimed. "The new has begun. The political church struggle is over. The struggle for the soul of the people now begins."[2] Müller, a hapless Nazi sympathizer, became known for his ineptitude, but in Wittenberg, his words were ominously accurate. Nazism was nothing less than a struggle for the souls of the German people.

As that struggle progressed, the Gestapo watched and harassed Confessing Christians. Confessing Church leaders fought bitterly with Protestant colleagues who bowed to Nazi pressure. As the systematic terror of the Third Reich grew, some Confessing Christians were arrested; a few were sent to concentration camps. Martin Niemöller, one of its most outspoken leaders, was in concentration camps for eight years. Dietrich Bonhoeffer, one of its seminary teachers, was executed in April 1945 for his role in the plot to kill Hitler.

Internationally, the Confessing Church quickly gained renown for its opposition to the Nazi regime. In 1945, Allied soldiers—appalled by the concentration camps and the full revelation of Nazi horrors—soon recognized Niemöller's and Bonhoeffer's names. The military defeat of Nazism had unmasked the immoral heart of its being to the world. The few Germans who had had the courage to oppose it precisely on the grounds of moral and religious conviction earned special respect. That respect put Stefanie von Mackensen back in the car to Hannover.

Yet, as the case of Stefanie von Mackensen illustrates, the Confessing Church story is not a simple one of good against evil, nor can it be understood outside the context of what happened to German Protestantism as a whole during the Third Reich. Although it held separate worship services and educated and ordained its own pastors, the Confessing Church never completely broke away from the German Evangelical Church, the Protestant church in Germany. The German Evangelical Church included three distinct traditions: the theologically strict Lutherans, the more liberal Reformed church, and the United church, which contained both Lutheran and Reformed elements. From its beginnings with Martin Luther, German Protestantism had aligned itself with the state authorities. The Confessing Church's struggles with the Protestant mainstream were bitter, particularly because Confessing Christians were challenging this traditional alliance of church and state.

Seen in this light, the Confessing Church marked the most radical break in German church history since the Reformation itself. And yet, despite initial postwar reverence for the Confessing Church, it was not a resistance movement against Nazism. Some Confessing Christians, it is true, gave their lives in the fight against Nazism. Others tried to the very end to make compromises with the Nazi regime. Confessing Church members included baptized Jews and Nazi party members, radicals and moderates. Like most German Protestants in the 1930s, most Confessing Christians were nationalistic. Many were anti-Semitic. The Confessing Church became divided between radical members who wanted to break entirely with the German Evangelical Church and moderates who feared that the radicals were using politics to divide the church. The only thing all Confessing Christians had in common was their opposition to the absolute demands of Nazi ideology on their religious faith.

In 1979, with plans to compile an oral history of the Confessing Church, I began to interview some of its survivors. Many spoke with me so frankly that I found myself not just recording what had happened in the Confessing Church but examining the factors that had prevented the church from resisting Nazism more decisively. I believe that, for many of those interviewed, the act of remembering became a moral act in itself. The emotions aroused in the people with whom I spoke led them to examine, morally and politically, what they themselves had seen and done—and, ultimately, to discuss what legacy they wanted, as Germans, for their children.

Obviously, the perspectives presented in the interview segments of this book are those of the individuals speaking. Human memory—particularly of a volatile subject like Nazi Germany—tends to revise and rationalize. This is one of the limitations of oral history. I think that it will be evident to the reader where rationalization occurs; in those cases where individuals' accounts do not correspond to historical evidence, I have noted that. I have tried to use historical and archival material to provide a chronological, thematic background as a factual context for people's recollections.

The Berlin Document Center was particularly helpful in checking the history of Nazi party proceedings against Confessing Christians who were party members. In addition, many of the people with whom I spoke were able to share diaries, letters, and other documents to confirm events or fill in gaps in memory.

In conducting interviews, I began with the assumption that these people's roles in the Confessing Church could not be understood without an examination of their attitudes before 1933 and of the events after 1945 which affected how they dealt with their own history. I asked what kinds of families they had come from, what they had been taught as children to believe, what their memories of World War I and the Weimar Republic were, what happened to them during the Third Reich and how they have dealt with that since 1945, and how they see themselves, morally and politically, today. I also spoke with them about the legacy of the Confessing Church in East and West Germany and was fortunate to speak with a number of people who lived and worked in East Germany after 1945.

I believe that the answers to these questions are important, not only for Germans confronting their history but for all of us. Throughout the world, religiously based moral values continue to play a role in political behavior. The story of the Confessing Church provides insight into the tensions between individual conscience and loyalty to the state, between moral beliefs and political responsibility. Even in a technological age, we still think of our moral being as that part of us which remains free and unique. But as the recollections of Confessing Christians show, however strongly our individual moral choices distinguish us from one another, they finally merge with the choices of others to form a whole, a collective impetus by which sociopolitical evil is either resisted or tolerated.

The story of the Confessing Church, then, is not of the triumph of good over evil. Good people do not always recognize evil. Even when they do, their behavior is guided not only by strength of conscience or love of humanity but by fear, nationalism, and human weakness. Yet the Confessing Church can still be recognized as a courageous attempt to do good, and its members were people whose religious faith prevented them from becoming blind followers of Hitler.

Their stories bear witness to the necessity not just of remembering history but of learning from it. They cover roughly the same period in which Stefanie von Mackensen lived. Born in 1894, she died in 1985. Her 91 years spanned a period that included two world wars and a series of German governments as radically different from one another as possible: the Kaiser's empire, the Weimar Republic, Nazi Germany, and the division of Germany into two countries, one a parliamentary democracy and the other a socialist state. Had she lived five more years, she would have witnessed what seemed impossible at the end of her life: the reunification of Germany.

But the focal point of her life, and of the lives of all speakers in this book, was those 12 years under Nazism, which forever changed the way in which they thought about themselves, their God, and their country. In this book, they recall that short, tragic era when good and evil wrestled for the fate of their souls.

I

OMENS

✥ 1 ✥

The Lost Empire

German Protestantism and the German Reich

THEY WERE BORN during the German Empire, in the final years of the reigns of the provincial German princes and of Kaiser Wilhelm II from the royal Prussian House of Hohenzollern. Toward the ends of their lives, Germans who remembered that era spoke of it in tones that evoked pictures of a lost, more civilized world, bathed in a calm and quiet light, like the final warm autumn days that precede a long winter. Perhaps their memories were so colored because those years were their childhood, a time that, for all but the most unfortunate, seems filled with new beginnings and possibilities. They saw the years between 1890 and 1914 as a golden age, ended with terrible finality by World War I. Like other Europeans, the Germans grieved for the past, site of their earliest memories and lost innocence.

Human memory and loyalty are affected not only by the past but by what follows it. Social stability and political continuity keep history in the past; instability and uncertainty keep its ghosts alive. In 1918, Germany's old order was gone, its borders altered, its Kaiser and princes in exile; and German devotion to that lost world assumed a life of its own. The period of national mourning over Germany's defeat did not exorcise the grief and bitterness of its citizens, but gave those emotions new forms, breathing them fervently into the next period of German history, as if attempting to resuscitate the dead.

So this is what they would remember: the German Empire. Otto von Bismarck had united 18 different German states; the largest was the kingdom of Prussia, covering two thirds of German territory. Prussia's capital was Berlin; its territory extended east to the Lithuanian border, south to the Austro-Hungarian empire, and north along the Baltic Sea. Its western outposts included the farmlands of Westphalia, the Ruhr coal fields, and the vineyards and castles that flank the Rhine.

The Confessing Church would become strongest in Prussia, and many Confessing Christians spoke of what it meant to be Prussian. They stressed virtues like industriousness, thriftiness, and loyalty to German traditions and culture. Prussia's bureaucracy was renowned for its efficiency and honesty; its military was respected for its discipline and feared for its power. In the eighteenth century, the French statesman Comte de Mirabeau had remarked that Prussia was not so much a state with an army as an army with a state. Not much had changed by the late 1800s, when an English visitor to Berlin noted that "nowhere in Europe were so many uniforms to be seen in the streets."[1]

The mentality instilled in the wearers of these uniforms was one of absolute, unwavering obedience to the German empire and its Kaiser. Martin Niemöller joined the Kaiser's Marines in 1910 at the age of 18; he later noted that

> I was never interested at all in politics as a Kaiser's officer because we didn't even have the right to vote. Everyone who wore a uniform, in Prussia or in the German Reich, had no right to vote. You received that right when you were pensioned. Then you became a citizen. No soldier could go to vote or was entered on the election lists. That's something you have to know to even begin to understand the people of that era. Officers and reserve officers were not interested in political issues. We simply remained true to our oath to the flag under which we stood.[2]

It is striking that Niemöller (and many other pastors) recalled their worldview at that time as being "apolitical."[3] In reality, it was not so much apolitical as politically restricted, bound to traditions and laws that required absolute loyalty. The mentality of soldiers who were not counted as (and did not consider themselves) citizens had ominous political consequences during the Third Reich, when German soldiers and civilians became known for following orders without concern for the consequences of their actions.

This kind of blind loyalty was instilled early. As boys, Martin and his younger brother Wilhelm had played soldier. As World War I approached, such children's games in Germany were incorporated into actual military preparation. Kurt Scharf, a Confessing Church pastor who later became bishop of Berlin, recalled that he, his brothers, and their classmates were allowed to participate in the Kaiser's Maneuvers of 1913 near the Polish border.[4] For days, the boys marched with the 54th Artillery Batallion and a group of infantry from Küstrin. They bivouacked, hid in the forests, and crossed the marshes and lakes of the region in pontoon boats. It was the greatest adventure of their boyhood.

Kurt Scharf was 11 years old at the time, too young to join the Kaiser's army when the real war began the next year. Wilhelm Niemöller was 17. As soon as he was eligible, he enthusiastically enlisted and donned his soldier's uniform with the same reverence with which, much later, he would wear his pastor's robes:

> We had sworn our oath to the flag under the Kaiser, and with that, everything was settled. It was never a problem for us; it shouldn't be made a problem now, in retrospect. If the Kaiser had called, we would have come. We would have gotten up at 2 o'clock in the middle of the night and said, "We're awake." Those were genuine loyalties.
>
> You should understand how I mean that. It's easy, after an experience of evil, to project the image of a dictatorship back into the Bismarckian era. It wasn't like that. What we did was of our free will—I signed up voluntarily in World War I— and we saw it as a matter of course. We had sworn it to Kaiser Wilhelm. Our oath stood, and with that, the matter was settled.[5]

They took their loyalty oaths with religious seriousness. Martin Niemöller, by the end of the war a decorated U-boat commander, refused to surrender in 1918 until convinced that the Kaiser had indeed abdicated. The incident displayed the stubborn will that Niemöller would later turn against Hitler; it also reflected the era and the church in which the Niemöller brothers had grown up. Their father was a prominent

Lutheran minister, and the brothers would eventually go into the ministry themselves. In that era, the move from the military to the ministry did not require an enormous shift in loyalties. Since Martin Luther's time, one of German Protestantism's foundations had been unwavering support for state authority. The biblical passage frequently cited to characterize the correct relation between the Christian and the state was Romans 13:

> Let every person be subject to the governing authorities. For there is no authority except from God, and those that exist have been instituted by God. Therefore he who resists the authorities resists what God has appointed, and those who resist will incur judgment. . . . Therefore one must be subject, not only to avoid God's wrath but also for the sake of conscience.[6]

In Lutheran theology, this view developed into the doctrine of two kingdoms, represented by the thrones of earthly rulers and the altar of God. Christians owed political obedience to the throne and religious subservience to the altar. German Protestants viewed their love for the Fatherland and loyalty to its leaders as patriotic and Christian virtues. The effect upon the German Protestant pastorate — at least in the eyes of one British churchman — was that their "belief in Christianity was so closely intertwined with a strong nationalism that it was difficult even for themselves to say where the one began and the other ended."[7]

This situation was grounded historically in the circumstances following the Reformation. After declaring their independence from the Roman Catholic bishops, Protestant parishes placed themselves under the protection of the provincial German princes. These princes remained the titular heads of the Protestant churches in their respective provinces until 1918. At the local level, many of the landed nobility became patrons, paying the living for their local pastor.

In his memoirs, Otto Dibelius (who, as church superintendent in Berlin, became prominent in the Confessing Church) described the patronage system and its effect upon the church after 1918. The patrons, he recalled,

> were in the truest sense of the word the lords of their lands; they felt themselves to be the guardians of the monarchistic tradition, particularly now that the monarchy had ceased to exist. But they did hope for a better future! And they particularly felt themselves to be the quiet lords of their evangelical church, in any case within their regional borders. They administered their patronage, some unwillingly and greedily, others, however, with seriousness, piety, and fidelity. Their fathers had built the churches. They kept them up, and built here and there a new chapel. They found it important that, during every worship service, the patron was prayed for. No pastor or teacher who fell out with his patron could retain his position.[8]

Even in parishes with no tradition of patronage, there was evidence of the church's traditional ties to the monarchy. During the 1930s, for example, Confessing Church pastor Kurt Scharf served a parish in the village of Friedrichstal near Berlin. The small red brick church there had been built in 1887 with money given by Kaiserin Luise Viktoria, and the Kaiser's round seal was engraved in the wall to the right of the pulpit.

Institutionally and ideologically, then, the German Evangelical Church was aligned with the state, a situation formalized over the centuries by law. Since 1794, the churches had been governed by provincial consistories, which included clergy and state representatives, the latter having the governing voice. After 1852, when church-elected synods of lay and clergy members were established, the church's independence to govern its own affairs grew; synodal approval was needed for state laws concerning church affairs.

But the overlap of church and state interest continued to be taken for granted. Most church people saw no need to alter it, since it gave the Evangelical Church a powerful, economically secure position in German society. Almost 40 million of the 65 million Germans living in 1910 were members of the German Evangelical Church. State laws provided for the collection of church taxes, and additional state subsidies were granted to the churches and their schools.

This legal structure provided the underpinning for how the Protestant clergy saw their role in German society. They came predominately from the middle or upper-middle class; their cultural attitudes tended to be identical to those of governing interests, the upper classes and the German monarchy.[9] Yet, like Martin Niemöller during his military service, most pastors viewed themselves as "apolitical," and they (and their church) were strongly biased against any church position that appeared "political." The discrepancy between this attitude and the church's de facto alliance with the state remained unexamined.

In part, church caution regarding political positions was based upon a legitimate fear of the clericalism that had flourished during the Middle Ages, when bishops and church princes held the cross in one hand and the power of law in the other. The move away from clericalism was an important step toward religious tolerance in a more liberal society. Changes in Prussian law during the nineteenth century reflected this. At the beginning of the century, all Christian Germans had to be baptized by six weeks of age. Such laws had been discarded by the end of the Bismarck era, when German citizens had the option of leaving the church altogether.

The clericalism present in the German Evangelical Church's ties to the monarchy and the state, however, was ignored. Loyalties to Kaiser and country were patriotic; this patriotism was part of the German culture. For many pastors it was as much a part of their upbringing as learning the German language had been. But the practical implications of the bond between throne and altar were not that different from the loyalty instilled in the Kaiser's soldiers. Rudolf Weckerling, a pastor's son who became a Confessing Church pastor himself, described his upbringing this way:

> At home, we learned that politics ruins the character. I learned a Christianity that was utterly without any relation to social life and reality. It was a pious niche, and otherwise you went along with everything. Total conformity.[10]

For Kurt Scharf's parishioners in Friedrichstal, the Protestant tradition was represented visibly by the massive parsonage and the simple dignity of the church with the Kaiser's seal. The pastor was an important symbol of church tradition. Villages like Friedrichstal represented an ideal for Germans, what they called a *heile Welt* — literally, an intact world. The stereotype of the fatherly pastor tending his flock and watching over this *heile Welt* was, essentially, what many parishioners expected in a pastor. In most German villages, the church tower was the first thing one saw from a distance. Architecturally, theologically, and sociologically, the church and its pastor were the heart and soul of the small world of everyday life.

Pastors enjoyed considerable influence. Particularly in rural areas, where the church was the main social institution — the site of seasonal festivals, church services, religion classes, and town meetings — the pastor was a powerful figure. The situation in the village of Mennighüffen in eastern Westphalia, described by Ernst Wilm, was typical:

> For 30 years this parish had had a Pastor Schmalenbach, who was a very talented preacher, a patriarch who led his parish in a grand fashion. He could be very strict. Socially engaged Christianity meant nothing to him; he was simply a conservative monarchist. He helped awaken a living Christianity in this parish. Church attendance was very high. The church was so full that one row sat and one row stood, in very close quarters. They changed every five minutes: those who had stood, sat down, and those who had been sitting, stood back up. For a newcomer who had to preach, it was disconcerting, because there was always motion.
>
> There was another pastor, Dütemeyer, who came after Schmalenbach, and he was there for 30 years, too. Then I arrived in 1931. At that time, out of 3,000 members in the parish, there were at least 1,500 every Sunday sitting in church. There was a children's service and Bible school with 300 to 400 children and confirmation pupils. The whole neighborhood was imprinted by the church. The pastor in his sermons had to involve himself with what was happening in the world. You couldn't keep silent; it was simply so. That was expected of the pastor and, I think, legitimately.
>
> My father had had the following experience. He came as a candidate for the ministry from Bethel and was with Schmalenbach in Mennighüffen. There he attended an election rally — this was around 1890 — where a conservative had spoken, and then Schmalenbach said: "People, you've heard this man, and I tell you, this is a man you can vote for." Then someone jumped up excitedly and said, "Now you know. Whoever is for our Lord Jesus should vote for this man!" Schmalenbach also worked against the [Social] Democrats when they held campaign rallies there.[11]

Despite claims of "apoliticality," then, a pastor's de facto alliance with the state effectively sanctified state authority and gave his own pastoral role additional importance. Such was the strength of this tradition that it often superseded sociopolitical differences between pastors and their parishioners. In Mennighüffen, for example, most of the parish members worked in a nearby cigar factory and, as Wilm recalled, "they just managed to get by in life." Politically, support for the Social Democrat party and socialist ideas had begun to grow there, as it had in many working-class areas toward the end of the nineteenth century — a trend that was anathema to monarchists like their pastor. Unlike Social Democrats in the cities, however, Mennighüffen's workers continued to fill the church on Sundays. At the time Wilm arrived there as pastor in 1931, "the Prussian loyalty to the ruler was sacrosanct. They couldn't free themselves that quickly from this sense of belonging to Prussia."[12] (It should be noted that they were not loyal, nor was their church, to the leaders of the doomed Weimar Republic. What Wilm described was the continued loyalty, widespread among pastors and less so in working-class and rural areas, to the Kaiser and the Prussian monarchy.)

The "Crisis Mentality," Nationalism, and Anti-Semitism

In the larger German cities, however, working-class allegiance to the monarchy had begun to decline by the end of the nineteenth century — a result of increasing industrialization and changing social patterns, marked by the rise of working-class political parties like the Social Democrats and the Communist party. Despite the differences between them, these two parties tended to be lumped together by conservative Germans and their church. Like other European churches, the German Evangelical Church viewed the growing Communist movement as a serious threat to social tradition and government authority. Their fears increased in the chaotic years immediately following World War I, when social unrest and strikes spread throughout the country and it seemed as if the seeds of the October 1917 Russian revolution had taken root in postwar Germany. The fate of the Russian Christian churches under the Bolsheviks heightened those fears.

The alarm of church leaders increased as the German Evangelical Church itself became the target of scathing attacks in working-class newspapers. In some cities, the Social Democrats organized campaigns to convince workers to leave the church and reclaim the part of their wages that went to the church tax. The phenomenon of a pastor sanctioning a political candidate to his respectful parishioners became more of an anomaly, at least in working-class areas.

Sieghild Jungklaus, one of the first generation of German women to study theology, became a pastor in the Confessing Church. She grew up in a parish led by her father in Pankow, a working-class area of Berlin. She later recalled the atmosphere there and its effect upon the pastors:

At that time, Pankow was a huge parish with around 65,000 Protestants and three pulpits, two churches, and a large parish house. We were at the Pankow Church of Hope. There were rented barracks, which had been built, in part, by the first settlers, with two or three courtyards in back. Of course, poor people lived there: workers and such, who had to suffer fairly early under the unemployment. That began very early. Naturally, the convinced Communists weren't people who went to church. That is correct. But — I'll put this very cautiously — the part of the parish where I grew up was more leftist, in any case. Whereby, later, they were very susceptible to National Socialism.

It's very difficult to explain. . . . Certainly my brother and I were strongly influenced, in our parents' house, in a specific direction: that is, all of us were raised in those days with a certain national consciousness. That extended to the workers' families, for whom World War I and its end were a very hard thing — much that had happened had done Germany a serious injustice. That was the general opinion; we heard that at school, and that was the opinion at home. Naturally, there were many parsonages then that were loyal to the Kaiser and the monarchy. Now my father wasn't like that. I believe that he voted German National, for you realize, the Social Democrats then were extraordinarily anti-Church. . . .

I recall that on every Reformation Day or thereabouts, the Social Democrats held a huge gathering at the large monument to Luther that stood by the Marienkirche in Berlin. There they propagated godless propaganda and called for people to leave the church. . . . Because of that, it wasn't possible to vote Social

Democrat. Even when one was not at all in agreement with the right-wing parties. For the generation of our parents, that just wasn't a possibility.[13]

In response, what German theologian and sociologist Karl-Wilhelm Dahm calls a "crisis mentality" had developed among Protestant pastors.[14] Even before World War I, they feared that their community stature was diminishing; working-class attacks on the monarchy and the church warned ominously of social disintegration, if not actual revolution. The events of 1917 and 1918 seemed to confirm their worst fears. How realistic those fears were is debatable. Church membership showed a small decline between 1867 and 1905 (from 65.3 to 62.6 percent of the German population). After that, there was a dramatic increase in the actual numbers that left the church for atheistic reasons, but it was not enough to affect overall church membership.[15] Most workers apparently chose to remain in the Protestant and Catholic churches in order to receive the still important social rituals of church baptism, marriage, and burial. But the direct influence of the clergy in other areas of their lives was slowly diminishing, as it was in most Western societies at that time, as secular philosophies began to exert their influence.

The changes wrought by the outcome of World War I only intensified the longing of many Protestant pastors for the days of the German Reich. The result was a pastoral nationalism that, as Eberhard Bethge later wrote, said "yes to a foreign policy of might, no to a domestic policy of emancipation, in the name of faith."[16] This nationalism was not the only factor that led many Protestant pastors to welcome the rise of Nazism. Among those pastors and church leaders who became early supporters of the Nazi party, anti-Semitism certainly played a role.[17] Like nationalism, anti-Semitism was so ingrained in many Christians that it went unquestioned. Only gradually, during the course of the Third Reich, did some Confessing Christians realize the consequences of this prejudice. As Helmut Gollwitzer, the son of a conservative Bavarian pastor, recalled,

> Just as the average Protestant was middle class and "national," he was also anti-Semitic. Today you can hardly speak of "harmless" anti-Semitism, but at that time we saw the antipathy toward the Jews as harmless. All of us. My father was theologically conservative, so the removal of the Old Testament didn't come into question for him. So how did he solve the problem? This way: I was raised to believe that, until the Jews rejected Jesus, they were a loyal people, a wonderful people. They were farmers and shepherds. Then God rejected them, and since that time they have been merchants, good for nothing, and they infiltrate everything, everywhere they go. And against that you had to defend yourself. In the Nazi party program it said that Jews should not be permitted to be citizens. Most Germans held that to be a matter worth consideration. . . . Certain kinds of restrictions on their civil rights — that was generally talked about and sympathized with.[18]

In their notion of an "Aryan" race, the Nazis took this conscious distinction between "Germans" and "Jews" further. In doing this, they drew upon racial prejudices and upon German national feelings. As Gollwitzer noted, the average Protestant was "national," a word often translated as "patriotic" or "nationalist," but with a far broader meaning in German. To be "national" in early twentieth-century Germany was to be both *völkisch* and *vaterlandisch* — to link one's identity to being ethnically

German and to the German Fatherland. This concept transcended mere political loyalties and carried cultural and geographical connotations as well.[19]

Centuries of emigration for religious and political reasons had created pockets of
German settlements throughout Europe, particularly in the Ukraine, Russia, Rumania, and Hungary. Although many descendants of these emigrants had never seen
Germany, they had retained their ethnic German identity in their new lands. After
World War I, many Germans viewed the establishment of Poland and the re-establishment of the Czechoslovakian border as the theft of "German" lands, since both
nations had sizable German populations. In addition, the terms of the Versailles
Treaty at the end of World War I prohibited the political union of Germany and Austria, which had a large German population. The presence of Germans outside the borders of Germany itself led German nationalists to emphasize their bonds with these
regions of German culture and language.

Some nationalists coupled this with the idealization of a racial German identity
and the vilification of Jews and other ethnic groups. A new wave of anti-Semitism
swept Europe in the wake of World War I, and in Germany it was focused upon the
Jewish immigrants who had fled pogroms in the Ukraine and Poland.[20] German
nationalists saw Germany's defeat in 1918 as a victory for Judaism, as one verse
making the rounds in Berlin in 1918 illustrates:

> *Ja, mein Christ, kannst du es fassen,*
> *Daß wir beid' mit Weib und Kind*
> *Nur noch Judensklaven sind?*[21]

> (Yes, my Christian, can you believe it that we two, with wife and child, are now only
> slaves of the Jews?)

For those Protestants who subsequently joined the Nazi-sympathetic church
group, the "German Christians," anti-Semitism and nationalism merged to form an
"Aryan" version of Christianity. Politically, however, the nationalism of most German Protestant clergy immediately after 1918 was exemplified by the German
National People's party, which, in its early years, was fairly heterogeneous, attracting
both liberal and conservative members.[22] At one point during the 1920s, 80 percent
of German Protestants supported the German National People's party.[23]

Interestingly, only 8 percent of German Protestants subsequently embraced the
more extreme racially oriented "folk religions" of the 1920s.[24] Like Helmut Gollwitzer's father, most Protestant pastors balked at altering their biblical tradition to
accommodate a German racial faith. In 1933, this would lead some of them to their
first clear stand against the Nazi regime.

But in 1918, German Protestants, like most Germans, were embittered by the
German defeat and by the terms of the Versailles Treaty, which, they believed,
unfairly blamed Germany for the war and saddled it with unjust reparations. In addition to the treaty's stipulations about the eastern borders, the Rhineland-Saar and
Ruhr regions were placed under French occupation. The German military was drastically reduced, and the Kaiser, in exile in Holland, was denounced as a war criminal.
Germans had a new, democratic government, but it had been imposed upon them;
and its initial task — paying war reparations to the victors of the war — was most

unpopular with the German people. All this contributed to German resentment against the rest of Europe.

Like many of the young men who had worn their uniforms proudly, Martin Niemöller was bitter. The officer's oath he had sworn no longer had any meaning; the empire he had pledged to defend was gone. He turned in his uniform and left the military; still loyal to the old order, he could not bring himself to serve its replacement. He began to study theology—a choice that was not, however, a retreat from resentment and nationalism. His church shared his feelings, and during the Weimar years, as Confessing Church pastor Günther Dehn later wrote, "the Church wanted to remain what it already had been for a long time: a piece of the past in a changed world."[25]

❧ 2 ❧

The Weimar Years

Postwar Resentment

A NEW EUROPEAN ORDER had been created, but many Germans believed that it was based upon the deliberate humiliation of Germany. Throughout the 1920s, German resentment festered like an unhealed wound. Every political crisis reopened it, and what the Germans called the *Schandvertrag* — the treaty of dishonor — was invoked as the cause of Germany's bad fortune. Over 60 years later, Stefanie von Mackensen's voice still grew bitter when she recalled how the Versailles Treaty had affected her. Newly married, she lived in Düsseldorf:

> In Düsseldorf, the left side of the Rhine was occupied by the French and the right side was free. My parents lived on the right side of the Rhine; I lived on the left side. Every time I crossed the bridge over the Rhine, they physically searched me. We weren't allowed on the sidewalks when a French officer was present. I lived through all these things, these small humiliations, and they exerted a powerful influence on my national attitudes. I joined the Nazi party in 1932. The youth today can't understand that at all. One can't understand it. One can only comprehend it when one knows the history that preceded it.[1]

The resentment Germans felt toward the treaty was nurtured by the Protestant church. The Versailles Treaty was made public in Germany at the end of June 1919, and the German Evangelical Church promptly declared Sunday, July 6, to be a national day of mourning. A lengthy statement was prepared to be read in churches throughout Prussia, which said in part:

> The demand that we acknowledge ourselves as the only guilty party in the war puts a lie in our mouths that shamelessly violates our consciences. As Protestant Christians, we raise our sacred protest before God and Man against the attempt to print this stigma upon our nation.[2]

In the words of various Protestant church people, Versailles represented "the blackest day in German history" and the "disgrace of the century" and had been brought about, among other things, by "the treason of the Social Democrats."[3] Protestant wrath at Germany's international humiliation merged with outpourings of loyalty to the Kaiser.

The German Evangelical Church entered the crucial Weimar years grieving over Germany's defeat and bearing distinctly promonarchical and antidemocratic sentiments. As Karl-Wilhelm Dahm observed, Protestant conservatism during the Weimar years was not the kind that aligns itself with established authorities, but a conservatism that remained loyal to a lost past.[4] Embittered nationalists put the blame for Germany's defeat not on the Kaiser and his military commanders but on the fragile new government that now saw itself compelled to observe the terms of the Versailles Treaty. The Republic's leaders varied in their commitment to democracy. Some were proud of the new constitution, which guaranteed a wide range of civil liberties; others had agreed to a democracy only because they hoped to gain more lenient postwar terms from the Allies.[5]

In 1919, however, most Germans longed not for democracy but for stability and order. The Weimar Republic, its birth accompanied by right-wing soldiers' uprisings and Communist attempts at revolution, was an uncertain government in a volatile environment. It was burdened by the social and economic costs of the war and the additional obligations of paying war reparations, which the victorious European powers had set at 132 billion gold marks.[6]

Weimar politics was characterized by resentment and in-fighting, and the economic instability and inflation of the early postwar period made the political atmosphere even more labile. In January 1919, one U.S. dollar bought 8.9 Reichsmarks; by November 1923, it purchased 4.2 trillion.[7] Savings and pensions became worthless, and the number of people on social relief rose dramatically. By the end of 1923, only 29.3 percent of the labor force was fully employed.[8] Even those fortunate enough to have full- or part-time work lived in a world of crazy money, where a kilo of butter cost 68 million Reichsmarks and a paycheck could become worthless overnight. Few families were left unscathed.

These pressures merged with widespread postwar bitterness in Germany to erode public support for the Republic and its leaders. Small extremist parties arose; within the German parliament, an ongoing battle for political power raged among the some 30 political parties that at various points were represented there. Under such circumstances, a stable coalition of governing parties was impossible. During its short existence, Weimar Germany was run by 21 different coalitions, whose leaders had the difficult task of governing the country and attempting to placate its political factions, whose attitudes ranged from the extreme right to the extreme left.

Most crucially, the Republic lacked the trust and support of an entire group of Germans whose loyalties rested firmly with the monarchy. As Helmut Gollwitzer recalled, the Weimar Republic

> was called the "unloved Republic." It was loved by no one. It was supported by the workers and a few conscientious liberal groups, as well as by the Catholic Center party, but loved, in the sense that people identified with it — that was extremely seldom. . . . My father, for example, said in 1918, "From now on, I will always be on the farthest right wing." He wasn't in the Nazi party, but he was sympathetic to them, and he experienced the year 1933 with great joy. To the extent that they were churchgoers, the Nazis from the entire area came to his church. We were "national"; "national" was identical to being on the right.[9]

Even those who supported the Weimar Republic became increasingly frustrated at the desperate social circumstances and at what they saw as undue foreign pressure on the Republic's leaders. Emmi Delbrück was married to Klaus Bonhoeffer, who would be executed, like his brother Dietrich in 1945, for their participation in the plot to kill Hitler. Both the Delbrück and Bonhoeffer families supported the Weimar Republic, and members of both families distinguished themselves in the civil service and political appointments. What Emmi Bonhoeffer recalled of the instability of those years was that

> We were very, very unhappy that the other countries supported our republican gov-
> ernment so poorly. In that respect, the pressure of the Versailles conditions was so
> foolish. A man like Brüning [chancellor of the Republic from 1930 to 1932]
> couldn't even consolidate the customs annexations for Austria, which would have
> meant a certain relief in the number of unemployed. Not even that. They put their
> thumbs down so hard that no respectable government could have held out. People
> were filled with scorn for this incapable government. The misery of unemployment
> was so extensive that even my father-in-law, who really can't be suspected of being
> a Nazi, said, "When Hitler puts bread on the tables of the first million unemployed,
> I'll put the flag out, too." He never hung it out, because he saw the means with
> which Hitler did it. But I tell that to explain how great the pressure of the unemploy-
> ment rate was. It is so easily shrugged off, but it was truly dreadful.[10]

The yearnings of many Germans for the restoration of social stability and interna-
tional respect for their nation defied easy solution. As people grew frustrated with the apparent ineptitude of Weimar leaders, they channeled their longings into the search for a Führer—a man behind whom all Germans could unite, someone who would embody the sense of purpose necessary for Germany to have a new future. Dietrich Goldschmidt, whose father was Jewish, recalled a discussion in his school:

> The teacher wanted to assure us that, so to speak, Germany would emerge from the
> crisis of suffering and mass unemployment that it was in, and it would experience a
> new rise and the Führer would come. I asked, "How do you know that, and how do
> we know that he is the Führer?" To which I received the answer: I didn't need to
> worry about that; one would recognize him, and it would come about.
>   In October 1932, I went to a mass demonstration. Hitler spoke in the stadium in
> Potsdam to the crowd gathered there; there might have been around 7,000 people. I
> stood in the top bleachers of the stadium, listened to him, and was so frightened by
> Hitler's screaming speech and the roar of the crowd that I left during the program.[11]

But Goldschmidt was an exception. Many Germans, even if initially skeptical, were pulled in by Hitler's oratory. One theology student recalled a friend's reaction when Hitler visited Heidelberg:

> I knew a man—a theological student—who said, "Hitler is coming to Heidelberg.
> I'm going. But he won't get me." . . . I knew this man well, and I thought a lot of
> him; there was something to him. He was someone who, normally, you couldn't
> fool. And he came back from Heidelberg and said, "I'm completely convinced by
> him." And it was true. Very strange. Hitler must have had a charisma, and unstable
> and ignorant people fell for him at once. But even someone who was educated, was
> a convinced Christian, who argued with everything—he came back and said, "He
> convinced me."[12]

Both at the time and in retrospect, some Germans viewed Hitler's rise as inevitable, as if fate itself steered events to make Germans more nationalistic, more violent, more resentful of other nations and of their own society's scapegoats — to turn them, finally, to the one political figure who appealed to all these fears and resentments.

New Developments and Old Loyalties

Yet, as historian Golo Mann has argued, nothing in history is inevitable. Although the Third Reich was rooted partially in the instability of the Weimar years, there were other aspects of Weimar Germany — positive developments, in Mann's words, "in embryo, which, sadly, never reached maturity or was forsaken. In the end, some things could have happened completely differently."[13] The Weimar era was one of new artistic, political, and social developments. Hitler brutally ended many of them in 1933, but the impulse behind them — which had welcomed, not mourned, the passing of the old order — went underground and formed the roots of resistance to Nazism.

Few of those roots were in the churches at that point. But some Germans for whom the Weimar period was one of new-found independence would later find an ally in the Confessing Church. One was 24-year-old Gertrud Staewen. For her, the Weimar Republic was a liberation:

> I come from Bremen. That connotes a stiff, northern German attitude and a patriotic home. My father was an important merchant. We lived simply, not luxuriously. Very strictly, in a kind of Christianity marked by pietistic, strict, empty commandments that you had to fulfill. My parents were puritanical and rigidly conservative. They weren't Nazis, thank God, the short time that my father was still alive then. He died of the decline of Germany. He was such a genuine German conservative that he couldn't comprehend the defeat in 1918 and the Kaiser's abdication.
>
> But he really couldn't understand me! When the time came, I would have loved to attend the university. I was the eldest. I wasn't allowed to, for that wasn't proper in our family. That's an important word: proper. My sister Hilda was allowed to study later, but that was after World War I, and my father had become poor. Then things looked entirely different, and the daughters had to learn something.[14]

The financial consequences of German defeat and the inflation of the 1920s brought women, of necessity, into the labor force. These developments coincided with the entry into public life of the first generation of German women to study at the universities. German women received the vote in 1919; in that year's elections, almost 80 percent of them voted, and 9.6 percent of the newly elected Reichstag delegates were women.

The increasingly visible presence of women in the labor force, in the arts, and on the political scene were signs of postwar social change, welcomed by some people and viewed with horror by others. Their symbolic cultural significance drew a strong reaction from the right wing; the Nazi tenet of *"Kinder, Kirche, Küche"* (children, church, kitchen) as the proper realm for female activities became one of its most publicized — and, it must be said, one of its most popular — slogans.[15]

But it held no appeal for Gertrud Staewen. Although she remained an iconoclast, the church would play a major role in her life. In 1918, the family pastor helped Staewen convince her father that, like her sister, she needed some kind of education. She was allowed to go to Berlin to train in volunteer social work.

Staewen eagerly entered the Berlin political scene. Every kiosk was plastered with posters announcing meetings, debates, literary readings. She attended Social Democrat rallies, Marxist debates, and meetings of workers' groups. She read everything, from pamphlets handed to her on the streets to the works of Dostoevski. She became part of the *Jugendbewegung*, a movement that loosely described a multitude of youth groups which had arisen around the turn of the century. About the only thing they had in common was some form of youthful rebellion against society. The course taken by individual groups depended upon what their young members were rebelling against and what they were seeking. Most were critical of society — particularly traditional institutions like the church — and most emphasized a return to nature. Staewen, like hundreds of German youths, made pilgrimages through the mountains and forests. The young Germans sang songs, recited Goethe, and took oaths of purity of mind and body. Such pilgrimages were philosophical as well as physical, and in the course of the 1920s, many groups became more ideologically rigid, some eventually turning to National Socialism.

Others combined their commitment to social reform with a reborn interest in religion. One New Year's Eve, Staewen attended a gathering of religious socialists. By temperament a devil's advocate, she had trouble remaining quiet at such meetings. One part of her longed for the intellectual community they offered; another part of her poked fun at the pretensions so often displayed. So it was on this evening. People stood up and expounded their theories or read poems or sections of novels they had written, as Staewen recalled ironically,

> to promote socialism and improve human beings. A great deal of totally idealistic rubbish that wasn't true was read aloud to make us all more Christian and more socialist.
>
> Finally I jumped up and got angry, and said that no novel had ever led a person to Christ unless it was by Dostoevski. For him I'd make an exception. Now, besides us, there were several men toward the back whom we didn't know. They were smoking dreadfully. As I spoke about Dostoevski, the curtain of smoke opened and a man stood up. At that time he was still quite young; he looked like a woodcut of a Swiss farmer. He asked me, "Do you know my friend Eduard Thurneysen?" I said, No, I didn't. Then he said, "Read him!"[16]

The man was the Swiss theologian Karl Barth. After the meeting ended in the early hours of the morning, he drew Staewen into a deep conversation. Barth and his friend Thurneysen, a practical theologian, would lead a large group of young Germans into the church opposition to Hitler.

The encounter with Barth brought Gertrud Staewen back into the Protestant church, but she remained well away from its mainstream. The various religious movements of the 1920s, from the religious socialists to the right-wing "Aryan" religious groups, were minorities within the church. Intellectually and sociologically, the Protestant church had changed little since 1918. The majority of parsonages during the Weimar Republic probably resembled this one, described by Martin Schröter:

I grew up in the classic German home. The major figure was Bismarck. My father liked to quote Bismarck, and the statement that politics was a dirty business—we took that in with our mother's milk. In 1927, we moved to Breslau; my first conscious memories, especially political memories, begin there. How enthusiastic we were when Hindenburg came to Breslau! To us, he was the representative of that Germany seen in my parents' house with many positive values. Much later, I realized that the other, left-liberal Germany of the 1920s had completely passed us by. Not a syllable of Tucholsky, of Brecht, of religious socialism. Not a syllable, although all that existed.[17]

Institutionally, the church's position in the Weimar Republic had not changed substantially. The Social Democrats had backed off from previous threats to abolish the church tax and ban parochial schools; the church made no major concessions under the Weimar Constitution, which guaranteed basic religious liberties. The changes that occurred after 1918 tended toward, not against, church independence. The powers held by the provincial princes, for example, had been passed on to church consistories; the highest church officials were now genuinely church, not state, representatives.

But the Evangelical Church had not chafed under its previous arrangements with the state; it had been a loyal supporter of the old system. The predominantly conservative Protestant leaders and pastors associated the Weimar Republic with Social Democrats like Friedrich Ebert, its first president.

Conservatives within the church trusted the Social Democrats only slightly more than they did the Communists. The church, as church historian Klaus Scholder notes, was "a correct partner of the republican authorities. But under the surface remained an ineradicable mistrust of the 'godless constitution' and the 'state without principles.'"[18] While the church did not work openly against the Weimar Republic, it made its position clear, as one pastor who worked in Frankfurt in the 1920s recalled:

In the old churches before World War I, the general prayer for the church included a paragraph where the Kaiser, his family, and the army of our land were prayed for. It was an established prayer. After 1918, this prayer was left out. The Kaiser had abdicated, each and every prince had disappeared from view, and there was a vacuum that wasn't refilled. Only when Hindenburg was elected Reich President [in 1925]—then, suddenly, we prayed once again for the authorities. That wasn't ordered; it just happened. All at once it was possible again, because Hindenburg represented the old Germany—essentially, the Kaiser's Germany. When he was elected after the death of Friedrich Ebert, a wave of enthusiasm went through the people.[19]

But Hindenburg, at 78, was too old to control the battling factions on the German political scene. Many Germans sincerely feared a revolution and were weary of Weimar democracy, which, as far as they could see, promoted nothing more than political mayhem. Ironically, the party that benefited most dramatically from such sentiments was Hitler's National Socialist Party (NSADP)—the Nazi party—which was responsible for much of the political violence. Its percentage of the vote in the Reichstag elections jumped from 2.6 percent in 1928 to 18.3 percent in November 1932.

The rise in the NSADP's fortunes was partly due to fear of increasing Communist strength. But while the German Communist party, led by Ernst Thalmann, increased its percentage in the Reichstag, its rise was not as dramatic: 10.6 percent in 1928, 13.1 percent in 1930, and 16.8 percent in 1932.[20] There had been regional Communist uprisings in the early 1920s in Berlin, the Ruhr region, Saxony, and Thuringia. All had been put down, but the prospect of revolution alarmed the German middle and upper classes and the Evangelical Church. Many people believed that Adolf Hitler was the only potential leader who could appeal to the same groups being wooed by the Communists — the working class and the millions of unemployed.

By the 1932 Reichstag elections, the masses were being actively courted. Change was in the air. Every night at the Sportspalast in Berlin, speakers for the different parties competed at the microphone for the audience's approval. It was a carnival-like scene. The Sportspalast held 20,000 people; tickets were sold for seats on the balconies. Bleacher seats on the main floor were cheaper, and then, for most of the crowd, there was standing room. Marta S., at that time a second-year history student at the university in Berlin, went there almost every evening with friends:

> By 4:30 in the afternoon the street in front of the hall was already full; at 5 the hall was opened. Party members circulated with petitions. . . . The programs started at 8 in the evening. Housewives and workers told how they had become Communists. I heard Ernst Thalmann there once; he didn't speak demagogically at all. No one left, and sometimes people would faint from the heat, hunger, and the crowd and had to be carried out. You saw how enormous the commitment and morale among the Communists were, and we thought that a Soviet Germany was almost there.[21]

Audiences at the rallies held by the moderate parties — the Social Democrats and the Center party — were, she remembered, more subdued. But on the platform, she recalled,

> the speakers had difficulty not to fight with each other. Their goal was to support Hindenburg, but that was the only thing they had in common. We knew that Hindenburg had a conscience, above all, that he had a sense of duty. But the readiness of the voters to work for him was missing. There was nothing there to electrify a young person. We were too young to know that the very time to support the middle is when it's weak. I was looking for a party that would prevent us from becoming Soviet.
>
> The Nazi rallies were like the Communist ones — packed full, with banners and singing. They were demagogues. We had learned to be distrustful of demagoguery, but we were pulled in anyway. Goebbels was a powerful, hypnotic orator. He had a sense for what the masses wanted to hear.[22]

Marta S. had been scarred by the Weimar years. Her mother, widowed in World War I, had scraped by during the inflation years by taking in boarders. Marta lived in an unheated room in Berlin. Every weekend, the different groups — the Nazis and their storm troopers or the Communist Red Front — marched with torches down the street below her window. When she left her room in the morning to go to the university, she walked past the human debris left by the war and the 1920s — disabled soldiers and unemployed men with signs around their necks, begging. When she went to the Sportspalast, she was moved most by the rhetoric of the Nazis as they railed against the Versailles Treaty and its humiliation of a once proud German people. "Fourteen years!" Adolf Hitler thundered at one rally in 1932, and people like Marta S. could list every humiliation they had lived through since 1918. "It's enough!" screamed Hitler, and the crowd rose to its feet, thousands of right arms stretching into the air, a mass gesture of defiance and reborn national pride.

There were Germans who felt nothing but repulsion for the growing political movement, but even they acknowledged the power it exerted over most of their compatriots. The Bonhoeffer family, recalled Emmi Bonhoeffer, was horrified at

> this petty nationalism, this arrogance combined with uncultured narrowness. It was so unbearable. There are people who had no idea what was going on, who nevertheless rejected Hitler simply out of some human instinct that this tree would bear no good fruit.
>
> But there's that saying, "Nothing is more successful than success," and he had immensely great success. This faceless mediocrity fled into that success, mixed with this pseudoideal of racial purity, and the idea of an oppressed people throwing off its chains. That was underscored by expressions such as Churchill used: "The lion has torn his chains." Then they felt like lions, terribly proud. But a lion is a noble animal, and Hitler, on the contrary, was a small, despicable boor. But the people warmed themselves in this sun. The lion tearing his chains! Magnificent! . . . In any case, most Germans did have the feeling that it was a great age.[23]

Those who welcomed Hitler's rise to power saw a new sense of order and purpose in the Nazi party. The working-class youths who had drifted aimlessly through the 1920s were now in uniform; when they marched down the street, they marched in step. Most important, they looked toward the future, not bitterly into the past. Stefanie von Mackensen was doing volunteer work in working-class settlements in Köslin, where she and her husband had moved. One day, she recalled,

> two unemployed youths came walking toward me in SA uniforms. To my astonished question as to how they had come to be National Socialists, they explained, "Yes, there's someone who is concerned about us, who's giving us something to do again, and who includes us in society. And that is Adolf Hitler."[24]

Von Mackensen knew that such settlements, filled with unemployed youths and war widows struggling to raise their families, were fertile ground for Communist ideology. If Hitler could lure them from that, was he not exactly the leader needed to resurrect Germany from the gloom of defeat and to prevent it from going the way of Soviet Russia?

The "German Christians"

It was not only on the political front that various groups promised Germans a vision for the future. Within the Evangelical Church, too, different theological trends emerged during the Weimar period; they help to explain why some German Protestants subsequently became pro-Nazi "German Christians" and others, opposing them, established the Confessing Church.

A pietistic revival movement had swept through many German churches in the late nineteenth century and enjoyed a resurgence in the 1920s. It had begun with a new emphasis on scripture and the Reformation confessions. Wilhelm Niemöller believed that the strength of this movement in Westphalia was one reason the Confessing Church later became strong there:

> During the last century, Westphalia had a so-called reawakening movement, a very remarkable phenomenon. Suddenly everyone became pious. No one stole anymore, and all the dreadful things that we think of as being part of human existence disappeared, and the churches were filled. New churches were built, because the old ones weren't large enough.[25]

The church-centered, scripturally conservative Protestantism of these Christians enabled some of them to oppose, fairly early, the "German Christian" attempts to adapt the Christian faith to Nazi political ideology.

But a different kind of revivalism also arose during the 1920s. It too preached the importance of traditional moral values, which it saw threatened by secular philosophies and the new cultural developments of the Weimar years. At the same time, the birth of extreme "folk religions," which mixed selected scriptural passages with reflections on nature, the Fatherland, and the German *Volk*, appealed to Germans who were reaching back to old cultural traditions as a bulwark against the uncertainty of the Weimar years. Nazi rhetoric used this theme. Hitler's speeches emphasized that the German people embodied, as no other people on earth, a deep spirituality and culture. These were the very qualities that, if harnessed, could restore the German Reich to its former glory.

Within the Nazi party itself, however, there was great ambivalence toward Christianity. The faith of true party believers was Nazism, and they viewed Christianity as a weak, outmoded superstition that would eventually disappear. The most rabid exposition of this view was Alfred Rosenberg's *The Myth of the Twentieth Century*, a bizarre blend of selected New Testament verses and citations from Hitler's *Mein Kampf*. Rosenberg's book, published in 1930, was aggressively anti-Semitic, anti-papal (it was censured by the Vatican), and, in its essence, anti-Christian. Rosenberg claimed that the German people were surrounded by enemies and had been infiltrated from within by two groups — the Jews, who sought to destroy the Aryan race, and the Christians, who wanted to sap its national pride. The honor of the German people was at constant war with the forces of internationalism, with which the Christian churches (particularly the Catholic Church) were identified. Moreover, Germany's churches compromised the ideals of *Volk* and Fatherland by their "shameful" worship of the cross, which, Rosenberg contended, had no place in the spiritual life of a proud people.

It may seem surprising that Rosenberg's book had any credibility at all among Christians. Indeed, his fanaticism was ultimately a liability, for even the "German Christians" rejected the scope of his attacks on the Christian faith. Much Nazi propaganda, however, hedged its criticism of the churches. The Nazis claimed to be attacking "negative" Christianity, which threatened to devour German moral principles. The alternative, as stated in the 1920 Nazi party platform, was "positive" Christianity, which would defend the supremacy of the German people.

Most Christians ignored the basic paganism of Nazism and focused, instead, upon the "positive" Christianity that the party promised. Even before it came to power, the Nazi party tried to manipulate kindred spirits within the German Evangelical Church. In 1930, a meeting was held to form a national "Christian-German Movement"; it was attended by a pastor, two of the Kaiser's sons, a Nazi member of the Prussian regional parliament (the *Landtag*), and two editors of Nazi newspapers—one of whom was young Josef Goebbels, Hitler's future propaganda minister.[26] But the "Christian-German Movement," although strongly nationalist (it aligned itself with the German National People's party, which formed a coalition with the Nazis in 1932), was not predominantly a church group. The Protestant group that emerged to embrace Nazi ideology, and that sought after 1933 to build and lead a Reich Church, was the "German Christians."

The "German Christians," formally founded in May 1932, hoped institutionally to unite the regional member churches of the German Evangelical Church into a national Reich Church. Theologically, they embraced the spirit of "positive Christianity." They were strongly anti-Semitic and supported the Nazi agenda as the political reflection of "true" German Christianity. Their preaching adopted the same triumphalist tone heard in Hitler's speeches. Joachim Hossenfelder, a "German Christian" pastor who became bishop of Brandenburg in 1933, proclaimed, "Christian faith is a heroic, manly thing. God speaks in blood and *Volk* a more powerful language than He does in the idea of humanity."[27] The German people were seen as God's chosen instrument at a crucial historical moment, with Adolf Hitler as the man who would lead them out of the wilderness.

Mainstream Protestants (and those who subsequently became Confessing Christians) viewed the "German Christians" as a politicized group whose faith was no longer based upon the Bible but upon Nazi ideology. As events would show, the Nazis used the "German Christians" as an instrument to gain control of the German Evangelical Church; when this failed, Nazi party support for the "German Christians" died. More rabid Nazis (including Alfred Rosenberg) opposed party support for the "German Christians" from the beginning. The "German Christians" saw themselves as the renewal movement of a church that had lost its national bearings and was in danger of losing its faith.

Hope, Anxiety, and the Birth of the New Reich

After 1933, as the practical consequences of "German Christian" faith for the church became evident, some of its early members left. But toward the end of the Weimar era, many felt that their refound national identity had been given a cultural and spiritual language. It seemed as though Germany at last had a sense of direction. Marta S. recalled how as a schoolchild she had felt ashamed to be German when her teachers talked bitterly of how the rest of Europe looked down on the Germans:

> We had the feeling we had no future. We suffered the consequences of World War I, which had broken out before we could walk, and we thought that we would never have a chance. What gets put into schoolchildren's heads doesn't go away quickly.[28]

Now she had the sense of exhilaration that Germany held its future in its own hands. Wilhelm Niemöller, who had ended the war as a defeated soldier, joined the Nazi party in 1925. Years later, he searched for the words to describe what he felt in 1933:

> We didn't exactly have the wish for revenge, I don't think it was that, but we wanted to regain our national importance. We didn't want to be somebody again—that sounds so much like ambition, it wasn't that either—but we wanted to be German

brothers alongside German brothers. Then along came this man who could hit things right on the target, and who stood for a united, great German Reich. That was the sweetest sound to our ears.[29]

On January 30, 1933, Adolf Hitler became Reich chancellor; by March 23, he was granted absolute power by the Enabling Act, passed by a Reichstag in which most of those who might have opposed him were conspicuously absent. (Many Communist delegates were already in the detention camps that preceded the concentration camps; 26 of the Social Democrats were prevented by the SA from entering the building.) The speed with which Hitler was able to dismantle German civil rights and its parliamentary system testified not only to his extreme ruthlessness but to the failure of many Germans to see what they were losing. In their enthusiasm at the birth of the new Reich, they retreated from the political responsibility that had burdened them in the Weimar Republic; in their adoration for the new Führer, they were relieved to become followers.

In the Evangelical Church, some members greeted the Third Reich with a mixture of hope and foreboding. Most, however, welcomed it. At the opening worship service for the new Reichstag members, held in Berlin's Nikolaikirche, Otto Dibelius preached; Hitler and Goebbels were absent, having chosen to visit the graves of SA "martyrs." Dibelius announced that "once order has been restored, justice and love must reign once more," but he also said,

> And when it's a matter of life or death for the nation, then the power of the state must be applied thoroughly and energetically. . . . We have learned from Dr. Martin Luther that the church may not get in the way of state power when [the state] does that which it is called to do. Not even when this [power] becomes hard and ruthless. . . . When the state carries out its office against those who bury the foundation of state order, above all against those who destroy honor with vituperative and cruel words that scorn faith, vilify death for the Fatherland — then [the state] is ruling in God's name![30]

Like Dibelius, most Protestant leaders welcomed the restoration of Germany's honor that Nazism seemed to promise, even as they sought to keep the church free of "German Christian" ideology. The inherent contradictions of this position left them completely unable to respond to the actual ways in which the Nazis exercised power. It blinded them to the fact that despair, not hope, had enabled Hitler's rise to power. The Third Reich would create a political system based on the worst that human beings are capable of, on base fears and prejudices, ambition and ruthlessness. The most self-destructive goals would be given the illusion of reasonableness, not through inherent rationality but through brute force. Now this brute force was at large and officially sanctioned, rounding up artists, writers, and racial and political targets in every walk of German life. Far from fulfilling the glorious prophecies of the rise of a new Reich, these developments were themselves omens for Germany's future, for a nation that one day would be held to account for what Nazism did in its name.

Gertrud Staewen was among the first Germans to taste what life under the new regime was really like. She had thrived on the changes for women in the 1920s, but they had altered her own future. She was now divorced, supporting two small children through a variety of poor-paying jobs. By 1933, she had written two books (one an oral history of working-class despair in Berlin) that were banned by the Nazi party. By May 1, some of her friends were already sitting in Gestapo prisons.

Nevertheless, Staewen and a small group of friends decided, on May 1, to go to Tempelhof Field in Berlin. The Führer had chosen this day for the inauguration of the new Reich. The airfield was filled with the brown SA uniforms and black SS ones. Banners flying the swastika waved over the platforms at the front of the field, where the dignitaries and speakers for the new Reich were illuminated by blazing spotlights. At the age of 88, her voice shaking, Staewen remembered the scene:

> I'll never forget that day from its beginning till the end. It was the most dreadful thing I ever experienced. What happened with the Jews was also dreadful — so when I say "the most dreadful" here, it's because there it unfolded right before my eyes. I saw the huge masses with their flags, brightly lit in broad daylight, and heard this constant trumpeting of the fanfare. He introduced it, this music, a braying, destructive, piping music. And the Tempelhof Field was filled to the last place with jubilant, screaming people. Only our group sat there and wept. Everyone else was simply enraptured.
>
> Then, as it began to get dark, he came. He was carried on the shoulders of the SS men, and others held onto his hands. He was carried upright through the masses of people, who cheered him and kissed his feet and — he came right by me. That one time in my life I saw him. And I knew, Germany is now dead, forever. Even today I don't want it to rise again. Since that day I wouldn't trust it for anything.[31]

✯ 3 ✯

Nationalism, Nazism, and the Churches: The Early Period

Gleichschaltung and Nazism's "Religiosity"

THE MASS DISPLAY of enthusiasm at Tempelhof Field on May 1 demonstrated the two kinds of responses Hitler drew from his admirers. One was jubilant hysteria, which Hitler's personal charisma triggered in those who believed in him. In rigid contrast were the rows upon rows of brown- and black-shirted SA and SS members standing in the broad center of the field. Their emotions were betrayed only by the hundreds of right arms that simultaneously jutted into the air and the hundreds of voices that bellowed *"Sieg Heil"* as one voice. Both responses represented Hitler's power: the spontaneous emotions of the masses and the controlled obeisance of his disciplined party — in the locked step, the uniforms, the unquestioning loyalty to his dictates.

Ultimately, Hitler's might relied upon his ability to unite all Germans behind the Nazi worldview and eliminate any hindrance to this goal. He made this clear in a speech on February 3, 1933 to a group of army and marine commanders. He would not tolerate, he said, "the expression of any principles that stand opposed to the goal. Whoever doesn't convert must be subdued."[1] For this, Hitler could not rely upon enthusiasm, which, like other emotions, is fickle. So began the systematic *Gleichschaltung* (literally, "switching into the same gear") of German society.

The *Gleichschaltung* of the German nation encompassed every level of society. Each citizen was affected, step by step, by a series of laws regulating everything from mandatory party membership for the practice of many professions to the requirement that civil servants replace the traditional German greeting, *Guten Tag*, with *Heil Hitler*. Oaths of personal loyalty to the Führer were introduced in the military and the civil service, where "non-Aryans" and politically unreliable persons were summarily fired or pushed into early retirement. All other political parties were banned. One by one, nongovernment organizations — artists' groups, youth organizations, sports clubs, women's groups — were incorporated into new organizations placed under Nazi party leadership.

30

In retrospect, it is astonishing how quickly German society was restructured to serve Nazi purposes, but it is important to recognize that many new structures were initially created parallel to, not in place of, old ones. It would have taken Hitler years to dismantle the bureaucracy he inherited; his tactic was to set up organizations that gradually took control over or absorbed the existing structures. In some parts of the civil service, this was accomplished fairly rapidly. In others, full control was not really achieved until after 1939, when comprehensive wartime emergency laws eliminated what little independence remained in the bureaucracy.

For the average German, this initially resulted in considerable confusion as to which office was responsible for what. Many civil servants became frustrated and fought to hold their own territory against what they saw as party-appointed incompetents. There was a police department, but also the Gestapo; there was a court system, but — when the Nazis did not like the verdict — special courts to deal with crimes against the state. Eventually, of course, the Nazis would have the last word, but in the early years they did not always have it. From 1933 until 1935, the prevailing attitude among many bureaucrats was to make whatever concessions necessary to the new regime, but to try to hold their own territory.[2]

The majority of bureaucrats, for reasons of conviction or career security, conformed to the demands of *Gleichschaltung*. Between Hitler's election as chancellor at the end of January and the end of April, the number of Nazi party members rose from 849,000 to 1,644,884.[3] Some Germans joined because of new professional requirements, but even in professions that did not yet require party membership, many Germans joined to advance their careers. In 1933, refusing to participate in *Gleichschaltung* required an inordinate amount of clear-sightedness and will. One of the few Germans to resist at this stage was a young secretary, Helene Jacobs.

Jacobs was not an active Protestant (although her resistance group later worked with Confessing Christians), nor was she personally affected by the Nazi racial laws. She was firmly committed, however, to the democratic ideals of the Weimar constitution. Her early resistance made her an outsider in the Third Reich, without such necessary papers as an "Aryan" identity card. She would remain an outsider even after 1945, when, as a result of her resistance against the Nazis, she had no official certificates or job records in a country that relied on them. As Jacobs later recalled,

> I had begun to study during that time. You received an obligatory book which you had to sign; I didn't do it. At the technical high school where I last studied, I couldn't take any exam. But I didn't want to get involved in that. It was so obvious to me that it [the Third Reich] wouldn't last. I thought, I'll just wait that long and then I'll continue. As a result, I didn't have any steady position. I worked for very little money for a Jewish attorney, and wasn't a member of any organization. Anywhere it said, "For Aryans only," I said, "What's that? There's no such thing." I kept myself away from such requirements.
>
> The point that aroused me so from the beginning was that we as a people had to show our unwillingness in some fashion, not just when the crimes began, but before, when it started, with this so-called "Aryan" ancestry. They distributed questionnaires and you had to say whether you had "Aryan" ancestors. Everyone filled them out. I said, "We can't go along with this; it's not legal. We must do something against this and throw the questionnaires away."

But today—the other people my age, they behaved totally differently at that time. Most of them built their careers then. When I said, "I'm not going to have anything to do with this," I isolated myself.[4]

The ultimate goal of *Gleichschaltung* was to capture the souls and minds of the German people. Hitler demanded not only obedience but a kind of faith. For Hitler, as historian Bernd Hey has noted,

everything was political. "The inner religious part of every human being was, in Hitler, perverted into political wishes and political will." Hitler absolutized politics and saw in the churches only a political power; he denied the reality of religion and faith. On the other hand, political power for him won "the luster of religious mastery." The religious sensibility of Hitler and his followers was channeled into political hopes; Germany's renewal became the National Socialist creed. In this way, political faith replaced religious faith, National Socialism became ever more a replacement for religion, and the party a substitute for the church.[5]

For Nazis, the *Volksgemeinschaft* (the community of German people) that Hitler sought represented an earthly version of a heavenly kingdom. All of his goals, from his plans to conquer Europe to the plan to eliminate "non-Aryan" peoples, were guided by this apocalyptic vision of a thousand-year German Reich.

This vision was incorporated by "German Christian" dogma, although, as some "German Christians" would realize too late, Hitler did not share their religious convictions. The Nazis used the "German Christians" as long as the latter appeared to be a viable political tool.

In the early months of 1933, the Nazi party even encouraged Germans to rejoin the churches, and the Evangelical Church rejoiced at the apparent reversal of a trend of declining membership. In 1932, 215,908 left the church and only 49,700 joined it. In 1933, 323,618 joined the church and only 56,849 left it.[6]

But for party stalwarts, such statistics, like the convictions of the "German Christians," were irrelevant. In the words of one SA member who left the church, he needed no church, "German Christian" or otherwise: "My religion is my Führer Adolf Hitler, my people and my Fatherland."[7]

Nevertheless, in the early years of the Third Reich, many Christians felt that their religious convictions were congruent with the Nazi worldview, and this illusion was nurtured by party propaganda. The article on religion in the 1920 Nazi party platform read:

We demand the freedom of all religious confessions in the state, insofar as they do not jeopardize its existence or conflict with the manners and moral sentiments of the Germanic race.

The party as such upholds the point of view of a positive Christianity without tying itself confessionally to any one confession. It combats the Jewish-materialistic spirit at home and abroad and is convinced that a permanent recovery of our people can only be achieved from within on the basis of common good before individual good.[8]

Church members whose initial attitude toward National Socialism was favorable read this as a guarantee of religious freedom. Stefanie von Mackensen was, in her own words, one of those individuals who were often in the party in good faith in the positive Christianity that Hitler had declared. . . . At first one basically couldn't see anything else there but a confession of Christianity, but that became falsified into an "Aryan" Christianity — at first hidden, later ever more open.[9]

But, of course, by declaring that "positive Christianity" should combat the "Jewish-materialistic spirit," the party's commitment to "Aryan" Christianity was explicit. This fact was not so much hidden as overlooked by a church in which anti-Semitism was very much taken for granted. Moreover, Nazi propaganda connected the "Jewish-materialistic spirit" to the dangers of Bolshevism, using the specter of Communism to fan the flames of racial hatred. Critics of the Nazi regime were often accused of supporting the Soviet cause. An anonymous letter sent to a Confessing Church pastor in May 1935, complained, "We were just barely rescued from Bolshevist chaos by Hitler and you don't need to throw sand in the eyes of the people with your Confessing Church politics."[10]

For the Nazi party, the key phrases in its article on religion were those that clearly stated the ideological limits of religious freedom. The goal of *Gleichschaltung* was not just absolute political sovereignty but ideological supremacy as well. The ideological conflict between the German Evangelical Church and the Nazi state was based on three issues. The first two, the tradition of state sovereignty over the church and the gradual trend toward church-state separation during the Bismarck era, presented conflicting demands and were a source of tension within the Protestant opposition to Nazism. The third, as became gradually clear, was the crucial question of the moral and political legitimacy of the Nazi state and its decrees. The conclusions that individuals drew about Nazism's legitimacy were decisive in determining not just whether but how they would choose to oppose it. For critics of Nazism who viewed the Nazi state as legitimate, albeit unsatisfactory, the choice would be to work within the limits of the Nazi system. Those who denied this legitimacy were led, ultimately, to resist Nazism actively. This difference would lead to some of the bitterest divisions within the Confessing Church.

The *Reichskirche* and the Formation of the Pastors' Emergency League

The initial conflict between the "German Christians" and mainstream Protestants was over the issue of the *Reichskirche*. Just as he wanted every organization under party control, Hitler wanted Germany's 28 regional churches united into a Reich Church. Many within the church had long favored a move toward unifying the churches under a central office, and Hitler's plan did not at first meet with much church protest.

The protests began with the question of who would preside as bishop over the Reich Church. Protestant leaders nominated Friedrich von Bodelschwingh, a respected Westphalian pastor who headed Bethel, a large charitable community for the mentally ill and disabled. The "German Christians," however, had already selected their candidate for Reich bishop: Ludwig Müller, a little-known pastor and former military chaplain whose sole administrative experience had been as regional leader of the "German Christians" in eastern Prussia. He was also an *Alte Kämpfer* —

an old fighter, the term used for early members of the Nazi party, and had known Hitler since the 1920s.

Protestant leaders were outraged by the "German Christians'" usurpation of their right to appoint their bishop and by the selection of the unknown, inexperienced Müller. Because both Müller and von Bodelschwingh were members of the Prussian church (the largest regional church, the Church of the Old Prussian Union included the Protestant churches in the states of Westphalia, Rhineland, Berlin-Brandenburg, and Prussia), the fight over ecclesiastical control centered there. In May 1933, representatives from the regional churches met and (after several rounds of voting failed to give either candidate a two-thirds majority) voted, 91 to 8, to elect Friederich von Bodelschwingh as their Reich bishop.[11]

With Müller's defeat, August Jäger, a lawyer from the ministry of culture, stepped in and placed the entire Prussian Church under police jurisdiction. A number of pastors were fired, suspended, or arrested, and the "German Christians" and Nazi party mounted a vicious campaign against von Bodelschwingh. Under this pressure, the leader of Bethel resigned.

Church elections were planned to be held in all regional churches on July 23, 1933 to elect delegates to a national synod that would officially elect a new Reich bishop. In a few regional churches, the Young Reformation Movement, an opposition group, placed its candidates on the ballot; but in many regions, the lists of candidates were almost exclusively "German Christian." The Nazi party openly supported the "German Christians." Three days before the elections, party chief Rudolf Hess ordered all party members to get their names on the elections lists in their parishes, reminding them that "participation in the election is mandatory."[12] On election eve, Hitler himself openly supported the "German Christians" in a nationally broadcast radio speech. Church members entering their churches to vote were confronted by rows of SA members wearing sandwich boards carrying the names of the "German Christian" candidates. Nationally, the "German Christians" won two thirds of the vote, giving them the majority in regional synods throughout Germany. This paved the way for synodal approval of Ludwig Müller as Reich bishop and for "German Christian" control of many regional churches.

The national synod meeting to confirm Ludwig Müller as Reich bishop was held in September 1933 and became known as the "brown synod," since so many delegates appeared in brown SA uniforms. Of the 229 delegates, only 75 were from the Young Reformation Movement. Throughout the meeting, they protested the decisions being made and were shouted down. When the synod passed the "Aryan paragraph," which required that pastors and their wives be free of "Jewish blood," the 75 walked out. Müller was elected Reich bishop.[13]

The machinations of the "German Christians," the police measures taken against the Prussian churches, and the Nazi party's role in the synodal election aroused a furor within the churches. Protestant outrage reached its peak after the national "German Christian" rally, held at the Berlin Sportspalast on November 13, 1933. Decorated with swastikas and banners proclaiming the unity of Christianity and National Socialism, the hall was filled. A series of speakers called for the removal of all pastors unsympathetic to National Socialism, the formation of a separate church for Christians of Jewish descent, and for implementation of the "Aryan paragraph" and the removal of the Old Testament from the Bible.

The "Aryan paragraph" became the focal point of early church protests — not, it should be noted, because of its anti-Semitism but because it raised the question of church independence. Protestant leaders were ominously silent with respect to the significance of the "Aryan paragraph" for "non-Aryans" and to Nazi racial laws in general. When the first nation-wide boycott of Jewish businesses took place on April 1, 1933, there was no protest from the Evangelical Church. Indeed, Berlin church superintendent Otto Dibelius (soon to be suspended by "German Christians" from office) responded angrily to U.S. church protests against the boycott. The boycott, Dibelius wrote them, was a "natural" response to "international anti-German propaganda" and to what he saw as disproportionate Jewish influence in German society.[14]

But Protestant leaders viewed the attempt to exclude "non-Aryan" pastors and members from the church as a serious curtailment of confessional freedom and as interference in church affairs. In 1933, the German Evangelical Church employed 18,000 pastors; 37 of them were "full Jews."[15] When the church protested the "Aryan paragraph," it was giving Hitler notice that it would not have its institutional prerogatives infringed upon.

The Sportspalast rally and the "Aryan paragraph" opened the eyes of a number of pastors who initially had been sympathetic to the "German Christians." After the Wittenberg Synod, a Pastors' Emergency League (PEL) was founded to help those who had been fired or arrested in the Prussian churches. The PEL was the precursor of the Confessing Church; its founders included Martin Niemöller, who had become the pastor of the *Annenkirche* in the wealthy Berlin suburb of Dahlem. The founding statement of the PEL pledged to protest all infringements on confessional freedom by the state and explicitly opposed the "Aryan paragraph." By the end of 1933, the PEL had over 6,000 members.[16]

In its opposition to the "Aryan paragraph," the PEL distinguished between Jews and Jewish Christians (that is, Jews who had converted to Christianity). Its concern was for the latter, who, it emphasized, were full, legitimate members of the Evangelical Church. But under Nazi pressure, some church leaders would retreat from this position. Few recognized the deeper question posed by the "Aryan paragraph" — namely, what the Nazi measures against the Jews should have signified to a religion whose founder, a Jew, had told his followers to love their neighbors.

One of the few who understood the implications of the "Aryan paragraph" was Hans Ehrenberg, a Jewish Christian pastor whose attempts to remain in his parish ended with his deportation to Buchenwald in 1938. In 1933, Ehrenberg prophesied, "The Church of Christ in Germany stands or falls in 1933 on the temptation to eradicate Judaism from itself."[17] In a letter shortly thereafter to Berlin Pastor Gerhard Jacobi, Ehrenberg stressed that the Jewish Christians in the German Evangelical Church were "a living monument . . . that belief in Christ is not a national religion."[18]

But for many Germans, Christianity had indeed become a "national religion." Even those critical of the "Aryan paragraph" continued to support the political policies of the new Nazi regime. None of them (as yet) could be considered a renegade in the Protestant tradition of support for throne and altar. Martin Niemöller had voted for the Nazi party in 1933. His church superintendent, Otto Dibelius, along with Bishop Meiser of Bavaria, Bishop Wurm of Württemberg, and Bishop Marahrens of Hannover, had also welcomed the political changes in 1933. The leader of the regional church of Westphalia, Karl Koch, had even been a delegate of the right-wing

German National People's party in the Reichstag from 1928 to 1930. All of these men were part of the early church opposition to Nazi policies toward the church. But they, and the PEL, limited their concerns to strictly confessional matters. When Hitler pulled Germany out of the League of Nations on October 15, 1933, the newly formed PEL sent a telegram of support "in the name of over 2,500 Protestant pastors who don't belong to the 'German Christians.'"[19]

The Beginnings of Church–State Tension

Yet the differences between church nationalists and the National Socialists were becoming gradually evident. The main factor was the blatant politicization of the church by the "German Christians." In fact, after the "German Christians'" electoral victory in the church elections and the Sportspalast rally, the issue threatened to split the German Evangelical Church. Most German Protestant leaders, proud of their theological tradition and its academic standards, viewed the "German Christians" as a sect. "German Christian" attempts to "aryanize" the Bible and rewrite various traditional liturgies to express the new *Volksgeist* led their critics to speak disdainfully of "the so-called worship services of the 'German Christians.'"[20] The theological differences and more serious incidents (of the Gestapo forcibly opening locked church buildings, for example, so that the "German Christians" could use them[21]) aroused concern in the international church community as well.

International protests about "German Christian" excesses were greeted with irritation in Nazi circles, and Hitler responded by abruptly changing tactics. Nazi officials began to emphasize the separation of church and state and to treat the church controversy as a purely internal church affair, having nothing to do with the Nazi party or the government.

There had been some talk in Nazi party circles of either forcing party members to join the "German Christians" or expelling people from the party who had not voted correctly in the July church elections. Both suggestions were vetoed in memos issued by Martin Bormann and Rudolf Hess.[22] Other party directives announced that the Nazi party intended to remain neutral on the church question and forbade party members from speaking publicly at religious rallies and from attending religious functions in party uniform.[23] It was the opposite of previous Nazi party tactics and shows the extent to which Hitler was prepared to abandon his erstwhile allies, the "German Christians." Indeed, some party insiders now scorned their representatives in the church struggle. Both interior minister Wilhelm Frick and cabinet minister Hermann Göring considered Reich bishop Müller a bungler,[24] and even Prussian church commissioner Jäger described Müller as "a very shifty rascal and a scoundrel."[25]

This internal party maneuvering, however, did nothing to defuse the fight within the churches. Ludwig Müller, maligned as he might be, was still Reich bishop, and enough state measures had been taken to threaten church independence. Many regional church offices were now held by churchpeople sympathetic to the party, and the sporadic arrests and interrogations of pastors by the Gestapo showed the limits on confessional freedom in Nazi Germany.

The stage was set for the convergence (in May 1934) of the various parts of the church opposition to the "German Christians" into the Confessing Church. Church opposition leaders were fairly united in their theological criticism of the "German Christians." Attempts to rewrite the Bible and remove the Old Testament did not win widespread approval among Germany's theologically traditional Protestant pastors and bishops. In addition, many shared Lutheran lawyer Heinz Brunotte's concern that "We have not received a state church . . . but we have received a thoroughly politicized church, in which political law continues to threaten to crush the law of belief."[26]

This was the spark that ignited the church opposition: It did not want the ideologically based religion of the "German Christians" infiltrating German Protestantism, discarding parts of the Bible, and reinterpreting scripture for ideological purposes. But in 1933 and 1934, it was not at all clear to most church leaders what this had to do with the Nazi regime itself. After all, Hitler, skillfully extricating himself from the controversies the "German Christians" had aroused in the churches, had emphasized that theological differences within the church were for church leaders, not the party, to resolve.

Reaching back for the certainties of Lutheran tradition, church leaders felt bound by their loyalties to throne and altar. Article 7 of the Augsburg Confession of 1530 had defined the church's role as preaching the Gospel and distributing the sacraments. As long as these two functions were fulfilled, the church existed, regardless of who controlled other church affairs.

For centuries, this had been the basis of the arrangement of German Protestantism with landed patrons. It did not, however, settle the troubling demands that Nazism was already making on the churches — demands, for example, for state control of church administrative boards or for pastors to swear loyalty oaths to the Führer. The Nazis' demands would ultimately be much higher, but in 1933, many within the church opposition were discussing what should be rendered reasonably to the Nazi Caesar. "Opposition" at this point was more an attempt to define church boundaries and protect the integrity of Gospel and sacrament.

In practice, this led to bizarre situations that would later haunt some pastors. In Ernst Wilm's parish in Mennighüffen, for example, the church elders had unanimously joined him in supporting the PEL. Eventually, over 90 percent of his parish members would sign the red membership cards of the Confessing Church:

> Part of it was that the false teachings of the "German Christians" were becoming more obvious. The Sportspalast rally in Berlin — such things opened the eyes of the parish. We didn't have a "German Christian" group in Mennighüffen. Later, more and more teachers, bank employees, and civil servants had to become party members, but the majority of them stayed in the church.
>
> The grotesque thing was that we had to devote almost half of our working time, until we hired a secretary, for people who wanted to trace their "Aryan" ancestors in the church books. They came constantly to the parsonage and asked for the birth certificates of their grandparents. Only the church books had the records of this, and they went back to around the 30 Years' War [1648].[27]

In 1933, the churches' refusal to comply with the state demand for proof of "Aryan ancestry" would have been an act of civil resistance that would have publicly questioned the legitimacy of the Nazi state itself. Not surprisingly, most church pastors did not even think of such an act, let alone its implications.

The question of the legality of Nazi decrees was already being raised in 1933, however, by lawyers and judges concerned by *Gleichschaltung* and its implications for civil law. The Nazi attitude toward civil law had been upheld by Carl Schmitt, a prominent state law professor. In an apologetic titled *"Lehre vom totalen Staat,"* Schmitt argued that, in a revolution, all old laws are automatically invalid. The laws of the new Nazi regime derived their legitimacy from the fact that Nazism represented "the only and unified will" of the people.[28]

This perspective, however, was not shared by a number of lawyers and judges. (Schmitt would subsequently retract his words and become an opponent of the Nazi regime.) It would take Hitler several years to transform the judiciary; in the early years, the Nazi subversion of the legal system was accomplished not so much by stacking the courts as by taking politically sensitive cases away from them. The list of "political" crimes grew, and these were put under the jurisdiction of the infamous *Sondergerichte* (special courts). Accordingly, the number of "political" crimes on the court dockets soared, from 268 in 1932 to 11,156 in 1933.[29] At the same time, the Gestapo took over cases that previously would have required a court trial. In February 1936, the concentration camps were put under Gestapo administration, and the civil courts lost any control over the Gestapo. (This meant, for example, that the Gestapo could rearrest someone who had been acquitted by the courts.)

Many cases affecting Confessing Church members landed in the civil courts, and in the first few years of the Third Reich, the civil courts still showed some independence. Heinrich Schmidt, a lawyer who worked for the Confessing Church, recalled that in 1934 and 1935, 70 to 80 percent of these cases were won.[30] When Karl Koch was removed by the "German Christians" from his position as president of the Westphalian church, he successfully appealed in a civil court for reinstatement.[31]

Fortunately for the Confessing Church, one of the most articulate critics of the Nazi understanding of revolutionary law was a lawyer and member of the church administration in Oldenburg — Wilhelm Flor. In an essay published in the October 1933 issue of *Junge Kirche,* the church opposition magazine, Flor noted ironically that in a revolution, "people who express legal reservations will be characterized as backward; it's said that they don't understand the spirit of the new time."[32] Nevertheless, Flor contended, Germans were not living under revolutionary law, and he proceeded to state the case that existing law was constitutional until it was constitutionally and legally changed.

In retrospect, Flor's arguments seem irrelevant; the Nazis exercised their power by trodding over the law, not by trying to make it constitutional. But since Flor represented the view of most German civil courts at the time,[33] he and a small group of other lawyers were able until 1937 to defend members of the Confessing Church in German courts on the basis of existing law — and win.

What Carl Schmitt saw as the source of state legitimacy was, essentially, mob rule, but it was mob rule in a nation that had developed compartmentalized bureaucracy to an art form. The disciplines of theology and of law were rooted in traditions so deep that, for purists, no new development would be accepted until it could prove its consistency with precedent. German lawyers and judges who wished to continue their careers furnished proof of "Aryan" ancestry and made other concessions to the new system—including remaining silent as their Jewish colleagues were disbarred and moved out of the civil service. Yet they would continue to show some judicial independence.

The long-term effect of this ambiguous situation was tragic, for many early critics of Nazi policies—particularly those in the churches—took the attitudes and occasional successes of the legal profession as a sign of political normalcy. Conscientious lawyers and civil servants failed, naturally, to thwart the course of Nazism. But in the early years of the Third Reich, they fostered the illusion that the Nazi regime was a legitimate government which could be dealt with through conventional means. Many individuals who subsequently resisted Nazism initially sought to uphold certain standards of morality and duty in the public sphere, even as these standards were being brutally violated by their nation's Nazi leaders.

Their tragedy was not merely that these standards failed to alter the course of Nazism but that Nazism rendered such standards irrelevant. *Gleichschaltung* and the growing power of the Gestapo ensured conformity through fear. At the same time, conservative nationalists within the government and the churches continued to believe that they shared a common goal with Nazism and could moderate its more extreme aspects.

Within the German Evangelical Church, these conservatives remained convinced that the church-state conflicts could be resolved through compromises with the state. In an 11-page memo written in January 1935, Paul Humburg (a Reformed pastor in the Rhineland Confessing Church) noted that most church leaders necessarily rejected the Nazi deification of blood and race as a violation of the first commandment. But, he contended,

> This finding does not need to mean that the church must necessarily come into conflict with the state, for this state does not carry out the aforementioned National Socialist theories 100 percent and, indeed, there are strong currents in the state and in the party which are hardly disposed to draw the conclusions resulting from these theories for the practical relation of the state to the church.[34]

Confessing Christians in the Nazi Party

The church opposition to Nazi policies, then, was hampered from the beginning by its own illusions regarding Nazi intentions. More seriously, however, it was bound by nationalist sentiments that led some church members to join the Nazi party. Most of them remained in the party, in the belief that their position could be strengthened if church interests were represented in party circles. Eberhard Bethge, a student of Dietrich Bonhoeffer and one of Bonhoeffer's closest friends, was a confidant of the group that later attempted to kill Hitler. After the war, he became a leading historian of the Confessing Church. Never himself in the Nazi party, Bethge recalled:

> There were several groups within the party—hawks and doves. Those of us in the Confessing Church—today, this is almost always left out—put great importance on having old party members with us. Some of these people today suffer a great injus-

tice. They were party members, and we didn't say, "Get out." We said, "Stay in," because when there was anything to be carried out in Berlin, somebody who had an early party number had to travel there and speak for us.[35]

Ironically, the practical uses of party connections became more valuable as Gestapo harassment of the Confessing Church increased. The low membership numbers of party members who had joined before 1933 showed them to be *Alte Kämpfer* ("old fighters"), and they had a special stature in the party. They were especially useful to the Confessing Church after 1935, when a growing number of Confessing Church members were forbidden by the Gestapo to travel outside the limits of their cities of residence. (Many people, for example, were forbidden explicitly to travel to Berlin.) "Then, too," Bethge continued,

> we wanted to prove that our attitudes were patriotic, and we did that through these people. We looked after these party members during the Nazi era and used them, and then after the war we let them fall, so to speak. One could, I think, yield to the illusion during the first three years of the Nazi period that even a pastor or a theologian could find his place in the party and, thereby, in the new German society which the party wanted. We were proud when one of us marched in an SA uniform in 1934. Then the difficulties of that became greater and greater.[36]

Herbert Mochalski, a young Confessing Church vicar in Silesia, joined the party in 1931 and also joined the local SA. In March 1935, he received a copy of a Confessing Church statement that condemned the Nazi view of religion. The statement, distributed in the Prussian churches by the Confessing Church leaders, explicitly denounced the "German Christians" and all "false gods" of race and *Volk*. After learning that pastors throughout Prussia planned to read the statement from their pulpits on March 17, interior minister Wilhelm Frick ordered police measures to stop it. Some 700 pastors were either preventively placed under house arrest or arrested after their church services for reading the declaration. Mochalski was among those arrested:

> At that time, I was still of the opinion that I represented true National Socialism and that it was the party that was betraying it. On the Saturday before the church service, the police chief came to me twice to make clear that I had to sign a promise that I wouldn't read the declaration. I refused both times. Then he said, "I'll have to come back tonight, then." It was clear to me what would happen, and I put on my SA uniform so that I would be arrested in uniform. To make it clear, you see, that here was an action taken against an *Alte Kämpfer*. That's how I still was. I was naturally making a protest. I found it scandalous that they would arrest an SA man, although it concerned church questions and not national or political questions. It was terribly embarrassing to the policeman.[37]

Neither the German Evangelical Church nor the Confessing Church ever decided to bar Nazi party members from church membership,[38] and for its part, the Nazi party itself never reached a clear stand on the issue, even as it distanced itself from the churches. Particularly in the early years of the Third Reich, the Nazi party was ambiguous in its treatment of members who were in the Confessing Church. As late as 1939, a case arose of a teacher who, as a Confessing Church member, decided to leave the party because of its views on religion. He lost his teaching job and appealed; the case went all the way to the Reichskanzlei in Berlin, where an assistant to chancellery head Hans-Heinrich Lammers reinstated him, noting that a teacher could not be fired for religious views.[39]

Such cases were hardly frequent, but they reveal the uncertainty within the Nazi party as to the significance of having Confessing Church members in its ranks. Party tactics to control critical members ranged from heart-to-heart talks to disciplinary proceedings. At the university in Berlin, Marta S. had joined the Nazi party. She had also become engaged to a young theology student who was in the Confessing Church and soon found herself in both groups:

> My husband always told me that I should know my own mind and know what I should do. I wanted only to represent my own point of view until it wasn't possible any more. Don't leave, let them throw you out — that's how we thought. . . .
>
> We had to register every Bible study with the party, but the party functionary himself came to the Bible studies, too. So we thought Christians could stay in the party after all. In the summer of 1934, the leader of the Nazi Women Students came and asked if I didn't want to succeed her as leader. They wanted someone who was a party member and a Christian. Fortunately I said no, because I needed the time for my studies. By the winter of 1935, I was relieved that I had refused. The wind had gotten colder; it had become clear to me that I would only have fallen between the wheels.
>
> I had other conflicts with the party, but it was another year before my misgivings were fully confirmed. Because I didn't remain silent in the meetings of the Nazi Student Union, I was kicked out. . . . I didn't want to leave the party, on advice of Confessing Church pastors, but to be thrown out instead, so that the party would have to show its true colors, which, of course, it didn't do. I received a letter from the party which stated that I was too "narrow and confessional," but that, because of my youth, they wouldn't bring proceedings against me.
>
> With that, I thought that I was no longer in the party, and I stopped paying my dues. But it became clear that I hadn't been ejected from the party, and that it could even be dangerous for me to leave. . . . I was invited once by the party leader at the university, and we talked until midnight. . . . He said I was too young and could always change my mind. Today, I think that he wanted to protect me. He thought I would be safer in the party.[40]

As Bethge noted, the Confessing Church encouraged people to stay in the party. As the account of Marta S. indicates, the possible political consequences of this option became apparent only gradually. But party membership had consequences for the very faith of these Christians and for their practice of their beliefs. Most crucially, it affected their decision to witness to their faith when this brought them into conflict with the party. Wilhelm Niemöller, a party member himself, recalled what he advised people:

> There was an entire group who were in the Confessing Church, were already in the party previously, and now asked: Can one, as a Christian, remain there? And, in general, we didn't aim to get the people out of the party. On the one hand, we had enough confidence to say, the more Christians in this party, the better the possible effect . . . and — I don't know if I'm saying this correctly — but, when conflicts arise and become unbearable, you shouldn't heat them up. Instead: Hold to the Lord of

the church, and the Lord of the church has the last word. And when any doubt arises — can you do this? can you do that? — then the Antichrist stands ultimately on the one side and Christ on the other, and then you should do what God commands.[41]

After Wilhelm Niemöller became active in the Pastors' Emergency League, the local Nazi party tried to throw him out. He viewed his fight to stay in as a matter of honor:

> I was truly in doubt, which has happened to me seldom in life. . . . Then all kinds of people came to me and said, "You have to complain; you can't just let this go. It's a confession of guilt if you take this." Among them was a councilor from the church consistory, a lawyer from our regional church. He said, "You absolutely must appeal this."[42]

Niemöller did, and won; after one year, he was readmitted to the Nazi party.[43] Another Confessing Christian summoned before the Nazi party leaders was Stefanie von Mackensen. At the beginning of the 1930s, her husband became vice president of the state government in Pomerania; both she and her husband joined the Nazi party in 1932. She joined the Confessing Church in 1934 and became administrative secretary of the Pomeranian Confessing Church, whose ranks included over 300 pastors and Dietrich Bonhoeffer's young theology students at his illegal seminary in Finkenwalde. Eberhard Bethge recalled that her initial appearance in Confessing Church circles was met with distrust, which was understandable in light of her husband's position. As a result of her family connections, however, she was able to help the Confessing Church until 1938, when her husband lost his job. "We belonged to those most under attack in Pomerania," Bethge recalled, "and every few days we came to Frau von Mackensen to talk about things, and she protected us where she could."[44] Initially, her activities had no repercussions for her husband, although, she said,

> That was, of course, my biggest fear. What did happen was the following. In Berlin they wanted to found an Emergency League [the PEL] to help the arrested lay members of the church. I drove to Berlin and was elected to the board of this group. When I returned, my husband — at the time, he was the second highest official in Pomerania — told me that a registered letter had arrived at his office from the interior ministry, which read, "In Berlin an Emergency League has been founded. Police observation of Frau Stefanie von Mackensen and Dr. Kroll [the other Pomeranian delegate at the Berlin meeting] is to begin at once." My husband had to give the order for police observation to the police director.
> But even that didn't damage my husband or have any apparent consequences. . . . I was often questioned by the Gestapo because I managed the church collections and they had been forbidden by Himmler. [Note: in 1937, Himmler banned many Confessing Church activities, including the collection of money.] I managed the accounts, and the collections were transferred into my account. I was also questioned because of our newsletters. It wasn't possible to make public announcements of Confessing Church positions, so this was done through thousands of newsletters that were given out to parish members. Distribution was slow and tedious.
> Once the local SA director mentioned that he might send me to a concentration camp for a while, but it never happened.[45]

It is a peculiar picture of political ambiguity in the Third Reich. Bethge described Stefanie von Mackensen as "the backbone" of the Pomeranian Confessing Church. Without her, he said, Dietrich Bonhoeffer would not have been able to carry on at Finkenwalde as long as he did. The Gestapo kept track of all her activities, but had apparently decided that the best tactic in conflicts with the church was to create no unnecessary martyrs and no publicity.[46] This strange situation finally ended in 1938, when von Mackensen got into a public argument with the provincial party governor, the *Gauleiter*:

> At a public gathering at which both my husband and I were present, the Gauleiter had said — in addition to other offensive comments about Protestant pastors — that the Christian churches were one big pigpen. I sent in a protest and told him that there was no more place for me in party gatherings if I had to hear smears against something that was sacred to me. With that, they began party proceedings against me. My husband lost his position. But they never said that he lost his position because of his or my beliefs, but because of "political undependability." They didn't start the proceedings against me because of my letter or its contents, but because I had sent the letter to the church hierarchy and it had been made public. The Nazis always tried to avoid saying that they persecuted people because of their beliefs; they always chose some other roundabout way.[47]

With the publicity gained by the letter, the limits of party tolerance had been reached. Stefanie von Mackensen, however, reacted uncertainly; she still separated the religious beliefs that had led her into the Confessing Church from her political beliefs:

> We Nazis in the Confessing Church often considered whether we shouldn't publicly leave the party. We then decided not to. We wanted to be shut out. We wanted to force the Nazis to declare that Christianity in the party was not an option. During the party proceedings against me, I was asked: "In the case of a conflict, whom would you obey? The Jew Christ or Adolf Hitler?" The questions were that pointed. That was no question for me. The answer had come at Barmen: Christ alone. . . . Then the council withdrew and returned to say, "The *Gauleiter* demands that you leave the party."
> That was a difficult question. I replied, "No. I won't do it. I have the same right to be in the party as the *Gauleiter*. When I joined the party, you knew that I was an active Christian. I haven't changed. If the party has changed, then the *Gauleiter* has the opportunity to throw me out. I would accept that at any time."
> I don't know if that reply was right. At the moment, it appeared right to me. Today, I would say that I should have left the party — but then it never would have been made public. I had to decide very quickly; I was sitting there before this council of high-ranking Nazi party members, and had to decide immediately. But then my husband lost his office, and I had to leave Stettin as well.
> It's very hard to explain to people today how we managed this. The national question always entered in, and one was German, wasn't one? We saw how Hitler marched into the Rhineland with his troops and freed the Rhineland. As an American, you won't be able to understand this. In retrospect, after all that happened, I don't understand either how I could do it. But we didn't see what was to come, and what happened.[48]

In fact, party records show that all charges were dropped against von Mackensen; she was reprimanded only for having shared her protest letter with Confessing Church leaders. It is not clear from the records whether her husband's demotion to a government position in Silesia was indeed the result of his wife's activities in the Confessing Church.

What is clear, from the records and from von Mackensen's own recollections, is that she viewed her argument with the party as a confessional dispute, not a political one. Like Wilhelm Niemöller, she argued for her right to remain in the party. Niemöller, von Mackensen, Herbert Mochalski, and Marta S. never officially left the party; they became passive members while they continued their activities in the Confessing Church. (Marta S. eventually was brought before a party court in 1942 for her "lack of interest.") It should be noted that in Nazi Germany many people in the churches viewed this arrangement as the safest one for those who had joined the party. The risks of passive membership were less than the consequences of openly breaking with the party.

And yet the discrepancy between Confessing Church membership and party membership would become increasingly evident. After Stefanie von Mackensen and her husband moved to Silesia, she was out of the Pomeranian Confessing Church. She re-established her connections to the Confessing Church only after the war. To the end of her life she remained vague as to the reasons why. It is certainly the case that, in the Silesian village where she lived, only coincidence would have brought her into contact with a Confessing Church parish. It is possible, too, that the tensions between her religious faith and her national loyalties had simply become too great. In 1938, with the growth of Nazi military might and its increasingly obvious plans to extend the German Reich throughout Europe, the most bitter disputes within the Confessing Church over national loyalty were only beginning.

But the question of national loyalty merely obscured a more profound issue. The majority of Confessing Christians were, after all, patriotic Germans. The real debate within the Confessing Church would be between those who would work within the system and those who would not, between those who recognized the Nazi state as their government and those who came to deny its legitimacy. The most crucial question for these Christians would be whether they, as Christians, were called not only to oppose Nazi policies toward the churches but to resist Nazism politically.

Ultimately, the resolution of this question did not rest on the issue of national loyalty but on how these Christians defined their faith and their church. In Adolf Hitler they faced a formidable enemy. As the records of party proceedings against Confessing Christians show, the Nazis were often willing to tolerate some degree of private faith as long as it did not interfere with the public image of the party. Hitler, however, had only scorn for it:

> I promise you that, if I wished to, I could destroy the Church in a few years; it is hollow and rotten and false through and through. One push and the whole structure would collapse. . . . I shall give them a few years reprieve. Why should we quarrel? They will swallow anything in order to keep their material advantages . . . we need only show them once or twice who is the master. Then they will know which way the wind blows. They are no fools. The Church was something really big. Now we are its heirs. We, too, are the Church. Its day has gone.[49]

II

THE
CONFESSING
CHURCH
IN THE
NAZI ERA

✣ 4 ✣

Convictions and Conflicts

The Early Divisions within the Church Opposition

THE WAYS in which individuals confronted Nazism depended upon their backgrounds and personalities as well as upon their political persuasions. Both theological and temperamental differences among the leaders of the various churches played a major role in the alliances and divisions within the church opposition to Hitler. The radically different situations of the regional churches in 1934 magnified these personal differences. Germany's churches were divided regionally along borders that often reflected confessional differences as well. Some regional churches were predominantly Lutheran; in others, the Reformed tradition had played a stronger historical role. In the Evangelical Church of the Old Prussian Union, the Reformed and Lutheran traditions had been united since 1817.

After the July 1933 church elections, "German Christians" successfully seized synodal control of most regional churches. Those in which they encountered the strongest opposition were the three largest Lutheran churches of Hannover, Bavaria, and Württemberg and the eight regional churches that made up the united Evangelical Church of the Old Prussian Union, in which the Lutheran tradition had been leavened by Reformed influences.

There were, of course, a fair number of stalwart Lutherans in the Old Prussian Union and a few Reformed or United parishes in the Lutheran regional churches. But, in general, institutional developments in these churches reflected the dominant confessional tradition of each church. Institutionally, German Lutheranism was more hierarchical than the Reformed tradition. The Lutheran bishops held more power than the church presidents in reformed regions (the presence of a bishop or president in a region indicated the dominant tradition there), and Lutheran preaching, based upon the theological doctrine of two kingdoms, was more explicit about church obedience to state authority. In the Church of the Old Prussian Union, where the Reformed tradition had had a greater influence, increased power on the lay and congregational levels of the church had been an early development.

The theological differences between the two traditions led to disputes within the church opposition to Nazism, and no one articulated or provoked these differences as much as the Swiss-born Reformed theologian Karl Barth. Barth, professor of systematic theology in Bonn until 1935, was instrumental in helping to write some of the most important early documents of the Confessing Church, and he wrote most of its founding statement, the Barmen Declaration of Faith. His greatest influence, however, was in guiding a number of theology students into the Confessing Church. Of the young Germans who began their theological studies in the late 1920s and early 1930s, even those who did not study directly under Barth in Bonn were influenced by his seminal works on church dogmatics and on the Letters to the Romans in the New Testament. Equally important and controversial was the fact that, by the time Barth left Nazi Germany in 1935, the acerbic professor was as well known for his outspoken criticism of Nazism as for his theological views.

To his followers, Barth would remain a hero. As Helmut Gollwitzer, one of his students, later claimed,

> If it hadn't been for Barth, Hitler would have had no difficulty with the church. To say it somewhat provocatively, Barth theologically prepared a church that had never had a wide range of opinions to ask if it really had a common confession. The word "confession" caught fire again. Barth made the phenomenon of heresy clear to a Protestantism in which there had been no differentiation between pure, true teaching — that is, orthodoxy in the best sense of the word — and heresy. At the same time, he was on the left politically. In him, national sentiments and Protestant nationalism hadn't become as hardened as in the older theologians and the students of other theologians.[1]

Barth taught that biblical scripture was the only source of revelation about God and, thereby, remained the only foundation of Christian ethics. In response to "German Christian" and Nazi ideological absolutism, Barth reminded his students that the Bible had to remain their guide and Jesus Christ their model. Individual Christians had the freedom, on the basis of scripture, to oppose the state when its dictates came into conflict with scriptural mandates. Jesus Christ — not Adolf Hitler — remained the spiritual head of the German Evangelical Church.

The Nazi state correctly recognized the challenge to its authority inherent in Barth's views, but the Nazis and the "German Christians" were not the only ones to feel challenged by Barth's teachings. The German Lutherans questioned its theological fine points and feared the institutional consequences of Barthianism, for the situation facing the three largest Lutheran churches at the end of 1933 was very different from that within the Church of the Old Prussian Union.

The Nazi state had directly intervened in the Church of the Old Prussian Union by appointing August Jäger to oversee the Prussian churches, and Jäger had ordered the arrest and suspension from office of some pastors. Having had its first taste of Nazi ruthlessness, the church opposition in Prussia, particularly in Berlin, was more critical of Nazi church policies and clearer on the necessity of church independence from the state. These member churches of the Church of the Old Prussian Union (which included almost half of the Protestant pastors in Germany[2]) eventually made up the core of the Confessing Church.

The bishops of the three Lutheran churches of Bavaria, Hannover, and Württemberg initially had to contend with "German Christians" who had gained seats on those regional synods as a result of the July 1933 elections. Nevertheless, these bishops remained in control of their churches. After the Sportspalast rally in November 1933, hundreds of people (including many who had won synodal seats in the church elections) resigned from the "German Christians," which further weakened "German Christian" influence in some churches.

These three regional churches came to be known as the "intact" churches in the church struggle. They were neither taken over by "German Christians" nor were they institutionally split by the battle raging between church and state. Although they were under pressure from the state and from the "German Christians," the three Lutheran bishops still had the upper hand and intended to keep it. To their thinking, this required a steady course down the middle — making concessions to the state where necessary and avoiding confrontations with state authorities.

Their personal convictions influenced this tactical decision. August Marahrens of Hannover genuinely believed that the church could and must find its place within National Socialist society. He had been a military chaplain in World War I and had remained with his unit in prisoner of war camp — an experience, one of his supporters later said, that made him welcome the rise of Nazism in 1933.[3] He had two sons in the SA and belonged, as he said in 1938, to those "who despite all disappointment hold onto the hope in their inner hearts that the difficulties between the 'Movement' [National Socialism] and religious proclamation can be brought to a positive solution."[4] Marahrens' presence in the ranks of the church opposition at all stemmed from his stand against "German Christian" ideology. Once the "German Christians" had ceased to pose a threat in his church, he was outspokenly supportive of many Nazi policies.

Bishop Meiser of Bavaria was a conciliator whose main concern throughout the Third Reich was preventing a schism in the German Evangelical Church (particularly after August Jäger tried to remove Meiser from office in October 1934 and divide the Bavarian church into two regional churches[5]). Meiser believed that the key to dealing with the "German Christians," as he admonished Barth early in 1934, was to avoid confrontation and work to preserve the "intact community" of the church.[6]

Bishop Wurm of Württemberg subsequently defied Hitler publicly on the "mercy killings" of mentally ill and disabled persons, and, of the three intact churches, Württemberg maintained the strongest ties to the Confessing Church in Prussia. But Wurm's perspective during the Third Reich — and after 1945 as well — was that he would have "welcomed it if . . . a peaceful relation to the state had been reached."[7] This goal, claimed Wurm, was thwarted, not by the Nazi regime but by the radical sectors within the Confessing Church. Wurm criticized these Confessing Christians because they

> didn't merely fight the intrusions of the state into church territory, but, as a power from below that assumed inappropriate authority, they fought the state as such. . . . They were too convinced that an arrangement with the state would simply drive the church to ruin.[8]

The differences among these three bishops and Martin Niemöller (who symbolized the radical group after his arrest in 1937) could not have been greater. Niemöller, asked in 1981 to comment on his differences with Wurm, recalled that the Württemberg bishop

> had such a need for peace. . . . Perhaps that's where my time in the Marines helped me; I never found a better comradeship anywhere in the world than on my U-boat. . . . You have to show people Christianity and Christians. Then, Christianity automatically becomes an active way of behaving for this comradeship, for such a

brotherhood. We created such a brotherhood in the Pastors' Emergency League, and with what we collected through lectures, sermons and collections, we supported all the "half-Jews" who had been thrown out. We didn't pass that money on to the church, but gave it to our cast-out brothers, in the name of the real church.[9]

For Niemöller, the "real" church, a confessing church, was a fellowship that supported those who had been cast out. For Wurm and the other Lutheran bishops, a confessing church concentrated on its confession and did not try to assume "inappropriate authority." These differences were obscured initially by the common front against the "German Christians," but Helmut Gollwitzer later recalled that, in 1936, Niemöller shocked him by warning, "Dear Gollwitzer, you must be clear about one thing. The real dividing line is not between us and the 'German Christians,' but between us and the middle."[10]

The majority of German Evangelical pastors were in the "middle"; they tried throughout the Third Reich to pursue a cautious course that endangered neither them personally nor their church institutionally. But Martin Niemöller and other radicals saw an active danger for the church in this caution, and, it seemed to Niemöller, their course was most exemplified by the behavior of the three intact churches.

Barth had raised the question of whether the three Lutheran churches could find common confessional ground with the besieged churches of the Old Prussian Union. This question became crucial in late 1933 and early 1934, when two measures further highlighted the differences among these churches. The first was a government order in December 1933 which stipulated that all church youth groups must be dissolved and the youth sent instead to the party youth organizations (for boys, the Hitler Youth; for girls, the League of German Maidens). The second was an order issued by the Reich bishop on January 4, 1934 titled "Regarding the Restoration of Orderly Conditions in the German Evangelical Church." This document paved the way for the attempted government takeover of the regional churches and included, among other provisions, automatic implementation of the "Aryan paragraph." It had been written, for the most part, by Prussian Church Commissioner August Jäger, who had not consulted "German Christian" church leaders. Even the "German Christian" president of the Evangelical Consistory in Berlin, Dr. Friedrich Werner, conceded that it was probably unconstitutional.[11]

The Church Leaders' Meeting with Hitler

Both measures obviously represented serious threats to all the regional churches, and the church opposition decided that the time had come to seek a meeting with Hitler himself. Meiser, Wurm, Marahrens, and Niemöller actually met with Hitler; before the meeting, they called a number of other pastors and theologians together to discuss what the church opposition should say to the Führer. The two-day meeting of this group in Berlin dramatically illustrated the divisions within the church opposition. The group included representatives of the church opposition from Rhineland, Westphalia, and Hesse, three "German Christian" theologians, and Friedrich Werner and Karl Barth.[12]

By all accounts, the discussions were stormy, with Barth at one point screaming at the "German Christians": "You have a different faith, a different spirit, a different God!"[13] Despite this, the group managed to draft a statement to Hitler: It demanded Reich bishop Müller's resignation, the lifting of the January 4 decree, and the establishment of a church-state arrangement that protected the status of the regional churches.

Two points are striking about the first meeting of the church leaders with Adolf Hitler. The first is that the memo presented to Hitler (which was signed by all participants of the Berlin meeting, from Barth to "German Christian" Werner) was notable for the church's tendency to assume all responsibility for the problems within its ranks and for its openness to compromises with the Third Reich. The second point is that all the church opposition leaders believed, apparently genuinely, that a meeting with the Führer himself would lessen church-state tensions. This optimism was based partly on their uncertainty concerning where Hitler himself stood on the issue. Except for his speech supporting the "German Christians" in July 1933, Hitler had kept his hand hidden while the "German Christians" and the church opposition fought with each other. As events of 1934 would show, his support for Müller and Jäger would last only as long as both men served Hitler's own ends—a stance that convinced some church people that Adolf Hitler was, as he himself claimed, a disinterested observer in the whole matter.

Another factor was certainly church openness to the general aims of the Nazi state. Several church leaders believed that, in matters of church affairs, Hitler was simply uninformed, and saw an open discussion with him as the opportunity to correct his views on the subject. Prior to meeting with Hitler, the church opposition had spoken with its own contacts in the Nazi regime—beginning with Reich president Hindenburg. The three Lutheran bishops, in particular, felt confident that several influential government members were sympathetic to their cause. Bishop Wurm trusted interior minister Wilhelm Frick and relied upon him to serve as a mediator between church and state.[14] In 1934, Leipzig mayor Carl Goerdeler was one of Hitler's confidants (he would eventually join the plot to assassinate Hitler) and had agreed, after meeting with Confessing Church lawyers Wilhelm Flor and Eberhard Fiedler, to persuade Hitler to get rid of Müller and Jäger.[15] Von Bodelschwingh had talked with Hindenburg and Reich finance minister Lutz von Schwerin-Krosigk; other Confessing Church allies in the government were Walter Conrad and Rudolf Buttmann in the interior ministry.[16]

The actual meeting with Hitler on January 25 should have dispelled any illusions about Hitler's attitudes toward the church and the tactics he was willing to use against it. In addition to Hitler and the four churchmen, Gestapo head Hermann Göring, chancellery head Hans-Heinrich Lammers, Frick, and Buttmann were present. Göring opened the meeting by revealing that the telephone in Niemöller's Dahlem parsonage had been tapped. The Gestapo chief proceeded to read the transcript of a telephone conversation Niemöller had had that morning with theology professor Walter Künneth, in which Niemöller referred to the church's contacts and joked that Hitler would receive the *letzte Ölung* (Niemöller's pun was that Hindenburg would "butter him up," but *letzte Ölung* also means last rites.) Göring then read from Gestapo files on the activities of the PEL to prove that the group was actively agitating against the state.

The Gestapo files were one of the first signals to the church leaders of how closely they were being watched, yet none of the four churchmen remarked upon this. Instead, they vainly protested their patriotism and loyalty to the state. When they finally raised the issue of Reich bishop Müller, Hitler noted curtly that Müller had been elected in church, not state, elections and told them that the church bore the responsibility for its problems. The only thing he had to tell them was that he would not tolerate political agitation against the state.

As historian Klaus Scholder has noted, each participant of the meeting later had a different version of what was said and, more significantly, drew different conclusions from it.[17] The meeting was not only humiliating for the churchmen, it reduced their access to government insiders. Walter Conrad lost his job only days later, and his colleague, Rudolf Buttmann, was out of the interior ministry by the summer of 1935. Not surprisingly, the church's other contacts within the government increased their distance from the church opposition.

The only man to emerge triumphant from the meeting was Hitler. He had succeeded, not only in blocking the issues the churchmen had hoped to raise but in sharpening the divisions already present in the ranks of the church opposition. The three Lutheran bishops were furious with Niemöller. As Wurm wrote Buttmann several days after the meeting, "This time the U-boat captain didn't torpedo the enemy, but his friends and himself!"[18] Niemöller, assessing the encounter for a group of PEL pastors, compared the meeting to a battle at sea. History's judgment, he told them, would depend on which side cried "Victory first and loudest."[19]

But Niemöller knew that the stakes were higher. Six days after the meeting with Hitler, Niemöller wrote Reich Bishop Müller that he viewed the church-state conflict "not as a question of power, but of the evangelical truth."[20] During the same week, the Lutheran bishops met with Müller and signed a statement (which Müller, elated, immediately released to the press) declaring their "unconditional loyalty to the Third Reich and its Führer" and their support for the Reich bishop. This ill-considered action was the result of their desperate wish to repair the damage done by the January 25 meeting and to revive the possibility of some compromise with the state. But, although Meiser and Wurm qualified their support for their statement afterward — and eventually disowned it — the damage had been done.[21]

The tensions between the intact churches and the Prussian churches were now in the open. In the Prussian churches, pastors spoke scornfully of the "capitulation of the bishops."[22] In response, around 1,800 pastors, mostly in the intact churches, left the PEL to stand behind their bishops.[23] The PEL itself came under increased pressure from the Gestapo, which had removed the PEL organizational files from Niemöller's parsonage the same day the Dahlem pastor was meeting with Hitler. In the days following, a number of PEL pastors throughout Prussia, as well as in the church of Hesse-Nassau, were subjected to house searches, interrogation, or arrest. In Berlin, Friedrich Werner, the "German Christian" head of the Evangelical consistory, declared a new rule that allowed him arbitrarily to move pastors to other parishes, put them on leave, or retire them — all without the right of appeal.

These measures alarmed and radicalized many in the Prussian churches. The tendency in the intact churches was to put the blame not on the government or the Gestapo but on the radical PEL members who had "provoked" these measures. Hitler's accusation of political provocation against the state had stuck.

Despite their conciliatory efforts, the intact churches were also coming under pressure. In addition to the ongoing problems presented by "German Christians" who had gained footholds in regional church administrations, a more serious threat came from Prussian church commissioner Jäger, who moved to absorb the regional churches into the Reich Church.[24] In March 1934, Bishops Meiser and Wurm once again sought a meeting with Hitler. The Führer told them exactly what he expected from the churches: an orderly, authoritarian, and hierarchical institution. Hitler could not comprehend the phenomenon of pastors and parishes refusing to obey official church authority; and ominously, Hitler warned them that the churches would eventually have to accept what he described as the "natural law" of "blood and race."

In their few meetings with Adolf Hitler and their many encounters with local Nazi leaders and the Gestapo, church leaders and pastors were certainly confronted with the ruthless, corrupt face of Nazism. Part of the church's failure to recognize the political realities of its situation was that church members, as people motivated by their religious faith, resisted being defined politically. The heart of this denial of a political identity rested not just in church tradition but in their own search for a new identity as a church. In the spring of 1934, many Christians throughout Germany were searching for a common theological identity — to see, as Gollwitzer put it, if they truly had a common confession.

These Christians shared a number of concerns and knew that their ability to survive as a Christian church would rest not just on what arrangement they worked out with the state but on the integrity and steadfastness of their beliefs. They were united in their opposition to the "German Christians." These common purposes pulled the various factions together in May 1934 at the first Confessing Church synod in Barmen, a suburb of Wuppertal in the Rhineland.

Barmen and the Meaning of Confession

In the period immediately preceding the Barmen Synod, tensions among the church factions had subsided somewhat. In part, this was due to Jäger's increased pressure on the intact churches; it was also due to Meiser's and Worm's realization that Reich bishop Müller and the official "German Christian" leaders could not be trusted. In Württemberg, Wurm was contending with his church's budget council, on which "German Christians" still held a small majority. In addition, there had been a reconciliation of sorts between Meiser and Niemöller, brought about largely through the mediation of von Bodelschwingh.[25]

Although church leaders acknowledged a common cause, a common identity as a church continued to elude them. The word "confession" was acquiring a new significance, not just as a statement of what Christians believed but as a "symbol of the church."[26] Yet, confessional differences between Lutheran and Reformed Protestants were so large that, as Scholder has noted, many Lutherans found it easier to come to terms with the "German Christians" than with the Reformed understanding of communion and liturgy.

Lurking behind these confessional differences were fundamentally different expectations as to the purpose a declaration of faith should serve. Theologically, the more radical members of the church opposition were looking for confessional clarity;

they wanted to send a message to the state that the Christian church had no room for Nazi ideology. The moderate members of the intact churches wanted the exact opposite. They were looking for common ground, for a Christian statement that would not exclude anyone, but, by addressing the spiritual yearnings of the German people, would bring the misguided "German Christians" back into the fold.

Despite these fundamental differences, the delegates to the Barmen Synod managed to agree on six fundamental Christian precepts. These six points became known as the Barmen Declaration of Faith, a document that emphatically opposed the "German Christians'" "Aryan" Christianity and that became the foundation of the Confessing Church.

The Barmen Declaration repeated Barth's claim that Christ, and the knowledge of him gained through the Bible, was the only authority of the church and that the knowledge of God gained through the Bible was the only source of revelation. In Barmen, the church declared that it would not alter this witness to suit the goals of any political party. Most important, the church denied that the state had a right to impose a totalitarian order on all aspects of human life, since part of the church's vocation was to give order and meaning to human existence.

The six theses of the Barmen Declaration were the result of hard work and long negotiations. The document itself was written by Karl Barth, Lutheran pastor Hans Asmussen, and Lutheran church councilman Thomas Breit. One eyewitness to the final negotiations was Hans Thimme, a young vicar who had been thrown out by the official "German Christian" administration in the Westphalian church. As an assistant to Westphalian Confessing Church leader Karl Koch, Thimme's first task was to help at the Barmen Synod. He vividly remembered the all-night session that preceded the final meeting of the synod:

> It was an extraordinarily tension-filled experience, to witness the heated debates, and to see how, especially throughout the entire last night, they negotiated. I had editorial and "runner" duties — I had to make sure that everything was as they wanted, that the technical things functioned — that was my job, basically. But I was there during the extreme suspense as things developed and as they finally agreed. . . . That night, unity on the six Barmen theses became possible.[27]

The next morning, the document was read aloud and approved unanimously by the 138 delegates. Thimme recalled that

> such a movement swept through the group that the men, frankly, broke into tears. Completely spontaneously, without our being told to, someone announced, "Now we will all sing '*Nun danket Gott*'! ["Now Thank We God"]. That was the high point of Barmen and, in a certain sense, the high point of my life, because with that, we had actually — and this was the decisive thing about Barmen — determined the church's identity.[28]

The Barmen Declaration had temporarily united the different groups within the church opposition. Many accounts of the meeting attest to an almost miraculous sense of unity. Stefanie von Mackensen, the only woman delegate, was present as a representative of the Pomeranian Council of Brethren (these were the local governing boards of the Confessing Church). She later described Barmen as "the experience of the spirit of God":

It was so overwhelming, how all the differences, the being against one another, that had so often been present, simply disappeared. It was overwhelming, how we were given the words decided upon in Barmen. All at once, we were freed from our isolation, and experienced a community that, until then, hadn't existed in the Evangelical Church.[29]

Barmen represented a major step in the history of German Protestantism, and it was a courageous statement. But its words concerned ecclesiastical independence. Whatever concerns the Barmen delegates had about the increasing persecution of the Jews and other totalitarian measures, those concerns were not mentioned in the Barmen Declaration. As Hans Thimme noted,

People later became agitated over what was not said in Barmen. And, of course, it's true. In Barmen, National Socialism wasn't directly addressed, anti-Semitism wasn't directly addressed, nor militarism or the authoritarian system as such. Indirectly, of course, Barmen contains some of that, but one has to understand that, in Barmen, it was above all a matter of the rediscovery of the identity of the church within such a divided church. Basically, we were not a church; we were a collection of different tendencies and confessional positions within a church awash in generalities. Barmen signified the discovery of the identity of the church, and presupposed that now, on the basis of this identity, clear, specific statements could and must be spoken. The failure or, to put it better, the omission of the Confessing Church is not what wasn't said in Barmen. Rather, the omission lies in the fact that this fundamental declaration from Barmen didn't find any continuity in practical consequences.[30]

Part of Barmen's significance was its signal of potential opposition to the Nazi regime. As one of the few places where some criticism of the Nazi regime had been voiced, the Confessing Church appeared, at home and abroad, as "the last refuge of freedom and independence in a land locked into gear and oppressed."[31] Yet, as Helmut Gollwitzer observed, the emphasis on a church identity that excluded a political role represented something else:

We totally deferred our political opposition to Nazism and tried to bring the church opposition to its feet. It's a very controversial decision. We did it from a tactical standpoint, but it wasn't just tactics. The amalgamation of Christian identity and national identity was almost complete in a large sector of German Protestantism. We hoped to bring our brethren away from this and to bring them to recognize the contradictions of being a Christian and a Nazi, and perhaps even to bring them away from this Prussian German nationalism. It was our view that this process needed time, that it was not our task to build a small anti-Nazi sect within the church, but, if possible, to bring the church to Christian consciousness and, thereby, to a Nazi-free space.

So we deferred our own political polemic against the Nazi state. After 1945, this was an accusation against us. I would still justify it today. Reich bishop Müller once said, "My goal is that there will be only National Socialists, above the pulpit and below the pulpit." Our goal had to be that those above and below the pulpit would see clearly the contradiction between Nazism and Christianity.[32]

Although the Barmen Declaration was confined to the religious realm, its words contained the theological seeds of broader resistance. The diverse groups at Barmen had achieved common ground, but the theological differences among them were, in the words of one Lutheran delegate, "artificially *bridged*, but not *overcome*."[33] The

Lutherans saw the Barmen Declaration as a church document to be pondered and elaborated upon, corrected and further developed theologically. The Reformed and Old Prussian Union delegates (and those in the PEL) viewed it as a full confession, as significant as the Augsburg Confession of 1530.[34] As the foundation of a Confessing Church, it gave church protests against Nazi infringements on the faith a *status confessionis.*

These were radically different interpretations of the document that, as historian Klaus Scholder noted, changed the Evangelical Church's understanding of church and state more deeply than anything else since the Reformation. Inevitably, responses of churchpeople throughout Germany differed. In Barmen itself, Pastor Karl Immer printed a booklet containing the Declaration and his own report on the synod. By the end of June 1934, 25,000 copies had been sold. Although the Barmen Synod was ignored by the Nazi press, word of the synod and its Declaration spread throughout Germany. "The experience of Barmen," said Hans Thimme,

> was simply a formative and far-reaching signal. . . . The amazing aspect of this initial period was in the spontaneity. . . . It was really, on the one hand, a kind of revival movement. I think one could say that. But it also expressed—I wouldn't say a direct protest movement, but an insecurity and dissatisfaction with some things within National Socialism that people rejected. First, they opposed all interference in the church. People were of the opinion that the authoritarian stance of National Socialism should at least have its limits at the church. That was one reason. Another reason was the use of force—that, for example, all the youth work had been stopped, that the organizations had been dissolved. There was a sentiment of protest against the totalitarian monomania of National Socialism. And this attitude of protest, without being active protest, expressed itself in that people gathered in the church as the last stronghold of freedom.[35]

The Political Repercussions of Barmen

As the words of Barmen were read and discussed in parishes, pastors and their congregations met with immediate consequences. At about the time the delegates met in Barmen, Anton L. had begun parish work in a village east of the Elbe River. The village, typical of the rural regions in eastern Germany, consisted of the farmers and servants who worked lands belonging to a nearby patron. Every Sunday the young vicar was invited to dinner at the manor, where the patron discussed theological issues with him. There were few Nazis in the village, Anton L. recalled, but both the mayor and the patron were uncritical of the Nazi regime.

Inspired by reports of Barmen and armed with copies of the Declaration, Anton L. put up signs on trees in villages throughout the district announcing a meeting in a local pub. "I was 22 years old at the time," he recalled, laughing,

> and here I was calling the parish together to inform them about the situation in the Protestant church. I described what had happened in Barmen and the Confessing Church. Together with a neighboring pastor, who was along the same lines as I was, thank God, we held a parish council meeting with the result that the council in [his] village decided to put itself under the jurisdiction of the Provisional Church Government [the governing board of the Confessing Church].[36]

In Anton L.'s own village, however, news of the Confessing Church was less well received. The governing council of his parish consisted of a few farmers, a representative of the patron, and the mayor. Under the mayor's influence, the group voted against joining the Confessing Church:

> The result was that they closed off the church to me. I couldn't preach in the church on Christmas in 1934. I was able to hold a Christmas Eve service in the forester's home for those who, despite everything, stood by me — that is, by the Confessing Church.[37]

The sequence of events that ended with Anton L.'s ouster from his parish was typical for Confessing Church pastors whose parishes were divided and whose local superiors did not support them. The church was closed off, sometimes by the Gestapo, and the pastor's salary (at that time, around 100 marks a month) was stopped. Anton L.'s immediate superior had already been replaced by a "brown" pastor, whose signature appeared on a terse order for Anton L. to leave the church and the village.

> I suspect I was denounced by someone who had been at the gathering I'd called. A few years ago, I was at the church consistory to look through my personal records, and there's nothing on record. It was simply on the basis of a suspicion.[38]

Outside the Prussian church, the results of Barmen were far less dramatic. Although Bishops Meiser and Wurm had attended the Barmen Synod and voted for the Declaration, the official church newsletters in Bavaria and Württemberg did not even print the Declaration. Prominent Lutheran theologians like Paul Althaus (an early member of the Christian-German movement) wrote lengthy, detailed criticisms of the document.[39]

Indeed, even as the Nazi regime intensified its political pressure on the churches, the intact churches energetically protested political repercussions as unfair and inappropriate. In a 1935 memo sent to Hitler, Lutheran bishops plaintively protested continued harassment: "The state continues to hit precisely that circle of Lutherdom which, in the course of German history, has proven itself to be the truest supporter of the state."[40] Even the more radical Niemöller attempted to clarify where the roots of his resistance lay. "It's not true," he wrote in a newsletter to PEL pastors after his meeting with Hitler,

> that the PEL stands in opposition to Adolf Hitler. On the contrary, it's been emphasized repeatedly on our part that this struggle has to do exclusively with church matters, and that any opposition in state matters is an outlandish lie.[41]

Elsewhere, Niemöller wrote that in no instance would the PEL "cover for individuals who fall *politically* out of line."[42] Niemöller's position was based partly upon his continuing patriotism, but it certainly reflected as well the cautious conviction, epitomized at Barmen, that Christian interests would be protected only to the extent that the church's motives remained religious. Politically based motives and goals were seen as corrupt and corrupting of faith. As the Confessing Church leadership emphasized in December 1934, "We don't wish to be a refuge for politically dissatisfied elements."[43] As the pink membership cards of the Confessing Church stated, "such a confession includes the obligation for loyalty and devotion to *Volk* and Fatherland."[44]

Politically, then, the self-definition of the church opposition in 1933 and 1934 was essentially that of the loyal opposition: called upon to defend church interests against the state, where necessary, but otherwise sharing a common purpose with the Nazi state. In the more radical sector of the Confessing Church, this attitude changed as church members came into more serious conflicts with the Nazi regime. Even in the early years of the Third Reich, however, political differences among the church factions were evident. In one essay dealing with the problem (published in February 1934), two Confessing Church pastors wrote that

> Correct church politics in the Evangelical Church is only possible as proclamation. Correct proclamation always works as a political act in the parish, church, and state. But proclamation may never be placed in the service of church-political or political goals.[45]

This perspective based the church's actions on biblical proclamation, but did not rule out the possibility that the effects of such proclamation would extend beyond the purely religious realm. From the point of view of many conservatives, however, any proclamation that had political consequences had already left the proper sphere of church activity. This sphere, argued one Lutheran pastor, was not so much "neutral" as "above partisanship" (*überparteilich*).[46] Neutrality implied that the church was not concerned with political affairs. This pastor contended that the church must indeed concern itself with political matters, but on a different level: The church's task was to rise above the mundane world of politics to bring God's word to all participants in the political realm.

The differences between these two perspectives had far-reaching consequences. In the spring of 1934, one of the major questions dividing PEL members and Lutherans was whether the Evangelical Church could include both PEL members and "German Christians." Could the two extremes theologically co-exist in the same church? The PEL's position was that they could not: A truly Confessing Church had no place for the "Aryan" ideals of the "German Christians." As Karl Barth had shouted in January 1934, the "German Christians" worshipped a different God.

Most Lutherans rejected this position. If the Kingdom of God were truly open to all, they argued, how could one justify a church that preached selectively and excluded a group because of its politics? (The Lutherans were concerned, of course, not just with this facet of belief but with keeping their churches together.) Even within the PEL, however, the radical step of shutting one group of Christians out of the church made many people uncomfortable. Gollwitzer recalled that he arrived only laboriously at the conviction

> that the church is not an auditorium where every religious interpretation has the same rights . . . there is a line between correct teaching and false teaching, and one has to draw that line. That was something new for us, and a bit hard to swallow. It contradicted our ideas of Protestant freedom, as well as of tolerance. Second, we had to see that the merging of nationalism and religion led to a falsification of Christianity, to the subordination of the Gospel to nationalism and to right-wing political interests.[47]

That was the crux of the matter. Barth's followers claimed that a church which tried to include both "German Christians" and their critics would lead, inevitably, to a "falsification of Christianity." Instead of remaining above party politics, the church was in danger of becoming subordinate to politics. At what point did Christians owe loyalty to the state and at what point did they have the obligation — precisely on the basis of scripture — to raise their voices against it? Gollwitzer recalled the differences on this point between "the middle" and radicals:

> I knew many people in the middle. Every hue of German Protestantism was gathered there. There were some people in the middle who pursued their local church struggle bravely. There were a very few who really came into a deep conflict with the Nazi party. But to belong to the middle, of course, was a presupposition for an easier arrangement with the party and the state.
>
> But for Bonhoeffer and for all of us, there was no alternative but to belong to the Confessing Church. Even in 1933, not to have belonged to the PEL or to have recognized the Council of Brethren would have meant to be in the "neutral" middle, which had many nuances. For us, it would have been impossible not to go into the Confessing Church, even though there was much in the Confessing Church that we didn't like.[48]

The path by which some people arrived at more open resistance to the Nazi state, Gollwitzer believed, occurred less in the Lutheran churches, partly because of the different circumstances there. While the Nazi persecution in the Prussian churches intensified (with such events as the March 1935 arrests of 700 pastors, described in Chapter 3), pastors in the intact churches were able to continue their work as before. For these pastors, criticism of the state seemed to be political provocation. In the Prussian churches, meanwhile, some Christians had had their first direct experience of Nazi terror. In Dortmund, Westphalia, one church choir decided to sing outside the Gestapo jail where its pastor was imprisoned. As one choir member recalled,

> First, someone poked his head out the window and told us to stop singing. Then an SS man came out and arrested some of us. We were singing "*Zerstören deiner Feinde Macht*" ["Destroy the Might of Your Enemies"]. I couldn't do anything; I stayed in jail that night. Then came my interrogation. Everything was designed to create fear and worry. The SS building was all closed in. Enclosed steps, locked corridors, closed doors. They dictated a statement and I had to sign it. The next day they released me and said, "You will hear from us." All that for singing a chorale. When I got home, I learned that someone had put a list of people who had been beaten and tortured by the Gestapo under my father's door. I had to comfort him. Who would do that? Why? It was all to create terror.[49]

Gollwitzer believed that the absence of such arrests in the Lutheran churches explained their continuing reluctance to oppose the state authorities:

> Apparently you have to come into real conflict with the state, and in this conflict stand in a position where you can't give in, where you have no alternative to evade the conflict through some moderate political stance. You have to come into conflict with the state in order to suffer a revision of all your prior loyalties and political convictions. I witnessed that in some people with some suddenness. When a church with a Confessing Church pastor would suddenly be occupied by a "German Christian"

pastor, the police took the Confessing Church pastor away, there was a quarrel in front of the church doors early on Sunday, and the parish would then have to move to an inn or a barn or onto the open fields to hold its worship service. Politically, that was a major enlightenment.[50]

The Political Identity of Confessing Christians

For some people, it was an awakening. For many, it was not. In the year following Barmen, many Confessing Christians did not feel that they were directly affected by the political crises occurring daily in Nazi Germany. In 1980, the choir member arrested in Dortmund expressed her feelings this way:

> I am not a political person. I still don't belong to a political party. So I saw only a spiritual thing there. Today, it's clear that it had a broader political aspect, but, at the time, it wasn't.[51]

The arrests of pastors and church members who acted on their religious convictions were not viewed in a political framework by which Christians could have connected these arrests to the growing oppression of Jews and others under Nazism. Martin Schröter, the son of one of those pastors arrested in March 1935, recalled the reaction of family and friends to the arrest:

> It was plainly a confessional matter; it was suffering for the sake of the faith. The Gospel was at stake and there could be no compromise. We were fully aware of that. That was really the most impressive part. I got two days free from school, because a cousin who was pastor in another village had also been arrested, and his wife was alone with their children. I — a 16-year-old boy — was told to keep her company in their house so she would have a man's protection! So it was half-adventure and half-reality, but in no sense did we see through it. We didn't even have the framework, so to speak, in which we could have politically categorized such a thing.[52]

At the same time, pastors who dealt with Nazi authorities were learning about the insidious nature of Nazi rule. One pastor in Hannover described how, in meetings with Nazi officials, "one would be pushed further, step by step, until he had crossed over the line, without noticing that his spine was being bent millimeter by millimeter."[53]

Despite such ominous experiences, a certain condescension toward the political sphere remained. Politics was corrupted and corrupting, and *Überparteilichkeit* — remaining above the political fray to address the larger spiritual questions — was the course that many throughout Germany chose to follow. Most pastors not only distrusted "German Christian" demagoguery but any call to political activism, including that from some sectors of the Confessing Church. The intact churches, in fact, tended to lump the PEL and the "German Christians" as opposite extremes. Both groups, they believed, sought a dangerous politicization of the church.

This criticism obscured the fact that all sectors of the church opposition were confronted by the same dilemma: how to maintain their position and defend standards set by Christian belief. Although the German Evangelical Church was one of the most powerful German institutions, many Protestants had an almost fatalistic sense of powerlessness. As one Christian wrote in his diary in 1932, "when an unpolitical person lands in a political age, it's almost as if he comes under the wheels."[54] In his 1961 memoirs, Berlin church superintendent Otto Dibelius remarked,

> To undertake anything against this position of power was completely ruled out — in any case for someone who stood far removed from political happenings, who felt no call in himself to concern himself with conspiracies, and who always learned of events only afterward.[55]

Yet, Dibelius had been a member of the German National People's party after 1918 and was one of those within the Confessing Church who had contacts in the Nazi regime. His recollection of his own emotions as Adolf Hitler came to power in 1933 was that "something new would have had to come. And if Adolf Hitler wasn't what we would have wished for, at least he was an energetic man who could truly handle the Communists."[56]

Whatever the claims for *Überparteilichkeit*, then, church attitudes toward politics in principle and the Nazi state in practice were ambivalent, reflecting the pulls of nationalism, church tradition, fear, and prejudice as well as the purely confessional motives the church claimed. But long after the initial receptiveness of some people to Nazism had waned and their opposition to some Nazi policies had grown, a fundamental distrust of "political motives" continued to influence church members' attitudes and behavior. As a lawyer working in the Evangelical Church consistory in Berlin, Elisabeth Schwarzhaupt tried to mediate between the "German Christians" there and the Confessing Christians who turned to her for help. (According to several people, she did help Confessing Christians in their battles with the official church.[57]) But, although in sympathy with the Confessing Church, Schwarzhaupt never joined it:

> Only with difficulty can I tell you why; it's very long ago. I only recall my impression of alienation [from it], and I suspect that I didn't want to join a church group simply because of my political opposition to Nazi ideology. I didn't want to be a Christian for political reasons. I constantly came up against the question: Are our motives Christian and church-related or are they political? Am I sitting in the church waiting for those phrases in the sermon that contain political aggression?[58]

While some Germans who opposed Nazism probably gravitated toward the Confessing Church, most Confessing Christians did not consider their membership a form of political protest. Ilse Härter, one of the first women to be ordained in the Confessing Church, commented,

> At the beginning, it was certainly the case that the question whether one, through belonging to the Confessing Church, was involved in a kind of political resistance, would have appeared to most people as absurd. Although there were certainly some who belonged to the Confessing Church because they weren't Nazis. But it didn't go so far that they then actively resisted politically. . . . The realization gradually developed that this theological decision also had political consequences. . . . During the entire period, the distinction was always made in the Confessing Church: one was arrested for "political reasons" and the other for "church reasons." It was fine when one was arrested for church reasons! But it was somehow suspicious when someone was arrested for political reasons.[59]

As a result, while Confessing Christians resisted the pressure to "Aryanize" their faith, they compliantly filled out their "Aryan" identity papers, with the help of church records. In general, they submitted without question to the demands placed upon them as German citizens. Martin Schröter recalled how this affected his own life:

> I remember that we went, very excited, to the large lectures during the "evangelical weeks" that took place then. I heard Asmussen there for the first time, Niemöller for the first time. In my class at school, where my fellow students and I stood for different worldviews, I got into arguments with them. . . . We felt ourselves to be confessors in the Christian sense and had no inkling, no antennae whatsoever, for the fact that, politically, something entirely different was being done to us. I remember our history lessons. Frederick the Great and his battles—that was the content of our history lessons. It was all war history, and we were made enthusiastic for it. So we became enthused ourselves. It was in that sense that I became a soldier [in 1939]. Of course, I wanted to study theology, that was without question for me, and there was no break there. I was pulled into the war with the firm conviction that that was the righteous thing, that we would win the war. For me, all that went unquestioned.[60]

Although it sought to create a purely religious space within the churches, the Confessing Church could not withdraw from the political life of Nazi Germany. Eventually, everything in the Nazi state had political consequences. Quite early, Nazi pressures reached even remote areas such as the villages Herbert Mochalski served in Silesia. The region was still without electricity, and when Mochalski met with villagers in the evenings, their primitive cottages were lit by acetylene lamps. After an hour, he recalled, the lamps would flicker and die as the people sitting together used up the oxygen in the room. Most of them were tenant farmers who worked the lands of the local patron. Mochalski reflected,

> I can't say that they were political. I hardly met anyone who spoke out politically. It was a church resistance in the parish. To what extent individuals saw it as political resistance, they never told me. But actually, it was political resistance because—and this was the reason for my second arrest—in this parish it wasn't possible to form a Hitler Youth or League of German Maidens group. The children all came to the evangelical youth group.[61]

Every week, Mochalski held four Bible studies; every Sunday, there were two services. All were filled. This was the political threat the Nazis saw in the Confessing Church: the ability of this defiantly nonparty organization to mobilize people, bring them together, and make them decide to send their children to church youth groups instead of to Nazi groups. As Hans Thimme recalled,

> The Westphalian regional synod met in March 1934 under President Koch and protested the law of Reich bishop Müller. . . . It met, I believe, on a Wednesday. It was broken up by the Gestapo; it was forbidden that [the meeting] be continued. That happened anyway. Those who belonged to the Confessing Church met that afternoon as a synod in another parish house in Dortmund and decided that a large rally should take place three days later, in the Dortmund Westfalenhalle [a large convention center].
>
> There were no press possibilities. The possibility of radio, of course, was even less. There was only word-of-mouth propaganda. . . . And three days later the West-

falenhalle in Dortmund was so overfilled that surrounding churches, too, were filled and overfilled. It was in the air.[62]

The rally in Dortmund, in fact, pulled in more than 25,000 people, many of them simple coal miners and other members of Dortmund church parishes. It is not surprising that the Nazi authorities saw this as a political threat. As Kurt Scharf noted,

> This kind of protest against totalitarian demands had the effect, from the very beginning, of political opposition as well. When a group within a totalitarian system resists on one single point, then they have come into political opposition to the total demands of such a system.[63]

The Growth of the Confessing Church

While the plans for a Reich Church had been stalled, the Confessing Church was growing. Across the country, pastors and parishes were signing the red cards (the early ones in the Rhineland were green), using the Barmen Declaration as their confession of faith. In western Prussia, the Rhineland, and Westphalia, the Confessing Church grew rapidly; in the middle and eastern provinces of Prussia, its parishes were more isolated. In the other regional churches, pockets of support for the Confessing Church emerged. Even in churches that had a strong "German Christian" presence, there were small but convinced groups of Confessing Christians.

Nationally, the Confessing Church was a minority in the German Evangelical Church. By January 1934, over 7,000 pastors—around 37 percent of the Protestant pastorate—had joined the PEL.[64] Most were serving parishes in the Church of the Old Prussian Union: in Berlin-Brandenburg, Westphalia, and the Rhineland. (By the end of 1934, 90 percent of the active Protestants in Westphalia—some 500,000 people—had red membership cards.[65] The official "German Christian" church administration in Westphalia admitted that its authority in that region did not extend beyond the walls of its own building in Münster.[66])

By 1936, PEL membership dropped to 5,226. (After the dispute about the bishops' meeting with Hitler, most of the PEL members in the intact churches had withdrawn.[67] In the other regional churches, the administration was in the hands of "German Christians"; in Schleswig-Holstein, for example, the "German Christians" had won 75 of the 79 synodal seats in the July 1933 elections. Even there, however, a small group of PEL pastors refused to recognize their "German Christian" bishop.[68])

Throughout Germany, PEL members were informed of developments in the Confessing Church through illegal (under Nazi press laws) mimeographed newsletters, couriers, and, increasingly, the *Fürbittenliste*, a list of church members and pastors throughout Germany who had been interrogated, arrested, or otherwise harassed by the Gestapo. Every Sunday, this list was read aloud in Confessing churches, and those on the list were prayed for.

By 1935, part of the Confessing Church had become an underground network. Because of his Jewish grandmother, Heinrich Schmidt was barred from practicing law and had offered his legal skills to the Confessing Church. As the churches came under more pressure, Schmidt became a courier for the members of the Confessing Church's Provisional Church Government:

Three lived in Berlin, one in Hamburg, and one in Frankfurt, and they weren't allowed to meet together or to leave their cities. They wanted to continue their work, and I was asked to keep the contact between them. Telephones were tapped. The mails were watched. The only way to pass on news in written form was if someone were allowed to travel around. Naturally, there were some meetings and the others traveled, but the Gestapo didn't know. I would set up the times and places, underground. . . . I did this until the summer of 1938. Then I was jailed by the Gestapo.[69]

Gestapo pressure on the Confessing Church was building. In the spring of 1934, Nazi authorities in Mecklenburg held a show trial of seven pastors (the so-called Schwerin trial). As a warning to other Confessing Church pastors, the three main defendants were given sentences of six, four, and three months in prison. In the other regional churches, August Jäger, who after 1934 was in charge of church affairs throughout the Reich, intensified his efforts to purge bishops, pastors, and theologians who did not conform ideologically. Jäger's goal remained a Reich Church, governed by "German Christians." In October 1934, Jäger attempted to seize control of the Bavarian and Württemberg churches. Bishops Meiser and Wurm simply refused to acknowledge his decree. In a foolish miscalculation, Jäger had both bishops placed under house arrest. Due to the prominence of both men and the attention the church struggle had been drawing abroad, the arrests drew strong protests from U.S. and British churches. More worrisome for the Nazis, however, was the response of the Bavarian and Württemberg populations. In Bavaria, minister president Siebert (who had warned Jäger that it was a mistake to move against Meiser) was visited by regional party leaders representing 60,000 members, who threatened "political consequences" if Meiser were not reinstated as bishop. One of the party leaders told Siebert that he had his hands full "keeping the farmers from leaving the party."[70] In Württemberg, 82 percent of the pastors supported Wurm in defiance of Jäger's order.[71]

Because of the outcry, both bishops were released within days. In München, a church service to support the bishops ended with this show of support described by a British eyewitness:

A moving scene followed. The congregation, having sung "A Mighty Fortress," left the church still singing and proceeded, some 2,000 strong, to Bishop Meiser's residence. Tumultuous cheering brought Bishop Meiser to the balcony, where he affirmed his own allegiance to the Führer and the Third Reich. They remembered Hitler, he said, in their prayers every day. The struggle was not political but ecclesiastical, and arose over the spiritual leadership of the church. The crowd sang *"Deutschland über alles"* and the Horst Wessel song [the Nazi anthem], but was dispersed by storm troopers.[72]

Buoyed by their apparent victory, Meiser and Wurm, joined by Marahrens, met with Hitler on October 30. The three bishops, still convinced that their problem was Bishop Müller, again told Hitler that the Reich bishop should resign. According to Wurm, Hitler replied, "Of course he can. Who's stopping him?"[73] Annoyed by how Müller and Jäger had bungled the Reich Church, Hitler washed his hands of them. Jäger had already resigned on October 26; Müller remained Reich bishop in name only. (He was arrested at the end of the war and committed suicide in March 1946 in a Berlin prison. Jäger became an officer in Poland and was executed there in 1948 for war crimes.[74])

The Dahlem Synod and the "Middle Ground"

The Reich Church remained partly constructed, like an unfinished cathedral. Church authorities supportive of the Nazi regime controlled many of the regional churches. For the three bishops of the intact churches, the struggle for control of their churches was ending, and they could try to carry on as before.

For the Confessing Church in Prussia, however, the struggle was intensifying. Westphalia, despite a church bureaucracy in Münster controlled by "German Christians," was predominantly a Confessing Church; most of Westphalia's pastors, including its church president, Karl Koch, essentially ignored any orders coming from Münster. In the rest of the Church of the Old Prussian Union, the Confessing Church stood as an outspoken foreign body within the official church structures. Most of its pastors remained under the jurisdiction of the Evangelical Church consistory in Berlin and received their salaries from it. Their relationship to the consistory, whose staff included both moderates and "German Christians," was affected significantly by the second Confessing Church synod.

At the very time that Meiser and Wurm were under house arrest, the Confessing Church held its second synod in Dahlem, Martin Niemöller's parish in Berlin. Under the shadow of events in Bavaria and Württemberg, the Dahlem delegates debated the practical options open to the churches and came to two controversial conclusions. The first, stated in Article 3 of the Dahlem synodal statement, was that the Confessing Church was the only legitimate church in Germany and that Confessing Christians and the "German Christians" shared no common faith. As Fritz Müller, one of Niemöller's colleagues in Dahlem, put it: "We are not leaving this our church for a free church, rather, we *are* the church."[75] The second conclusion was that, as the legitimate Prostestant church in Germany, the Confessing Church was entitled, when necessary, to educate and ordain its own pastors, establish its own administration, and govern its parishes. This article of the synodal statement established *Notrecht*, literally, "emergency law."

The principle of *Kirchliche Notrecht*—the church rules of order in times of emergency—was debated heatedly, for it was an important step in increasing the Confessing Church's independence from the official church administration. In an act of defiance, the Confessing Church exercised this right at once. Shortly after the Dahlem Synod ended, it ordained four young pastors whose official churches had refused to ordain them because of their Confessing Church activities. Among them was Hans Thimme:

> When *Notrecht* was proclaimed in Dahlem, they wanted to demonstrate that they were challenging the church administrative authorities, and for that reason I was ordained in Dahlem on the Sunday following [the synod], along with three others, as a demonstration of church *Notrecht*. It was an act of church governance, which only

the church officials or the official church administration took note of per se. Because now, through *Notrecht*, the Confessing Church was also assuming the rights of the church leadership, this ordination was performed as a demonstration.[76]

In the eyes of the official church, Thimme's ordination itself was legal, because he had taken his ordination exams from the official church. Problems of legality arose, however, if he were to be given a parish. After Dahlem, theology students who took their ordination exams from Confessing Church boards were not recognized at all by the official church.

This illustrated the confusing status of Confessing Church pastors. Despite *Notrecht*, most of them were never completely out of the official church. Pastors who had held office before 1934 continued to draw their salaries from the official church administration. If they had been removed from office by "German Christians," they still had legal recourse until 1937, and, as has been noted, many won reinstatement. Parishes, too, even when they elected to join the Confessing Church, remained part of the official German Evangelical Church.

When a parish joined the Confessing Church, then, it often had to perform both official church and Confessing Church duties — taking up a collection for the official church during the service, for example, and one at the door for the Confessing Church. *Notrecht* was to have the greatest consequences for young theology students who, as the church struggle began, were taking ordination exams and looking for positions. Official church authorities, hoping to shut out what they saw as the Confessing Church troublemakers, acted decisively to keep them out of church positions. In cases like that of Hans Thimme, the only option for the young Confessing Church pastor was to work in what were, for the church and eventually for the state, illegal activities. Thimme was taken on as an unpaid assistant by Westphalian church president Karl Koch, lived in Koch's house, and was supported by Confessing Church collections and the Koch family. At the same time, Koch had been ousted by "German Christians" and was appealing in a civil court. After he won his appeal, he continued as president of the Westphalian church, although the official administration under him was partly "German Christian."[77]

For the representatives of the intact churches, where the plight of young illegal pastors was not an issue, *Notrecht* was too problematic, and they criticized the Dahlem Synod as having been controlled by the radical wing of the Confessing Church. The contrast to the unity displayed at Barmen was striking. On the morning of the final vote in Dahlem, almost half the delegates were absent; of those present, 52 voted for the controversial articles and 20 against them. Meiser and Wurm, of course, were still under arrest; delegates from their churches and from the Hannover Lutheran church voted for the establishment of *Notrecht* with the qualification that it be used only as a last resort. They warned that it would inevitably lead to "difficult conflicts" with the state.[78]

For the Lutherans, however, the major problem with the Dahlem Synod was that it represented precisely what they had tried all along to avoid: an attempt by one part of the Evangelical Church to shut out another. One Lutheran delegate charged that, in separating itself from the "German Christians," the Confessing Church had relinquished "the freedom and the willingness to preach to the supporters and followers of the National Socialist Movement."[79]

Other delegates at Dahlem worried that the Confessing Church was assuming a power it did not really have. Pastor Ernst Otto, leader of the small Confessing Church in the heavily Nazi region of Thuringia, warned that

> it would be an empty and ludicrous fiction to claim that we take over the leadership of the church in Thuringia . . . in the whole of Thuringia, we have only 1,000 members in Confessing parishes.[80]

Otto was not the only member of the Confessing Church to temper his support with what he felt to be a necessary touch of realism. In Berlin, suspended superintendent Dibelius, a member of the Brandenburg Council of Brethren, commented that the Dahlem statement was "fundamentally in order and the goal is correct, but the shot goes too far.[81] In his memoirs, Dibelius recalled the words of a Brandenburg farmer, who told him, "Herr Pastor, don't fool yourself; when the going gets tough, you'll be standing completely alone!" "The time simply hadn't arrived," Dibelius concluded, "in which one could base such a—from a human standpoint, futile!—fight of the church against the state."[82]

For that, of course, was what the theological arguments and conflicts all came down to: the apparently futile battle the Confessing Church was trying to wage against the Nazi state. In the history of the Confessing Church, the Barmen Declaration would be given the more lasting significance. The Dahlem statement, in contrast, made many church members uneasy precisely because it more specifically committed the church to a political position. For some, Dahlem was the logical extension of Barmen; it simply established as policy what Barmen had implied. But others believed that Barmen's *Sola scriptura* and *Solus Christus* should have prevented the church's attempt at Dahlem to redefine itself on the basis of the political circumstances in Nazi Germany. In Dahlem, church members took sides that remained firm even after 1945, and after the synod, the more radical members of the Confessing Church were often called Dahlemites.

Not surprisingly, the consequences of the Dahlem Synod were quite different in the intact churches, the Prussian churches, and those churches under "German Christian" administration. One pastor worked in Hesse, where the bishop was a "German Christian." As he recalled, after Dahlem, his situation was one of

> half-illegality. We continued to receive our salary and accepted certain things. It was simply so that a large part of the pastorate in Frankfurt remained "neutral." They weren't "German Christians." They simply tucked in their paws, laid back their ears, and hibernated. We tried to pull them out and bring them over to our side, but we succeeded in very few cases. Then we had to break with them. Through the decisions of the Dahlem Synod, we were pledged to leave those brothers behind who didn't commit themselves to the consequences of the [Barmen] Confession. We refused to recognize our bishop and held a large gathering where we officially dissociated ourselves. The more the political pressures increased, the more difficult things became. I couldn't work any more with youth. That was taken out of my hands.[83]

The underlying question which troubled church leaders and Nazi authorities alike was at what point the Confessing Church's activities and protests would challenge the legitimacy of the Nazi state itself. Even after the Dahlem Synod, the SS did not yet perceive that this was happening. In a lengthy memo, dated February/March

1935, the Gestapo gave its assessment of the struggle between Confessing Christians and the "German Christians" as

> above all an internal church fight, in which each of the two parties has assured its loyalty to the state . . .
>
> In the background of the debate stands the general problem of the relation between church and state, of political and religious worldviews. It had to come to a dispute, because here, two fundamentally different interpretations of this problem confronted each other. On the one side is the opinion that religion (including church law) is to be totally separate from political worldview (Motto: the church must remain the church! — the point of view of the Confessing movement.) On the other side, the transformation of the church, according to a political point of view, is being striven toward (Motto: church within the state — Thesis 1 of the "German Christians.")
>
> Both sides must be granted that, at least as far as their genuine adherents are concerned, they do not stand opposed to the state. Nevertheless, there is no doubt that, on the part of the Confessing movement, the number of inner opponents of National Socialism is large, simply because here the church is more important than the state.[84]

The memo speculated on the possible damage the Confessing Church could do to the Third Reich and listed the most dangerous categories of church members, with the names of several Confessing Church members under each category. These categories of potential "enemies of the state" included Jews, Marxists, Democrats, Free Masons, and foreigners (Karl Barth was named here). But the biggest threat posed by the Confessing Church, the memo concluded, was the adverse publicity, particularly in the foreign press, generated by events like the house arrests of Meiser and Wurm:

> All these consequences have certainly not been intended by the originators of the church debate (excluding the enemies of the state named above). But they offer evidence that the overall church dispute presents a severe national danger, which must, without fail, be countered as quickly as possible.[85]

Some Confessing Christians already recognized that the real threat facing them was Nazism. Helmut Gollwitzer was a member of the more radical wing of the Confessing Church. For him and others, as he recalled later,

> the "German Christians" had become insignificant, and it became clear to us that we were now directly confronted with the state. There's a saying, "You beat the sack when you mean to beat the donkey." The "German Christians" were the sack that we beat, but we meant the state. The Gestapo knew that, but they always had to be careful to make our activities appear to be an internal church conflict. . . . But in 1936, it had become clear. The Confessing Church and the state stood in opposition to each other, with no cushion in between.[86]

Inner-Church Tensions Increase

By 1936, the Gestapo was increasing its pressure on the Confessing Church. At the same time, the distance between the intact churches and the Confessing Church was growing. At the beginning of 1935, the church opposition to the "German Christians" formed a Provisional Church Government to govern church affairs. Initially, this was an attempt to offer the Nazi regime a church-controlled alternative to the Reich Church, one that would win state recognition for the Confessing Church and, at the same time, be controlled by the Confessing Church and intact churches.[87]

The first Provisional Church Government was headed by Bishop Marahrens of Hannover. (Its other members were Westphalian church president Koch, Reformed pastor Paul Humburg, Lutheran Church councillor Thomas Breit, and lawyer Wilhelm Flor.) Marahrens' goal was to have the Provisional Church Government recognized as the legitimate church leadership, and he hoped to render *Notrecht* superfluous. At the same time, however, the Nazis had appointed Hans Kerrl, a Nazi bureaucrat from the interior ministry, to oversee church affairs. Kerrl established a Reich Church Committee to supervise the regional churches and named Wilhelm Zöllner to direct it.[88]

Marahrens attempted to make some arrangement between the Provisional Church Government and the Reich Church Committee; this course was opposed angrily by many within the Confessing Church's own governing Councils of Brethren. At the fourth Confessing Church synod in Oeynhausen in February 1936, the split among the various factions became final. The Lutheran churches, presented with what they saw as unacceptable demands from the Councils of Brethren, withdrew from the Provisional Church Government.[89] In Oeynhausen, the radicals had the stronger hand, and the newly elected Provisional Church Government that emerged there represented a more homogeneous position — essentially, that of the Dahlemites. (It was led by Pastor Fritz Müller of Dahlem, joined by Pastor Hans Böhm, Berlin superintendent Martin Albertz, Pastor Otto Fricke of Frankfurt, and Pastor Bernard Forck of Hamburg.) Officially, the Confessing Church consisted thereafter of those churches and individuals who placed themselves under the jurisdiction of this Provisional Church Government.

After Oeynhausen, Hans Thimme later recalled, the different church factions "stayed together as a Confessing Church, but they went their separate ways."[90] Although the intact churches claimed to be on the same side as the Confessing Church, bitterness toward the intact churches remained from the debates over the course of the first Provisional Church Government. In 1937, for example, Dahlem Pastor Eberhard Röhricht noted that 206 pastors from Berlin-Brandenburg were in prison, while only two in Hannover, one in Württemberg, and one in Bavaria had been imprisoned.[91]

The more radical Confessing Church theology students in Berlin circulated open letters which angrily contrasted Marahrens' diplomatic route with the activism of the Dahlemites: "The gun with which we are being shot down," one student wrote bitterly to Marahrens, "is being loaded by you in Hannover."[92] Marahrens responded that he was protesting state pressure as bravely, and, he maintained, more effectively than the radicals in Berlin. He reminded them that he had protested the imprisonment of some Prussian pastors in early 1935, and he believed their subsequent release was not only a sign of the effectiveness of working through proper channels but of Nazi flexibility in responding to the church.[93]

Claiming that such flexibility was an illusion, Confessing Christians began to distance themselves from the intact churches. The sympathies of Martin Fischer, a newly ordained pastor in Berlin, lay somewhere between those of the Dahlemites and the intact churches, but as a member of the Berlin Confessing Church, he knew where his loyalties should be:

> I was asked, for example, if I would take a parish in Freiburg. That was in an intact church. It was a matter of honor that you didn't go from one of the divided churches to the intact ones. So I refused.[94]

In Mecklenburg, where Christian Berg had been one of the defendants in the Schwerin trial, Bishop Rendtorff had aligned himself more with Marahrens' course. When Berg left his parish in 1936, he bypassed his church superiors and made his own arrangements for a successor:

> This was the question for me: if I simply leave, then my church administration in Schwerin, a "German Christian" administration, will put a Nazi pastor in my place. I couldn't endure that, so I arranged with the Confessing Church administration that they send me a young confessionally loyal vicar. I let him live in my house, let him participate in the Bible lessons and preaching. And when I left, my patron saw to it that he was elected and installed as pastor of the parish. It made the Nazis in the higher church council in Schwerin unbelievably angry, but they couldn't do anything about it. They couldn't push a pastor out of his house, and the patron protected him, too. . . .
>
> According to the letter of the law, he was illegal. But it happened in many places in Germany, where individual parishes, instead of obeying the orders of a "German Christian" administration, simply went around them.[95]

Increasingly, however, Confessing Church radicals came into conflict not just with "German Christians" but with, as Martin Niemöller had put it, "the middle." But who was the middle? Although Niemöller focused his enmity on the pastors and bishops in the intact churches, even in Dahlem there was no unanimity on the proper course for the Confessing Church. The Dahlem parish, although it symbolized Confessing Church activism, was itself divided. Niemöller and his two colleagues, Fritz Müller and Eberhard Röhricht, did not see eye to eye on everything. Asked in 1981 how many parishioners had supported him, Niemöller replied,

> I would say everyone who came to church. Naturally, that was a minority. In Dahlem we had, from 1931 to 1933, an average Sunday attendance of around 600 people. The number of souls in Dahlem was at that time 10,000–12,000, that is, those who paid the church tax.[96]

But, as Elsie Steck, the church secretary then, recalled,

> There was a whole sector who found Niemöller's course too radical, and who held to the other Dahlem pastors, and who were absolutely in favor of working together with the official church. There was a whole group. They were by no means all in agreement with Niemöller's course.[97]

Relations between Niemöller's followers and more moderate parish members, Steck said, were fairly hostile. Above all, between the pastors themselves and between their wives. The longer it went on, the worse it got. Each had his own party. These different parties were represented on the parish council.

Earlier in Dahlem, it had been the case that the confirmation children were divided among the pastors according to their address or the year of their birth. During the church struggle, the families who stood with Niemöller sent their children to a special confirmation class that Gollwitzer and Helmut Traub held. In time, it developed that Niemöller's followers came more to his programs, and also that the children's worship service wasn't for everyone anymore, but rather for each faction of the parish. . . . People put pressure on each other. . . . For example, the administrative tasks changed, I think, every year from one pastor to another. Each time the one pastor had the administration, he also put together the parish newsletter. Then he would literally "mislay"—only briefly—the programs of the others. There were taunts.

On the other hand, the parish had the two churches—Annen and Jesus Christus—and the pastors did take turns. They did preach in both churches, although the intercessory services [for the Confessing Church] were all in the Annen church. As I recall, the collection was taken twice. They announced that the collection would be according to the official collection plan, but that an extra collection would be taken for the Confessing Church. Of course, that was often much more than what came into the official collection.[98]

Faith and Concepts of the Church

At the end of the early period of the Third Reich, then, the Confessing Church was not a unified block of resistance to Nazism, but a scattering of individuals and parishes whose common creed was a Christianity undefiled by Nazism. How they practiced that Christianity was affected not just by the conflicts they had with the state but with each other. What continued to divide these Christians was an essential question of individual and institutional identity: To what, in their confession of faith, were they committing themselves and their church? Should the church be a heterogenous institution encompassing, and preaching to, a variety of viewpoints? Or should it be an institution that had no fear of drawing the line at what was clearly non-Christian, even at the risk of shutting some members out?

The answer to these questions led to the deeper issue of how Nazism should be resisted. Even here, perceptions of what was morally right differed. There were some moderates who felt they helped the Confessing Church by working within the system. One was the lawyer Elisabeth Schwarzhaupt, who worked at the Berlin church consistory. She recalled:

We had hopes of maintaining an intact church administration during the period of the National Socialist government. In 1934 and 1935, I didn't imagine that this government would last very long. . . . Of course, it was always tacking into the wind. When I think back to petitions that I drew up at the time, you began with a declaration of loyalty to the state until you pushed in what you really wanted. . . . We were able to achieve isolated things, but always in a roundabout way. Under Werner's leadership and during the war, more couldn't be achieved. . . . The sense that [we] saw in our work was, above all, to maintain the structure of a church administration so that in better times, when the National Socialist influence subsided or some kind of change of government came, an appropriate administrative structure would be there.[99]

But the deeper problem, often obscured or forgotten when Germans considered their behavior long after 1945, was that for many — if not most — in the church opposition, declarations of loyalty to the state were quite genuine. These Christians disagreed with the "German Christians" and with Nazi attempts to seize control of the Evangelical Church. But there are numerous open professions of support for various Nazi policies scattered throughout church statements of the period. They show that there was true support in the churches for some Nazi policies. The troubling historical evidence suggests that the churches refrained from criticizing the Nazi regime, not just because they wanted to remain "apolitical" but because they often agreed with it.

A few Confessing Christians later accused more moderate members of the church of having hindered the cause of church resistance. Kurt Scharf, reflecting in 1981 on the Confessing Church's failure to stop the evil around it, said,

> before pastors and parishes felt the length and breadth of injustice, and that took years, the precious initial state, in which something could have been done, had passed. . . .
>
> If a far greater number of the neutral pastors, together with their parishes, had held to the Confessing Church from the beginning, the persecution of the Jews wouldn't have reached the extent that it did. We could have worked in the initial stages with totally different decisiveness and power, including the power of numbers. We in the Confessing Church were particularly angry at the neutral pastors, because we thought that they knew better, better than those who had been dazzled.
>
> Of course, I must add: If we had shown our protest more powerfully and more publicly! If we had brought it forward not only in sermons or in synodal decisions, in declarations and announcements from the pulpit, but if we had gone into the streets, arm in arm, with the Jews! The Confessing Church, in its huge confessional gatherings from 1934 on, set masses within the church in movement. That's why it's my opinion that if the others had joined in, and if we had had the experience of the effectiveness of public demonstrations like those at the end of the 1960s, then in 1933 and even in 1934, the disaster could have been held off.[100]

Had Confessing Christians been more politically active, could they have united others to oppose Nazism more forcefully? This question troubled and divided many who had been in the Confessing Church, to the end of their lives. The most haunting question is what early, public resistance by men of Meiser's and Wurm's stature might have achieved — for the Nazi regime, in the early years, did back down on some points where public opinion turned against it. (Following the uproar over Meiser's and Wurm's arrests, the Nazis dropped Jäger and Müller.) What would have happened had they used their influence, not to seek compromises with Hitler but to lead the members of their churches in opposition against the Nazi party or — as Scharf suggests — to support the Jews?

Yet, given the realities of the church at the time, such questions are hypothetical. It was only after much time and painful experience under Nazism that some Christians like Martin Niemöller and Kurt Scharf believed that the church should have taken a more prophetic — and openly political — role in opposing Nazism. The irony is that the struggle of the Confessing Church to remain free of Nazi ideology was for many a struggle to remain apolitical. They felt that the church, come what may, was called upon to be the church and nothing more. If they fulfilled this task for the church, God would take care of the rest. As Otto Dibelius wrote in his memoirs,

> Niemöller once accused me, 25 years later: I had never been a man of the Confessing Church, rather always merely a man of the church. That was 60 percent correct. But what, then, did I want to be other than "a man of the church?"[101]

5

Daily Life and Work

EVEN IN TOTALITARIAN SOCIETIES the rhythms of daily existence continue. But the structure of a dictatorship is like a spider's web, its strands interwoven and extending into the farthest corners of society. For those who become caught, the perception and practice of daily routines is abruptly altered. Others evade the web, however, and are able to maintain the illusion that life goes on as before.

Looking back at the Nazi era, our perceptions of what daily life must have been like are influenced, inevitably, by what we know of Nazi crimes. Historically, we think of everday life in Nazi Germany as inseparable from the political realities of Nazism. Yet, for many Germans, private life and political reality remained separate spheres. This separation, deliberate or unconscious, served as a kind of psychological protection. The apparent normalcy of their own private lives enabled many Germans to ignore what was happening to the Jews and other victims of Nazism. As long as their own lives continued in a more or less reasonable fashion, they rationalized, things couldn't be that bad.

Not all those who constructed their lives on such rationalizations were Nazis. The diary of the novelist Jochen Klepper, a visitor of Confessing Church services, portrays his desperate attempt to sustain a private sphere until 1941, when orders for the deportation of his Jewish wife and stepdaughter drove the three of them to suicide. In March 1933, Klepper bitterly examined himself and his compatriots:

> Tired 30-year-old, 40-year-old compromisers, made anxious by a primitive struggle to exist. However we turn it—that's who we are! . . . What a retreat into the private realm. To whom should one appeal in this age? What does this so grandly constructed national revolution bring? The atmosphere of a pogrom. But I flee into the bourgeousie [sic]. It's not easy for the bourgeousie to maintain itself in the middle of two revolutions.[1]

Like Klepper, many Christians retreated into the private realm, into a "bourgeousie" that, for Klepper, represented stability and security. Institutionally, the German Evangelical Church's battle with Nazism was somewhat similar to this: It was not only a struggle for church independence but for the institutional integrity of the church. At least for the conservative nationalists in the church opposition, this posture reflected their attempts to preserve the church as it had been before 1918.

Through the very process of coming into conflict with the Nazi regime, in some ways the German Evangelical Church would be changed profoundly. But changes were occurring even before 1933—changes that played a crucial role in the church struggle with Nazism. The most important one was the emergence of women pastors. After 1927, when women were allowed to study toward a full theological degree, the number of women students at theological facilities rose from 77 (in 1926) to 330 (in 1931).[2] The church struggle with Nazism was just beginning at the time that these women entered the service of the church.

The Women of the Confessing Church

The women met with considerable opposition. Although most of them hoped to be ordained and given parishes, in 1933 no regional church was ordaining women. Although they had the same theological training as men, women were examined separately and were "consecrated," not ordained. Their pastoral duties were limited explicitly to working with women and children. Women were not permitted to lead parishes, administer the sacraments, or, in some regions, preach. They had to retire when they married. In Berlin-Brandenburg (the regional church most open to the women), a woman had to work seven years before she received her full salary — which, even then, was 70 percent of the salary received by a man beginning his duties as a vicar.[3]

The most daunting obstacle women faced, however, was the deep-seated prejudices against women that prevailed in German society and in most of the Protestant church. In 1933, Annemarie Grosch began her theological studies in Berlin. As she recalled, even in the most radical sector of the Confessing Church, women were hardly treated as equals:

> I studied completely in the dark, without knowing what I would be able to use it for. . . . We lived in Dahlem, in Niemöller's parish. So I came right smack into the beginning of the church struggle. Politically, my family was essentially united, but that didn't mean that we agreed on church matters. To that extent, I had to keep everything that I later experienced in the Confessing Church somewhat secret at home, because I didn't want to jeopardize my theological studies. My parents said, "You've gotten on the wrong horse; nothing will come of that under Hitler." Which was basically obvious. Neither of my parents was really interested. As long as it didn't cost anything, so to speak, one could let the child go ahead. But I suddenly turned into someone who practiced it seriously, and that was disagreeable for them. They didn't like it, but they let me go ahead . . .
>
> At that time I went to Niemöller, in 1933, and asked him about studying theology. The first thing he said to me was: "Can you cook pea soup?" A typical picture of a woman, although cooking pea soup had nothing to do with studying theology! . . . Then I asked Niemöller about the "German Christians" and he said — this was in April or May of 1933 — "Oh, by the time you're finished with your studies, the 'German Christians' will have long since disappeared into oblivion." But when I finished, he was sitting in a concentration camp.[4]

Like Niemöller, most Confessing Church leaders expected that the chief responsibility of the women emerging from seminaries would be to cook the pea soup at church suppers. Moreover, these women were beginning their professional lives at the very time that the Nazi regime began to restrict the women's rights achieved during the Weimar Republic. The Nazis' ideological view on women was not just the stereotype of *Kinder, Kirche, Küche.* An important element of Nazi ideology was the concept of *Gemeinschaft*—"community"—and the Nazis had very specific ideas of where each German fit, or did not fit, into the ideal Nazi community.

The core of this idealized community was the *Bauerntum*, those men and women who worked the land. Nazi propaganda romanticized German farmers as "the bearer of the people's hereditary health."[5] The Nazi slogan *Blut und Boden* (blood and soil) represented the new "Aryan" ideals of racial purity and wholeness. Within this context, a woman's function was to bear "Aryan" children. As one parish helper who completed her schooling in 1936 recalled:

> They did try to influence us. One very good teacher, who came out of the Christian Student Union, was so influenced by National Socialism, perhaps through her brother, that she had read a great deal about *Bauerntum, Blut und Boden,* and so on. She passed that on in our German class. I had four sisters who all went to the same school. Later, with my second-youngest sister, it was the case that this teacher told the children: "It depends primarily on all of you becoming wives and mothers. You must give the Führer a child." The texts that were read all went in this direction: "The main thing now is that children be born."[6]

Various Nazi programs put these ideological views into practice. In the *Lebensborn* program, unmarried mothers who could provide proof of their own racial purity and that of their offspring's father were cared for in one of seven homes established by the SS. The children were provided for and their adoption facilitated by the state—The *Lebensborn* program was the SS counter to abortions in Nazi Germany—estimated at 600,000 a year[7]—but it was also a glorification of "racially pure" motherhood So was the Mother's Cross, introduced at Christmas 1938: German mothers with four or five children received a bronze cross; those with six or seven children, a silver cross; and mothers with eight or more children were presented a gold cross personally by the Führer himself.

Because the Confessing Church was virtually the only institutional realm in which an attempt was made to keep women's groups independent of Nazi control, it became a place where women could find alternatives to the rigid ideological precepts then governing their lives. Since the birth of the Confessing Church coincided with the emergence of the first generation of women theology students, logically many of these women would join the Confessing Church. Indeed, as other career possibilities were blocked off, the German Evangelical Church became one of the few places where women could continue their careers. The lawyer Elisabeth Schwarzhaupt, who had been a vocal critic of Nazi views on women, found a position at the official church consistory in Berlin after her career in the judiciary was thwarted:

> from the summer of 1933 on, I was no longer entrusted with a new task. . . . I negotiated many times with my superior in the head regional court in Hamm, but I never received any really clear information. It became clear to me that he didn't have the courage to employ me further, although, according to my grades and qualifications, I would have been entitled to it, because he knew that Hitler had said, "A woman should not be a soldier, judge, or statesman," and the whole tendency of National Socialism was that women should return to the home, should concern themselves with the household and children. . . .
>
> Then I got the idea from a head consistory member at the chancellery of the Evangelical Church in Berlin to apply there.[8]

Although positions in the church were open to them, women usually met the same reaction that Ilse Härter did when she began her apprenticeship as a vicar in a Confessing Church parish in the Rhineland: "I was sent to a pastor who greeted me right at the door with the words: 'Just so you know from the start, I didn't want you and I can't teach you anything either!'"[9]

Many of the barriers these women faced broke down rapidly. The Confessing Church needed such women so much, particularly during the war, that their fight for ordination during the Nazi era was more successful than it might have been under normal circumstances. The women's own courage overpowered many of the prejudices that initally faced them. As Annemarie Grosch remembered,

> I myself experienced something very interesting in my parents' social circles. In March 1933, when I moved from Krefeld to Berlin, I was, as they put it so stupidly, "introduced into society"; this was customary. Then I was asked, "What would you like to do?" I said, "Study theology." Then I always noticed how they smiled so condescendingly and thought, "Oh, well, she should study, but she doesn't seem to be very gifted. . . ."
>
> But in 1937, 1938, that had changed completely. When they heard what I was doing, Oh! Then they had a tremendous respect and were speechless with astonishment. With that, it became clear to me: It's not the official institution of the church that instills respect in people, but rather there, where they notice that someone is serious and genuinely prepared to put something at stake. That is where the church wins plausibility.[10]

Gestapo Surveillance of the Churches

Despite their courage, a number of Confessing Christians nevertheless complied with many of the Nazi regulations governing their activities. For example, Confessing Church meetings and other activities had to be registered with the Gestapo, and at many meetings, a Gestapo officer was present taking notes. As Dahlem secretary Elsie Steck remembered,

> Niemöller held a so-called open evening every Monday, in which he would share with the parish what had happened during that week. The parish knew what was going on. The open evenings were held in the large hall of the parish house. At first, they had been in the parsonage, but that was much too small, and then they were in the large hall. The Gestapo had decreed that only those with the red cards could come in at all. We had to promise to check everyone, and the Gestapo official listened in as well.[11]

It was a typical scene in Confessing Church parishes throughout Germany. In Westphalia, said Hans Thimme,

> aside from the worship service, we held parish meetings. In Oeynhausen, it was taken for granted that we held a parish meeting every three to four weeks in the parish house. . . . We always had prominent people who could report on all parts of Germany. [The parish meetings] were the information cells. . . . Naturally, a spy always attended. We always counted on that, but we behaved rather freely nonetheless.[12]

Some Confessing Christians were members of parishes in which the majority of parishioners and their pastor had no ties to the Confessing Church and were either "neutral" or "German Christian." For these Christians, the Councils of Brethren sent young vicars to hold meetings, Bible studies, and worship services. These gatherings had more of an underground character. After being banned by the Gestapo from Silesia, one young pastor came to Berlin, where the Council of Brethren assigned him to care for several such groups. He recalled:

> In Charlottenburg, in the Trinity parish, the Confessing members who didn't have a pastor couldn't use any of the church rooms. I took care of two house Bible circles there. One was at a carpenter's; he lived on Stuttgarter Platz. The other was at a doctor's house on Bismarckstrasse, near the Deutsche Oper. . . . Here it was, so to speak, not illegal but, in any case, more unofficial. Our task was to proclaim God's word, and to strengthen the people, and, of course, to inform them about Confessing Church matters. . . . These house Bible circles, I would say, had perhaps 12 to 15 members. . . . There was certainly a whole group of these in Berlin.[13]

Occasionally, if the Confessing faction in a parish was large enough, the Council of Brethren through its contacts in the official church, maneuvered a position for one of its young pastors. For a brief time, Ilse Härter worked in such a parish in Berlin:

> They [the Council of Brethren] told me only that I should build up the Confessing parish there . . . the pastor in Wannsee might have been a bit younger than I. In any case, he was a rather shifty customer, who had been active in Switzerland and, as I learned from friends there in 1948, he had been deported from Switzerland because of Nazi intrigues. . . .
>
> I was maneuvered into this parish in a funny way, if I recall correctly, in the position of parish helper with "special duties." This pastor had agreed to that. He must have known, basically—he knew that I was a vicar—he must have known, then, that the Brandenburg Council of Brethren and the Provisional Church Government, which had arranged all this with the presbytery, had connected it with a very specific goal. . . .
>
> He belonged to the "other" side. In my presence, for example, he denounced people over the telephone to the *Reichssicherheitsamt* [the central office for the Gestapo and the SS]. That's the kind of customer he was. Moreover, he didn't do much in the parish. Practically, I did the work. I held the church instruction classes and did the parish and hospital visits.[14]

There were different degrees of risk within the Confessing Church. In particular, the Nazis focused on the church's youth work, since they saw this as a direct challenge to their own efforts to indoctrinate German youth. It was no coincidence that the weekly meetings of the Hitler Youth were held on Sunday mornings. In many cases, Gestapo regulations "permitting" church youth activities were formulated so that actual compliance was impossible. To receive permission to hold youth outings, for example, churches had to submit—months ahead of time—a list of participants, their dates of birth, whether they belonged to the Hitler Youth, how long the activity would last, where it would take place, and a detailed description of what was planned. Those youth who were not given written permission from their Hitler Youth leader were not allowed to participate.[15]

Not surprisingly, the effect of such requirements was often that the churches had to cancel their youth programs. As one parish newsletter announced,

The planned retreat could not take place, unfortunately, since it was not possible to draw up a complete list of participants by November 27, 1937 and give that to the Gestapo. Because of that [the Gestapo] refused permission for the retreat.[16]

When church workers did hold youth activities, they did so with the troubling knowledge that they might be putting at risk not only themselves but their young participants — often only 13 or 14 years old — as well. After one such meeting, the pastor reported:

Several visits by the Gestapo took place . . . around 15 youths who went to the apothecary after the talk were detained there by the police and their names were written down, because they had appeared as a group in public.[17]

In another case, the youth were interrogated directly by the Gestapo:

We had a blossoming youth work. Then my vicar was transferred, and in a confrontation with a young "German Christian," he was arrested. He was imprisoned. When my youth heard that, they were very moved. They wrote him, and one of them wrote another letter of comfort, and that was noted by the lawyer who had to read the letters in the prison, and he notified the Gestapo. They searched the house of this youth and found illegal pamphlets from the Confessing Church. With that, it was my turn. I had a five-hour interrogation at the Gestapo. That wasn't so pleasant. But then they got to the youth work, and they summoned the entire youth group to the Gestapo.

    We sat in the parsonage the evening before. I said, "Boys, now we're going to play it through. I am the Commissar, I interrogate you, and you answer." I just wanted to loosen them up, so that they knew that they could answer, that they had a clear conscience, and that they should say only what was really to say, should tell only the truth. It went well. They all got off. But my vicar and myself were still summoned to court because of our youth work.[18]

A surprising number of youth continued to attend Confessing Church activities, but the effects of Gestapo harassment, even for those who were not arrested, were disheartening. As one parish worker recalled:

It was hard to gather the children. We were not allowed to do anything other than tell Bible stories and sing songs in which the word "God" had to appear at least once. We were not allowed to play games with the children if they didn't have something to do with [religion]. . . . My friend was even summoned to the Gestapo because she violated this prohibition. She had invited the children at Christmas to my large room in the parish house and had written, "Bring your dolls along." Because of this card she had to go to the Gestapo. There she was told, "What do you want? You have the Bible, that's thick enough. You don't need dolls, too. Tell the biblical stories, we can't forbid you that, but then that's enough." One needed a lot of imagination to bring the children and youth into the parish.

    One needed imagination to get the work going at all. I was very discouraged at the onset of this period. . . . I had the feeling that nothing would come of this work. Very few children attended. So I went to my pastor and said, "You should be paying me less." . . . He answered: "When someone does such work, it's much harder when the work is so limited. It would be much easier to have a large troop around and work with that." . . . Then, when I said I couldn't get anywhere because of the countermeasures from the state organizations, he said to me: "Were you ever in a medieval city with a fountain at the market place? Did you see whether the fountain flows at night or if it is turned off?"

"No," I said, "it's always running." "Yes," he said, "that's how we have to see ourselves, that there is a fountain in the town that runs day and night. When the people aren't thirsty, they walk past it. But they always know: if I'm thirsty, there is a fountain that flows."

And so I worked on, as hard as that was.[19]

Kinds of Faith

A deep, steady faith not only led these Confessing Christians into their initial conflict with Nazism but sustained them as the scope of that conflict widened. Faith was a concrete reality for those in the Confessing Church. It is doubtful that they would or could have otherwise persevered as they did. Their faith enabled many Confessing Christians to break out of set political and ideological patterns. They took God and their duties as Christians seriously.

The recollections of Heinrich Vogel illustrate this dedication. Vogel was not only pastor of a church in Dobrikow, a village in Brandenburg, but also director of the Confessing Church seminary in Berlin. Together with two other pastors, Vogel had written the statement that had led to the arrest of 700 Confessing Church pastors in March 1935:

> We discussed among ourselves what needed to be said. I retreated to my hotel room for an hour and wrote this message, which wasn't merely directed at the new heathenism but consciously against the totalitarian state. Let me tell you how it was. I was truly aware of the immense responsibility, that here a text should be written in which the church dared to speak in God's name. I still know how I thought, "You could sooner justify a war than to write a false sentence." What do they know today, what do they have today from all their discussions, how they talk about God and God's word, as if about an interesting problem. God is no discussion object! He is God. That is an enormous difference.
>
> Now, I sat there in my hotel room with my paper and wrote. . . . Afterward, I returned to my friends, read it to them, and I can still hear how one of them laconically said, "So, we'll all end up in jail." And that's what happened. The totalitarian state noticed indeed that it wasn't just the *Myth of the 20th Century* being attacked, but its totalitarian demands, and it reacted by arresting 700 at once, namely, all those who read the statement.[20]

By the time Vogel's words were to be read from the pulpits, he was back in his own parish. He, too, was arrested:

> I remember still, an old, well-behaved man from the neighborhood came to me, you could feel sorry for him, the poor fellow; he had the task of putting this either/or to the pastor of Dobrikow. I said, "No, you know, the police don't decide what will be preached from my pulpit." He said, "But think of your wife and children." I said, "That's been done." So I went along, I couldn't do anything else, but he felt much worse about it than I did.[21]

Such firmness in confrontations with Nazi authorities sometimes won respect, and even hidden help, from local officials. As an illegal pastor in the "German Christian"-controlled church of Hesse, Rudolf Weckerling was regularly summoned to the local Gestapo headquarters:

> But it was all relatively merciful, because the Gestapo was very bourgeois. Basically, it was hard for them to understand, because the pastors were all somehow conservative nationalists, and the people as well. Usually they were not convinced Nazis, but simply continued to work [under the Nazis]. We often had to contend with the Gestapo—house searches, etc. We had one Gestapo official who was a convinced Christian mission member, evangelical, and he always sent his daughter ahead as a warning that he was coming.
>
> You have to imagine how chaotic this was. He may have been in the party, but we were in an area that was still very traditional with respect to the church. . . . It's often imputed that everything was centrally controlled. That's what they wanted, but locally, it was hardly carried out. It took a while to develop that and put it in place.
>
> I experienced that during my interrogations. I had many interrogations. Later, when I came out of prison, there were new people trained by the Gestapo, and then I noticed that this quasi-idyllic period of the first years—that was over. Suddenly a very sharp new wind was blowing.[22]

Gestapo tactics grew harsher as time passed. By 1936, the *Fürbittenliste* included the names not just of outspoken pastors but of ordinary lay people; the Gestapo grew determined to stop Confessing Church activities. One active lay member, for example, was arrested and sent to a concentration camp;[23] in Prussia, the Gestapo forcibly arrested a pastor's wife, leaving her two small children alone in the parsonage.[24]

The randomness and the brutality of the Gestapo's harassment of Confessing Christians increased the terror among church members. This was certainly a deliberate part of Gestapo tactics. In a society where virtually all opposition had been subdued, the continued activities of the Confessing Church were an affront to Nazis who believed that Germany's future rested on Nazi ideology and not on an outmoded Christianity. An example of Nazi tactics against the Confessing Church can be seen in the case of Herbert Mochalski, the former SA member whose Bible studies in the remote villages of Silesia were drawing more people than Nazi indoctrination meetings were. As this letter, written by the regional Nazi leader of adult education, illustrates, Mochalski's activities infuriated local Nazis:

> The last [Nazi party] evening instruction class was attended by around 30 men. A migration of people occurs, however, when these so-called Bible studies take place. . . .
>
> Because this is so, because our entire struggle for a transformation of the people to the National Socialist way of thinking will remain elusive as long as these Bible studies with their church-political reports exist, we ask for permission to pull this place apart. We plan to take part in one of the next Bible studies. As usual, they will send us out of the hall, if not already by the end of the Bible study, then in any case before the "interesting" reports (read *incitement*). It can then be absolutely counted on that, when we refuse, it will come to the fatal confrontation that we are longing for, so that we can prepare an end to this mischief once and for all[25]

Even in heavily Nazi regions, however, Confessing pastors found groups of Christians who remained loyal, despite persecution by Nazi officials. In Thuringia, a stronghold of the "German Christians," Nazis had been part of the regional government coalition since 1930. Only a handful of Confessing Christians existed, and most were unable to gather in churches for Sunday worship, meeting instead in private homes for Bible studies.

One of the few pastors in Thuringia to work for the Confessing Church was Friedemann M.[26] After he passed his theological exams in 1936, the "German Christian" bishop of Thuringia called him and two other young Confessing pastors in and told them bluntly that in a Nazi state there was no place for them. The three found tiny groups of Confessing Christians willing to support them; that support consisted, essentially, of room and board:

> It was difficult for me. I made my hardest trip home. My father had died in World War I and we had only a cottage. My family needed a man who had a job. We had lost all our money in the inflation years, and all that I had saved at the end of my studies was 25 marks. I lied to my mother, and told her I would soon receive word of where I would be working.[27]

Through the help of Ernst Otto, an older, established pastor who led the Confessing Christians in Thuringia, Friedmann M. was given a small church controlled by a baron sympathetic to the Confessing Church. The landed nobility, with their estates far out in the countryside, exerted considerable control over their small realms. In some areas, patrons were able to curtail the power of local Nazi officials. Some patrons, of course, were enthusiastic Nazis themselves; others, like Ruth von Kleist-Retzow, who protected Dietrich Bonhoeffer's Finkenwalde seminary, had opposed Hitler from the beginning. In any case, the Confessing Church sent some of its young illegal pastors to "safe" pastorates that had been established and were protected by a patron opposed to Nazism.

How safe these parishes remained depended, of course, not only on the patron but upon the tenacity of local Nazis and how tightly the region was controlled by higher Gestapo offices. In the case of Friedemann M., his patron was able to support him until 1941 — quite an achievement in Nazi Thuringia. Nevertheless, it was a dangerous time. The young pastor was regularly summoned to the local Gestapo for questioning. He made a point of holding services and Bible studies in different houses, never in the same place two times in a row:

> One night, there was a Nazi party meeting. One of the Nazis got drunk and told the police that they should shoot me on sight if they saw me out on the street at night. One of those who had been at the meeting came afterward to warn me. After that, a farmer walked me home every night after the Bible studies.[28]

Within the Confessing Church, younger pastors and vicars, like Friedemann M. and Mochalski, ran the greatest risks. Pastors already established in their pastorates before 1933 continued to receive pay and enjoy some job security, even after they switched their allegiance to the Confessing Church. Otto Dibelius, for example, forced into early retirement by the Nazis, remained active in the Berlin Confessing Church and continued to receive his pension from the official church consistory. The established position of people like Dibelius ensured them of some degree of support from the official church bureaucracy.

This was seldom the case for the young pastors who, having completed their studies and often their exams in the Confessing Church, had no legal standing in the official church. When in trouble, their only recourse lay in what other Confessing Church members and the Councils of Brethren were able to do for them.[29] As the number of arrests grew, the Councils of Brethren tried to assist the families of those arrested, offering information on what Gestapo prisoners could receive and advice on finding lawyers and financial help.[30]

The financial needs of illegal pastors were particularly pressing. A young pastor barred from an official pastorate was totally dependent upon the collections gathered in Confessing Church parishes and the private financial support offered by parish members (or, as in the case of Hans Thimme, on being supported by an official pastor who still received his full salary from the church).

The Gestapo singled out the young illegal pastors and students of the Confessing Church and hounded them constantly. When these young pastors were placed in parishes, local Nazi authorities began a steady stream of harassment that often culminated with a pastor's forcible removal from his parish and banishment from the region. In some instances, it went beyond that. In October 1935, for example, a young vicar in Wielitzken was attacked and badly beaten by a gang of SA members. Although he recognized and brought charges against his attackers, local Nazi authorities claimed that the attackers were "unknown" and that they would not pursue the case due to "lack of public interest."[31]

By October 1934, according to the Confessing Church, the number of disciplinary actions against its pastors stood at 1,043.[32] These ranged from interrogations to arrests. The purpose of these actions was to intimidate; the Gestapo often ended interrogations, for example, with ominous warnings about the concentration camps. The Nazis reacted more brutally and decisively, however, when attacked publicly by the church, particularly when those involved were already at risk — through their illegal status, forbidden political affiliations, or, most notably, when they were not "full Aryans."

The "Hitler Memo"

One of the earliest such confrontations concerned the so-called Hitler memo. In May 1936, the Provisional Church Government drafted an outspoken letter to Hitler criticizing the deification of the Führer and the totalitarian structure of the Nazi state and explicitly objecting to anti-Semitism and the growing persecution of the Jews. These elements of Nazism, the memo stated, contradicted Christian obligations to love one's neighbor. Church leaders did not publicize the letter, but sent it privately to Hitler himself. Despite their efforts to keep it secret, however, copies of the letter were passed to several ecumenical contacts and a representative of the U.S. State Department[33] and eventually released to the foreign press.

With the publication of such sensitive charges in the foreign press, the Nazis reacted. They arrested Friedrich Weissler, a Jewish lawyer who worked with the Provisional Church Government, and Ernst Tillich and Werner Koch, two young theologians who had contacts with the foreign press and occasionally served as couriers for the Confessing Church. They also arrested Heinrich Schmidt, the Dortmund lawyer who worked for the Provisional Church Government and who had worked with them on the memo. Schmidt recalled,

> we thought that there were many unjust things in the Third Reich which he [Hitler] simply didn't know about. We wanted to make clear to him that there was a large number of people not willing to follow him. We spent many meetings on this memorandum. We made only statements that could be proven — not only on ecclesiastical matters, but we also talked openly about the persecution of the Jews, that men and women were jailed without court hearings, that there were concentration camps to which people were sent without being sentenced. A number of political questions, aside from the ecclesiastical questions. This memo was sent in June 1936 to Hitler. Whether he read it or not, we don't know.
>
> The memo was not to be published because we hoped to reach Hitler without him setting up his propaganda apparatus against the church. . . . The release [to the press] turned out to be a good thing, because it showed there was opposition to Hitler. Weissler had talked about it one evening to friends who were journalists and shown it to them. One of them [Tillich] copied it and leaked it. The preliminary group had wanted to publish it, but in their own time. . . .
>
> At first, nothing happened on the Nazi side. On October 6, Weissler was arrested by the Gestapo, and in November, I was arrested, too. In January, I was released, and Weissler was taken to the concentration camp in Sachsenhausen, in the village where Kurt Scharf was pastor of the congregation. Weissler was a Jew; his parents were born Jews, and he had been baptized as a child. After he had been in Sachsenhausen for four weeks, his wife got the message that he had hanged himself. She immediately said, "My husband wouldn't kill himself." At that time, Frau Weissler was allowed to see his body. That was arranged by Scharf.
>
> Before she was taken to her husband, she was told that she would only be shown his face. If she wanted to find out whether he had really killed himself, she would have to remove the shroud. As she was in the hall with all the corpses, the guard said, "This is enough. You must leave." As she was about to leave, she grabbed her husband's body, pretending to embrace him, and she tore the cover off. Scharf could see that he had been murdered.[34]

There is an interesting legal footnote to the case: with Schmidt's encouragement the Confessing Church leaders filed a brief in one of the civil courts accusing persons unknown of Weissler's murder.

> Later, we found out that two SS guards were jailed a few weeks later for the matter, and that one had hanged himself in jail. . . . I'm telling you this to show you that, even at the time, some people still maintained that there was justice. Franz Gürtner, the minister of justice, was able to keep some of the civil courts uncorrupted.
>
> Today, we see the concentration camps from the perspective of what happened during the war. In 1933 and 1934, people were killed — so-called enemies of the state — and the courts had no way of interfering because no one took it to court. The relatives were told they had died of sickness. If some people had taken some steps, some people — not many, I know — would have followed more closely what happened in the camps. The judges and prosecutors were often not Nazis but conservative nationalists.[35]

The Hitler memo exemplified the different fate that awaited Jews who worked in the Confessing Church. Whereas Koch and Tillich, like Weissler, were also sent to Sachsenhausen, only Weissler was murdered; as Koch recalled, Weissler was immediately put in a separate barracks and they did not see him again.[36] Koch was released from Sachsenhausen in 1938 and Tillich in 1939, but, as a Jew, Weissler was doomed. In this respect, Heinrich Schmidt was fortunate. Although he was, according to Nazi racial laws, a "one-quarter mixture," Schmidt had falsified identity papers on him when he was arrested. "If the Gestapo had had the computers of today," he said, "I wouldn't have had a chance."

Persecution and Solidarity

The incident showed the greater dangers inherent in Confessing Church activities that more directly confronted the Nazi state. There were other activities in the Confessing Church that, from the beginning, entailed more risk. One was the job of courier, since it involved traveling (which was already controlled, albeit sporadically, by the mid-1930s) and carrying information too sensitive to be sent through the mails, which were often censored and confiscated. Both Werner Koch and Heinrich Schmidt served as couriers for the Provisional Church Government.

Another courier was a young Dutch woman, Hebe Kohlbrugge. Initially, Kohlbrugge had come to Nazi Germany out of enthusiasm for National Socialism; she quickly became disillusioned and joined the Confessing Church in Berlin. In 1938, she asked Kurt Scharf if she could help in one of the parishes. He sent her to one of the church's most outspoken foes of Nazism, Günther Harder, a pastor in the village of Fehrbellin, some 45 kilometers northwest of Berlin.

By 1938, Martin Niemöller was imprisoned in Sachsenhausen, and every evening church bells in Confessing parishes throughout Germany were rung for him. Kohlbrugge, working with Harder's youth group, began taking the children to ring the bells. The attraction of pulling church bells was soon drawing 20 to 25 school children and youth every evening. It did not take long for the Gestapo to summon Hebe Kohlbrugge and order her to leave the country. Kohlbrugge, however, took advantage of the ambiguity that still existed in some sectors of the bureaucracy. A government official in Potsdam, saying that they didn't want problems with citizens of other countries, told her she could stay. When the Gestapo returned and asked Günther Harder if she'd left, the Potsdam official again affirmed that she could remain in Germany.

A courier mission for the Confessing Church led to her arrest and deportation. To deliver copies of Niemöller's sermons throughout the province of Brandenburg to other Confessing pastors, Kohlbrugge was given Otto Dibelius' car, and was stopped by a policeman because one of the headlights did not work:

> This policeman was a very alert one. He looked at all my papers: a Dutch girl, with a Dutch passport and license, in the car of a pastor who lives in south Brandenburg, traveling in north Brandenburg. So he went to the police and said, "Look at this funny business, and she had packages in the car." . . . So there I was, and I was taken to prison. That was the end.

Coming the first time into prison is a terrible shock. I was absolutely alone, the only woman in the prison. I was 21 years old. Of course, I had no trial, but I was interrogated for hours and hours, and that was very hard. I wasn't beaten, but they tried to thoroughly upset me. "Sit still! Why are you putting your hands together?" — It was that the whole time, and then a question in between. The whole time they shouted loudly, that I had to sit differently, or that I had to look to this side or that side, so that, in the end, I didn't know where I was.

"They wanted, first of all, to know why I hadn't left the country. Second, what these packages had been in the car. I didn't have much to hide, because the Confessing Church worked quite openly. Of course, there were things we didn't do openly, but those were the things they didn't ask. They knew I'd been working with Harder, they knew everything, so I hadn't much to hide.[37]

A week after her arrest, her interrogator asked if she had any complaints and gave her a train ticket. The Dutch ambassador had intervened; she was to take the first train to Holland and was banished "forever." In Nazi Germany, Kohlbrugge recalled ironically, "everything was forever."

Within this atmosphere, with its risks, interrogations, and the growing awareness within the Confessing Church of the full scope of Nazi brutality, deep bonds of trust formed between the different sectors of the Confessing Church. In a church tradition that had been strongly hierarchical, the rigid barriers among members of different ages, classes, and callings became more flexible. This new sense of fellowship — between students and professors at the illegal Confessing seminaries, between young illegal vicars and pastors and their older, established colleagues who sat on the Councils of Brethren — reflected the serious responsibility Confessing Church members bore for each other.

This responsibility was most crucial in the illegal seminaries that the Confessing Church had established to train its young pastors. Annemarie Grosch recalled the camaraderie among her fellow students at the *Kirchliche Hochschule* in Berlin:

We were a sworn-in community, so that I never had anxiety at any theological exams — for when you must first hide together before it starts, then that's much more important than the whole exam anxiety, isn't it? We tried from the beginning to have our lectures near the university, so that we could attend both. But we were rather well known in the theological faculty at the university as the "gang," because we always arrived at the last minute, hot from running and completely out of breath. Simply from that, they knew that we always had to run back and forth. From the beginning, we had the Gestapo at our heels; they always found us, wrote us up, and sealed up the place where we had had our lectures, and then we had to find a new place.[38]

One of Grosch's teachers was Heinrich Vogel, the stubborn pastor of Dobrikow and director of the *Kirchliche Hochschule* (the Confessing Church seminary) in Berlin. He compared his life and those of his students in that era with the lives of the persecuted Christians in the catacombs of Rome:

but you mustn't imagine these catacombs as they were in the age of the Romans, rather sometimes a student's room, then the bedroom of a pastor, then the back room in some remote pub. We had to change continually, because the Gestapo was always after us. We had to be very careful. We had to find out whether the waitress in the pub was, perhaps, an informer, and how it looked in the neighborhood around the student's room. We couldn't use a place very long, because then the danger was that it would get out. The students, too, had to appear a certain distance after one another, not all at once, because that would have been noticed.

That's how we existed for years. But, despite everything, I think back on those years with pleasure. As you can imagine, it was such an excellent group of students. They were all young people who were setting their entire future at stake, eventually their freedom and their lives, in order to study theology. And all were shaped through the decision, that "either/or" under which we all stood: either the cross or the swastika. . . .

The *Kirchliche Hochschule* existed for two years. Then Herr Himmler attacked with a decree that threatened us with annihilation, eventually with the concentration camp.[39]

The Himmler Decree of August 1937 seriously escalated the legal pressures on the Confessing Church. It focused on the already vulnerable young pastors and students by making the giving and taking of Confessing theological exams illegal and declared the seminaries — from Bonhoeffer's Finkenwalde in Pomerania to the *Hochschule* in Berlin — illegal as well. Although these activities had not carried the sanction of the official church since December 1935, and were thereby illegal de facto, the Himmler Decree, as a Gestapo regulation, declared them to be criminal activities, punishable by imprisonment. As Vogel recalled.

Now we stood before the question: What should we do? What dared we do? Because it wasn't just us teachers, but our students as well, who were threatened with concentration camps and all that. Could we justify that? There were two schools of thought among us. The one was that we should change the education of the future pastors into nothing but apprenticeships; that is, to distribute our students among pastors who were suited to educate them theologically. . . .

The others, for whom I was the speaker, were of the opinion: No, we must continue, whatever the danger. We decided, then, to go on. I was in the good position not just to have to speak radically but to have to practice it at once. It was, namely, my turn the next morning.

I was in the process of discussing this with my students. We had stationed a watch in the house across the street. So we held the lecture. I had hardly begun when my watchman came and said to me, "The house is surrounded. The street exits are occupied, and at one of the street exits a Gestapo wagon is standing with enough empty places for us."

I told the others. I said, "So, it's our turn. We have to reckon with this any moment. Until they arrive, as long as we have time, we're going to proceed."

They didn't come. God in heaven, I really don't know, even today, what miracle happened. They didn't come. At the last minute, they must have received other orders. I said, "Friends, we're going to stop now and change our meeting place."[40]

Despite the Himmler Decree, the *Kirchliche Hochschule* and several other illegal seminaries continued to meet secretly until the Gestapo forced them to close. But the practical and psychological pressures on those who illegally taught or worked illegally in other areas had become enormous. Pastors, teachers, and church workers who served on examination committees were now as subject to imprisonment as the young pastoral candidates whom they examined. Confessing Church leaders worried about pastors breaking ranks — in extreme cases, by giving information to the Gestapo. Immediately after the Himmler Decree, the Berlin Council of Brethren sent a warning to all its pastors:

> From the standpoint of honor of a Christian and German man, it is ruled out absolutely that a pastor of the Confessing Church offer himself to the police as an informer on his colleagues. . . . The honor and fellowship of the status of pastor forbid any pastor to contribute, in any form, to a colleague's imprisonment for church or church political reasons.[41]

The threat of Gestapo interrogation and imprisonment was magnified by the fears and pressures of daily life. Many people were compelled to lead two existences, one in the Confessing Church and the other in the official church. Heinrich Vogel described his dual life as pastor and director of the *Kirchliche Hochschule* as

> an unheard-of burden. If I hadn't had a wonderful wife it would have been impossible, because I was always gone, and then afterward, I was in prison. My wife cared for the household and children, the parish, gave the confirmation classes, and called together the pastors from the Confessing Church in the entire region, of which I was leader. In this way, I could continue this double and triple existence. But particularly in the responsibility for the carrying out of a *Hochschule* teaching post, it was dreadful. Sometimes I thought, if only the Gestapo would move in, so I don't have to hold my lecture tomorrow! You can't take that literally, of course; I was happy when they didn't move in. But you understand what I mean. By normal academic standards it was impossible, irresponsible. . . .
>
> Yet, how often my wife and I thought back in gratitude on those times. Of course, we were in danger day and night, that's true. I saw the Gestapo prison from the inside. . . . We lived for nine months without any salary. Shortly before Christmas,[42] with five small children at that time, we received the message that my salary was totally cut off. That was in connection with the Czech crisis [Note: the Sudeten crisis, in September 1938] as the threat loomed of an invasion of Czechoslovakia, and with the prayer liturgy.[43]

National Loyalty and Political Criticism

The incident of the prayer liturgy was an example of a controversy within the Confessing Church triggered by national and international events provoked by Hitler. In the late summer of 1938, as a German invasion of Czechoslovakia seemed imminent, people throughout Europe feared that war was inevitable. In response, the Provisional Church Government wrote a liturgy to be used in special worship services to be held on September 30 in Confessing parishes throughout Germany. This "prayer liturgy" emphasized, through selected hymns, readings, and prayers, the church's desire for peace. In its confession of sin, it also lamented the sins committed by Germans and their leaders.

In the eyes of the Nazi authorities, this was treason. Nazi anger at the prayer liturgy was compounded by the publication, at the same time, of a letter that Karl Barth, living in Switzerland, had written to a Czech theology professor, Josef

Hromádka. Barth urged all possible resistance to a German invasion, writing that "every Czech soldier who fights . . . will be doing this for the Church of Jesus."[44]

Barth's letter and the controversial prayer liturgy set off a chain reaction within the churches. The Provisional Church Government disassociated itself from the Barth letter; the bishops of the intact churches disassociated themselves from the prayer liturgy and the Barth letter; and the official church consistory used its power to punish the leading pastors of the Confessing Church, including Vogel, by stopping their salaries. Ironically, the last-minute agreement between Hitler and Neville Chamberlain at Munich temporarily stayed the threat of war, and the prayer liturgy was never used. But, as Vogel remembered,

> I had signed it. The opposition thought it could bring us to our knees with hunger — which totally misfired. And indeed, not in the least thanks to the Pomeranian landed nobility; I should put a good word in for them in this respect. I got to know others, but, you know, there were those who understood what was at stake, and who were prepared to sacrifice. They packed packages, sent us hams. When it was over — after 10 months, this ruling that cut off the pastors' salaries was lifted — we still lived off the rest for a while.[45]

For Confessing Christians, issues like the Sudeten crisis and the growing threat of war again raised the uncomfortable questions of national loyalty and obedience to the Nazi state. These questions were particularly crucial in light of the Nazi remilitarization of Germany. As early as 1936, for example, civilians were drafted for what, essentially, were preparations for war. Even before the Sudeten crisis, Annemarie Grosch, like other Confessing Church students, had been drafted,

> since Hitler had demanded that all students do something military. That had already begun in 1935, with small-caliber shooting. I learned to shoot with small-caliber weapons. Furthermore, we had to choose to participate either in an apprenticeship with the Red Cross for a quarter year or in something that we didn't know, which was called "Communications." That lasted only three days. Our whole group of women in the Confessing Church naturally wanted to do what was shortest. We all signed up for "Communications" and none of us knew what it really was until we were ordered after three to four months to a place in Berlin. Oddly enough, it was the post office. There we were sworn in and then we heard what it was: the building of the military air force broad-casting system. So we were helpers for the air force. We were instructed, had regular drills, and had to participate in maneuvers. We called it "the store" among ourselves. That's how it came about that a whole group of women students from the Confessing Church landed in the military. I was on duty the night the war broke out and during the Czech crisis the year before.[46]

By drafting Confessing Church students, the Nazis showed a chilling contempt for their opponents in the churches. The members of the Confessing Church, so often denounced in the Nazi press as traitors, watched and questioned by the Gestapo, could be used for Nazi purposes. Chilling, too, is the assumption (and the fact that it proved to be true) that there would be no resistance.

The Nazi authorities could be influenced, however, particularly when they feared public protest. When Heinrich Schmidt, along with several other Westphalian members of the Council of Brethren, was rearrested in the summer of 1938, the outcome was unexpected:

> The central Gestapo office had fingerprints and files on us. The vice president of the Council of Brethren asked me, "What does this mean?" I said, "The concentration camp." But three or four weeks later, we five had to leave Westphalia. I was banished to a village in the Thuringian Forest, now in East Germany, and was not allowed to leave the village. What I tell you now I learned only after the war. We were supposed to be sent to a concentration camp. Because one of the pastors [in Dortmund] knew that, he had gathered a group of miners and went to Berlin and threatened riots in Dortmund if [we] were taken away. And they succeeded. I saw the documents to prove it only a few months ago. Somehow, the pastor had influenced Himmler or someone like him. This happened in October 1938, around the Czech crisis, and the Nazis might have been worried about domestic unrest.[47]

In any case, Nazi persecution of the Confessing Church, whether through laws like the Himmler Decree or through the more common tool of the Gestapo, increasingly confronted Confessing Christians and their church with the question of political resistance. This, of course, had been the question that had paralyzed some within the churches all along. Some Christians, particularly in the intact churches, charged that the Confessing Church had exceeded the legitimate realm of its activity in the 1938 prayer liturgy. But for people like Heinrich Vogel, Heinrich Schmidt, and Werner Koch, the church could not remain passive and silent in light of Nazi injustice. Having acted upon this belief, they entered the political realm, if not by intent, simply by virtue of the political risks they took. Whatever their reasons, whatever the issues involved, they would suffer political consequences. Yet the official church and some parts of the Confessing Church, trying to defend themselves against charges of political provocation, withdrew support from those members who had resisted "politically"—at the very time that persecution of more active and outspoken Christians was intensifying.

Nowhere was this clearer than in the debate that arose over the content and purpose of the *Fürbittenliste*—the intercessory lists, read every Sunday in Confessing Church services, of those members who had been arrested, banished, or forbidden by the Gestapo to preach or to travel. These lists were distributed and read not only in the Confessing strongholds in Prussia but in Confessing parishes throughout Germany, including some in the intact churches. The bishops of the intact churches believed that the purpose of the *Fürittenliste* should be explicitly limited. As Hannover's Marahrens wrote his pastors, the lists were not to be viewed or used as "pressure from the church public upon state organs."[48]

But within Prussia, too, there were differences of opinion on the lists. The *Fürbittenliste* rarely included the name of someone whose activities posed political problems for the church. This became most evident after the July 1944 attempt on Hitler's life; then the names of those implicated who had Confessing Church connections (most notably, Dietrich Bonhoeffer) remained absent from the lists. Even earlier, however, the Lutheran bishops removed Martin Niemöller's name from the list in their churches,[49] and Werner Koch's name did not appear for what were, probably, politically based objections.[50]

The debate over the *Fürbittenliste* went beyond attempts to weed out politically questionable names. It highlighted the divisions within the Confessing Church on how to view the Nazi state itself. Some conservative pastors contended that the church, to be evenhanded and truly Christian, should pray for the state as well as for those in its prisons.[51] Particularly after the war began, the practice of praying for the Fatherland ostentatiously supplanted or was added to the *Fürbittenliste* in some churches. But even in more radical Confessing Church circles, the purpose of the lists, and the real intentions of those whose names appeared on them, remained problematic — as this Council of Brethren memo illustrates:

> We are asked again and again whether the brothers and sisters who stand on the *Fürbittenliste* have gotten into trouble really only for the sake of the Gospel, or whether they are not being punished, and rightly so, for political offenses. . . .
>
> The decision on the question of whether the Gospel is being followed or not rests with [the church] alone. In all these decisions — and much more so in criticism of them — attention must be paid so that the *Fürbittenliste* are not viewed and used as a demonstration against the authorities or as a means of stirring up the parish.[52]

Even if the church did not want the *Fürbittenliste* seen as political provocation, the Nazis saw them as such. The reading of the *Fürbittenliste* joined the list of other punishable offenses. In Brandenburg, vicar Liselotte Lawerenz was arrested:

> It was a hot iron. I had discussed with [Kurt] Scharf how I should behave. We agreed that I should mention the arrested local pastor and [Martin] Niemöller by name. . . . So I did it according to plan, but after that afternoon, they told me at the parsonage that the police had asked about me. At first, nothing happened, but at the end of November I received a summons to the infamous Police [Gestapo] headquarters at Alexanderplatz. The interrogation concerned the service and the mentioned *Fürbitte*. . . .
>
> Then [the Gestapo officer] told me that I was arrested. . . . The women's prison was full. I was crammed into a cell with eight people. There were places to sleep, one bunk bed and a cot. For the others, straw mats were spread out on the ground. . . .
>
> On the ninth day, I was summoned . . . this time to a court interrogation. I had nothing to hide. The judge referred to a liturgical pamphlet that they had obtained from Fehrbellin, and in which the general *Fürbitte* had been entered. I think that [the judge] was not a fanatical Nazi, but had understanding for my situation. In any case, I was released![53]

As Liselotte Lawerenz' account indicated, Gestapo spies regularly attended Confessing Church services. In some case, they forbade the reading of the *Fürbittenliste*. Following one such service, held in Dahlem in violation of Gestapo orders, all 250 of those attending were arrested.[54] Not surprisingly, the reading of lists with several hundred names of persecuted Christians had a galvanizing effect on Confessing congregations, particularly in 1937 and 1938 as Nazi brutality was exercised more and more openly.

There were a number of signs that Nazi ruthlessness against the churches was intensifying. The arrest of Martin Niemöller in July 1937 shocked Confessing Christians, many of whom had assumed that the Nazis would avoid attacking a man of

Niemöller's stature and fame. At his trial in February 1938, Niemöller was indicted for reading forbidden announcements from the pulpit. However, the additional charges on his warrant of arrest — inciting unrest, provoking the state, and encouraging traitorous activities — reflected the real reason the Nazis wanted him out of the way.

The court was lenient; the seven months that Niemöller had served in prison while awaiting trial were equated with his sentence. He was fined and released, but Hitler, furious that Niemöller was free, ordered the Gestapo to rearrest him as a "special prisoner" of the Führer himself. Niemöller was sent to the Sachsenhausen concentration camp and, in 1941, to Dachau, where he remained until the end of the war.[55]

Niemöller's imprisonment was another signal to the Confessing Church that its activities, religiously motivated as they might be, had political implications. But in defending Niemöller at his trial, Confessing Church lawyer Horst Holstein emphasized Niemöller's national loyalty, not the sins of the Nazi state that had provoked Niemöller.[56] When a British film company made a film fictionally portraying the Niemöller case, Berlin Council of Brethren member Hans Böhm wrote Arthur Duncan-Jones, the dean at Chichester Cathedral and a British supporter of the Confessing Church, to protest:

> We fear that here the purely churchly activities of Pastor Niemöller will be misused for political purposes. That would suit neither the wishes of Pastor Niemöller nor the concerns of the Confessing Church. . . . We are fighting for the Church of Jesus Christ and wish for no allies whose goal is of another nature.[57]

Confessing Church realists, of course, knew that any open profession of political opposition to the Nazi state would be imprudent, if not suicidal. As war loomed and Nazi propaganda stirred national loyalties and revived the anger at Germany's defeat in 1918, patriotism stirred in the churches as well as in the general population. Yet the desire of Confessing Christians to make sure that their beliefs and actions were nonpolitical was based as much on their understanding of the Christian faith as on political tactics. In practice, this was "a difficult problem," as Pastor Christian Berg recalled:

> I saw to it that I didn't preach politically, but I addressed public issues and the consequences of that which I proclaimed became urgent, so to speak, by themselves. I left it to the thoughtful members of the congregation to draw the political consequences of that. . . . As a preacher, one should destabilize all human power through one's sermons, in order to proclaim and make firm the Kingdom of God in its uniqueness. That would be my view.[58]

But the attempts of more conservative Christians to separate their religious motivation from its political consequences succeeded neither on paper nor in reality. People acting entirely out of religious convictions can indeed suffer political consequences, and this was certainly the situation of the Confessing Church in Nazi Germany. The real problem with the church's protestations of political innocence was its simultaneous attempt to weed out the politically suspect from its ranks. This attempt undermined the work and lives of those Confessing Christians whose activities could (and, in some cases, did) land them in concentration camps.

The *Kirchliche Hochschule* Trial

In 1941, the Nazis finally closed down the *Kirchliche Hochschule* in Berlin. Despite the Himmler Decree and the Gestapo's continued harassment of faculty and students, the faculty had continued to teach as well as they could; and the Council of Brethren in Berlin had continued, illegally, to examine candidates for the ministry. In May 1941, 23 people involved in the illegal examinations were arrested. Among them were Heinrich Vogel; Günther Dehn (another professor at the *Hochschule*); Berlin Confessing Church superintendent Martin Albertz and his wife; Council of Brethren member Hans Böhm and his wife; youth worker Barbara Thiele; examining committee members Günther Harder and Elisabeth Grauer; and Albertz' two secretaries, Ilse Arnheim, a "full Jew," and Grete Michels, a "half Jew."

The trial was held in December 1941 in a Gestapo court. The course and outcome of the trial revealed the psychological and political pressures present in the courtroom. Fehrbellin pastor Günther Harder, a defendant himself, kept careful notes that reveal much about what happened.[59]

As in Niemöller's trial, the defense lawyers tried to play to the prejudices of the Nazi judges, defending Hans Böhm — "to Böhm's open torment" — as a national patriot whose wooden leg from World War I showed the depth of his allegiance to the Fatherland. The defense attorney let loose, according to Harder,

> an entire arsenal of German national breast beating, so that dear Barbara, in the recess, wept for grief that she wasn't being defended for her faith but with this breast beating. That the only thing that was of use were amputated legs.[60]

Albertz' and Böhm's wives, as well as Barbara Thiele, were defended as innocent accomplices who, in supporting the work of their husbands and pastors, had unknowingly and unwillingly broken Nazi laws. Barbara Thiele and Elisabeth Grauer, in fact, had been members of the Council of Brethren's examination committee for several years (Grauer had led the examination of women candidates). Yet, as Harder wrote with astonishment, according to the defense lawyer, they had done only what the men had told them to do, "although Barbara, like Frau Böhm and Frau Albertz had said, well and plainly, how deeply their commitment to the Confessing Church was founded in [their] parish work and consciousness."[61]

Although the defendants were found guilty, most of their sentences were commuted to the time already served in the Gestapo prison. With that, Vogel and most of the others were released. (Vogel believed that the relative leniency of the court indicated the judges' sympathy for the Confessing Church.)[62]

Martin Albertz, however, was sentenced to 18 months. As Günther Harder wrote in his notes, the judges were severe with him because he had not offered any "national qualities" in his defense statement and because he had continued to hire and support two "non-Aryan" secretaries secretly — which, in Nazi Germany in 1940 and 1941, took considerable courage. Albertz' office, in fact, was a refuge and meeting place for several Jewish members of the Confessing Church (these people were baptized Christians but were "non-Aryans" according to Nazi law). Four "non-Aryan" women worked at various times as secretaries to Albertz. As "non-Aryans," their fates were far more tragic than those of the other Confessing Church members who came to trial. Although Arnheim and Michels, like the other women, were sentenced to the four months already served, Elisabeth Grauer recalled that they were "simply held longer by the Gestapo and eventually deported to the east." Only one of the Jewish women who worked in Albertz' office survived the Third Reich.[63]

The nationalistic tone of the Confessing Church defense lawyer and the sarcasm that Albertz and the two Jewish women had to endure in the courtroom haunted Günther Harder, who believed that the Confessing Church, instead of trying to excuse its behavior to the Nazi judges, should have directly attacked the legitimacy of the Himmler Decree. Wrote Harder, "The agonizing question is this: whether we really can continue legitimately to say that we have church leadership."[64] During the course of the trial, Günther Dehn had asked him,

> "Are you, too, as horrified as I by *how* the defense is going?" Most of the men and the lawyers . . . said again and again that, of course, they hadn't wanted to violate the Himmler Decree. . . . Our Confessing Church has become a very poor church, in the form of the lowest, most bitter vassal.[65]

Yet, it was obvious that a clear, public stand would have led to the concentration camp. Vogel, during his seven-month imprisonment before the trial, was haunted by the certainty that he would be sent to one of the camps:

> At that time, I was rather bad off, psychologically—the wife, the five children, etc. In addition, I have a great deal of imagination and ability to reflect. That's not good for an imprisonment. Basically, I'm much more one of the old hounds of hell, hunted by reflection and imagination, a fearful man, rather than someone who thirsted for heroic achievements. But I know situations where I didn't have any other choice.[66]

Despite such fears, Vogel and the others had continued their activities, risking imprisonment, even being sent to the camps. This conscious choice, based upon their faith, was viewed by the Nazis as an act of resistance. Nonetheless, many Christians still refused to wrestle with the implications of this for the church. The question of resistance simmered within the Confessing Church. Events like the 1941 trial of the examining committee members held up a mirror to the Confessing Church. Günther Harder, like other radicals, was deeply troubled by what he saw.

The Legalization Controversy

After the 1937 Himmler Decree, the official church administrations in the Rhineland, Westphalia, and the other churches in the Old Prussian Union offered to legalize pastoral candidates who had been educated and examined in the Confessing Church. Young pastors who had taken their theological exams in the Confessing Church could be re-examined by a board of the official church. If they passed this examination, they could be placed by the consistory in a parish and would be ensured a regular salary and pension.

For the Berlin consistory, legalization meant a flow of new pastors to fill the growing number of vacancies. Throughout Prussia most young pastoral candidates had gone into the Confessing Church. Legalization was tempting to the illegal pastors for a number of reasons. After the war began, legalization offered financial security to their families. As Illegals, they were among the first to be drafted. If they were killed in action, their widows and families were not entitled to a pension from the official church.

Of the entire Protestant pastorate, 45 percent of the ordained ministers and 98 percent of vicars and candidates to the ministry had been mobilized by October 1944.[67] The ranks of young Confessing Church Illegals were hardest hit. By the summer of 1941, wrote Eberhard Bethge, 270 of the 300 Rhineland Illegals and 132 of the 154 Brandenburg Illegals were on the front. Of the approximately 150 students who studied with Bonhoeffer, over 80 were killed in the war.[68]

Even before the war, however, the financial difficulties of the Illegals, and the difficulties that the Confessing Church had in raising enough money to support them, led some Confessing Church leaders to support discussions with official church representatives on the legalization question.

The troubling question was what ideological and practical concessions the illegal pastors would have to make. In Westphalia, the legalization controversy almost split the Brotherhood, the group of illegal pastors and candidates. Westphalian Confessing Church leader Karl Koch had worked out an arrangement with the church consistory in Münster that, Koch contended, enabled the candidates to remain active as Confessing Church pastors. Koch was named head of the consistory committee that would re-examine the Illegals and saw this as a guarantee that they would not have to yield on crucial tenets of faith. At the same time, the consistory declared that every theological professor in Münster — including some "German Christians" — would be given a turn on the committee.

This was unacceptable to many of the young Illegals, and a heated debate arose. Hans Thimme, who had worked as Koch's assistant, was drawn into the controversy because he headed the Brotherhood of Confessing Church students in Westphalia. Thimme, then and later, supported Koch's position. Thimme's own situation differed from that of the Illegals in that, although he had been ordained in the Confesing Church, he had taken his theological exams in the official church, before the Confessing Church had begun to examine candidates separately. Thimme's perspective was this:

> I myself, since I was already legal through the normal channels, and because I sensed the creative possibilities one had as a pastor of the Confessing Church in a parish, was of the other opinion: that if these legalization measures could be completed without pressure on their consciences, and there was the possibility of entering parish work in a good, orderly way, then that was such an opportunity that one had to acknowledge it, for the sake of service to the parish.[69]

Eberhard Bethge has noted that the crux of the legalization issue, for those directly affected, was whether to rescind their support for the synodal decisions made at Dahlem. If, as the Confessing Church had decided at Dahlem, it represented the true Protestant church in Germany, then its pastors should stand firm and resist the tempting benefits of legalization. If the Confessing Church was not the true church (and there had always been dissension on this point), then, in light of the difficulties facing them as a result of the Himmler Decree, Confessing Church pastors and students could consider the legalization option seriously.

A number of factors led some illegal pastors to reconsider their relationship to the official church. The conflicting loyalties that pulled pastors toward both sides in the debate are evident in this statement, written by 18 illegal pastors in the church in Saxony:

> the constitutional church, as it exists today, has become a very questionable structure. It appears as if a spirit alien to Christ may well win the upper hand in it. . . . Indeed, it can be a question today whether the Church of Jesus Christ isn't present in a better and more complete form on the edge or even outside this constitutional church. We acknowledge, then, the questionability of the German Evangelical Church and the evangelical regional churches.
>
> Nevertheless, we believe that we are still called to serve in this constitutional church. . . . As men who have studied theology and entered the pastorate, we are called to serve in the constitutional church as long as we do not know for sure that the Church of Jesus Christ is no longer present in it and cannot be restored again in it.
>
> The question today is whether the Christian church as a public institution in the Third Reich will be able to remain at all. We do not have to answer this question; rather, God will do that, through the course of history. But we want to take pains to comply with Christ's commandment: "Render unto Caesar what is Caesar's and unto God, what is God's," in its duality and entire weight. The obligation to loyalty and obedience to the Führer must be taken totally seriously by us. We would bear a heavy guilt before God if our negligence or our obstinacy made it impossible for the Christian Church to find room in the Third Reich.
>
> [The Confessing Church] may not end its struggle before God puts an end to it himself. . . . loyalty to the task given us is simply not the same as stubborn holding fast to weapons that have become blunt. . . . We know that we belong to the Confessing Church, are bound with all its members and are co-responsible for its general fate.[70]

For many Illegals, the question of legalization was settled when they were drafted into the German army in 1939. The war quickly cut the ranks of theological students and young pastors. There were around 2,000 theological students in the last prewar semester in 1939; by February 1940, there were 38.[71] For various reasons, quite a few of the Illegals in the Confessing Church were eventually legalized. Bethge estimated that in Westphalia, for example, some 80 percent of the illegal candidates took the reexamination.[72]

The most steadfast opponent of legalization was Dietrich Bonhoeffer, who urged his students, even after the war began, to hold fast to the course decided upon at Dahlem in 1934. For Bonhoeffer, it was a serious matter of confessional truth. In this matter, as in others, he was explicit that the Confessing Church should not yield on any point to the Nazi state or those elements in the official church that cooperated with the state. "Don't let us talk ourselves into this," he beseeched his students,

> that over there in the ranks of the consistory we would be free for all the essential questions! There we would have yielded all inner authority, because we would not have stayed in the truth.[73]

Bonhoeffer's warning, "Whoever breaks from the Confessing Church separates himself from salvation," made the decision facing the young Illegals immensely difficult. (Few of Bonhoeffer's students became legalized, although it is hard to say what would have happened had they not been drafted as soldiers.) The legalization question forced these young pastors and students to choose consciously, on a crucial matter, between compromise and resistance. One of Bonhoeffer's students who did, in fact, become legalized, spoke in 1982 and asked to remain anonymous; he had never told some of his fellow Finkenwalde students what he did. Shortly after the Himmler Decree, the patron of the church where he had been working as an illegal vicar presented him with a choice. The parish position had to be filled with a pastor approved by the consistory. Either he would take the legalization exams — and the patron would see to it that he got the position — or the patron would have to find someone else. Decades later, the decision he made in 1938 continued to arouse anguish:

> Of course, it was a matter of conscience, but I think today — one can say, of course, that it was opportunistic or whatever. They told me, "Take this re-examination, then we can fill this position and have some peace, and, moreover, you don't need to promise that you won't read the *Fürbittenliste* or take up the [Confessing Church] collection."
>
> [The consistory] didn't ask any more what had been in the past. They were probably just happy that someone had taken up their offer. . . . In respect to the parish, I didn't regret it. . . . It wasn't at the cost of giving up all Confessing Church activities. I didn't have to sign anything, I didn't agree to any commitments, and, as I told you, everything else went its way: proclamations from the pulpit, the *Fürbittenliste*, prayers, and collections. I continued to do all that. . . . But how can I say it? The contradictions are so schizophrenic. But we thought then, if one retained this spiritual freedom. . . . The "German Christians" were long gone. It was just a formal proceeding, if you wish. Bureaucratic, you know? It didn't have any ideological demands, as was the case in 1933 and 1934. No, the consequence, of course, is that I was thrown out of the Confessing Church by the Council of Brethren by [Martin] Albertz, who understood me nevertheless.[74]

The man received all his personnel files back from the Berlin Council of Brethren. Legalization meant a break, institutionally and also personally, from the leaders of the Confessing Church:

> Yes, to the extent that they were no longer, how should I say it, the disciplinary officials for me. I continued — you can see that from the round letters and the *Fürbittenliste* — to receive the material [from the Confessing Church] and was kept informed. The contact was there, the collections for the Confessing Church went, as before, to the Council of Brethren, but, of course, I was cut off from the "young brothers." There I had cut myself off, that's true. . . . I took a different path than they did; they regretted that and the attempt was made — Bonhoeffer sent two people to me, perhaps to try to change my mind, but the decision had been made. . . .
>
> It's a little hard for you to understand how such a thing is possible. You say, either/or, don't you? . . . Whereby, I would say again, the decisive thing is basically in what respect and under what blessing one perceives his service as pastor. Not the administration of personnel files and the placement of the pastor.[75]

Yet, of course, the two men whom Bonhoeffer had sent saw it, like Bonhoeffer, as an either/or question:

Oh, well, of course they did, naturally, there was this distinction. This famous saying — theologically, by the way, absolutely wrong, if I may say so — from Bonhoeffer: "Whoever separates himself from the Confessing Church, separates himself
from salvation." Theologically, you can't demand loyalty to that. But it's understandable from his own position . . . this was put into practice very differently. None
of my colleagues in this church district, the community of brothers at the grass roots
said, "You've broken away from us." . . . That, I would like to say, is the decisive
answer to your question. The brothers.[76]

How his colleagues and fellow students reacted depended, in part, on how
severely they themselves had come under political pressure:

That played a role, too, didn't it? The stronger the fronts were, you see, with the
political things, the more that led to the reaction: "We will no longer sit with you at
the same table." Naturally, it's a difficult situation. I can't give any numbers on how
many did this legalization. I don't know. There were two others [Confessing Church
pastors] in our church district; they didn't do it. But theirs was not the situation that I
had — with this matter of the parish position. If it hadn't been for that . . .[77]

It is difficult for people, when they reflect on their behavior during the Nazi era,
to articulate what really motivated them. What does become clear from such recollections is that concessions made to the official church became, by extension, symbols
of acquiescence to the Nazi regime, thereby creating a layer of guilt that permeated
all attempts to explain.

Judgment and Accountability

This layer of guilt and of judgment — the distinction between those who "separated
themselves from salvation" and those who didn't — was already forming during the
course of Nazi Germany. It would influence not only people's memories after 1945
but their pattern of behavior during the remaining years of the Third Reich. One
woman, a parish helper, was summoned to the Gestapo because of a pamphlet she
had distributed:

It was oppressive to go through so many doors, and one door after another closed
behind me. I was asked where I had received this letter and to whom I had given it.
The questions were phrased in such a way that, without lying, I could make the matter seem harmless. I really didn't know where I had gotten the letter. Someone had
put it with my things, and I had passed it on to very many people. I didn't say that,
but I thought of a few people who I knew could stand up to being questioned. I
searched my memory and named a few people, and then I had the feeling that I had
said enough. . . .
    I was finally released, with the warning not to tell anyone. I went to my boss —
somehow I had to get rid of it — and told him everything. He said to me, "*Finally*
you belong to the respectable people!" It came from his heart, was so refreshing. . . .
It did me some good. Then I really did notice that all the "respectable" people had
been summoned by the Gestapo.[78]

In Baden, a young woman theologian, who had been interrogated several times
by the Gestapo, recalled running into a church social worker:

He said, "I hear you're not doing well." Someone had told him what I had gone through under the political authorities. "Ha!" he said, "You should have done as I did. You see?" He flashed a big party badge. That someone can do that, say, "On the outside, I do this, and inside, naturally, I'm completely different" — I was never able to do that. There were people, though, who could do that. I don't hold that for entirely genuine. But I have to admit, some people in our church administration did it, too. I know this for certain. They did it because they had a National Socialist finance department that controlled all the salaries and expenses, and they wanted to get along with this finance department to some extent. They wanted to bring them around to give permission for this and that. . . .

I don't consider it honest, but then, I wasn't in their work. I don't know what I would have done. I don't believe I would have done it. But I know of many of these people in the church administration, they were not Hitler supporters at all. They were only so on the outside. It wouldn't be my way, but I have to accept it. They were that way.[79]

Looking back, Hans Thimme described such people (of whom there were many) as "tired." There was, he recalled, "a general paralysis, the effect of which was that the beginnings in Barmen later just sank into a vast, resigned, apathetic exhaustion. People went to church, people stayed with it, but — this tiredness."[80]

The threat of Gestapo interrogation, of imprisonment in the dreaded Gestapo prisons or the camps, rumors about beatings and torture, and the concentration camps — all spread like a shadow over people's consciousness. Legalization and other concessions were, in a sense, the construction of political safeguards, attempts to create pockets of security for individuals and their families.

With the Nazi machinery of terror in full operation, members of the Confessing Church increasingly were unsure as to who might be a Gestapo informer. As a result, the most important information — about concentration camps or small resistance groups, for example — became limited to small circles within the Confessing Church. As the woman in Baden noted,

With people on whom one could depend, one could speak clearly. . . . We met together once on the street, on one of the bridges that goes over the Neckar. Now, when you met someone, you remained standing and spoke with one another, and we stood for a long time by the railing and looked down into the water and spoke with each other. The traffic flowed past us; sometimes someone walked by. There I said, "Now we can talk openly with each other and name names. Now no one is listening." Those of us who belonged to the opponents of the regime had to be careful.[81]

The *Fürbittenliste* showed, in sheer numbers, the long arm of the Gestapo, but even then, the lists offered only a partial picture. The *Fürbittenliste* from January 4, 1939 contained 283 names.[82] The German statistics yearbook for 1938 gives the total number of various police measures taken against Protestant religious workers as 4,468; this figure did not include the number of Gestapo interrogations.[83]

The systemic terror of Nazism threw the conscientious citizens in the Confessing Church into an emotional maelstrom. It was powered by emotions that swelled and paralyzed them — by the ties of nationalism, fears for their families and for themselves, and the desire to live and work without coming into conflict with Nazi authorities. In this dilemma, there was little peace for the Confessing Church pastors or parishioners.

A few, distraught at the hesitation of some Confessing Church leaders to challenge the Nazi regime more openly, left the Confessing Church. In August 1938, Gustav Heinemann, then a young lawyer and member of the Rhineland Council of Brethren, announced his resignation from the synod there. His criticism of the continuing attempts of many Confessing Church leaders to compromise with the official church, to find its place within Nazi Germany, described the tragedy of the Confessing Church:

> We have done nothing to awaken a genuine and credible readiness to give up the official church. . . . How much have we declared unbearable, and yet we bear it! . . . We are neither as an organization nor as individuals prepared for anything other than that which we have had for generations. . . . In the best case, we are waiting for a great and utterly unignorable signal to break away. It will not come. There will only be signals in small doses, which will not bring us to a complete break.[84]

Some of the heroism that emerged in the Confessing Church came from those people who charted an individual course and followed it. One was Kurt Scharf, pastor of a parish in a village so peaceful that it seemed to be on the edge of the world. Scharf, a member of the Council of Brethren since 1934 and author of countless newsletters to other Confessing pastors, was disciplined for the first time in 1934 by the Berlin consistory. Shortly thereafter, the "German Christian" church officials in Berlin began their efforts to remove him from his parishes so that a pastor could be sent in who was more compatible with the consistory's purposes and with local Nazi officials.

In 1938, following the Sudeten crisis and the prayer liturgy controversy, the consistory suspended Scharf from his pastorate. When Scharf refused to acknowledge the suspension, the consistory brought proceedings against him. The court's verdict in January 1939 quoted the prayer liturgy and denounced the Confessing Church,

> which through its position of rejection of National Socialism, through its connections with international Protestantism and democracy, and through its declarations of battle against the constitutional and legally recognized organs of the legitimate church leadership, has inflicted the worst damage not only on internal church life but regrettably on the troubled relationship between the state and the Protestant church in Germany as well.[85]

Despite the court verdict, Scharf refused to leave his parishes. When the consistory sent a replacement for him, he continued to hold services in the church. When the Gestapo sealed off the church, Scharf and the parishioners loyal to him met elsewhere.

The Scharf case did split his parishes. While several parishioners, including the organist, testified against him,[86] the consistory received over 1,000 letters supporting Scharf;[87] but once the war began, open support for him dwindled. At Easter 1940, for example, only eight children were sent to Scharf for confirmation; the pastor sent by the consistory confirmed 45.[88] At the same time, the consistory sharpened its attacks on him, accusing him of subverting "the closed ranks for *Volk* and Fatherland" in his refusal to leave his parishes.[89] The words of the final verdict against Scharf, in July 1940, described his offense:

The fact remains that here, in a concrete case, a pastor believes that he doesn't need to obey legal decisions. . . . It is not up to the spiritual decision of the accused whether he wants the norms of the state laws to be valid for the realm of the church or not. This is what the accused will not recognize.[90]

Scharf believed it important to hold out as long as possible, not only for the sake of his parishioners but as a witness to what the Nazis were doing. The back window of his parsonage faced the concentration camp of Sachsenhausen. As Scharf recalled,

At first, in 1933, there was a small concentration camp in Oranienburg on the grounds of a former brewery. The first prominent prisoners — from political groups, the Berlin art and literary scene, cabaret singers, Jewish and leftist artists — were sent there. This Oranienburg camp didn't exist much longer than a year. At the end of 1934, labor troops from a concentration camp in Emsland [on the Dutch border] began to build the concentration camp at Sachsenhausen. The forester in Sachsenhausen at that time refused to release the lands for it. He didn't want his trees in such a wide area to be felled, but they went ahead and began construction anyway. The camp was occupied from 1936 on. Most of its inmates were transferred in from the camp in Emsland. They called themselves the *Moorsoldaten* ["Moor soldiers," because of the swampy moors surrounding the camp in Emsland]. They brought their marching song, the *Moorsoldaten* song, with them to Sachsenhausen. I often heard the prisoners singing it on the highway from Sachsenhausen to Oranienburg, when they were led, that is, driven, to their working posts.

In the concentration camp were Jews, then the so-called sect members — Jehovah's Witnesses, Adventists. They were identified as religious prisoners with a purple triangle, whereas the prisoners from the Confessing Church were listed as political prisoners and had a red badge. The Jews wore the gold star; there were also homosexuals and gypsies among the inmates.[91]

The concentration camp became part of the daily lives of Scharf's parishioners:

It lay between my two parishes, between the main parish in Sachsenhausen and the adjunct parish in Friedrichstal. The borders of the concentration camp were a few hundred meters from my parsonage. From the fields behind my house, you saw the towers and the boundary walls, after they had been erected. But above all, the businessmen, the manual workers, and certain delivery firms came into the camp to provide services for the SS officers and SS troops there. The manual laborers also did repairs in the officers' apartments. Through that, they were aware of what happened in the camp.

When the prisoners were taken to their work place, one saw them — emaciated, wraithlike. Parish members and school children often put bread unobtrusively on the street curb, out of pity, so that the prisoners could grab it and get a little more nourishment. This happened even during the war, when food was rationed.

At the beginning, Sachsenhausen was, for the most part, a prison, but it developed quickly into a labor camp. Near the camp, a huge brick factory was constructed, and labor troops were sent to work in the military industries, like the Heinkel aircraft factory in Oranienburg. Right on the border between Oranienburg and Sachsenhausen was a huge metal foundry. After the beginning of the war, the confiscated church bells were delivered there and melted down for weapons. Labor troops from the camp were sent there as well, and it was hard labor in such plants.

There were no gas chambers in the Sachsenhausen camp, but they had a crematorium. When the prisoners died as a result of the treatment in the camp—not enough food, overwork, and the gruesome treatment—then they were cremated. We could see the number of prisoners who had been murdered by the perpetually smoking chimneys of the crematorium. Their bodies were burned when they were murdered or when they ran, out of desperation, into the barbed wire or were shot while fleeing. The camp leaders would claim that someone had wanted to flee and had been shot, whereas in truth they had been chased around the camp and shot.

It was very hard for those of us who lived in the south part of the parish after the Russian prisoners of war were brought in. They arrived totally exhausted. They had been transported for weeks, standing and closely penned up in cattle cars—and when they were unloaded at the train station, they just fell out. This always took place at night, under the glare of spotlights. A tower of corpses rose beside the still living bodies that tumbled out onto the platform. The living prisoners would be driven by the SS men with whips and dogs into the camp. Those who collapsed got a kick that snapped their necks. Our people saw the smoke climbing out of the crematorium day and night.

Our parishes knew what was happening there. The knowledge about the procedures in the camp lay like a poison cloud over our parishes. Because of that, the recognition grew quickly that this war would work its way out on us like the judgement of God. That's how we saw the bombing raids on Berlin after 1942. . . . Our parishes saw the burning churches and the burning cities as God's judgment for what had been done in 1938 to the Jews and their synagogues.

In such situations, the word of God has an immediate impact. We didn't have to add much interpretation to the biblical text. . . . A text like the one from the Revelations of John, which announced the horrors of the end of time and, then, again and again, descriptions of the times during which the parish had tranquillity and could spread itself out under God's protection—we experienced that as our reality![92]

If the parish saw the destruction of Germany in the war as God's punishment for the evils of Nazism, it was in large part due to the message Scharf preached to his flock, a message found not only in his sermons from that era but in records of the disciplinary proceedings against him, which listed his "offenses:" He insisted upon staying in his parsonage to serve the Confessing Christians in Sachsenhausen and Friedrichstal. He was accused of "individualism" in refusing to acknowledge official church orders. In Sunday services, he announced the number of prisoners in the concentration camp. He rang the church bells for them every evening. He prayed publicly for the "persecuted brothers and sisters of Israel."[93]

He made his parishioners aware of the suffering in the concentration camp. Like most Germans, they were, on some level, already aware. From Scharf's description it is obvious how visible that suffering was to the surrounding population. Scharf's task, and that of Confessing Christians like him, was to make them aware on a deeper level, ultimately, on the level of accountability: that the suffering of those in the camps had consequences for Germans outside them.

The inmates of Sachsenhausen heard the church bells ring nightly and knew that, in that moment, they were being prayed for. The parishioners in Sachsenhausen and Friedrichstal heard the bells and knew that their pastor stood firm, pealing a message to God and humanity, in protest against Nazism, in solidarity with the suffering of the Nazis' victims.

The bells of the Confessing churches reverberated long after the war, in people's memories. Their echo testified to the courage and resolution of many within the Confessing Church, but it also troubled many Christians. The question that haunted them was whether, had they acted differently, they could have halted the series of events that culminated in mass murder.

✤ 6 ✤

The Murder of the
Institutionalized Patients

IN NAZI GERMANY, a selection process took place on both sides of the barbed wire. In the concentration camps, prisoners were graded like livestock. Those who were healthy and strong were put to work. All who were ill, too old, too young, weak, and not useful were "disposed of," "eliminated," "erased." In Nazi Germany, there were many euphemisms for murder.

The most insidious aspect of Nazi ideology — the selection process between weak and strong, between "Aryan" and "non-Aryan" — became a fundamental part of life in Nazi Germany. Hitler's goal was to transform the Germans into a "pure" race of *Übermenschen*, who would be physically, culturally, and intellectually dominant.

Yet, where there are *Übermenschen*, there will be *Untermenschen* — whole groups of people viewed and treated like animals. In Nazi propaganda, Jews and other "enemies" of the Fatherland were invariably portrayed as subhuman, Neanderthal-like figures. So, too, were people with physical and mental disabilities, and they were described in terms that suggested racial regression, the potential downfall of the entire German nation. The text of a typical Nazi poster of the 1930s appealed, as well, to German pocketbooks:

> Everyday, a cripple or blind person costs 5–6 RM [Reichmarks], a mentally ill person 4 RM, a criminal 3.50 RM.

and, concluding with a drawing of an attractive "Aryan" couple surrounded by five small children:

> a worker has 3–4 RM a day to spend on his family.[1]

This crude appeal to prejudice was supported by the science of eugenics, at that time intellectually respectable. The eugenics movement, which spread internationally in the late nineteenth century, was based on Charles Darwin's and Gregor Mendel's observations of the process of natural selection in plants and animals. The idea of the survival and adaptation of the fittest led to hopes, among eugenicists, that the human race could be made healthier and more intelligent by breeding out hereditary weakness and disease.

Nazi ideology drew early from eugenic theories to construct and condone its concept of a superior race. In July 1933, a law was passed ordering the compulsory sterilization of individuals with hereditary weaknesses. Under Nazi law, the range of genetic weaknesses was wide, including epilepsy, all kinds of birth defects, blindness, deafness, personality disorders, some orthopedic problems, mental illness, retardation, and alcoholism. Professionals who encountered such problems — from dentists to midwives to schoolteachers — were required to register these cases with Nazi officials. Under the 1933 sterilization law, between 200,000 and 350,000 people were sterilized.[2]

Even before 1933, however, there were ominous signs that some German eugenicists were concerned with more than just ensuring that institutionalized patients not pass their weaknesses on to coming generations. In a 1920 essay, Arthur Hoche, a professor of psychiatry, and Karl Binding, a lawyer, argued for the euthanasia, or mercy killing, of institutionalized patients, "within the proper limits."[3]

The term they chose to describe severely disabled patients was "life unworthy of life," a phrase that raised a fundamental moral question. Hoche and Binding distinguished between patients whose earthly use could be easily seen and those whose lives appeared to serve no purpose, who were a burden on their families and, when they lived in institutions, on the state. If they could not work, if they served no purpose, if they were doomed to spend their lives being cared for, then was not their death a welcome and beneficial alternative for all concerned? With such arguments, the eugenicists prepared the way for the "mercy killing" of those "unworthy of life."

The euthanasia discussion posed an immediate challenge to the churches, since the German Evangelical Church, through its Inner Mission, owned and operated hundreds of hospitals, orphanages, and institutions for the mentally and physically disabled and the elderly. In 1931, the Central Council of the Inner Mission issued a statement opposing euthanasia. The same statement, however, described the approximately 30,000 patients in church-supported institutions as "the victims of guilt and sin."[4] Other statements from that era, by pastors and church institution leaders, expressed similar prejudices in unmistakably moral tones.[5] Hereditary and mental diseases carried a number of stigmas, only one of which was the social prejudice against people who were "unproductive."

Even before 1933, then, a kind of selection process occurred, by which healthy, nondisabled Germans distinguished themselves from members of the population who were mentally ill or disabled. As Friedrich von Bodelschwingh (the nephew of Bethel leader Fritz von Bodelschwingh) observed in 1966, euthanasia proponents simply denied the moral consequences of their position. Hoche and Binding spoke

> not of the "killing" but rather of the "destruction" of life unworthy of life, for, in his [Binding's] opinion, it's not a matter here any more of a real life. Life that no longer has any value for the sovereign is not even capable of being killed; one can only "destroy" it.[6]

The prejudices that undergirded this worldview made the churches' fight against euthanasia difficult. Few leaders of church-supported institutions supported euthanasia in any form. Their life's work had been based on a deep respect for life and upon the Christian mandate to minister and care for those less fortunate. But in countering the psuedo-humane arguments for "mercy killing," church leaders met with considerable prejudice, even among Christian groups. As Paul Braune, who led the Inner Mission's fight against Hitler's euthanasia program, later wrote:

This consenting or, for the most part, neutral position on the murder of the invalids, mentally impaired and epileptics was spread so extensively among the populace that, even in circles very capable of better judgment, I met only a slight shrug of the shoulders when I told of my fight against euthanasia. . . . Again and again, I was met with the thoughtless words: Is it really so terrible, when such invalids are freed, gently and painlessly, from their suffering? Even Christian-oriented circles didn't comprehend completely how [I] could set [my] life and existence at stake for such hopeless, or even inferior and pitiful, human beings.[7]

For the churches, the euthanasia program became one of the most haunting aspects of the Third Reich. For the Inner Mission, church institutions were an essential part of Christian ministry. Yet, the same divisions that had plagued the churches in their struggles with Nazism arose here as well: between those who wanted the church to protest publicly and those who hoped to end the euthanasia program by reaching some arrangement with the Nazi state.

The Euthanasia Program

At the beginning of 1939, ostensibly in response to the anguished letter of the parents of a severely handicapped child in Leipzig, Hitler empowered a special Reich Council,[8] under the jurisdiction of the interior ministry, to deal with the question of "mercy death" for the severely handicapped. Actually, plans for a euthanasia program had long been part of the Nazi program. In 1929, at the Nazi convention in Nuremberg, Hitler had proposed the annual "removal" (literally, *Beseitigung*") of 700,000 to 800,000 of the "weakest" Germans as a means of rapidly improving the overall health and capabilities of the German race.[9]

In the spring of 1939, Nazi officials began to consider which institutions could be converted into euthanasia centers. Some 20 Nazi officials, doctors, and directors from several institutions met to plan the beginning of the program. One of the six institutions finally selected was the church-supported home of Grafeneck, near Stuttgart, which was placed under state control.

With these preparations under way, the interior ministry began contacting institutions. In August 1939, the ministry ordered doctors and midwives to register all births, from 1936 to 1939, of babies with birth defects and sent out forms that the attending doctor was to fill out and return to the Reich Council. This was the beginning of the children's euthanasia program, under which some 5,000 children would be killed. In October 1939, Hitler signed a brief personal order assigning his personal physician, Karl Brandt, and Reich chancellery director Philipp Bouhler the task of

extending to specified doctors that those who, according to human judgment, are incurably ill may be granted, after a critical examination of the state of their health, a "mercy death."[10]

Hitler's memo was postdated September 1, 1939, to coincide with the beginning of the war.[11] Indeed, one rationale given for the program was that the deaths of institutionalized patients would free medical facilities and beds for wounded soldiers from the front. Several thousand patients were killed under SS command in the first months of the war; one group of patients was herded into a Prussian forest and shot down by SS soldiers.[12] But as far as institutional directors were concerned, the official euthanasia program began in October 1939 when forms were sent out to several institutions in Baden and Württemburg.

It is unlikely that the first institutions to receive the forms were aware of their purpose. For each patient, a form was to be filled out giving in detail the nature of the patient's illness, the length of time already spent in institutions, and the patient's racial status. The cover letter told institution directors that filling out the forms was a necessary statistical measure and that a mass transfer of certain patients to other institutions might be necessary because of the wartime demand for medical facilities. Three state-appointed experts would review the completed forms, select those patients to be "transferred," and provide for their removal from the home institution.

The completed forms were sent to the Reich Council, where the three "experts" "evaluated" hundreds of forms each day, marking each one with a red cross for death or a blue cross for life — without ever having seen any of the patients whom they were condemning to death. Under the auspices of the Reich Council, a bus firm was established and outfitted with special buses with covered windows. The buses, often staffed with SS members, picked up the selected patients and drove them to one of the euthanasia institutions, where special gas chambers and cremation ovens had been constructed. Although some patients in the first months were killed by morphium-scopolamin injections, gassing by carbon monoxide was determined to be a better method,[13] bringing death in about 20 minutes. One employee who watched described the "mercy death" that resulted:

> Here I made the observation, through the observation window placed on the side, that the people died an agonizing death. The length of my observations lasted only around three minutes, for I couldn't bear the sight any longer.[14]

Families were notified only afterward that their relatives had been moved to other institutions, and those who pursued the matter were told that visits or other contacts with the patient were impossible because of wartime restrictions.[15] Shortly thereafter, the family of each patient received a letter saying that their relative had died unexpectedly of heart trouble, pneumonia, or a similar disease and had been cremated immediately for precautionary health reasons.

Families, doctors, and staff members at the original institutions suspected quickly that what was happening far exceeded the mere transfer of patients. Their inquiries at provincial government offices were deflected, however, either with denials or with refusals (on the basis of wartime "secrecy") to answer questions.

There were some doctors and state institution directors who supported euthanasia, were aware from the beginning of what was taking place, and approved it.[16] Some were even invited to witness the "euthanization" of their patients or were placed on the lists of doctors who helped with the program.

But others were horrified by their suspicions. They began trying to get confirmation of it, and, in the meantime, tried to prevent the removal of patients from their institutions. Ludwig Schlaich, head of the church-affiliated Stetten home in Württemberg, had been drafted at the beginning of the war and was with his unit when the first forms arrived at Stetten. Schlaich's unit was stationed in the area, and his sympathetic officer gave him frequent leaves, so that Schlaich, despite his military status, was able to follow what was happening.

At first Schlaich and the two assistant directors at Stetten tried to stop the buses from coming, even appealing to Rudolf Hess.[17] Schlaich, like other opponents of the euthanasia program, argued with officials that no law existed that had ordered or regulated what was happening. In fact, that was the tactic behind Hitler's secret order to Brandt and Bouhler. In the initial months of the euthanasia program, distraught institution directors like Schlaich searched for the government's legal basis in removing patients, while the government hid behind denials, based upon the Führer-ordered secrecy of the measures.

Meanwhile, the buses continued to arrive. Many doctors tried to negotiate with the bus personnel. In one instance, the bus stood in front of an institution for four hours while doctors argued with the bus driver and another staff member argued frantically on the telephone with a bureaucrat in Stuttgart.[18] The bus finally drove off with 11 patients; the doctors' stalling tactics had rescued four patients from the list.[19] In another case,

> on the day of the transport, 15 more patients could be fought free by negotiating with the transport leader. But still, on this day, 41 mentally impaired patients had to get on the buses after an affecting farewell.[20]

As the program continued, some wary doctors simply refused to fill out the forms. Inspector Hermann, the courageous director of a home for deaf and dumb patients near Ravensburg, sent the blank forms back to the interior ministry with a letter:

> I know the purpose of this planned economic census. I know of the many reports of death. . . . I can't conscientiously keep silent and cooperate. . . . I am prepared to accept the consequences of my disobedience.[21]

Shortly thereafter, a commission of government-appointed doctors arrived at Hermann's institution and filled out the forms themselves. Hermann, by arguing with the commission, was able to get some names removed from the list. Of the 110 patients in his care, 18 would be killed.[22]

Although forbidden to do so by the interior ministry, doctors and directors at the institutions affected began notifying relatives of those patients particularly endangered to see if the families could take them back home. They also began to spread word of what was happening, so that the euthanasia program quickly became generally known.

Indeed, the top secret status of the euthanasia program, officially maintained by the Nazis until the end, was a sham. Annemarie Grosch, who worked in a Confessing parish in Berlin at the time, recalled that she heard about it very early. She later told of her father's reaction:

> He himself had a Jewish cousin, whom he told in 1934, "See to it that you get out." He was that pessimistic at a time when the Jews themselves, to a great extent, didn't think of all the evil yet. . . . Then, in 1939, I came home from an information evening in the Dahlem parish and said, "Now they're giving fatal injections to the terminally ill."
>
> My parents already lay in bed. My father sat up and said, "That's not true!

That's exaggerated!" It was utterly unimaginable for him, for a man who had the first edition of Hitler's *Mein Kampf* and had read it before 1933, and, therefore, knew Hitler's thinking. . . . My father could believe anything of Hitler, but he held that to be simply impossible. That went so far beyond all the terrible notions that he had.[23]

Unbelievable as the euthanasia measures were, detailed knowledge of the program spread among the staffs of affected institutions, families, and the patients themselves. The impairments of the people whose lives were "unworthy of life" ranged, in fact, from severe disabilities to short-term psychiatric problems. Except for those on the very first transports, many patients understood enough of what was going on to fill them with panic. Eyewitness accounts and recollections compiled by Ludwig Schlaich shortly after 1945 show that even severely disabled or retarded patients showed their fear of the dreaded transport buses; indeed, transport personnel sometimes had to use force to get patients, kicking and screaming, into the buses. Patients appealed pathetically to relatives and institutional personnel to save them. "Yesterday the car was here again," one patient wrote to her sister,

> and eight days ago, too, they took many away again where one wouldn't have thought. It was so hard for us that we all wept. . . . now I want to ask you if you would stand up for me so that I could come to you, for we don't know whether they won't come again next week.[24]

Another patient wrote to her family,

> I live again in fear, because the car was here again. . . . Those are not guesses, what I tell is all true, the government doesn't want so many institutions anymore and they want to put us out of the way.[25]

When the buses arrived, patients often tried to hide. The most wrenching scenes came when they were led onto the buses. Schlaich described one who wept, "How can I help it, that I am this way and that they are doing this to me?"[26] and another who faced the bus "with wide open, fear-filled eyes, pale as a corpse, who beat her arms in the air and screamed, 'I don't want to die!'"[27] Word of such scenes spread rapidly in the villages surrounding such institutions, and staff members who worked in euthanasia institutions met sometimes with open hostility from local people.[28]

While some Nazi officials retreated into officially sanctioned secrecy about what was no longer secret, others presented the case for "mercy killing" in coldblooded terms. One man appealed to a family friend, an SS official, to save his institutionalized sister. He received this reply:

> I can understand completely your pain about the expected fate of your sister, but I ask you to consider that, for the mentally ill who suffer, as your sister does, from such difficult disturbances, an earlier peaceful death does indeed mean deliverance as opposed to perhaps years of bodily and spiritual agony. I personally believe that Christian love for one's neighbor takes a false path in the careful maintenance of the mentally ill, and that it is more Christian and humane to release such invalids from their pitiful fate. . . . I personally believe that, in this sense, medicine has occupied itself with a false consideration for humanity, and that in this area there will be changes in this view in the near future.
> I can only advise you, in this case, to turn personally to the institution's direc-

tors in order to learn if your sister is in a position at this time where her discharge from the institution could be arranged.

Should that not be the case, I ask you, dear colleague, to keep in mind that at this moment the finest and healthiest of our young men are giving their lives, daily and hourly, for our people in the war. The death of each one of these men brings a vast amount of pain and suffering to their families and friends. When one considers this, the blow of fate which affects one family, on the basis of the fulfillment of the above measures, [i.e., euthanasia] can indeed be borne more lightly. . . . You will understand that, on the basis of my explanation, it is impossible to make exceptions in an individual case through whatever possible connections.[29]

The Church's Response

The only recourse the directors of the institutions had was to try to rescue their patients by negotiating with the transport team that arrived to take them away. "While the buses waited before the doors of the institution and the screams of fear of our unfortunate patients echoed through our buildings,"[30] as Schlaich recalled, he and others like him went down the transport lists and tried to give reasons why various patients should be spared. One might have influential relatives, another was a good worker and indispensable to the institution's workshops, another was a decorated World War I veteran and should be spared out of respect for the Fatherland.

But this strategy, while it did rescue some lives, was a stopgap measure. Moreover, it was morally abhorrent for conscientious doctors, since it forced them, albeit for tactical reasons, to calculate the "worth" of the human lives in their care. Faced with an impatient SS transport leader and the bus waiting before the door, there was no way to rescue all the patients whose names were on the list.

Their only real hope was an end to the entire program. Institutional doctors and directors, frustrated by the limitations of what they could do, put their hopes in two influential institutional leaders: Pastor Paul Braune, the vice president of the Central Council of the Inner Mission and director of the Lobetal institution near Berlin, and Fritz von Bodelschwingh, the leader of the 3,000-patient community of Bethel in Westphalia.

Braune had realized the significance of the interior ministry forms and the reports of patient transfers from the beginning. In 1985, his widow, Berta Braune, who worked with him in Lobetal, remembered his words when he first saw the forms: "Now they're going to try it out with the sick, and then they'll go on to all those who are disagreeable to them."[31] Spurred by various reports and inquiries from Baden and Württemberg that were being sent to the Inner Mission, Braune began tracing reports of patients' deaths, talking with relatives, contacting institutions, and amassing information that led him inescapably to the conclusion that mass murder was being carried out.

Braune compiled his facts and wrote an eight-page memo, which he sent to the interior ministry in July 1940, pointedly condemning the euthanasia of patients:

How far does one want to go with the extermination of so-called lives unworthy of life? The mass actions up to now have shown that many people have been taken who were in large part clear and of sane mind. Where does the limit lie? Who is abnormal, antisocial, who is hopelessly ill? . . . It is a dangerous venture to abandon the integrity of the person without any legal foundation . . . Will it not endanger the ethics of the entire population, when human life counts for so little?[32]

But, although Paul Braune was vice president of the Central Council that oversaw the work of the Inner Mission, he wrote and signed the memo alone. The other Central Council members were far more hesitant to confront the Nazi state — as was Braune's friend and colleague, Fritz von Bodelschwingh, the Reich bishop candidate in 1933. (Von Bodelschwingh, whose father had founded the huge Bethel institutions in Westphalia, directed Bethel until his death in 1946.) As Berta Braune remembered,

> My husband had made the first visits to the government people alone, and then fetched von Bodelschwingh, as he should. I remember that he said, "I have to, now; Bodelschwingh's name is known worldwide. He has to help now.[33]

But von Bodelschwingh, although he agreed to use his influence with Nazi officials, did not sign the memo. Nor did the Bethel leader help Ludwig Schlaich, who wrote von Bodelschwingh for advice about rescuing the patients in Württemberg. Von Bodelschwingh wrote him

> some friendly sympathetic letters, but asked, however, that I not use his name . . . excuse me, when I say how we felt at the time — but he left us alone, didn't even advise us as to what we should do. We understood indeed that he didn't want to endanger his Bethel patients, but it was painful, nevertheless.[34]

As events would prove, von Bodelschwingh was committed to rescuing his patients in Bethel and saving the Bethel institutions themselves. But the leader of Bethel was also a nationalistic German who had sworn a loyalty oath to the Führer; in any system of government he probably would have been an obedient citizen.

Despite their differences, Braune and von Bodelschwingh both wanted to force the Nazi state to admit that euthanasia had no legal basis and was immoral. Having compiled proof of what was going on, they hoped to persuade government officials to bring the euthanasia program to a halt. Their hopes rested on the "not insignificant number of civil servants from the former old Prussian institutions, who indeed now wore the [Nazi] party insignia, but still thought along the same lines as we did."[35]

How these civil servants really thought, what they knew, and when they knew it can never be known, but, whatever they thought of the euthanasia program, they did not stop it. In March 1940, Paul Braune visited a contact in the interior ministry. As Braune wrote in 1947, the official

> was horrified at how openly I spoke about these things, which were handled there only as matters of strictest secrecy. He called my attention to the fact that I was playing with my life if I concerned myself further with these matters. It was exactly as if I wanted to lay myself down in front of a steam roller to stop it.[36]

This minister knew of the euthanasia program, but, according to Braune, Reich Justice Minister Franz Gürtner did not. Many within the Confessing Church saw Gürtner as a man of integrity who had attempted to keep the civil courts independent of Nazi party pressure.[37] When Braune and von Bodelschwingh visited him in June 1940, Gürtner was outraged to learn of what was happening. "It is a fatal affair for a

Reich justice minister," Gürtner told them, "when he is told by the most credible sources: in your domain [people] are being murdered on a conveyor belt, and you know nothing of it!"[38]

Gürtner promised to help the two men. Having established that the program had no legal foundation, he sought to stop it, but nothing came of his efforts, and Gürtner died in January 1941. Another contact for the churchpeople was State Secretary Friedrich Kritzinger, who offered sympathy for their cause but let them know "that a stop to the measures was almost impossible."[39]

Berta Braune believed that the various government contacts were "men of integrity":

> We had a Herr Jakobi at the interior ministry; my husband had ties to him through a Christian student group to which my husband and Jacobi belonged. He was a man of integrity . . . there is no doubt at all about that. What does it mean here "to collaborate"? You know, things were so difficult, and each person stuck his neck out. . . . We had two other men with whom, when Braune had questions, the agreement was: "I'll go out and leave the files on the table." These things helped my husband.[40]

Braune, of course, genuinely believed that he would be able to achieve his goal — an end to the euthanasia program — through these contacts:

> That was the main thought of my husband as he ran without ceasing from government post to post. He had negotiations with the interior ministry, the employment ministry, the health ministry — these were all questions that affected these ministries, where it had to do with the people who were with us. . . . He intentionally informed the parents of patients in our home who were generals and officers. We had a small house for youths from noble families. Every possible noble name was represented there, and the parents could be informed personally, and at the time of the euthanasia program one family took its son back. Those are little things. But Braune's principle was to inform many within this good group in the government, so that they knew and would keep their ears open.
>
> Naturally, he had to leave them their freedom. They had to decide, of their own free will, whether they would use [this information] or not. . . . That was Braune's mission, and von Bodelschwingh's, too. Bodelschwingh sat again and again on the higher committees, in the church and the state. He never really broke with a state, nor did my husband. [Braune] said, "If you no longer want me, then throw me out."[41]

Both Braune and von Bodelschwingh tried to work through contacts in the Nazi system, but von Bodelschwingh was later criticized more severely. This is partly because Braune took some risks where von Bodelschwingh hesitated and because many people believed that von Bodelschwingh's prominence could have enabled him to do more. As the leader of Bethel, von Bodelschwingh was internationally known (during the economic crisis of the 1920s, for example, financial aid from Bethel's supporters in the United States had helped keep the institution afloat) and respected. Although he had lost the battle for the office of Reich bishop to Ludwig Müller, von Bodelschwingh was viewed by many as "the secret bishop of Germany." He was well known, widely respected, and had numerous contacts, including high ones in the Nazi regime.

Yet, on the euthanasia issue, he seemed to pull back, though not when it came to

Bethel's patients. Von Bodelschwingh was among the institutional directors who refused to fill out the forms. In this sense, the means by which the Bethel leader fought the euthanasia program were the same as those that were tried by Schlaich and a handful of other directors of institutions. Von Bodelschwingh notified the families of patients, and when the forms arrived in Bethel in June 1940, he refused to fill them out. He used every possible contact to save his patients. Hermann Göring's brother-in-law, for example, was a patient in one of the Bethel institutions, so von Bodelschwingh tried to influence Göring, the Luftwaffe head. In February 1941, when the Nazi doctors' commission arrived in Bethel to proceed with the selection process von Bodelschwingh had refused to carry out, the Bethel leader spent hours arguing with them. At the Nuremberg war crimes trial in 1947, Karl Brandt, Hitler's personal physician, testified that von Bodelschwingh was the only man who had convinced him that euthanasia was evil.[42]

Whatever effect von Bodelschwingh's efforts had on the consciences of Nazi officials, the fact remained that his tactics were private. For whatever reasons, von Bodelschwingh refused to attack the regime publicly or speak out on the euthanasia program. In fact, some of von Bodelschwingh's communications with Nazi bureaucrats on the euthanasia issue were conciliatory to the point that they gave the impression the Bethel leader was prepared to compromise. One letter, given to the regional president of Westphalia, stated that, if the state did not stop the euthanasia program,

> we must stand by our request to release us from any participation in the carrying out of this action. We will naturally submit to an intervention of the state which occurs without our initiative. If [an official doctor] wants, for example, to obtain the files to review the patients, files and oral information would be made available to him.[43]

In addition, von Bodelschwingh discouraged the leaders of the Confessing Church from taking a public stand against the euthanasia program,[44] arguing that public attacks would close his channels of influence and result only in his arrest, thereby leaving Bethel's patients unprotected.[45]

Paul Braune, having alone signed the Inner Mission memorandum, was arrested by the Gestapo in July 1940. For Braune, as Berta Braune recalled later,

> it was a call of faith to write it and to take responsibility for this memo. I ask you—I thought at the time, why can't the others sign it, too? And I think that today. But I believe that that's a totally fruitless thought.[46]

Although Braune's memo was the obvious reason for his arrest, the Gestapo claimed otherwise and did a cursory house search. Berta Braune remembered one Gestapo officer, sitting in her dining room and reading the memo, shaking his head and saying, "This just isn't possible."

> I said, "Yes, wouldn't it be more important to tend to *this*, to what is happening here, than to pick Braune up? What will you get out of that? . . . The arrest warrant for my husband was interesting; it read: "For sabotaging state measures in an irresponsible manner."[47]

As Paul Braune sat in the Gestapo prison on Prinz-Albrecht-Strasse in Berlin, several other Protestants began protesting the euthanasia measures. In Württemberg,

Bishop Wurm wrote interior minister Frick in July 1940; having received no reply, Wurm wrote another letter to Frick in September, which was widely publicized:

> Must the German people be the first civilized people to regress to the practices of primitive peoples in the treatment of the weak? Does the Führer know of this matter? Has he approved it?[48]

Wurm was not the only church leader to speculate that errant Nazis in the government were carrying out extreme measures without Hitler's knowledge or approval. As Ludwig Schlaich wrote to Josef Goebbels in September 1940, a number of people had told him, "If I weren't convinced that the Führer knows nothing about this, my trust in him would vanish.[49]

Another prominent church member to raise his voice was Lothar Kreyssig. Kreyssig, a Brandenburg judge and Confessing Church member, was forced to retire after he questioned the legality of patients being moved to Hartheim, a euthanasia institution in Brandenburg, and after he issued an arrest warrant against one of Hartheim's directors. "Everyone knows as I do," Kreyssig wrote Gürtner, "that the killing of the mentally ill will, in the near future, be just as known as an everyday reality as the existence of the concentration camps. It can't be any other way."[50]

The responses of Nazi bureaucrats remained evasive. Most letters were sent to interior minister Frick, whose standard reply, as he wrote to Wurm in the fall of 1940, was that the secrecy of the program necessitated secrecy as to its legal foundation. With the exception of Gürtner, government officials preferred to evade the issue. The Nazis insisted that the program (and its "legal" foundation, namely, the Hitler memo postdated to September 1939) had to remain secret because of the war. Paul Braune was assured that the euthanasia measures would be carried out "in a decent way."[51]

Lacking any concrete reaction from the regime, and isolated within the church, the staunchest opponents of euthanasia opted to go it alone. "I knew," Paul Braune wrote in 1947,

> that the official church leadership at that time, which had been informed by me, would hardly find itself prepared for energetic opposition against such measures of the State. I was therefore prepared to lead this fight essentially alone.[52]

In Westphalia, von Bodelschwingh continued his battle to save Bethel's patients and won assurances from the Nazi doctors that Bethel would be spared; "You need fear no disturbances for the next time," Brandt told von Bodelschwingh.[53] Still, in September 1940, the order arrived to prepare the 13 Jewish patients in Bethel for transport. Hastily, von Bodelschwingh wrote the patients' families, several of whom came to pick up their relatives, and asked the local Jewish community if it could take the others. The Jewish community in the surrounding city of Bielefeld, however, consisted of a few hundred Jews who had not been able to emigrate. At risk themselves, they were in no position to take the Bethel patients, seven of whom were subsequently transported and killed.[54] Similarly, the 14 Jewish patients in Braune's Lobetal home were deported in 1942, as Braune reported in a letter to von Bodelschwingh.[55]

Despite the growing unrest in the church about the euthanasia program, the Confessing Church synod, which met in Leipzig in October 1940, decided—in the tradition of church bureaucracies everywhere — to appoint a commission to study the issue. No wonder Schlaich and other concerned institution directors, meeting in December 1940, came to the conclusion that they were "utterly helpless," since people like von Bodelschwingh, "who had tortured themselves with these questions for months,"[56] still had not found a way to stop the euthanasia program.

Public Protest in the Churches and the "End" of Euthanasia Measures

By the end of 1940, 35,224 patients had been murdered, and some people in the Confessing Church began to insist that the church openly oppose what was happening. One of them was Ernst Wilm, the pastor of the Confessing parish in Mennighüffen. For Wilm, the church's silence on the euthanasia program was "the most serious chapter of my life" — not only because of Wilm's outrage at the murders of the patients but because of Fritz von Bodelschwingh, in Wilm's words, "was my spiritual father."[57] Wilm's father had worked in Bethel, and Wilm himself had been a vicar in Bethel under von Bodelschwingh.

After the Leipzig Synod, Wilm and another pastor, distraught at the Confessing Church's failure to take a stand, came to von Bodelschwingh with a copy of the Leipzig newspaper. As Wilm recalled, there were 10 black-bordered obituary notices,

> and at least six were of people who had been killed. That was obvious from the details that were named — that the bodies had been burned at once, and from the words, "We cannot understand his death." Later these death notices weren't allowed to appear at all. . . .
>
> And Pastor Fritz said, "I know all this, but let me handle it alone." We said, "If you're doing that for the patients in Bethel, we understand. But it's not just the Bethel patients. In Saxony, East Prussia, West Prussia, Pomerania, Württemberg, and Brandenburg they're already being murdered."
>
> "Yes," von Bodelschwingh told them. "I know that."[58]

In the summer of 1940, Wilm had tried to persuade some of the leading members of the Confessing Church in Westphalia to protest the euthanasia program publicly. Although Paul Braune had compiled proof that patients were being murdered, neither Wilm nor his fellow Confessing Christians knew at the time about the Braune memo,[59] and some of those at the meeting told Wilm that the church needed more information before it could make a public statement. Wilm protested that it was an "indisputable fact" that the Nazi state was murdering institutionalized patients, continuing,

> It is not entirely understandable to me, when we in the Confessing Church still cry for proof and even declare that, until we have it, we can't say anything. . . . We cannot and may not wait any longer for that. If we are convinced that [we] may not keep silent in this matter, then each one of us is challenged, no matter what the others do.[60]

Wilm's urgent appeal was blocked by the group that, supported by von Bodelschwingh, continued to support private negotiations with government contacts.

The difference between Wilm's position and that of church moderates reflected the same divisions that had plagued the Protestant church opposition from the beginning of the Third Reich, based on attitudes toward the political Nazi state and differences as to how the institutional church should address issues publicly.

Another difference, however, was between the roles and responsibilities of parish pastors like Wilm and institutional directors like Braune and von Bodelschwingh. As Berta Braune argued,

> My husband, too, sometimes spoke in his sermons up to the limit of frankness, so that I continually presumed that the Gestapo would come and ask about it. But that is only one side of the role of the institution director. The other is this: to protect those who cannot stand up for themselves, to take note of their situation, and to do them justice, like a father in his family. . . .
>
> The pastor in the pulpit has the task of preaching, proclaiming, of calling his parish members to decision, but he has no one for whom he especially must care. The institution leader, symbolically portrayed, is like the old Italian robed Madonna, under whose robes everything moves that can't help itself, that is weak and suffering.
>
> The institutional directors had this function. Because of that, they were, in a special way, interwoven with the state. The entanglement with state matters always brought a theologian who wanted to preach in an honest, open, and truthful way into difficulties: How can I continue my work, which the state supports or for which it pays subsidies, so that nothing happens to the weak ones? The main concern was always the human being, the challenged person, the person who was in a situation where he couldn't defend himself. . . .
>
> When I imagine the additional burdens that lay in Bodelschwingh's hands, and in my husband's hands, in the overall realm of the institution director — it's not at all comparable with that of a parish pastor.[61]

The institutional leaders were not only responsible for their patients; they represented the church in their debates with Nazi officials about euthanasia. They, and the church hierarchy, actively discouraged individual pastors from protesting the murders of the patients. As it turned out, the most outspoken critics of the euthanasia program were the more radical parish pastors. Privately, their church agreed with them; publicly, it said nothing. Max Lackmann, an assistant pastor in Westphalia, spoke out publicly, as did a Württemberg pastor, Adolf Staudacher. Both were sent to Dachau.[62] And on New Year's Eve 1940, Ernst Wilm addressed his congregation in Mennighüffen on the year that had passed. Wilm explicitly protested the murders of "innocent sick people upon command of the government," telling his congregation how

> We received the urns from the murder institutions with the letter of lies: "So and so has died of this or that illness, and the body was cremated immediately due to danger of an epidemic." We couldn't stand at the grave and say, "After it has pleased Almighty God to call our sister from this life," when we knew that she had been murdered! We had to stand in front of the patients and say publicly, as the church: "This is murder. This goes against God's commandment and God's will." . . .
>
> My elderly father, who sat in this service, was terribly upset afterwards and said, "You should have talked about that first with Bodelschwingh. You shouldn't have said that here and now." I said, "Father, I've already talked with Bodel-

schwingh. He won't do it. He doesn't want to." I had also spoken with Schniewind[63], and he had told me, "Yes, Brother Wilm, the church has to speak out, but then Bodelschwingh has to go to the pulpit, Wurm has to mount the pulpit, Dibelius has to mount the pulpit, and then the rest of you can mount the pulpit." But that never happened. . .

I wanted to stand up for the patients, and I didn't want the church to remain silent in the face of such crimes, as it did afterward on the crimes against the Jews. Not one single word about the murders of these patients went out to the pastors of Westphalia, either from (church president) Koch or from von Bodelschwingh. One has to be clear on that. . .

Here I must defend myself against the accusation, also that of my own father, that I should have yielded to Pastor von Bodelschwingh's request and remained silent. To that I say: I had fought for weeks and months, in conferences and meetings, and spoken with Bodelschwingh personally. But there is a limit, when silence has to have an end, when we can no longer remain silent about dreadful crimes, because otherwise we make ourselves guilty of them.[64]

Ernst Wilm and Max Lackmann were unknown pastors in village churches. No notice was taken of Wilm's outspoken sermon except by local Gestapo officials, who hesitated to take any measures against the popular pastor. The result of the opposition of more prominent churchmen like Bishop Wurm was, as Ludwig Schlaich observed, that the Nazis

no longer dared to pick up patients directly from homes of the Inner Mission to the extermination institutions . . . more often they took the detour of first moving the invalids to a secular institution.[65]

And there they were murdered. The only noticeable effect of the moderate course taken by such powerful leaders as von Bodelschwingh was that it made the Nazi directors of the euthanasia program more cautious. (It also probably rescued the life of Paul Braune, who was released from the Gestapo prison in September 1940, after Gürtner and other government officials intervened.)

The euthanasia program continued. In May 1941, homes for the elderly received the interior ministry forms.[66] Then, on August 3, 1941—one year after he had been informed about the murders of the patients[67]—Clemens Graf von Galen, the Catholic bishop of Münster, became the first prominent clergyman to mount his pulpit and openly challenge the euthanasia program and its ideological foundation:

Do you or I have the right to live only as long as we are productive? . . . Then someone has only to order a secret decree that the measures tried out on the mentally ill be extended to other "nonproductive" people, that it can be used on those incurably ill with a lung disease, on those weakened by aging, on those disabled at work, on severely wounded soldiers. Then not a one of us is sure anymore of his life. . . .

Woe to humanity, woe to our German people, when the sacred commandment "Thou shalt not kill" is not only violated, but when this violation is tolerated and carried out without punishment![68]

Von Galen's sermon was reprinted and distributed throughout Germany; the British air force printed it and dropped copies over German villages. The controversy was finally in the open. On August 24, 1941, 21 days after the bishop's sermon,

Hitler signed an order ending the euthanasia program. A total of 70,273 patients and children on the lists had been murdered; the actual number was probably higher.[69]

Like many of the Nazi regime's actions, Hitler's order was a tactic to placate the population. Euthanasia continued until the end of the war. In the same month as Hitler's order, the staff at Hadamar, one of the euthanasia centers, celebrated the cremation of its 10,000th corpse with a special ceremony, followed by music, dancing, and a great deal of drinking.[70] The difference made by the Hitler order was of scale; and the quick murder of patients was replaced, in many cases, by prolonged deaths coldbloodedly designed by Nazi doctors. Large groups of patients were kept in small rooms with no heat and under catastrophic hygenic conditions. Some were given drug overdoses that caused painful deaths; others were put on specially designed diets that Nazi doctors ensured would result in a "gradual, slow death after the passage of about three months."[71]

Having completed their work in the institutions, the euthanasia doctors moved on to inspections and experiments on concentration camp inmates; the staff members of the euthanasia institutions received jobs commensurate with their experience — in the death camps.[72] In the East, institutional patients continued to be brutally murdered, and the scientific techniques developed in the euthanasia program were refined and perfected until, in the gas chambers of Auschwitz, it would be possible to "eliminate" 15,000 to 25,000 people a day.

The Ethics of Public versus Those of Private Protest

The patients of the Inner Mission institutions fared differently under the euthanasia program. Although, after 1945, both Lobetal and Bethel claimed that they had rescued all their patients, this was untrue: in both institutions, the Jewish patients were deported and killed. Ernst Klee, who documented the euthanasia program in his book *"Euthanasie" im NS-Staat*, discovered that a Polish nurse in a 1966 war crimes trial testified that a busload of Bethel patients was transported and killed in a Polish institution in 1943 or 1945.[73] But it is nearly impossible to trace the actual numbers of patients transfered from church to state institutions and then killed. Even before 1933, the state often ordered the transfer of patients whose expenses were paid by government programs from private institutions like Bethel to state ones.[74]

In any case, it seems clear that open, public opposition was crucial in stopping a major part of the program. As Ernst Wilm noted,

> I'm of the opinion that Hitler stopped it because the unrest had become so great among the population and also among the soldiers at the front. He lived from secrecy, with these murders, and when the secrecy wasn't there anymore, he became afraid. Hitler couldn't keep his crimes secret any longer. . . . The pamphlets with von Galen's sermon and other information about Hitler's crimes were dropped over land by British planes, and many, many people knew the dreadful things that were happening. There wasn't anything to keep secret anymore.[75]

In October 1943, the 12th Synod of the Confessing Church issued its first public protest against euthanasia. Why did it take the leadership of the church so long to protest publicly the murders of the patients? One clue is implicit in Paul Braune's postwar comment on opposition to euthanasia. The only foundation establishing clear, unwavering opposition to euthanasia, he wrote, had to be based on the fifth commandment.[76] Arguments based on legal, humane, or medical considerations led to ambiguity, for it was possible, from all three perspectives, to make a case for the mercy killing of an incurably ill or severely handicapped person. Only the straightforward words "Thou shalt not kill" stated unequivocally that under no circumstances did the state or individuals appointed by the state have the right to end a human life.

This commandment was the basis of the opposition of Christians like von Bodelschwingh, but it was not the foundation of their strategy to stop the euthanasia program. Tactically, their moral opposition to euthanasia was subordinated by the decision, made in good faith, that the best way to save the lives of patients was to avoid provoking the Nazi state. Even when they argued personally with Nazi officials, church representatives avoided arguments based on faith. As Schlaich wrote, since "religious considerations only awakened their antipathy, we almost completely renounced stating such considerations to them."[77] The alternative, Schlaich wrote, would have been

> either to leave our patients in the lurch — and that's what it would have come to, if we had ended up in a concentration camp — and assuage our consciences, or to try at least to rescue as many of our patients as possible.[78]

The decision to abandon moral arguments was no doubt more realistic. When one church representative reminded a Nazi bureaucrat of the fifth commandment, the Nazi official replied caustically that "the fifth commandment is not any law of God, but a 'Jewish invention' that the Jews, 'the biggest murderers in the world's history,' use to weaken their enemies."[79]

In basing their strategy on the political realities in Nazi Germany, however, the church representatives became entangled in a serious dilemma. Privately, von Bodelschwingh tried fervently to convince Nazi doctors like Karl Brandt of the evil of what they were doing. Publicly, there was a terrible silence, which revealed unwelcome truths about the church's ability to resist on what was a clear moral issue. At no other point during the Third Reich would full knowledge of what was taking place, coupled with the unambiguity of which position was right for the church, confront the church with such immediacy. Speaking to the Westphalian Confessing Christians in the summer of 1940, Ernst Wilm warned,

> Do we really believe that afterward, when all the invalids have been murdered and it's universally known, that the accusation: "and you knew and said nothing" — that the church, able to speak out so well and loudly when it concerned her constitution, fell silent against this dreadful injustice, that she stood up for her pastors, but not for these poor and suffering people — do we really believe that we won't be confronted with this accusation?[80]

Had von Bodelschwingh spoken out publicly and attempted through his foreign contacts to win international condemnation of Hitler, his stature might have saved him from the concentration camp and turned the public tide against the euthanasia measures earlier. There is no way of knowing, however. In analyzing the behavior of men like von Bodelschwingh, we are left only with the judgments of those who knew them. The leader of Bethel, recalled Berta Braune,

> was a tremendous counselor. He shared his pastoral care with every person who needed it, and then things were not swept under the rug, but they did remain private. This genuine thoroughness in thinking things through was based on his taking people seriously. . . . Throughout his life, my husband was forever grateful that he had this encounter [with von Bodelschwingh] . . . even when there were a thousand other difficulties.[81]

Ernst Wilm, too, believed that von Bodelschwingh's motives in trying to change the hearts of Nazi officials were sincere:

> You've asked me: what was Bodelschwingh's reason? The first reason was that he didn't want to arouse the evil lion. He still had hopes of rescuing his patients, and that hope was fulfilled through his talks with Dr. Brandt. . . .
>
> Bodelschwingh wanted to protect his patients against this horror. . . . Another reason that's given is that he didn't want to upset his patients. You can't say anything to that, although I believe that they had already known for some time. . . . But a third reason with Bodelschwingh, and this was hard for me, was his antipathy toward the Dahlemites, against this somewhat more radical group in the Confessing Church. He had the suspicion that the Dahlemites used the murders of the patients to fight the Nazis, that this was a good opportunity for the Confessing Church to make the crimes of the Nazis clear to Christians. . . .
>
> But, even today, I'm of the opinion that a public statement of the Confessing Church would have done more than this silent, reticent struggle in Bodelschwingh's sitting room. For the terrible thing about the murder of the patients was that it happened secretly. That's how — in this silence — Hitler was able to do this thing at all. . . .
>
> You can't overlook the fact that Fritz von Bodelschwingh staked himself, body and soul, for his patients, and with that, staked his freedom and his life. It wasn't cowardice with him, it was singly his concern for his patients, and his belief that he could rescue the lives of his patients better through quiet negotiations than by public declarations of the church. He also wanted to rescue a man like Dr. Brandt from his own depravity. But his path wasn't right. He should have broken his silence and called the entire church to resistance in this matter.[82]

Had von Bodelschwingh behaved differently, would more patients' lives have been saved? Did Braune, later, regret that he had not circulated his memo openly, instead of taking it privately to government officials? In 1986, Berta Braune replied,

> No. I would say, there was really nothing else to do. It is truly a sad chapter. What would have happened is that the institution leaders who spoke out would have been taken away, and with that, the way would have been cleared for the annihilation of the institutions. That's how I see it. I cannot believe that shouting it to the world would have helped the patients somewhat, and that was the point . . . the euthanasia would have been carried out a great deal faster. Whether that's correct, I can't say. No one can say.[83]

The Third Reich continued its ruthless course. Ernst Wilm, believing that the murders of patients in institutions had indeed been stopped, gave thanks in his 1941

New Year's Eve sermon. Then, in January 1942, Wilm heard a troubling new rumor and repeated it to the churchwomen's group in Mennighüffen:

> that the doctors in the psychiatric ward in Hadamar (that was the institution where one of the patients from our parish had been killed, and many others from West-phalia), that there the doctors who were ordered to carry out these killings had refused and were threatened, but still refused. Then SS doctors were brought in and they did it. I spoke about this, and one woman repeated it to someone from the *Orts-gruppenleitung* [the local Nazi leadership]. And there he said, "So, now we have him!"
>
> I was arrested on January 23, 1942 and interrogated, basically, only because of this story about the killings of the patients. They asked me about little things: why I didn't say "Heil Hitler" when I came to the confirmation pupils. It was ludicrous. And they said, "You're stabbing the army in the back with such stories." I replied, "You're stabbing the army in the back when you murder children and sick people behind the backs of the men and fathers who are out there."
>
> I came to the police prison in Bielefeld and sat there until May. Then came the command, signed by Heydrich[84] and with that, I came to Dachau and served my time there.[85]

When Wilm arrived in Dachau in May 1942, he received the inmate number 30,156.

❖ 7 ❖

The Confessing Church and the Jews

The Role of Anti-Semitism

ALTHOUGH THE MURDER OF the institutionalized patients was the forerunner of the genocide of the Jews, there were important differences between the status of the Jews and that of Nazism's other victims. Even today, these differences condition our thinking about Nazi Germany. The Nazis planned and carried out the murder of hundreds of thousands of gypsies, disabled children and adults, homosexuals, and political opponents. But it is the Jews who are remembered above all. Genocide evokes a deeper and more lasting horror, and the Holocaust — the murder of the European Jews — has become the primary symbol of Nazi evil.

In part, this distinction is based upon the symbolic significance the Jews had for Germans, and for Christians in general, long before 1933. The very fact that the persecution of the Jewish people could reach genocidal proportions, without a massive outcry from their fellow citizens and with the participation of the thousands of Germans who worked in the camps, reveals how deeply anti-Semitism was embedded in the hearts and minds of ordinary Germans. This is why attempts to explain anti-Semitism merely on the basis of economic or political resentment, for example, fall short. Throughout Europe, outbreaks of anti-Semitism can be linked indeed to specific periods of economic or political uncertainty; but the irrational undercurrent of anti-Semitism was always there, waiting to be tapped, manipulated, and fanned, ultimately, into the flames of the Holocaust.

For this reason, it is difficult to evaluate what older Germans say about their own memories of the Jews in Nazi Germany. Certainly much of what is said cannot be taken at face value. Anti-Semitism, like all prejudice, often operates on the unconscious level. After 1945, the denial of responsibility for what had happened to the Jews necessarily meant the denial of one's own anti-Semitism. Even Germans with a record of resistance to Nazism often seem to have limited access to their feelings, let alone their memories, on the subject. It is as though the shame and horror aroused by the Holocaust has blocked all memory of one's own place in the event. Only the scars are left, and scars tell us only how people have absorbed the experience, how it has given them new political and moral insights, or, in some cases, merely hardened old prejudices.

Sometimes, however, memories emerge that pull back a curtain to give a picture of how people felt about the Jews. A pastor who grew up in the countryside of Hesse recalled,

> Part of my childhood memories is how the cattle were driven past my parents' home to the cattle market. Those who had control of the cattle trade were all Jews. We enjoyed seeing how they bargained. They approached each other with a slap of the hand. When nothing came of it, they did it again; it was interesting to watch it. . . . In every village, it was the Jews who had the trade and traffic in their hands. They had the cattle business, the grain trade, and they had general stores where you could buy everything. . . .
>
> Now it couldn't be helped that this also had very negative effects, namely, that there were also unscrupulous people among them who slit the farmers' throats . . . the farmers had simply become the slaves of the Jews. They never got anywhere . . . the Jewish question ate away at those in the countryside. . . .
>
> The rich, wealthy Jews founded the university in Frankfurt, the first German university without a theological faculty! In journalism, medicine, law, proportionally there was an enormous preponderance of Jews. Naturally, that was tied to the fact that other careers were closed off to them. There were reasons for everything.
>
> I came to Frankfurt in 1926. That was the world I found here: with a strong undercurrent of anti-Semitism among the people. Many went about their business. In the parish, I had gardeners and other people who had large commissions with the Jews, with the large firms, and they had a high opinion of them, but the basic mood was against them.
>
> At first, we had, as in other cities, a *Judengasse* [Jewish alley] here. That was a ghetto. The Jews had to live in this street up until the previous century. The Jewish emancipation [Note: In the mid-1800s, Jews in most parts of Germany received civil rights] removed many restrictions, and the Jews had access to everything and could settle freely. But they remained together in this quarter of the city. The east end was Jewish; the old synagogue stood there. In the west end, too, the Jews had spread out; the modern liberal synagogue stood there.
>
> All that sat very deeply within the people. In the last century, strong anti-Semitic currents emerged. . . . It was all already there. It's not at all the case that Herr Goebbels invented all of it; rather, the entire ideology and also the rhetoric were there. They [the Nazis] had only to take it and carry it to its conclusion.
>
> So one can't overlook the fact that, when 1933 came, there were not a few good Christians who had no objections at all if the Jews got pushed back a bit. That didn't start with concentration camps; it began with propaganda. But people said, "Oh, the cheeky Jews, let them get what's coming to them."
>
> That was possible. We really had a "Jewish question" here in Germany. No one wants to know about that anymore.[1]

Many Germans argued that Jews held too much power throughout German society and, at the same time, accused the Jews of refusing to assimilate and become "Germans." Many of the "facts" in anti-Semitic propaganda were erroneous. The Jewish emancipation achieved after 1848 was brief; only after 1869 (after the electoral victory of the Liberal party) did some emancipation measures become actual law in Prussia. With this, Jews were permitted for the first time to enter the civil service. Between 1869 and 1933, the number of Jews in the public sphere increased as a matter of course (since it had been closed to them previously).

In 1933, only 1½ percent of the German population was Jewish,[2] and the actual number of Jews in influential positions was far less than popularly assumed. Although many Germans blamed the uncertainties of the Weimar years on too much Jewish influence in the government, for example, only 4 of the 250 government ministers during the entire Weimar Republic were Jewish.[3] Yet, in April 1933, Berlin church leader Otto Dibelius wrote,

> In the last 15 years in Germany, the influence of Judaism has strengthened extraordinarily. The number of Jewish judges, Jewish politicians, Jewish civil servants in influential positions has grown noticeably. The voice of the people is turning against this.[4]

Widespread fears about the "infiltration" of German culture by the Jews, out of proportion to reality, indicated the deeper psychological factor in anti-Semitism. Periods of virulent anti-Semitism occurred throughout European history, particularly during the nineteenth century. Frequently, they occurred during periods of political uncertainty, when unreasonable prejudice plays a greater role in political behavior (for example, the German stock market boom and subsequent crash in the 1870s). The very intensity with which the Jews were attacked in times of political uncertainty revealed how deep and irrational anti-Semitism was. In the 1880s, German philologist Paul de Lagarde compared the Jews to a dangerous form of bacteria, breeding uncontrollably to spread cultural weakness and disease in the German people, and he recommended the forced deportation of Jews to Eastern Europe.[5] Other writings compared Jews to spiders, worms, and other insects that lived in darkness.[6] As early as the 1840s, the "Jewish question" was discussed as a biological or racial problem.[7]

Such attitudes, of course, made the gas chambers possible. When an entire people is compared to bacteria or insects, it is not surprising when talk turns to "exterminating" them or of "disinfecting" society. In addition, anti-Semitism fed on German desires for cultural and moral stability (and later superiority). Throughout Europe, it was strengthened by the anti-Semitism prevalent in Christian churches. In Germany, this was particularly illustrated by the polemics that Martin Luther had written against the Jews in the sixteenth century.

Hitler and other leading Nazis were hardly religious, but they drew freely from Luther's anti-Semitic writings, and they did so with scarcely a word of protest or contradiction from the leaders of the Protestant church. In *Mein Kampf*, Hitler had written: "In that I defend myself against Judaism, I am fighting for the work of the Lord,"[8] and a number of church leaders agreed that the fight against the Jews was, indeed, a defense of Christianity. As Dibelius' 1933 article indicates (and Dibelius was hardly an exception), a number of church leaders, even within the church opposition to Nazism, felt that the attempt to "put the Jews in their place" was both an understandable goal and a legitimate one. As Helmut Gollwitzer recalled,

> In 1933, it was still possible to get the attention of pastors and parishes when you simply told about the ill treatment that the SS dealt out to people, whether they were Jews or political opponents, because that contradicted Hitler's claim that there had never been such an unbloody revolution. But up till the passage of the Nuremberg laws in 1935, there was really a resistance, an aversion, to singling out the Jews for special concern. Only then did it become clear to many people: If the Jews still wanted to live here, what would they live from?

But this way of thinking was embedded in the Christian tradition: It was hard on the Jews and one had to pity them, but they had brought it upon themselves somehow. Either because there had been Jews who had dominated the business sector or because they had immoral business methods or — this was a reason for those in pious circles — that it was the wrath of God which now, after such a long time, had turned upon the Jews.[9]

Before and after 1945, some church members distinguished between "Christian" anti-Semitism and the racial anti-Semitism of the Nazis.[10] The history of the Christian church has been shadowed for centuries by an anti-Semitism that, at its most benign, was a passive hatred of the Jews and their religion; at its worst, it led to the Spanish Inquisition and the pogroms throughout Eastern Europe. European Christian theologians, even those whose work was not explicitly anti-Semitic, left this part of church doctrine unquestioned and unexamined. (Only after 1945 did Christian theologians begin to examine the role of church anti-Semitism.)

Although there were differences between the anti-Semitism present in scholarly theology and the racially based ideology of the "German Christians," "passive" anti-Semitism retained an active potential. An example of this was Adolf Stoecker, an influential, socially concerned Protestant leader toward the end of the nineteenth century who helped found the Inner Mission; he was also rabidly anti-Semitic. Stoecker and other "Christian" anti-Semites were not averse to using racial anti-Semitism to gain a wider hearing, and citations from their work later appeared in Nazi and "German Christian" pamphlets. "Christian" anti-Semitism, far from being a distinct, less malignant force, was interwoven with popular and political anti-Semitism throughout Europe.

Moreover, it played a role in making Nazism "respectable" in church circles. Christian protest against Nazi anti-Semitism was directed more against the excesses of the SA and SS, against vandalism, against businesses, and against violence toward individuals. "Anti-Semitism is justified," one German pastor argued, "but this anti-Semitism must remain within the biblically set limits."[11] Just as many nationalistic Protestants approved Nazi nationalism, they gave a kind of moral permission to Nazi anti-Semitism by passively accepting the most murderous part of Nazi dogma.

Some Christians, like Dietrich Bonhoeffer, began to recognize that brutal treatment of Jews violated the Christian doctrine of love for one's neighbor. Bonhoeffer's early awareness of the deeper significance of the "Aryan" laws prompted him to write a thorough analysis of the problem ("Die Kirche vor der Judenfrage") in 1933. Heinrich Vogel and Heinz Kloppenburg, a theologian who joined the Confessing Church, also published articles warning the church not to yield to the Nazi regime on this point. Their thinking, although far ahead of that of the rest of the church, still failed to confront the anti-Semitism within Protestant theology. Confessing Church pastor Ilse Härter, reflecting on the theological work done in the Confessing Church, wrote in 1989,

> It becomes clearer to me how tied down our ideas were because, basically, critical work on the Bible was taboo. People sought refuge in the scripture, and blamed the questionable theology of the "German Christians" on the results of liberalism. In any case, we naturally noticed that there were anti-Semitic tendencies in the New Testament. . . . But no professor pointed out to us (I didn't hear any) that we should question the anti-Semitism in the New Testament.[12]

As a result, the Evangelical Church's (and the Confessing Church's) defense of the Jews and Jewish Christians (baptized Jews) was confused, ambivalent, and intimidated by Nazi pressure.

The anti-Semitism of Stoecker and other "Christian" anti-Semites did not focus explicitly on racial differences. The Protestant attitude toward the Jews, essentially, was to convert them. The only real contact the church had with the Jews was through the *Judenmission*, the mission to convert the Jews. There was even some respect among church leaders for traditional Judaism. Adolf Stoecker himself viewed orthodox Jews as "the people of the covenant," and in his late anti-Semitic speeches, he excluded the "just and modest Jews" from his attacks.[13] Friedrich von Bodelschwingh (father of the man who led Bethel during the 1930s) shared these sentiments. Christian wrath, as he wrote to Stoecker, should not be directed against observant Jews but "only the Jews without religion, who . . . together with the lapsed Christians are one in their hatred of the cross, the throne and the altar."[14]

Von Bodelschwingh's words reveal the element in "Christian" anti-Semitism that subsequently made it so useful for other anti-Semitic groups in Germany: the linking of the Jews with political enemies. The nationalism of Protestant pastors, their distrust of the Social Democrats, fear of communism, monarchism, and essential conservatism—these beliefs were, in their opinion, the direct opposite of the "secular" and "Jewish" forces threatening German culture and faith: liberalism, secularism, socialism, antimonarchism.[15]

In this context, the Jews were blamed for a number of crises, even when their purported role in one would logically eliminate their role in another. In 1819, German farmers rioted and burned Jewish businesses, blaming the Jews for industrial changes. Following the attempted revolution in 1848, Jews were linked to the workers' movement; thirty years later, after the stock market crash, the Jews were blamed for controlling all the money. In 1918, an "international Jewish plot" was blamed for the terms of the Versailles Treaty.[16]

Perhaps the reason that anti-Semitism was so consistently and successfully used as a political tool was that Judaism remained, for most Germans, something foreign and therefore threatening. The Jews were "the other," linked with the political threat of the moment, and, whatever the political circumstances, they were invariably portrayed as the enemies of nationalism.[17]

Even assimilated Jews (in general, those who had converted to Christianity) were not always accepted as real Germans. Despite the Protestant position that whoever was baptized was a full Christian, church discussions of the "Jewish question" reveal the depth of ambivalence on the matter. On the one hand, a church newspaper editorial in 1874 rather laboriously arrived at the conclusion that Christian baptism did render the Jews "German" (not just Christian):

> The Jewish question is not a religious question, but a national one. The Jews in Germany are not Germans but Jews, they are another people and remain another people, they will never become Germans as long as many of them don't become Christian, and, in so doing, remove themselves from their national past.[18]

Sixty-one years later, at the Confessing Church synod in Steglitz, one synodal delegate argued against this conclusion. "A Jew does not become a German through baptism and belief," he said, and advised his colleagues to leave difficult questions like that of intermarriage between baptized Jews and Christians (obviously, he had accepted the Nazi premise that there was a difference between the two) up to the Nazi state.[19]

Many Jews who had converted to Christianity held such attitudes themselves. These Germans, suddenly "non-Aryan" under Nazi law, had long ceased to identify themselves with Judaism. Dietrich Goldschmidt, son of a Jewish Christian father and a non-Jewish mother, recalled that his father, an historian who lost his job at the end of 1934 because of the "Aryan" laws, was "baffled" by what happened to him:

> I think one could say it that way. . . . My father also said, "Oh, we wouldn't have all these annoyances with the Jews if so many Eastern European Jews hadn't immigrated here after World War I. . . . If that hadn't happened, things wouldn't have reached this difficult stage."
>   That's utter nonsense. He completely underestimated it. *We* completely underestimated it. To a certain extent, my father is a typical case of a baptized Jew who was fully assimilated, who couldn't imagine that he wouldn't be accepted as assimilated by the other side. That was a very widespread error.[20]

Many such Germans, bewildered at the situation in which they found themselves, stubbornly asserted their own nationalism — as if, once the Nazis could be convinced of Jewish patriotism, everything would be all right. These assimilated Jews, through their assertions of national loyalty, tried to distance themselves from the Jewish community. Jewish men took their World War I medals or baptismal certificates to the local Nazi headquarters to convince Nazi bureaucrats of their national loyalty.[21] Some took initial comfort in the illusion that the Nazi racial laws would affect only "full Jews." And, of course, "full Jews" were affected hardest and earliest by the racial laws, which, by the end of 1933, had removed them from all civil service positions and barred them from the universities.

But, based upon the ideology that even small amounts of "Jewish blood" contaminated "Aryan" purity, the racial laws categorized all Germans on the basis of their racial heritage, regardless of religious confession. Under the Nuremberg laws, passed in September 1935, a "non-Aryan" was a person with at least one Jewish parent or grandparent. A "full Jew" was a person with three to four Jewish grandparents or a person with two Jewish grandparents who was married to a "full Jew" or a member of the Judaic faith. Even a baptized Christian who fell within these first two categories was classified as a "full Jew."

The racially determined "mixtures" were classified according to degree: people with one Jewish parent were "first-degree mixtures," or "half-Jews"; people with one Jewish grandparent were "second-degree mixtures," or "quarter-Jews."[22] Around 2,000 racial laws were passed during the course of the Third Reich, 1,219 of them before the *Kristallnacht* in November 1938.[23] [Note: The Protestant church differentiated, in word and deed, between Jews who had converted to Protestantism and those who had not. For purposes of clarity, I will use the term "Jewish Christian" to refer to those people, whatever their degree of racial classification under Nazism, who were members of the Christian faith and "Jew" to refer both to members of Judaism and to secular Jews. Frequently the word "non-Aryan" appears in church documents and interviews. The term is distasteful, in that it uses Nazi terminology. But I quote it when necessary, and when it appears in interviews, since it does clarify the degree to which people were affected by the various racial laws.]

The Church and the "Aryan Paragraph"

It is understandable, then, that persons affected by the Nazi racial laws were confused initially about their own status in Nazi Germany. Yet even as they took false comfort in the hope that they would not be affected, what Jochen Klepper called "the silent pogrom"[24] had begun. Heinrich Schmidt, a Confessing Church lawyer, noted that,

> Before 1933, my family didn't take Hitler's anti-Semitism seriously. . . . I had a Jew-ish grandmother. We couldn't imagine that perhaps we would have difficulties in the Third Reich because of her. I studied law. In 1933, I took my first state exams, but I couldn't continue my studies because of my Jewish grandmother. . . . My family, therefore, was "non-Aryan," and we couldn't work in the civil service. But other-wise we weren't hindered.[25]

Statistics for the number of Germans affected by the racial laws vary greatly. In 1933, the Nazi regime listed 500,000 religiously observant Jews, 50,000 nonreli-gious "full Jews," 200,000 "half-Jews," and 100,000 "quarter-Jews."[26] But some church estimates put the number of Jewish Christians at around 1½ million.[27] Of these, 88 percent were Protestant.[28] Some Jews hoped that church membership would exempt them from racial restrictions. The number of Jews who converted to Protestantism jumped from 241 in 1932 to 933 in 1933 (in the Catholic Church, 89 converted in 1932, compared with 304 in 1933).[29] Until 1939, when baptism of "non-Aryans" was forbidden by the state, around 300 Jews converted to Protes-tantism each year.[30]

For the mainstream Protestant church, and even within most of the Confessing Church, the question of church advocacy on behalf of non-Christian Jews did not even arise. Dietrich Goldschmidt recalled that

> the idea that, from a Christian consciousness, one had to stand up for the Jews occurred to very few people. . . . The Jews were "damned." This teaching that the Jews had condemned Jesus, the teaching that God had indeed made a covenant with the Jews but that this covenant was void after the murder of Jesus, and that the Christians are the people of the new covenant — that pops up even today in the heads of pastors.[31]

The Protestant church's primary concern, then, was for baptized Christians who were suddenly "non-Aryan" under Nazi law. Because this was the area in which the Confessing Church came into conflict with the most rabid area of Nazi law, what to do about Jewish Christians became one of the most sensitive questions in the church opposition. The 1933 Civil Service Law removed "non-Aryans" and politically unre-liable civil servants from office (in Prussia, 28 percent of the higher civil service offi-cials lost their positions; elsewhere, the number was smaller).[32] Because pastors were included in the civil service structure, the "Aryan paragraph" became church law, requiring pastors to establish proof of their racial purity. While, initially, this affected only pastors and higher church officials, its potential consequences for all Jewish Christians were ominous.

The early disagreement within the churches over how to respond to this require-ment was not even between those who wanted to help Jewish Christians and those who did not, but between those who acknowledged the problem and those who pre-ferred to ignore it. The sentiments of the latter group were voiced by Bavarian Bishop Meiser, who, just two weeks after the passage of the Nuremberg racial laws in 1935, warned his colleagues preparing for the Confessing Church synod in Steglitz not to discuss it:

> I want to raise my voice against a martyrdom that we bring upon ourselves. I look toward the upcoming Prussian synod with some worry if it wants to broach such matters as, for example, the Jewish question.[33]

Despite the fact that one reason for the founding of the Pastors' Emergency League (PEL; the 1933 organization that evolved into the Confessing Church in 1934) had been the "Aryan paragraph," there was dissent even within the PEL on whether Jewish Christians could belong or not. On membership cards and ballots, some mem-bers crossed out Article 5, which stated that the "Aryan paragraph" represented "a vio-lation of the confessions";[34] and in Baden, one "non-Aryan" pastor was barred from membership by the local PEL.[35] After he appealed personally to Martin Niemöller, he was given membership, whereupon another pastor wrote to Niemöller to protest.

The issue led regional church governments throughout Germany to seek the advice of theology professors: Was the "Aryan paragraph" theologically consistent with German Protestant doctrine? Theological faculties met and wrote statements, which they submitted to church leaders. These statements of theological opinion, not surprisingly, often arrived at contradictory conclusions — representing, essentially, the prejudices of the professors who wrote them. The theological faculty at Marburg opposed the "Aryan paragraph." The faculty in Erlangen avoided the issue; the "Aryan paragraph," they decided, was an inappropriate means toward a justifiable end (that is, limiting Jewish influence). The Erlangen faculty proposed the establish-ment of a separate church for Jewish Christians — an idea that would be raised period-ically in other parts of the church.[36]

Such reactions, with the obvious implication that racial heritage was indeed something that divided baptized Christians from one another, showed the extent to which racial anti-Semitism was part of Protestant thinking, despite church protests to the contrary. The expectation that pastors and church workers should show proof of "Aryan" identity became a matter of course in some churches, although the Confess-ing Church never asked for such proof.[37] Ilse Härter, sent as a Confessing Church *Vikarin* to work in an official church parish in Berlin, recalled that the parish govern-ing board asked to see her "Aryan" identity card:

> I then told Herr von S.: I'm not bringing an "Aryan" pass, because if I would do that, I would distance myself in practice from the Jews. In other words, I refused. The affair with the "Aryan" pass ended in that von S. said, "Now, we can just write down that you don't look like a Jew" and that the Presbytery was convinced that I wasn't

Jewish. I told them that they couldn't be so sure, because, during my studies in Tübingen, the Nazi student organization told me once that I looked Jewish, just because I had brown hair and brown eyes![38]

Even Martin Niemöller's opposition to the "Aryan paragraph" reflected primarily a concern for church independence. Niemöller's 1933 attack on the "Aryan paragraph" was hardly a defense of those affected by it. "Whether it's congenial to us or not," he wrote,

> we have to recognize the converted Jews as fully entitled members through the Holy Spirit. . . . This recognition demands of us a high measure of self-discipline as a people who have had a great deal to bear under the influence of the Jewish people, so that the wish to be freed from this demand is understandable.[39]

There were others in the Confessing Church, like Lutheran pastor Hans Asmussen, who, while seeking to keep the church free of state interference, actually defended the racial laws:

> Our racial laws draw a firm and unbridgeable dividing wall between Jews and non-Jews. The Jews did that long ago and, through that, have kept their race pure. That's what we want, too. But what the Jew holds for correct when he does it, he sees as an injustice against him when others do it. . . . We want nothing to do with the Jewish race. . . . The Jews may keep their religion as they wish. . . . They live in our land, and we are the masters in our land and want to remain so.[40]

Asmussen and Niemöller would rue such statements later.[41] In the course of the Third Reich, both men came to recognize how such prejudices fed the swell of Nazi terror against the Jews. But the effect of such statements in the early years of Nazism was to minimize the ominous significance of the racial laws and the actual violence against Jews. Having aligned themselves with anti-Semitic ideology, many Christians were unable to break out of this cycle of rationalization.

In this light, the courage and clearsightedness of those who did immediately protest Nazi racial policies is all the more remarkable. One of the first to protest was Ina Gschlössl, a religion teacher in Cologne and one of the first women to complete theological exams. In July 1933, she and three other women vicars were denounced for making "unseemly remarks" about Hitler and for defending the Jews "in a manner and fashion . . . which lacks all understanding for the national standpoint."[42] All four women were dismissed at once; Gschlössl was not given another job by the official church in Rhineland until after 1945. After 1938, Gschlössl worked illegally to help Jews and Jewish Christians in Cologne.

In Berlin, Marga Meusel, a parish worker who had become active in helping Jewish Christians, wrote a lengthy memorandum (in May 1935) describing her activities and the growing "helplessness and despair" of those affected by the racial laws.[43] The situation of the Jewish Christians, Meusel wrote, constituted "an accusation against the Confessing Church,"[44] which, in her opinion, willfully ignored its responsibility toward them. Meusel had difficulty finding church leaders willing to listen to her. The editor of the Inner Mission's publication refused to print an article Meusel wrote about the plight of Jewish Christians,[45] and when Meusel and a Jewish Christian co-worker, Charlotte Friedenthal, turned to von Bodelschwingh, he, too, refused to help them.[46] The two women finally found an ally in Berlin Confessing Church leader Martin Albertz, who became active in helping Jewish Christians and who employed Friedenthal in his office until 1941, when, with the help of Dietrich Bonhoeffer, she escaped to Switzerland.[47]

Meusel proposed the establishment of a church office devoted to helping and advising "non-Aryan" Christians. She was joined by others who believed that Nazi racial ideology posed dangers for the very essence of the Christian church. In 1933, Dietrich Bonhoeffer addressed the importance of this matter and tried to convince the fledgling church opposition that it should be concerned for both Jewish Christians and all others persecuted under Nazi racial laws. Bonhoeffer felt so strongly that he called upon Christians to leave the church if the "Aryan paragraph" were adopted—a call that found little response, even from Karl Barth, who advised Bonhoeffer to hold his fire until the situation worsened.[48]

Both Barth and Bonhoeffer have been criticized for the ambiguity of some of their statements and for latent anti-Semitism (in the sense that they essentially supported the mission to convert Jews to Christianity instead of respecting the Judaic tradition as such).[49] Nonetheless, in 1933 and 1934, they were virtually alone in acknowledging the problem of anti-Semitism in the church and in addressing the Nazi racial laws. Bonhoeffer's friend and biographer, Eberhard Bethge, contended in a 1985 interview that Bonhoeffer actually began to examine critically the anti-Semitism in Christian scripture and thought during the course of the Third Reich. As Bethge said,

> I've reread all the Bonhoeffer material with regard to the aspect of Bonhoeffer and the Jews. I've established, I believe, that my own awareness of the centrality for Bonhoeffer of the Jews—not just [our] deaconical obligation to them but their theological task—was much farther than I myself had realized. Now I'm trying, theologically, to discover where that began, that he never deviated from a Christocentric, innermost faith. In his *Ethics*, he truly confronted our weakness, when he said, "The Jews hold the question of Christ open." That stands in the *Ethics*. We've read that for 30 years without really reading it. Now, suddenly, I see that. That, too, was something he sensed. His development from 1933 to the end can truly be established. He can't solve that now; we must solve it.
>
> Recently, I wrote about Christology and the first commandment, and [my] basis thesis is that Christ is Christ because, in Him, the first commandment is realized. That's why He's Christ. That means that, when a different god is made out of Christ—a Hellenistic or Teutonic or Jerry Falwell-made American god—then the first commandment is being violated. The Jews have the continuing task of reminding us of the first commandment. I'm trying, too, to describe how Bonhoeffer could pray to Christ, and the difference between a prayer to Christ that really worships a new god, or one that means the first commandment and the dethroning of other gods. . . .
>
> I'm trying to establish how some could confess the first thesis in Barmen *("Solus Christus")*, and still be and remain anti-Semites. There lies the deficiency, and there's where the future work lies. The sociological and political roots of the confessors at Barmen have to be examined more closely. I believe that Barth, too, was prepared to admit that even *"Solus Christus"* didn't erect any barriers against anti-Semitism.[50]

Most Confessing Christians addressed these uncomfortable theological questions only after 1945. In this respect, the church struggle against Nazism enabled most Christians to see the catastrophic effects of anti-Semitism only after the Holocaust: most were incapable of seeing this before 1945. As Helmut Gollwitzer noted,

> We, too, had to learn that we had grown up with these prejudices theologically. At first, we thought that the Jews deserved our human pity, and that the Jewish Christians needed our brotherly solidarity . . . [that] we had to help the Jews in Germany because they were a threatened people.
>
> In the meantime, Karl Barth had progressed further theologically. His basis for demanding that we help the Jews was that they are the people of God. That was a new basis for understanding the Bible, Judaism, and, with that, for understanding anti-Semitism as well. The view that anti-Semitism was merely the antipathy of a majority against a minority had to be abolished.
>
> It became more complicated because Hitler killed the gypsies as well, but . . . if he hadn't waged this complete campaign against the Jews, he wouldn't have been able to treat the gypsies in the same way. The Jews are truly the key. That is the essential point with the Jews, theologically and biblically: How do we go about unlearning this part of the Christian tradition? That remains one of the most provocative questions in German [*sic*] Christianity today.[51]

Theologically and politically, the fates of Christians and Jews were bound together. But the tendency of most Germans, including those within the church, was to put even greater distance between themselves and the Jews. Left to themselves, Jewish Christians formed their own groups. The Jewish Christian pastors founded the *Paulusbund*; in 1936, the "Reich Association of Non-Aryan Christians" was founded and grew quickly to 80,000 members.[52]

Some church leaders hoped that, through these organizations, the Jewish Christians could solve their own problems. Throughout 1935 and 1936, the church avoided a firm defense of Jewish Christians. One respected Bavarian churchman, Freiherr von Pechmann, heeded Dietrich Bonhoeffer's call and left the church to protest its silence on the persecution of the Jews. But he did not leave the official church to join the Confessing Church; even the latter was too silent for him.[53]

In September 1935, Marga Meusel, together with Heinrich Vogel, Bonhoeffer, Martin Albertz, and Franz Hildebrandt (a Jewish Christian vicar in the Confessing Church who subsequently emigrated to England) tried to put the "Jewish question" on the agenda of the Prussian Confessing Church synod held in Berlin-Steglitz. They were thwarted, not just by conservatives like Bavarian Bishop Meiser but by Westphalian Confessing Church leader Karl Koch, who threatened to leave the synod if the issue of the Jews was brought up.[54]

In its final statement, the Steglitz Synod issued a mild declaration criticizing the Nuremberg racial laws passed two weeks earlier. The wording, declared Martin Niemöller, was "a very wanting or less than wanting minimum" of what needed to be said.[55] Indeed, among some sectors of the church, the reaction to the racial laws was one of relief: With clear regulations established, people reasoned, the individual terrorist activities of the SA would come to an end (they did not consider that these were being replaced by state terrorism).[56] Among those affected by the comprehensive laws passed at Nuremberg, there was also some relief, if for a different reason. The Nuremberg laws and the regulations for their implementation, wrote Jochen Klepper in his diary, "will seem atrocious in later eras — to us, in the expectation of something much more horrible, they seemed mild."[57]

The Confessing Church's failure to take a stronger stand at Steglitz, Meusel wrote afterward, was not only a "tragedy . . . but a sin of our people, and since we are members of our people and answerable before God for his people, it is our sin."[58] But the concept of sin, and for that reason the concept of possible moral action, was still centered on the responsibility of individual Christians, not on the church's collective responsibility. Dietrich Goldschmidt described the dichotomy between these two realms in his own experience as a Jewish Christian member of the Confessing Church:

> As a matter of principle, the German bourgeoisie — to which the overwhelming majority of pastors and parish members belonged — was anti-Semitic in the sense that [the Jews] didn't "belong" to the church. So one basically didn't have anything to do with them. The guilt of the Christians and the church rests in the fact that the commandment to love your neighbor was interpreted or taken to mean that one looked after the Christian brothers and sisters — those who had been baptized. That means that when Christians came into conflict with the state or with the police, the church or the parish took care of them as long as it had to do with the church. They didn't look after these people when it was a political matter. The Christians in the church cared for Christians when something happened because they were Christians. When a Christian attended to politics, that was no longer something with which the church concerned itself. . . . In this sense, the responsibility for society, the responsibility for the Jews, Social Democrats, communists, gypsies, atheists, the responsibility for all these was not a responsibility of the church. . . .
>
> To this extent, the Christians were honest: whoever was baptized, belonged. I was baptized, and I belonged. . . . That means that I was accepted. For a young man of 20, when he finds friends, that's important.[59]

Individual Jewish Christians could find acceptance, even refuge, in their own parishes, where some Christian sense of responsibility for parish members still functioned. But Nazism was organized, systemic evil; in the Nazi system, the efficacy of individuals who behaved in morally responsible ways was limited. In addition, many Christians (and Jews as well) found it difficult to believe what was happening around them. As some individual parishes devoted their efforts to their own members, their view, inevitably, turned inward, and publicly, Confessing Church leaders were painfully cautious.

The Church and the "Non-Aryan" Christians

The ambivalence of Confessing Church leaders like Karl Koch in Westphalia was the despair of people like Bonhoeffer and Meusel. The people most betrayed by this caution, however, were those pastors and lay members affected by the "Aryan" laws.

The number of such pastors, estimated variously as between 33 and 90,[60] was small; the total number of Protestant pastors in Germany in 1933 was 18,000.[61] That may have been part of their problem, for the church's tendency, after the passage of the racial laws, was to view the new status of "non-Aryan" pastors as an exceptional situation. As such, reasoned church leaders, the plight of Jewish Christian pastors or those with "non-Aryan" wives hardly merited the uproar being made by people like Dietrich Bonhoeffer.[62] Both the official church and the Confessing Church leadership refrained from taking an official stand on the matter, leaving the practical considera-tion of what to do about these pastors up to regional leadership.

The responses of regional church leaders was not heartening. Westphalian church leader Karl Koch noted that, while he personally opposed the "Aryan paragraph," there were, nevertheless, some parishes that did not want "non-Aryan" pastors. In such cases, Koch recommended,

> the only course for the church is to ask such pastors, for the sake of love, to renounce the holding of their office and, in so yielding to the sentiments of the German peo-ple, to glorify the way of God.[63]

Like other Jewish Christians, most pastors affected by the "Aryan" laws were so patriotic, and even anti-Semitic, that they bowed quickly to Nazi pressure. In the Hannover church, "non-Aryan" Pastor Paul Leo wrote in a resigned mood that

> the Jew must affirm his fate as the member of a non-German people, without resent-ment, and that he has to acknowledge the measures of the authorities as long as they don't subjugate his conscience. So he must (especially as a Christian) accept, without outrage, that the state sees it necessary to limit the Jewish influence in public life.[64]

The inclination, both of church leaders and their Jewish Christian pastors, was to yield to Nazi pressure, and the issue of "Aryanism" was one in which the Nazi methodology of terrorizing people into silence had been perfected. The racial laws were only one form of intimidation. Local SS and SA groups and the Nazi press were proud when they discovered another "non-Aryan" trying to hide under the guise of respectability. In particular, *Der Stürmer*, the notorious Nazi propaganda newspaper, and its editor Julius Streicher, were merciless in uncovering and publicizing the pres-ence of Jews in the church and elsewhere. Several Jewish Christian pastors served their parishes without incident until articles about them appeared in *Der Stürmer*. In each of these incidences, church officials sought the quickest solution: They urged the pastors to resign their pastorates.

For at least one pastor, Hans Ehrenberg, the pressure to resign only added to his terrible loneliness as a Jewish Christian in Nazi Germany. *Der Stürmer* attacked him in 1937, quoting pacifist statements that Ehrenberg had made in 1919.[65] Ehrenberg wrote a long letter to his fellow Confessing pastors, pleading for their support:

> What do I need now? To talk things out, otherwise I will be isolated, practically speaking. Discussion, because in this simple way the service [that is, his service to the church] can be maintained. . . . I need neither advice nor outside help. But I need Christian brothers who show that they aren't only looking out for their own way. . . . I need *room*, meant here totally externally, room for me to live, for my marriage, the raising of my children in the family. . . . I can hardly live now in one single place without gasping for breath.[66]

But Westphalian church leader Koch, despite pleas from Ehrenberg and from his supporters in the parish, told the besieged pastor that there was no other way out: He would have to resign his pastorate. In a reply to Koch before his resignation, Ehrenberg wrote poignantly: "I don't know what I still have to go through. But I am comforted that there is no death — and haven't I been dying in my pastorate for a long time now?"[67]

Ehrenberg, like most of the other Jewish Christian pastors, was able to emigrate to England through the help of Dietrich Bonhoeffer and Bonhoeffer's ecumenical contacts there. But Ehrenberg and several others did not get out before the *Kristallnacht* in November 1938 and were subjected to several months in Buchenwald before they emigrated.[68]

In light of the fate awaiting them in Nazi Germany, they were fortunate to get out. The belief of church leaders that, of all the options, emigration was the best for all concerned certainly played a part in the decisions of people like Koch. Yet the failure of their church to stand by them left some Jewish Christians bitter to the end of their lives, for it signified that, even in the Confessing Church, there were Christians who did not acknowledge their responsibility for the fates of the Jewish Christian pastors (and of ordinary parishioners). The Confessing Church vicar sent to replace a Jewish Christian pastor who emigrated to England explained the situation coldbloodedly in 1982:

> He really couldn't be kept on there. He really did look like — excuse me, that I say this — like a Jew, you know? The Council of Brethren couldn't keep him on, because the parish, too, said, "We'll have such difficulties here, with the SS or whatever. . . ." He hadn't yet been ordained, I believe. So he was recalled, and I had to replace him, as an "Aryan," so to speak.[69]

The church's failure to stand by its Jewish pastors was an ominous sign for ordinary Jewish Christians, who could turn only to their church for help. Increasingly, the patterns of daily life and work were being torn apart by the machinery of the Nazi racial laws. No matter what they did for themselves or where they turned for help, those affected by the racial laws were often doomed or rescued by chance. The story of Gertrud S., a Jewish Christian woman, is related here at some length to illustrate the fortuitousness of her surviving the Third Reich:

> I was born in 1910. I am an illegitimate child; my mother and father were not married. . . . At that time, that was a dreadful thing for a family. The marriage couldn't take place because my father came from a pious Jewish family. In those days, that was taboo. Of my mother, I know only that she never married and that this relationship with my father lasted for years. Today, one would just say, very normally, "There's a child on the way." That was me.
>
> I was put in a foster home. I had the great opportunity to be taken in by a pious woman, a widow with three children who were very much older than I. I believe that this period of my life is part of the reason I later decided to take up social work, although I also had artistic tendencies. . . .
>
> I entered the *Mutterhaus* [a lay Protestant order for women] in 1929, at the age of 19. We were trained in this *Mutterhaus* as kindergarten teachers and child-care workers and were sent out from there into parishes. In 1932, I came to N. and

worked there until 1937. Basically, I was left undisturbed, because I never had any reason to talk about my family background.

There was a nurse there who was somewhat envious of me. I am a person who can approach people easily, and I had many contacts with the neighbors very quickly. And then this nurse found out from somewhere that my father was a Jew. One day, the village mayor, who was very attached to me, came and asked me point blank: "Sister Gertrud, is your father a Jew?"

I must say, at first I was taken aback completely to get such a question. I said, "Yes, that's correct." He was very upset, but he said, "You must leave your work at once." He had come during the kindergarten hours. I sent the children home. At that time, we had a council of women from the Red Cross, who supported the kindergarten. I sent them word, and also sent the news to my *Mutterhaus* in Mannheim. The *Mutterhaus* told me to come back to Mannheim at once: "We'll see what happens. . . ."

Naturally, the entire village had been stood on its head, since they hadn't had any idea of all this. Everyone was outraged. When I had moved there in 1932, I had been picked up at the train with a carriage decorated with flowers. Now I was taken, in a subdued atmosphere, with the same wagon to the train. All four of the women on the council accompanied me. They were on my side. I had hardly gotten back to the *Mutterhaus* when the entire women's group visited me. They had changed their yearly outing in order to come to Mannheim and wanted to go from there to Heidelberg. We went together to Heidelberg and, up above at the castle, we had our picture taken as a group. This photograph appeared in *Der Stürmer* with the subtitle: "Wanton wives visit a Jewess and allow themselves to be photographed with her."

Politically, I wasn't shaped or oriented in any sense. I should add, though, that our *Mutterhaus* had a note in the regulations for sisters that we should neither be politically active nor visit events of that kind. We had to remain "neutral," then, a directive that I find unthinkable even today. During this time, it became more and more clear what it meant to have my father a Jew . . . and also what it meant for him. There were the articles in *Der Stürmer*; every Sunday they preoccupied me terribly. Only now did I become conscious that I belonged to such an "inferior race," so to speak.

This brought me into an internal state with which I could cope only with great difficulty. I developed an inferiority complex. It's strange; I still think about it today. On the one hand, I wanted to live as a Christian, because I had been baptized a Christian and grew up as one, from childhood on. And yet such articles in the Nazi press impressed me more forcefully than what I knew of the Gospel, what I heard in church, or had otherwise been taught. For a long time, I was distraught by the fact that I had had to give up the work I loved and leave the children forever.

In Mannheim, the Gestapo visited me again and again to ask what I was doing. The *Mutterhaus* wanted to put me to work there at the house. You have to remember, I was very young. I wanted to do something else; I wanted to learn practical nursing. So I left the *Mutterhaus* on my own initiative. I want to emphasize that. My *Mutterhaus* didn't put me out, rather, I took it upon myself to leave. But it was fairly difficult to find a *Mutterhaus* that would take me in. I always laid out my situation at once so they would know who they were dealing with.

Later, I learned that my *Mutterhaus* tried to help me. It seems that sums of money were paid out that never reached me. I don't know why. They knew that I was someone who had to live utterly without relatives or other means. But they couldn't help. . . .

So I resigned from the *Mutterhaus*. There was a Hessian deacon in Darmstadt who gave me the chance to work as an apprentice nurse. He knew my situation. . . . But what happened there was that, every week, the Gestapo car drove up and asked me — friendly, always friendly — what I was planning to do. And, every time, that created a strange situation among my fellow apprentice nurses: "You must have done something illegal if they come all the time." Finally, the house director said that it would be very difficult to enroll me as a student nurse in a hospital, since all the doctors there were required to join the Nazi party, and I would hardly find a professor willing to teach me nursing.

This was very hard on me. I had to go somewhere. I had no relatives. My foster mother was the widow of a civil servant and received her pension from the state. It would have been terrible for me if I were to go home and, because of me, her pension was stopped. At that time, that was already happening. My friends were all teachers, so I didn't dare go to them either. You know, simply through this sense of inferiority, which I had gotten used to, I felt pushed out. There was no place to turn.[70]

The increasingly strict racial laws imprisoned Jews in their isolation. This paralyzed some and drove others to suicide. In 1942, Jochen Klepper noted the number of suicides in Berlin; the Jews, he wrote, had to wait

one week and a half for a funeral: the overload due to the 20 to 30 Jewish suicides per day, of which the German people, because of the isolation of the Jews, learn nothing.[71]

Nazi propaganda had succeeded diabolically in convincing Jews like Gertrud S. that they were inferior. But the resulting sense of helplessness — Gertrud S.'s feeling that she had nowhere to turn — stemmed from more than her own psychological state. Although in this interview Gertrud S. showed understanding for the risks faced by those who might have helped her, the fact remains that there were few offers of help. As the Jews were pushed to the outside of German society, many ordinary Germans closed their eyes to the Jews' plight.

Finally, a pastor with connections to church homes in Switzerland and Austria found a place for Gertrud S. in a sanatorium in Austria. As the situation there worsened, she moved on and eventually found a position near Montpellier, in the South of France, as domestic help in a family. She stayed there for two years; then she was interned with all other Germans in the area in a camp at Gurs in the Pyrenees. The purpose of the internment, under command of the German Gestapo, was to separate the "Aryan" Germans and release them. The camp then served as a transitory camp for Jews who were eventually sent to concentration camps in the east. Once the "Aryan" Germans were released, says Gertrud S.,

the Jews and half-Jews had to go back into the barracks. . . . In October, the last Jews arrived from Baden. They came from old folks' homes, hospitals, and there were women with children. . . .

This was in 1940. I helped in the camp, above all with the children. We lay in barracks without windows; there were just small holes in the wall. There were some 60 of us women, and we lay there in the straw. It was an impossible situation. Some of the mothers were hysterical. . . . We tried to get a special barracks for the children. That was approved, with the help of the Cimada.[72]

We received help from them — children's beds, and so on. I had a little kingdom there. I was even allowed to go with the children into the forest outside the camp, surrounded, of course, by policemen or soldiers. That I could live to see that — that one could occasionally get out to pick a flower in the forest. . . . I was in the camp for six or seven months. I know that the young people my age were all sent to Poland and never seen again.[73]

Gertrud S. escaped their fate; the family in Montpellier managed (probably through a bribe) to win her release from the camp. She was taken in by another family as household help and survived the war in France. Yet, despite the persecution that linked her destiny with that of millions of Jews, as a Jewish Christian, Gertrud S. felt a distance between her situation and that of the Jews. In the camp in Gurs, she recalled feeling "shut out" when the Jews prayed together or lit candles:

Today, I would join in with joy, but at that time, I had become somewhat narrow through being a deaconess, and I had my own prejudices against the Jews. That is the false training of us from that era. . . . One saw the Jews as anti-Christian, and, you know, the fact that my parents had never married — that, too, locked me into such rigid feelings.[74]

As the fate of Gertrud S. illustrates, even leaving Nazi Germany did not ensure the rescue of a Jew. But in general, the farther the Jews could emigrate, the safer they felt, and, for many, emigration remained their only hope. At the same time, it represented the abandonment of hope. Despite increasing persecution, many Jews could not imagine that their situation might worsen. Who, indeed, could have imagined, even in 1938, that in several years millions of human beings would be rounded up, stripped of what little they still possessed, and murdered in gas chambers? Hope was important, not only in considering a possible future but in enduring present hardship. In 1936, Jochen Klepper's Jewish relatives urged him to try to send his two step-daughters abroad. "We cannot and cannot see the good in it for them," Klepper wrote, "even when their future here in Germany appears so threatened. . . . When I think of the children staying in the country, faith stirs within me; when I think of their emigrating, all falls silent."[75]

Particularly for those affected only secondarily by the racial laws, the uncertainties of creating a new life abroad seemed greater than the risks of staying in Nazi Germany. This was the case for Dietrich Goldschmidt, whose father was of Jewish descent. He recalled the debate about emigration within his own family:

In the winter semester of 1933–1934 I began studying mechanical engineering at the Berlin Technical University. I was still admitted. At that time, Jews or "non-Aryans" could study only with a yellow student card. . . . At first, I chose this course of study out of interest. Without a doubt, I would have dropped it after several semesters and chosen one of the courses of study more oriented toward the humanities. But under the circumstances, I had to be happy that I was admitted to study mechanical engineering, with the assumption that, as a qualified engineer, I would be able to emigrate.

At that time, my family had no other ties abroad. One has to remember, from the perspective of those times, that people of Jewish descent with "Aryan" spouses (my mother was "Aryan") were not initially endangered.[76]

Nevertheless, Goldschmidt's family began to consider emigration early. His brother, a lawyer in Hamburg, lost his position in June 1933 and emigrated to London. His sister, too, went to England as a domestic worker. After the *Kristallnacht* in November 1938, his father also emigrated to England. Goldschmidt himself decided to remain in Germany and continue his studies:

> With reason, with understanding, I should have said to myself, "Man, get out of this country." After 1938, at the latest. . . . But what I have to add is that, of course, after the war broke out, since my father was gone, my mother and I were no longer immediately in danger. [Note: as a "full Aryan" separated, practically, from her husband, Goldschmidt's mother was in no danger. Goldschmidt himself, a "first-degree mixture," did not realize at the time that he would eventually suffer under the wartime Aryan laws.] Because we had no personal connections, no organization would have stepped in for us. We weren't prominent political refugees, we weren't immediate racial refugees. Switzerland would have sent us back at once, and where else should we go? So both of us stayed here. Both of us, my mother and I, survived.[77]

The differences between Goldschmidt's situation and that of Gertrud S., although both were the offspring of Jewish fathers and "Aryan" mothers, illustrate differences of chance. Gertrud S. was increasingly isolated; Goldschmidt, on the other hand, had a group of friends that alleviated some of the loneliness of his family's situation. In general, however, Jews were being detached, step by step, from the community around them. The Confessing Church's own failure, in some cases, to maintain fellowship with Jewish Christians was all the sadder since, in the Christian religion, the community of believers is an important symbol of faith.

Increasing Terror: The *Kristallnacht* and the Deportations

The *Kristallnacht* was a brutal signal, not just of Nazi intentions but of the extent to which ordinary compassion in German society had become numbed. (The term *Kristallnacht*, meaning "the night of broken glass," was coined by the Nazi press, which boasted about the German streets being covered with the glass of Jewish store windows. Because it is a Nazi phrase, many Germans today prefer to refer to it as the November 9 pogrom). According to the Nazi press, the pogrom of November 9 was the spontaneous anger of the German people in response to the assassination of a German embassy attaché in Paris by a Jew. In fact, the pogrom was planned and carried out by the SS, which duly reported the extent of the damage to Hermann Göring: 191 synagogues burned, 815 businesses destroyed, 36 Jews killed, and 36 wounded.[78] It was one of the few times that the SS underestimated its own "success"; other estimates for the amount of damage and the number killed are higher, placing the number of destroyed businesses alone, for example, at 7,500.[79]

Some 20,000 Jewish men, including four Protestant pastors, were arrested by the SS and taken to concentration camps.[80] Most of the Jews arrested in conjunction with November 9 were released weeks or months later after promising to emigrate; the price of emigration was their life savings and businesses and a large emigration fee.

The pogrom had a cataclysmic effect on German Jews; no longer was any kind of future for them imaginable in Germany. The reactions of non-Jewish Germans ranged from horror to a shocking equanimity. The Confessing Church vicar who had replaced a Jewish Christian pastor was still serving that parish in 1938. He later recalled his reaction to the *Kristallnacht* in a voice furtive with guilt. "You know," he said, "it didn't move me colossally." Then, his voice dropping even further, he attempted to explain:

> That's probably hard to understand. We had a few Jews in the area. There was a vet-erinarian, of whom it was reported that he had been picked up. It was also said that in S. the synagogue had burned down. But. Perhaps one had to have been in Berlin, to have seen it. At that time I was in a parish in the countryside. . . . Why it somehow didn't upset me inwardly I can explain only in retrospect: that the range of vision was too narrow. We stood under observation. . . . I frankly admit to you that some-times you had to push yourself not to be a coward. . . . I had married in 1936, and then, perhaps, one isn't so — I'm speaking unguardedly here, but I'd rather say it that way than weigh every word on the scale. When you have a child, then you're not as courageous as the Catholic priests are, with their light luggage.[81]

The ruthlessness of the November pogrom clearly terrified many people into silence. Another pastor, recalling the reaction of his parishioners, said,

> Now it could be seen. The Jews were driven together here and led through the entire city, with hands raised in the air, to the *Festhalle*, and there they were beaten — dreadful stories. Some people said then, "No, that's not what we wanted." But it was too late. No one dared anymore, really, to open his mouth.[82]

Many people recalled the remorse, the sense that things had gone too far. There was also, according to many accounts, horror at the violence against the Jews, at the rampant pillaging of Jewish businesses. Unfortunately, this horror subsided quickly. In Dahlem, said Helmut Gollwitzer,

> The *Kristallnacht* or, more accurately, the pogrom of 1938, had a politically enlight-ening effect. . . . Even families loyal to Hitler were outraged. When their children had been on the Kurfürstendamm [the main boulevard in Berlin] and pocketed something from the wares of the plundered businesses, they took it away at once and said, "That such a thing could happen in Germany!" There was a moment of deep indignation that went through the middle class. But then the political situation sharp-ened, and then the war broke out. Otherwise, it might have had a more far-reaching effect.[83]

Despite their horror, few people recognized that the *Kristallnacht* revealed the inevitability of mass murder. As Dietrich Goldschmidt said:

> The murder, to the extent that it then happened, or that one would murder people at all — only very few people saw that coming. I myself had an aunt. . . . This aunt said, "Dieter, the star is coming, it will definitely come, and before that happens, I'll kill myself." She really did commit suicide; she feared the coming persecution and didn't want to submit to it. She was in her seventies when she took her life.[84]

In Potsdam, noted Goldschmidt, the people he knew were shocked by the pogrom, adding,

I always get angry that people don't know why it's called *Reichskristallnacht*. . . .
There was a Reich Farmer's Day, a Reich Craftsmen's Day, there was the Reich
Garden Show. In this sense, that there were numerous connections with national
events, the people said, then, *Reichskristallnacht.* Sarcastically. . . . It is a sarcastic or
ironic comment. This connection has been forgotten . . . the attempt was to distance
oneself, through irony, from that which had happened.[85]

Goldschmidt's own memories of November 9, 1938, were these:

By chance, my parents had left for a week . . . so they weren't there. I was at home
alone . . . policemen searched our house, very superficially, and took a Finnish knife
from my room. That's a knife with a solid handle made of horn, that I had gotten as
a present at some time from my brother. It was a badge for the Hitler Youth or something similar. This knife was taken, and I had a pair of brown hiking pants; they
were taken too. As I recall, that was all.

Then they took me with them. I can't say anymore whether that was in the car
or with the streetcar. . . . I was then put in a waiting room at the police station in
Potsdam. After many hours, someone came and said that I could go home . . . the
"wrath of the people" hadn't meant me, a "mixture." Then I asked about my pants
and the knife. No, that would remain confiscated. That was all. . . .

As I remember, I didn't see anything like broken glass or burned out synagogues. My parents were spared, since, when they returned home a few days later,
everything was over. The only thing that my father demanded, which I could understand, was this. I had an unusual desk. This desk had a drawer in the front, and the
back of the drawer could also be opened without it being noticed from the front. This
back part hadn't been discovered [by the police], and in this back section I had bun-
dles of material from the Confessing Church and such things. My father demanded
that I sink it all in a gulley, a drainage ditch, and I did that.

Naturally, we heard about these things. Above all, the son of a close friend was
among those taken to a concentration camp. . . . I can't say exactly, but he was
released, with a shaved head, after about five or seven weeks, like the others. He was
thin and had obviously suffered. . . . The significant thing was that those released
from the concentration camps had been ordered to say nothing about their time there.
I assume that he also felt so humiliated that he didn't want to talk about it. . . . So at
that time, I didn't hear details of it.

But I drove frequently with the streetcar to Oranienburg [near the Sachsenhausen concentration camp] because friends of ours lived right next to Oranienburg.
. . . When I was on the way back from Oranienburg in the train, men with closely
shaved heads got in. These, then, were those who had been released from the concentration camp. I can't remember that there was ever an unfriendly comment made
to these people. As far as I can recall, people observed them with a certain air of
oppression; the people standing around showed, from their position, that they didn't
want to talk about it or have anything to do with it. I don't remember that people
were especially friendly to them, nor do I recall that people rebuffed them in any
way.[86]

Ilse Härter, recalling the reactions to the *Kristallnacht*, commented that

The prohibition against speaking about concentration camp imprisonment existed
from the very beginning for every prisoner. That's why those released came to us
theologians when they felt that they had to talk about it, for they knew of our duty to

keep it confidential. I think that, after the pogrom, the anxiety grew — and, because
of that, so did the silence. Many repressed everything, so as not to become the victims of their fears.[87]

In any case, the public outrage over the *Kristallnacht* subsided quickly. Laura
Livingstone [the sister-in-law of British Bishop Bell, Bonhoeffer's friend in England]
worked in Berlin until 1939 to help Jews. After the war, she wrote her impressions of
people's reactions to the pogrom:

> I had the impression that the population was deeply ashamed of what had happened.
> At that time, I even had the hope that now the Germans would finally understand
> what kind of government they had, and would try to free themselves of it. These
> naive hopes were not to be fulfilled.[88]

On the contrary, as Dietrich Goldschmidt recalled, most Germans continued to
view many aspects of Nazism positively:

> the persecution of the Jews, this escalating persecution of the Jews, and the 9th of
> November — in a sense, that was only one event, next to very many gratifying ones.
> Here the famous stories of all the things Hitler did come in: "He got rid of unem-
> ployment, he built the *Autobahn*, the people started doing well again, he restored our
> national pride again. One has to weigh that against the other things."[89]

Livingstone, like other people trying to help the Jews, was deeply disappointed
by the failure of both the official church and the Confessing Church to protest what
had happened. The silence of the churches in those November days was all the more
striking since the church had occasion, immediately after the pogrom, to speak out,
not only on the following Sunday but on Repentance Day, in that German church
year on the Wednesday following the *Kristallnacht*. Yet, the number of sermons that
protested the violence against the Jews were few. In Dahlem, Helmut Gollwitzer
preached one. In Württemberg, Pastor Julius von Jan preached another; he was
beaten afterward by a band of thugs and imprisoned for four months. When another
outspoken pastor, Otto Mörike, tried to get Württemberg Bishop Wurm to reprint von
Jan's sermon and distribute it to all pastors, Wurm refused, although he agreed to
help von Jan's family.[90] Wurm, in fact, wrote Justice Minister Gürtner to protest the
pogrom, but qualified his protest by adding, "I contest with no word the right of the
State to fight Judaism as a dangerous element."[91] (Wurm later wrote that he would
regret these words "to the end of my life."[92])

At the *Kirchentag* of the Confessing Church, a national meeting held from
December 10 to 12, 1938, delegates issued a statement of concern "for our Christian
comrades in faith among the Jews," but that, once again, limited church concern to
Jewish Christians. One reason for the silence within the Confessing Church, according to Albrecht Schönherr, was that the different groups within the church opposition
were still preoccupied with their differences of opinion. Schönherr, who later became
the presiding bishop of the East German church, was one of Bonhoeffer's students; in
a 1986 interview, he noted that the Confessing Church had just emerged from the
prayer liturgy controversy over the Czech crisis. No one, Schönherr recalled, wanted
another battle within the church over a response to the *Kristallnacht*:

We had pushed it [the prayer liturgy] through in the Prussian church and received an outraged attack from Bavarian and the others. That damaged us greatly. Above all, it crippled the church in regard to the "Jewish question." When the *Kristallnacht* happened, in 1938, the church should have done something, and it didn't. No one dared anymore, because we knew that people wouldn't come along on it. We had simply become too divided.[93]

The events of November 9 did move some people to urge the church to act. One was Paul Braune, the leader of Lobetal, who protested the euthanasia program. Shortly after November 9, Braune drew up a list of measures he felt the church should take to support Jewish Christians in light of the pogrom. Braune made an appointment with state secretary Kritzinger, his contact in the Reich chancellery, to discuss the measures; on December 1, he sent his proposals to von Bodelschwingh, with the request that Bodelschwingh also sign it. Berta Braune said:

The memo was a very realistic deliberation over what would happen to those who remained in the country, since all the others were emigrating. No one thought, in 1938, that they would be murdered. Such things didn't come into our range of vision at all. So my husband wrote this memo and sent it to von Bodelschwingh. In an accompanying note that I found in the archive is the request of my husband: "Dear Brother, I would prefer that you sign this as well."

Von Bodelschwingh didn't do that . . . von Bodelschwingh held himself out of the "non-Aryan" issue. Perhaps that is typical of his manner; he had far too many other things. They [the Jews] weren't central for him. I believe that they had very few Jews within the institutions. To what extent that played a role, I can't say.[94]

But a sense of urgency grew among many members of the Confessing Church and in many parishes; and private attempts to help the Jews continued. As Wolfgang Gerlach has noted,[95] the more restricted the Confessing Church became by the state (particularly after the arrest and trial, in 1941, of the Berlin seminary's examination committee), the freer it became on an illegal, unofficial level to do what it had been afraid to do institutionally. In a sense, the growing oppression within Nazi Germany gave the more radical members of the Confessing Church a greater sense of legitimacy. It must be noted that they received some financial and other support (such as official cover-ups for their activities) from the more cautious leaders of the church. People like Otto Dibelius, fearful of committing the church to a stand that would bring them into conflict with the state, were willing to help privately. As Helmut Gollwitzer commented, recalling the help he received from wealthy individuals in the Dahlem parish,

Many Germans are goodhearted and sentimental, just like many other people. Later, in the organized help for the Jews, we received help in individual cases, even from people in Nazi circles. And pity in any case, when the excesses were shocking, and that all the more so from Christians. "They are human beings, too," they'd say. You could always get somewhere with that.

Nevertheless, I have to say that Hitler had great success with . . . the negation of the consciousness that Jews were human beings. . . . My first wife[96] was half Jewish. During the final months of the war, she did forced labor at Siemens, and she told me that the workers spontaneously demanded separate toilets for the Jews and half-Jews forced to work there. Afterward, I asked her whether the command came from above. "No," she said, "the people demanded that on their own."

I can imagine that the same people, if they had encountered a truly suffering Jew, would have given him something and had pity on him, and would have said, "One really shouldn't carry it that far!" They wouldn't have held to be true what had already happened.[97]

The Grüber Office

Much of the Confessing Church's help for the Jewish Christians was channeled through the Grüber office, run by Berlin pastor Heinrich Grüber and set up by the Provisional Church Government of the Berlin Confessing Church. Grüber's office began its activities in September 1938, although Grüber had worked for several years with Marga Meusel, Laura Livingstone, Martin Albertz, and other Berlin Confessing Church members to advise and help Jewish Christians. They had worked to send Jewish children to British families, and after Jewish children were forbidden to attend German schools, Albertz had helped set up "family schools" for them in some parishes. There the children were taught by some of the women theologians in the Confessing Church. The Grüber office was set up to coordinate the activities of the different groups and individuals, particularly those of the Reich Association of Non-Aryan Christians, which was eventually absorbed into the Grüber office.

Most of Grüber's work, however, consisted of trying to help Jews and Jewish Christians emigrate. By 1938, about 150,000 German Jews had left Nazi Germany;[98] after that, emigration was almost impossible. (Eventually, half of Germany's Jews rescued their lives through emigration.[99]) Several months before Grüber established his office, the number of Jewish Christians seeking his help or that of the Confessing Church had increased dramatically;[100] the situation became even more acute after June 1938, when the first large group of German Jews was arrested and sent to concentration camps.

For the short period that the office existed — Grüber's office was shut down by the Gestapo in December 1940 — Grüber and his co-workers operated in a shadow realm between legality and illegality. The Gestapo made no secret of its observation of Grüber's activities, but, as far as Grüber's work in helping Jews emigrate was concerned, Nazi officials approved. From 1938 to 1940, emigration was still the favored solution to the "Jewish question."[101]

This led to some uncertainty among church workers as to the political legality of their activities. In 1937, Laura Livingstone had met with SS Oberführer Werner Best. "Since the work which you are undertaking has nothing to do with politics," Best told her, "I have nothing against your project."[102] Some of those approached by Grüber for help wanted to make certain that their assistance would not get them into trouble with the state and wrote the Reich Church office to check on Grüber's status with officials there. The letter was forwarded to Gestapo head Reinhard Heydrich, who replied that Grüber's work presented no problems.[103] In their efforts to find emigration possibilities for Jews, Grüber and some co-workers even received visas to travel abroad — which, by 1938, were difficult for any German to obtain. As late as March

1940, Grüber traveled to Switzerland on a visa personally approved by Adolf Eichmann to seek permission for Jochen Klepper's daughter to emigrate to a Swiss family who had offered to take her in (the Swiss government refused; Klepper, his Jewish wife, and daughter committed suicide in December 1942[104]). One of Grüber's most influential helpers was industrialist Gerhard Simson, a baptized "full Jew." Even Simson had a special Gestapo stamp on his Jewish passport permitting him to travel; he used the passport to emigrate to Sweden shortly before the war began.[105]

[Note: Some historians have contended that Nazi approval of Grüber's activities is evidence that, as late as the period between 1938 and 1940, the mass murder of the Jews was not yet planned. They claim that Nazi policies regarding Jewish emigration make sense only if we assume that the "final solution" was not planned until after the war began.[106]

The problem with such theories, of course, is that they have also been proposed by historical apologists for Nazism, who put the blame for the death camps not on the Nazis but on those countries that refused to accept any more Jewish refugees — thereby (according to the twisted logic of the apologists) giving the Nazis no other "option" but to murder the Jews. These historians regard the *Kristallnacht* as the culmination of Nazi measures to convince the Jews to emigrate.

But the euthanasia program was started in August 1939; simultaneously, the technology for mass murder — the development of the gases that would also be used on the Jews — was developed. There is no proof that the Nazis planned from the outset to use these gases on the Jews. The Wannsee Conference in January 1942 is often given as the official date of the Third Reich leaders' decision to murder the Jews. But Auschwitz had opened in September 1941, and the vehemence of Nazi propaganda and brutality, as well as Hitler's own words in *Mein Kampf*, illustrate that the readiness to murder had been there from the beginning.]

The hope of Confessing Church workers that other countries would open their borders was unfulfilled. At the Evian refugee conference in Switzerland in July 1938, Switzerland, France, England, the United States, and other countries announced new restrictions on emigrants. The Australian representative announced, "Since we don't have a real race problem, we have no wish to import one."[107] Grüber's attempts to help Jews emigrate were also hindered by the ecumenical office of the official German Evangelical Church, which, at foreign meetings like the one at Evian, worked to block the credentials of Confessing Church representatives like Martin Albertz. (The conflict here was over which church — the official church or the Confessing Church — would be recognized as the "official" German Evangelical Church at foreign meetings.[108])

Despite these difficulties, Grüber's office helped 1,138 Jews emigrate before August 1939;[109] by the time the office was closed, the total number helped by Grüber and his contacts was probably between 1,700 and 2,000.[110] Grüber had 35 co-workers in Berlin and an additional 26 contacts throughout Germany who tried to help the Jewish Christians and Jews in their regions. As emigration became more difficult, Grüber and his associates turned their efforts toward obtaining false passports, rationing cards, and identity cards for Jews, and, eventually, to finding hiding places for Jews who could not get out in time. (On October 23, 1941, an order from Heinrich Himmler banned all further Jewish emigration.)

Helene Jacobs, a member of the Dahlem-based "Kaufmann circle," which helped Jews, recalled that Grüber worked not only to help Jewish Christians but any Jew who approached him for help:

> That's why he was arrested, because he spoke out in outrage against the first deportations in Stettin. He had permission only to care for "non-Aryan" Christians. That's why he ended up in the concentration camp. For the most part, his office was run by those who were affected themselves.[111]

Of the 35 workers in his office, only 12 (including Grüber himself) survived the Third Reich.[112] Grüber was sent to Sachsenhausen in December 1940, and later to Dachau. After the Gestapo closed his office, the efforts of church people to help Jews and Jewish Christians were entirely underground.

The Underground Resistance of the Confessing Church

Particularly in Berlin, this ministry to the Jews was performed through "Bible studies" — virtually the one activity for which the Confessing Church had Gestapo permission to gather. Helga Weckerling, who was preparing for the ministry in Berlin, described the Bible circle she led at the Kaiser-Wilhelm-Memorial Church in downtown Berlin:

> We had a mixed group of Jewish women who had been baptized, but there were also some who had not been baptized. We didn't distinguish so strictly. Everyone could come who was interested. . . . Officially, nothing else besides Bible study was allowed, but of course we passed on information. Our central point was the Bible study, and that was very important, simply to develop a fundamental position on the role Jews had played in our history and the responsibility toward them that was demanded of us . . . basically, we knew very little about them individually . . . and there was no answer from those who were deported. . . .
>
> We couldn't gather in the public rooms of the church. . . . It was a very intensive work. We always held the meetings in homes, because the Jews couldn't go outside with their yellow stars. Some were deported. We helped prepare them for their deportation. It is horrifying to say that, although we couldn't imagine what they faced. They hoped to come to Theresienstadt. [Note: the "model" concentration camp, supposedly less brutal than the other camps.] We held everything we heard for rumor; the Jews did that, too. You see that from the fact that they took along all kinds of things for the "transport" — cosmetics, etc. . . .
>
> We studied the Exodus story with them. It was a work that, today, no one would understand. It's hard to imagine what that meant when, all at once, these people disappeared. We collected food coupons and were able to hide some people. It was all very difficult, because, for example, the neighbors noticed when someone wasn't registered. We tried to make sure that everyone had food coupons, and that wasn't so easy, especially in villages.[113]

The purpose of her work, said Weckerling, was "to understand part of their fate and bear it with them. Rescuing these people was impossible." For most of the Jewish Christians in these circles, she said,

It was already too late. We had one family, for example, in which the man was a hero in World War I. He truly believed that because of that nothing would happen to him. And it was too expensive for many to make their way abroad. These were more middle-class Jews — secretaries, teachers, and so on. The Jews who came to us were mainly the so-called "half-Aryans" or those in "privileged" (that is, mixed) marriages.[114]

As Elsie Steck, the secretary in the Dahlem parish, remembered, one purpose of these circles was to prepare the Jewish Christians for their deportation:

Beforehand, we went to them. Gollwitzer took his briefcase with the things for the Eucharist, and I went along, when they knew ahead of time that they would be picked up. Moreover, there were "courses" offered for some selected "non-Aryans." They weren't ordained, but they were prepared so that, if they stayed alive in the camps, they could be approached by other Christians.[115]

The fact that these Confessing Christians "prepared" Jews for deportation, praying with them, training them to give the Eucharist to others in the camps, sometimes even accompanying them to the train stations and town squares where the Gestapo had ordered them to appear for deportation, haunted some people for the rest of their lives. Weckerling says today,

We were never sure whether we were doing the right thing or not. We had been brought up differently, and it was war — and then, it's hard to undertake something against your own country. Later, when young people asked us, particularly abroad, why we hadn't resisted more, I tried to explain to them how hard it is, particularly during a war, to do something illegal that could lead to punishment.

We were simply too cowardly. That's what I would say today. That is the great guilt we have taken upon ourselves. It was due to the war. We lived in contradiction. We were against the government, but our men were on the front. My two brothers were also soldiers.[116]

At first, Elsie Steck recalled, the Confessing Church circles did not realize that the Jews were all being sent to their deaths:

At that time, it was said that very many went to Theresienstadt. The fact alone that we "educated" them shows that we didn't think they were going straight to their deaths. . . . Only after someone told Gollwitzer in the sacristy that he had delivered the gas there [to a camp] himself did we know. . . . Gollwitzer, of course, knew a great deal more.[117]

But, of course, the fact that people differentiated between Theresienstadt and the other camps showed an awareness that many Jews were, indeed, going to their deaths.

The question of knowledge and accountability is problematic, as many of these accounts illustrate. For many Confessing Christians, and for Jews themselves, the rumors about the camps were hard to believe. Annemarie Grosch could not recall exactly when she first heard details about the mass murders:

In retrospect, it's very difficult to say. We knew some things, but we never knew the entirety. We knew more than others, but we actually learned the extent of the horrors after 1945. For no one ever came back from the camps, and when people did return from a concentration camp, they had to sign that they wouldn't talk, and they were much too afraid to talk. Despite this, we did know some things through the open evenings in the parish with Niemöller, and these evenings continued with his successors.[118]

Niemöller's main successor was Helmut Gollwitzer, who (as Steck noted) knew a great deal. Several of the officers who eventually formed the conspiracy to kill Hitler passed information to the Confessing Church through Gollwitzer. But the question of knowing, Gollwitzer emphasized in 1980, was not just a matter of information:

> The instinct for survival told every German clearly what form of opposition would be tolerated and where it became dangerous. Worrying about church matters was a concern of the "Aryan" people. We "Aryans" were permitted to live. And the Jews were not permitted to live. A totally different standard of justice was valid for the "Aryans." If I stood in prison, in the interrogation room or the corridors of the Gestapo police prison on Alexanderplatz and a Jew was led past me, I knew that that was totally different. He was condemned to death. I was not; perhaps I would come back. Every German knew that.
>
> That's why the experiences in the church were enlightening to people who initially sympathized with Hitler. But the sharper the persecution of the Jews became, the more one had to repress what was happening to them. When I told people about it, how often they said: "Please, don't tell me anything! I don't want to know. I shouldn't know!" Simply knowing was dangerous. One could betray oneself; one might express, without stopping to think, one's horror. That's why a great proportion of the people held this knowledge away from themselves. And after 1945, they could, in a subjective sense, correctly say: "We didn't know." Because they didn't want to know. That belongs to the principles of a regime of terror, and here they worked.[119]

Despite this, there were Confessing Christians who tried to hide Jews and provide the necessary papers so that they could exist underground in Nazi Germany. It was dangerous; collecting extra food rationing cards, for example, was prohibited, and those caught could be imprisoned. In most cases, a Jew living underground had to move from one hiding place to another to avoid arousing the suspicions of neighbors and Nazi officials. Some Jews were rescued this way; one, Max Krakauer, was hid by 61 different families.[120]

One woman who hid a Jew was Marta S., the Confessing pastor's wife who had also been a member of the Nazi party. [Note: When I began searching for people who had hidden Jews, Liselotte Lawerenz gave me the address of Marta S. Pastor Lawerenz did not herself know that Marta S. had been in the party. In the course of my interview with her, Marta S. began to speak quite frankly about her early enthusiasm for Nazism and her gradual disillusionment with it and about Nazi party proceedings brought against her in 1942 for "disinterest." The version she told me corresponded exactly to that in party documents I was later able to obtain from the Berlin Document Center.

Liselotte Lawerenz was a reliable resource on other points and was present at the meeting in Halle. Ilse Härter, a close friend of Hannelotte Reiffen, recalled that Reiffen attended two meetings of the Illegals in Halle, one in January 1943 and the second (where Marta S. met Reiffen) in March 1943.

Nevertheless, it may be difficult for readers to believe that the same person could join the Nazi party in 1932 and hide a Jew 10 years later; readers will have to draw their own conclusions. It is not impossible. As Helmut Gollwitzer told me, even some Nazi party members in Dahlem were willing to help Jews privately. My own wary conclusion, based upon my interview with her, was that she did. I have included Marta S.'s story because she illustrates—more than any other person interviewed for this book—how Germans succumbed to Nazism, why it remains so difficult for them to wrestle with that, and how complex some of their lives were during the Third Reich.]

I participated in an illegal seminar in Halle. For the entire day, they discussed whether one could use illegal means, for example, false papers, to rescue Jews. One Dahlem pastor described that that was his daily bread, and that there was no way around it. Another pastor . . . held prayer and trust in God as the only permissible means.

As we were leaving, Hannelotte Reiffen [a *Vikarin* from the Rhineland, active in the Berlin Confessing Church] said to me, "Can you take a Jew in? It's a matter of life and death. Better today than tomorrow." For that, there could only be a yes. When she came the following day, I was frightened. She looked so Jewish that the other inhabitants of my house could denounce me at once. Luckily, no one in the village had ever seen a Jew, and since she was from Bavaria, everyone thought that that's what the Bavarians looked like. She was with us from March till May of 1943. . . .

The Jew was around 45 years of age, completely exhausted, because she couldn't get food coupons anymore, since she would have been arrested doing it, and she had run around for days in the cold, since she was in danger if she stayed at her apartment. I could make it believable in the village that she was there for a rest, because she looked terribly weak. She was in very bad shape. During the entire time that she was with me, she never slept more than three hours at a time. She was so afraid. She wanted to help me in the garden, although she was too broken physically.

I couldn't speak to anyone about it. . . . The mayor didn't require an official registration from my guest, although that was a requirement, basically. I could still make it conceivable during the second month that she had gotten an extension on her vacation, but no one would have believed me after eight weeks. The prospect that she couldn't stay continued to rob her of her sleep. Just in time, Hannelotte Reiffen found another parsonage. . . . In different places, she survived the period between 1943 and 1945, but she died soon after the war.[121]

Ilse Härter, who had left the Rhineland to work in the Berlin Confessing Church, moved to Württemberg in 1942. Württemberg was an intact church (its bishop was Wurm), but a group of pastors there, led by Hermann Diem, had formed a group, the "Society," that was sympathetic to the Confessing Church. After he was drafted in 1942 into the military, Diem asked Härter to take over his parish in Ebersbach, southeast of Stuttgart. As Härter recalled,

We didn't have any Jews in Ebersbach. But the Society had set up a service to help the Jews. They created the possibilities that Jews who were persecuted elsewhere could go underground in Württemberg, that is, live there illegally. In addition, we collected food coupons, which we sent to Berlin for other underground Jews. In December 1942, I had to give a talk in Berlin. I drove there and, at the same time, took very many collected food coupons, which I passed on. . . .

I was supplied with food by the people in Ebersbach. They said, "We don't want to know, but we know that you can use this for your work." That was primarily for the care of the Jews. . . .

We actually did have parish members who understood that the theological decision of the Confessing Church against the "German Christians" had political consequences. There were also parish members who declared themselves willing to take in Jews who had gone underground. They knew that that was a part of political resistance. Of course, we had too few who were in that position or who were prepared to take someone in.

There were people with whom one could speak completely openly about it. . . . But it wasn't the majority. One knew in the parish that one couldn't speak with everyone about it.[122]

In some cases, parish initiatives merged with other sectors of political resistance to Nazism, sometimes through coincidence. Helene Jacobs, the stubborn opponent of Nazism who had worked for a Jewish lawyer, was hiding an artist in her apartment who forged false papers for the Grüber office. Gertrud Staewen, the aspiring writer, had been receiving money since 1936 from Karl Barth and his circle in Switzerland to pass on to those helping the Jews in the Confessing Church. Staewen and Jacobs met each other in Gollwitzer's Bible circle in Dahlem, where they also met Franz Kaufmann, a prominent Jewish lawyer. As Helene Jacobs recalled,

He was truly a very extraordinary person. He came from a rather ambitious family. He had been with the administrative court and now had a non-Jewish wife, and they had a child. It was a so-called "privileged" marriage. He could have kept himself completely out of things.[123] But he couldn't stand it. . . . Untiringly, he thought about how one could help the people, through illegal hiding places, and so on. He was constantly thinking about it, and also used his connections that he still had from earlier days. He still thought, one has to appeal to people's consciences and then they would stop all this. . . .

I wanted to keep my democratic world; he wanted to maintain his Christian world. He belonged to those Jews who were already fairly assimilated. . . . When people asked him, he said, "I have to do this for the sake of the church." I said, "I have to do this for the sake of the state." That was a considerable difference between us.[124]

As Staewen recalls, she, Kaufmann, Jacobs, and another woman, Melanie Steinmetz, decided

to form an illegal circle to help the Jews. You must understand what a torture it was, because everything had to happen very secretly. . . . As a result, many people didn't know at all that we were doing this, just as we didn't know that others were also a part of it.[125]

Their work was supported by Karl Barth in Switzerland and by Adolf Freudenberg, a "non-Aryan" official in the German state department who, after his dismissal from the civil service, became active in the Dahlem parish. Freudenberg emigrated to Switzerland in 1939 and served as a bridge between the German resistance groups and their ecumenical contacts abroad.

The group distributed the passports and food coupons, forged by the artist hidden by Helene Jacobs, to Jews. Staewen collected Mother's Crosses, the Nazi gift to women who had many children; the crosses were given to Jewish women trying to leave Germany with false papers, in the hope (which was borne out) that border guards would be less suspicious of a woman wearing such a symbol of Nazi achievement. But their work often pushed them to despair. In 1982, Staewen tearfully recalled one Jewish woman she helped who was finally deported to the camps:

> She was utterly exhausted . . . and waited simply for her fate. We thought and thought. We had no hiding place where she could have stayed all the time. We could help a little to feed and visit her. When I heard that she would be deported the following day, I began to howl, "Isn't anyone going to murder these fellows?" Then she said to me, very calmly, "Should the last German person I know be filled only with hate?" I'll never forget that, for the rest of my life.[126]

Finally, the Kaufmann group attempted to bribe the Gestapo to rescue the lives of Jews. Staewen said that the group was approached by a Gestapo official who told them that he knew of their activities, but that for a bribe he would not only remain silent but would use his influence with another high official to buy the lives of Jews already in the camps. Jacobs met the man once:

> It was gruesome, the way he telephoned with his Gestapo connection. . . . Word had gotten around Dahlem that perhaps such an action would be possible, and a whole group of people had given me the names of relatives or friends who had already been deported, whom one believed could now be rescued. I didn't believe it. . . . This man certainly just wanted the money. . . .
>
> He picked out some for whom we should pay. But that didn't happen in any of the cases. It was a set-up game between the two of them; it was completely mendacious. . . . It was so repulsive. . . . I can't describe to you how repulsed I was, and how sad I was that Kaufmann got into this.[127]

But as Jacobs realized afterward, Kaufmann was being closely watched by the Gestapo at the time; he may have hoped to avoid arrest through the Gestapo contact. As Staewen recalled, a large amount of money changed hands:

> He wanted a huge amount, I think 250 marks per person just to tell us whether they were still alive or not. We picked out nine for him . . . and I included the names of three who I knew were already dead. He listed them, and it was exactly correct. So we thought, good. He came back very soon. Now he needed much larger sums; he "could try to get the people out of the concentration camps for us." We said that we didn't believe it. He said, "It'll cost you, though." I don't know anymore the exact sum. But it was between 2,000 and 4,000 marks per person, a great deal. We didn't have money, but there was still a lot of money in Dahlem. We pulled in a lot; people gave it to us when we said that we needed it. . . .
>
> Then we took those thousands to him and heard nothing. Nothing. We never heard from the man again, either. Later, he was hanged by the Russians.[128]

(Jacobs and Staewen remembered the outcome of the attempt differently. Three of the people whose lives were "bought" did, indeed, survive the camps; Staewen believed that, in the case of one woman, the man made good on his promise to have her picked out. Jacobs, however, did not believe that the woman's survival was due to the Gestapo man's intervention.)

The Official Church's Silence

The intensity of their efforts, and the daily tragedies with which those Confessing Christians working to help the Jews were confronted, were in marked contrast to the pronouncements of the official German Evangelical Church. After 1939, when emigration had become virtually impossible, Jewish Christians received even less support from their church (the official church was utterly silent on the plight of the non-Christian Jews). In fact, in 1939, proposals for the establishment of a separate church for Jewish Christians were revived. In 1939, the five regional churches led by the "German Christians" officially forbade "non-Aryans" from being church members, telling pastors that if they wished to offer services for "non-Aryans," such services could not take place on church property.[129] In March 1939, Heinz Brunotte, a church lawyer in the administration of the official Protestant church, proposed giving Jewish Christians "guest status": Jewish Christians could continue to participate in the "spiritual life" of the church, he suggested, but should be barred from "public church rights" — essentially, any kind of public ceremony.[130] (Brunotte's goal, as he wrote in 1968 in a defense of his actions, was to guarantee Jewish Christians a "fixed status," which, he noted, "could not be reached at that time without certain limitations."[131])

Nothing came of Brunotte's proposal. In January 1941, the Gestapo banned the Protestant *Judenmission*, and on September 5, 1941, Jews were required by law to wear the yellow star in public. The church's Spiritual Confidential Council, an advisory board led by Bishop Marahrens of Hannover, could not agree on a church position in response. As a result, no official guidelines immediately emerged from the Protestant chancellery in Berlin. The regional churches and individual parishes had to decide for themselves how to treat the "star-wearers." The Hannover church, led by Marahrens, responded by "releasing" Jewish Christians from the obligation to pay church taxes.[132] In October 1941, the Lutheran church leaders in Saxony (there were two church administrations there, one for Lutherans, the other for "Evangelicals") ordered their churches not to permit "star-wearers" into worship services. In Breslau, Käthe Staritz, a vicar who worked openly with Jewish Christians and secretly for Grüber's office, publicly defended the right of the Jewish Christians to attend church. She was sent to a concentration camp, with no word of protest from the official church administration there (she was, however, on the Confessing Church's *Fürbittenliste*.)[133]

Isolated protests against the church order to exclude Jewish Christians came from Wurm in Württemberg and others in the Confessing Church. In the fall of 1943, the Prussian Synod of the Confessing Church protested the exclusion of the Jewish Christians, and, in August 1943, the Confessing Church Synod acknowledged its guilt in being silent about the injustices against the Jews.

The overall mood within the church, Brunotte later recalled, was one of "deep hopelessness."[134] In December 1941, the chancellery of the German Evangelical Church in Berlin, in agreement with its Confidential Council, issued a statement recommending

> that the baptized non-Aryans remain separate from the church life of German parishes. The baptized non-Aryans will have to find the ways and means themselves

to create such arrangements which could serve their special worship and caritative needs.[135]

There was no mention of the deportations, which had begun in October 1941 (Auschwitz had been opened in September 1941). In April 1942, a member of the official church chancellery met with Adolf Eichmann to get Eichmann's permission for Jewish Christians to hold worship services in the concentration camps. Eichmann refused, telling him that "a Jew was a Jew,"

> whether baptized or not. . . . He could, however, assure me that the entire Jewish question here in the Old Reich [that is, within the pre-1939 German borders] was only a transportation question.[136]

The meeting with Eichmann was the last instance on record in which the official German Evangelical Church concerned itself with the "Jewish question" during the course of the Third Reich. Writing in 1968, Brunotte argued that no one could blame the official church chancellery for not doing more for Jewish Christians:

> Here was done what could be done. . . . No church office could effectively have helped any more. . . . With the final deportations of the German Jews to the extermination camps in the East, the problem of church care for the non-Aryan Christians was extinguished.[137]

The bluntness of that final sentence holds the essence of the church's failure to help the Jews more than it did. It was not just helplessness but callousness that kept the church from being more outspoken on behalf of Jewish Christians and Jews. The 1941 chancellery statement barring "non-Aryans" from Christian services referred to the "withdrawal" (as if this were voluntary) of Jews from German society and concluded:

> This is an indisputable fact, which the German Evangelical Church, bound by its obligation to bring its own Gospel to the German people and into [German] life as a member of the public sphere, cannot disregard.[138]

Believing that they had to behave within certain bounds to retain the church's place in German society, many members of the church hierarchy became convinced that they were powerless to take any other course.

The Confessing Church's record was better than that of the official German Evangelical Church, but it, too, fell short. Considering the question of what the Confessing Church did on behalf of the Jews, Ilse Härter wrote,

> Perhaps the fact that so little was said by the synods — there were other statements — to the Jewish question was because the older Confessing theologians, who perhaps were influenced by men like Stoecker, thought that they had to be cautious here. People like Asmussen, because of their "two kingdoms doctrine," differentiated between what our task was and what the state's task was. Concern that the synods were being watched, and that [a statement] might make any work for the Jews utterly impossible, also played a role. This fear was entirely justified. . . .
> More people than one thinks gave practical help. Would that have been possible had the Confessing Church protested better? I don't know. On no account do I wish to excuse the Confessing Church. We all became guilty, even those of us who helped the Jewish people. We didn't scream it out, because we knew, indeed: If what

we do becomes known, these people will go to their deaths in any case, just as our path would lead to the concentration camp. Whereas, when we help secretly, perhaps they will survive. But show me the person who can be at peace in that situation.[139]

Helene Jacobs recalled that Franz Kaufmann, seeing Jews picked up by the Gestapo, asked, "Should we live on as if nothing had happened?"[140] This was the question that haunted so many Confessing Christians, before and after 1945. As a "non-Aryan" who escaped the labor camps until 1944, Dietrich Goldschmidt recalled that the question was difficult, even for him:

> I lived in Berlin until the end of October 1944. We knew of [deportations] and received the names of people who had been deported. . . . There were a few post-cards [that is, from the camps], and we never knew how seriously to take them . . . these were certainly intended to calm people, the friends, here. But still, there was a contradiction within us, so to speak, which said, "it could hardly be that they've survived," and yet still hoped, "but it can't be that they kill millions of people." The fact that we know today — that just among the Jews there were six million killed — that was something incomprehensible to us during the war.[141]

Goldschmidt escaped from the labor camp in April 1945, after the camp leaders fled in fear of the advancing Allies. For three weeks, he and his wife roamed the country-side. During these travels, he met several people who had escaped from concentration camps:

> There, for the first time, I heard in detail how people had been killed in Auschwitz, that is, about the gassings. . . . But I have to repeat that, up to the point that I've told you, anyone could know who wanted to! I have to emphasize that, when people say, "We didn't know anything," then one has to ask, "Did you want to know?" Then the answer will be, "No, I didn't want to know," if they're honest. For, if one had wanted to know, then one brought oneself into a dreadful situation. Then one's conscience would have been summoned: Something has to be done. Or one would have had to say, in good conscience: "Now I can't do anything. So it's better that I don't know anything. Then, at least, I can live this horrible life further."
>
> Perhaps you know T. S. Eliot's *Murder in the Cathedral*. There's a place where the archbishop comes from France, and the choir, the women of Canterbury, don't want him: "Yet we have gone on living, living and partly living . . . leave us and leave us be." This phrase has stayed in my memory. Don't burden us with any knowledge; living, partly living, we want to get through.[142]

To know was to abandon the false comfort of "normalcy," to rise above the mesmerized passivity of those who continued to believe that the Third Reich existed through an act of fate — both accidental and unstoppable. The ideological tangles of Nazism continued to hold many Germans captive. Even when they were aware of the terror being carried out in their name, they could see no other possibility, for themselves or for their country — particularly once the war began.

❦ 8 ❦

The War

The Mentality of People in Wartime

WAR HAS BEEN USED to extenuate any number of moral lapses, and not just for soldiers. War's hardships drive individuals into private retreat, where they become less concerned with the moral relevance of their lives than with simple survival. Their governments expect them to sacrifice. Food, fuel, and clothing may be rationed; civil liberties may be restricted or abolished. In the larger interests of the nation at war, territory previously private is claimed, and those who protest are spurned as traitors. Many citizens become morally passive, echoing the cry of Eliot's Canterbury choir: "Let us live, half-live."

Germans lived with the consequences of this long after the Third Reich had been reduced to ashes. They could not evade the question of their own role in the course of Nazism, before or after September 1, 1939; but there were very few Germans who did not suffer greatly as a result of World War II. Many families lost someone at the front, and many more lost family members, homes, and possessions in the bombing raids on German cities or on the refugee treks from the east at the end of the war.

Engulfed by personal loss and widespread destruction, many (if not most) Germans were reluctant, after 1945, to examine the question of their own guilt. Memory reduced their experiences under Hitler to the war years, and the horror and sorrow accumulated then left little room for anything else. If they mourned for the Jews and others who had been murdered, it was more comfortable to do so as fellow victims. Their own lives wrecked by the cataclysm of the war, many Germans preferred to believe that they, as much as anyone else, had emerged from the Nazi years as victims. With that, they reasoned, the moral slate was wiped clean.

It is understandable that ordinary Germans (including those in the Confessing Church) were preoccupied increasingly with their own problems as the war dragged on. To some degree, however, this had been the case since 1933. As Peter Steinbach has written, the Nazi era was "a way of life in the long period of great loneliness,"[1] where the pressures of life under a dictatorship led to individual isolation from any normal sense of collective responsibility. The war only magnified this problem, coming, like a bill long due, to all those who had refused or failed to see Hitler and the Nazis for what they were. Hans-Bernd von Haeften, an official in the *Auswärtigen Amt* (Foreign Office), member of the Confessing Church, and eventual conspirator to kill Hitler, put it more provocatively. After the November 9 pogrom in 1938, he decried the silence of the Confessing Church, writing that Christian passivity was rooted in the Lutheran belief that

155

the world is simply of the devil, [which] has very substantially contributed to letting it go to the devil all the more. Given up for lost by the church, the world makes itself powerful, and draws its order of values out of itself. Today, we know what comes of that.[2]

In September 1939, Martin Niemöller, 47 years of age, in his third year of Nazi imprisonment, wrote to a military commander whom he had known in World War I asking to be released from Sachsenhausen so he could serve in the German Wehrmacht. In his biography of Dietrich Bonhoeffer, Eberhard Bethge wrote that Bonhoeffer and several other Confessing Church leaders had encouraged Niemöller to do so. They were fearful that, under wartime conditions in the concentration camps, Niemöller might not survive.[3] But in 1981, Niemöller explained that his motives in 1939 were also patriotic:

> My sons had been drafted, and their father, who had been a career soldier, sat behind bars — that is, behind the walls of a concentration camp — and I wanted to be with my sons, to defend the German Reich as my Fatherland with my sons. . . . My oldest son was 17 at the time and studied theology in Marburg; my second son was a medical student, or would have been; and my third, who was still relatively young, was just 15 years old. And I thought, now I can sit here in my cell and worry about my three sons who are out there, and I sit here and can't do anything, where it probably concerns the very existence of Germany.[4]

All the bitterness of the German defeat in 1918 rose within him, and Niemöller brooded that, were Germany to be defeated again, "then my Fatherland is gone — and, at that time, that still meant something: 'Fatherland.'"[5]

Martin Niemöller was not the only Confessing Christian to distinguish between loyalty to the Fatherland and allegiance to Adolf Hitler, either at the time of the war or afterward, when they tried to describe their role in the war. Some 1,500 Confessing Church pastors and Illegals served as soldiers.[6] Eventually, 45 percent of all ordained Protestant pastors and 98 percent of unordained vicars and theological candidates served in the German military.[7] In fighting for the Fatherland, they inevitably fought — whatever their motives — for Hitler.

The Loyalty Oath Controversy

For Confessing Christians, the dilemma of living with anti-Nazi convictions and national loyalties was hardly new, but the war increased their difficulties in grappling with this troublesome issue. The loyalty oath controversy that had confronted Confessing Church leaders at several points during the 1930s is an example.

By virtue of their status as civil servants, church pastors and officials were required by Nazi law to swear an oath declaring personal loyalty to Adolf Hitler — as were religion teachers and professors at public schools and universities (this was the official reason that Karl Barth lost his position at the theological faculty in Bonn). In practice, however, the church did not always enforce the oath requirement. Demands that it do so intensified when nationalistic fervor was running high — after Hindenburg's death in 1934, for example, and after the Austrian *Anschluß* in the spring of

1938. On both occasions, "German Christian" leaders in the German Evangelical Church demanded that all German Protestant pastors swear a loyalty oath to the Führer. The Confessing Church's ambiguous response revealed how difficult it was to risk controversy on the issue of loyalty to the German head of state.

Radical Confessing Christians rejected it, but more conservative Protestants argued that the loyalty oath represented nothing more than a vow of national allegiance which any pastor could take in good conscience (although the wording of the oath, "I will be loyal and obedient to the Führer of the German Reich and nation, Adolf Hitler," made this interpretation questionable). Eventually, the Confessing Church took a position that enabled its pastors and officials to take the oath. Since a Christian's ultimate allegiance was to God, wrote church leaders, no earthly leader could expect or demand complete allegiance. By virtue of being Christians, church members were promising that nothing would go against God's will. For Confessing Christians, the unspoken implication was that they could and would refuse to follow Nazi dictates when these ran contrary to Christian precepts.[8] But there was no escaping the fact that the Confessing Church had found a circuitous way for its pastors to comply with the letter of the law, if not its spirit. For those pastors still uneasy about the loyalty oath, the Prussian Confessing Church Synod decided in 1938 that individual pastors taking the oath could attach a personal declaration of their own interpretation of this vow.

The Confessing Church's conflict here was more with the "German Christians" than with Nazi officials. The "German Christians" used the issue to wage a propaganda battle with the Confessing Church, and the Nazi party withdrew conveniently from the scene. At the height of the controversy in 1938, for example, Hitler deputy Martin Bormann wrote all Nazi regional directors that the oath was to be handled as an "internal church matter" and that party officials should take no action on it.[9]

Eventually, most Confessing pastors did take the oath. By June 1938, the percentage of those who had taken the loyalty oath in the regional churches in the Church of the Old Prussian Union ranged from 60 to 89 percent, except in Westphalia, where only 21 percent took it.[10] The few pastors who refused to do so were accused of risking a potentially dangerous conflict with the Nazi regime over a matter the church viewed as resolved. In 1941, the Confessing Church's attempt to place Ilse Härter as a parish worker in an official parish failed because Härter refused the parish's demand that she take the oath:

> I had all kinds of discussions with the Confessing Church people, with [Kurt] Scharf and Dibelius, in fact. In 1938, when the requirement for an oath from the pastors had come up, the Brandenburg Confessing Church had established a written declaration of loyalty. They wrote down their understanding of the oath and then sent this interpretation of the oath to the authorities responsible, saying, "When this is acknowledged, then we can swear the oath." And, apparently, people then took the oath with this declaration. In 1941, Scharf thought that I could swear it along with this, too.
>
> Then I told him that was mindless. For it was already 1941. Through the events that had happened in the meantime, it had become clear that Hitler didn't give a hoot about these church interpretations of the oath . . . It was totally clear that [the church's] version of the oath would be thrown in the wastebasket and that the oath meant a complete obligation to Hitler, and I resisted that. . . .

> I stood by my refusal, and the consequence was that the people in Wannsee said that I had to stop my work. So, practically, I was thrown out.[11]

Otto Dibelius summoned Härter and scolded her:

> He sat there with his impressive demeanor and said, "What protection must we still bring to bear for you? The Provisional Church Government, the Brandenburg Council of Brethren, the Bishop and the General Superintendent?" To which I replied that further "protection" wasn't necessary, since I was remaining by my decision.[12]

In the Hannover church, Härter's brother-in-law, Winfried Feldmann, lost an associate pastorate because of his refusal to swear the oath.[13] Both Härter and Feldmann lost their positions because of the church's stance, not because of any actions taken against them by the Nazi party. When the Confessing Church made clear that it saw no grounds for civil disobedience on the point, it may have been choosing its battles (this was certainly how Kurt Scharf saw it). But on the oath question, the church had yielded to the Nazi state on a political point that concerned private conscience.

Pastors Who Became Soldiers

This set the tone for the entire question of Confessing Church loyalties in wartime. There was virtually no discussion in the Confessing Church about the legitimacy of becoming a soldier, for example. While the prospect of fighting a war for Adolf Hitler troubled some people, national loyalties were still seen as something separate from Nazism. Confessing pastors decided that they would fight for Germany, not for Hitler. This attitude was based on the illusion that the consequences of their actions could remain as pure as their intentions. Among many Germans, there was no real enthusiasm for the war. As Helmut Gollwitzer recalled, in Dahlem:

> First, something positive: 1914 didn't repeat itself in 1939. The population was deeply depressed. One even heard at table discussions that Hitler was distressed about the lack of enthusiasm for the war among Germans.[14]

The trauma of World War I still sat deeply. In 1938, wrote Martin Broszat, Hitler was already worried that the German people would not support a war and exhorted the Nazi propaganda press to steer the public toward a more belligerent mood.[15]

The underlying gloom as the war broke out began to shift after Hitler's spectacular successes in Poland, France, and Holland. And the basic readiness to fight for the Fatherland remained — as did the belief that pacifist tendencies or criticism of the Nazi regime would only hurt Germany's cause, which had become the cause of those in uniform and their families. These sentiments were described by Dibelius in his memoirs, as he analyzed his own feelings toward the prayer liturgy controversy during the Czech crisis in 1938.

The liturgy, drafted when war seemed imminent, was controversial because it prayed not for German victory but for those whose countries would become battlefields, and it called upon Germans to resist the temptation to hate and want revenge for the defeat of 1918. Dibelius supported the liturgy. "And nevertheless," he wrote, "something was absent":

The [words of] pastoral consolation for the soldiers who had to march, and for their relatives, was missing. Lacking, too, was a sense for the fact that the church, even in the dreadful fate of a manifestly unjust war, must know itself bound with its people. National Socialism had driven this feeling thoroughly out of the theologians in Germany — but along with it, the sense in their fingertips of the effect which such a prayer liturgy, especially if war didn't break out, had to have on people. Whoever, like I, had to send three sons to war, had to feel that.[16]

Dibelius and Martin Niemöller each lost two sons in the war; almost 2,000 pastors' sons died.[17] Almost 3,000 Protestant pastors, vicars, chaplains, and theology students died on the front,[18] and half of the Confessing Church's Illegals fell in battle.[19] When Dibelius and others later spoke about the war, their emotional loyalties were to the loved ones they had lost, as well as to their nation. Understandably, they needed to believe that these had died not for the commands of a crazed Führer but for something meaningful. In explaining Martin Niemöller's motives when he tried to enlist, in 1939, Wilhelm Niemöller denied even nationalistic motives for his brother's behavior,[20] and Eberhard Bethge recalled that Wilhelm Niemöller was "furious" with him over a remark of Bethge's:

He had estimated the number of Protestant pastors who had fallen in the war at around 1,855. For the sake of the confession to Christ, however, only about 21 Protestant pastors died. I used these numbers to compare: 1,855 fell for Hitler, and only 21 against Hitler. He was furious. He couldn't bear this discussion at all.[21]

That was how they saw the role of soldiers after 1945. But what were the motives and mentality of those Confessing Church men as they went to war? Bethge recalls that, for those illegal pastors who suffered under the fact that they were not recognized as legitimate pastors,

to be an officer was a possibility to get bourgeois recognition once again. In 1938, 1939, that had almost disappeared. Suddenly, now, we could prove that we would don the gray uniform for the Fatherland and that we would fight well. . . . Many Confessing Church pastors went relatively happily and willingly.[22]

Albrecht Schönherr, one of Dietrich Bonhoeffer's students in Finkenwalde, recalled,

The people differentiated between National Socialism and national duty. That was one thing, and the other thing, I should say, is that, naturally, we were also afraid. When you think that in this war, one shouldn't have even touched a weapon. It was already clear, basically, that this was a criminal war. But to have the courage to risk one's life on that point — we just didn't have that. One has to see that much of what has been disguised was simply fear.[23]

Out of fear, patriotism, or a mixture of motives, many Confessing Church pastors enlisted. In Breslau, Heinrich Albertz was one of the Illegals:

It was an interesting thing. I wasn't at the peak of health; when the war began, I didn't have to become a soldier. It was the third of September 1939, in Breslau. Of 30 Confessing Church pastors, suddenly 20 were gone. They weren't drafted; they went voluntarily. For me, at the time, it was an unbelievable blow.[24]

The percentage of voluntary enlistments varied, of course. From his vantage point in Dahlem, Helmut Gollwitzer believed that relatively few pastors or Illegals from the Confessing Church enlisted voluntarily. But he also recalled the kinds of pressures they were under — not just internal pressures of conscience but the Nazi pressures on active Confessing Church pastors, particularly on the Illegals.[25] For them, voluntary enlistment was not necessarily a sign of deep patriotic loyalties. As Gollwitzer noted, at the onset of the war, the Gestapo developed a new tactic against the illegal pastors: They were registered as "unemployed" and, with that, sent directly to the front. Moreover, their families had no right to widows' pensions or other war benefits when these men died. For this reason, Dibelius attempted — futilely — to persuade Berlin consistory vice president Friedrich Hymmen to grant these illegal Confessing Church pastors official standing in the church, so that their dependents would be entitled to church benefits if they were killed.[26] In some churches this was done quietly, by the side.[27] But, as Gollwitzer said,

> This, of course, was a serious charge against us, when an illegal pastor — and they were good people — was suddenly sent to inspect panzers in Westwald. . . .
>
> In addition, conscientious objection had no tradition here. It was not only that it meant risking one's life, but also that we were not at all prepared for it. I can tell what happened to me. In the first week in August 1939, I spent a week in Switzerland with Karl Barth and other friends. Pierre Maury [an ecumenically active pastor who later headed the French Reformed Church] . . . was there, and Visser t'Hooft [a Dutch ecumenist who helped found the World Council of Churches] from Geneva. We saw that war was imminent. Karl Barth wanted the ecumenical world to tell Christians in Germany: This is an unjust war.
>
> Naturally, we hesitated. Perhaps it was partly rationalization, but we found theological and political grounds to prevent this from being done. Barth was very angry. He then asked Pierre Maury and me: "You'll face each other, Christian brothers and friends! What will you do?" I said, "Jesus will show me. I don't know."
>
> I returned to Germany. The war began. . . . Hermann Stöhr [the secretary of the German branch of the International Fellowship of Reconciliation], with whom I had mutual friends, had refused to go . . . ; he was offered various alternatives: an office position, as a medical orderly, and so on. He refused everything, and was shot. He still got word to us that he didn't see his path as an obligation for all of us. He had simply felt himself called to refuse it.
>
> I had been banished from Berlin on September 3, 1939. Several generals had managed to get me drafted into the Wehrmacht, because banishment was frequently the prelude to being sent to a concentration camp and because a Wehrmacht uniform kept you out of the concentration camps. My orders to the Wehrmacht came on December 5. All this with the fate of Hermann Stöhr in my head. I'm not sure what clinched the matter for me, my cowardice or my theological reasons. Only God knows. A deeply devout woman in the parish let me go with the promise: "You should be there for your comrades. The Christians there need us too, and you will never shoot a person for Hitler." As it was, it was my intention never to do that, and so I went.[28]

Like Gollwitzer, Karl Steck observed that refusing military service simply did not occur to most people (and the few who did refuse, like Hermann Stöhr, were executed). Steck, a professor of systematic theology (he married Gollwitzer's secretary, Elsie Steck, during the war), was partly responsible for the education and examination of illegal Confessing Church pastors in the "German Christian" controlled church in Hesse. Steck was able to work with the young ministry candidates until the war began. Then he was banished from Hesse by the Gestapo, and the young Illegals under his care were drafted,

> one after the other. Many are no longer living. But I can't recall that we really debated questions about military service and the Wehrmacht and the Nazis. We crept into the Wehrmacht. I was in prison for a short time. I was banished, then I was drafted, and, with that, I escaped a trial before the *Sondergericht* [Gestapo court]. My military superior declared that I was indispensable, that I couldn't attend the proceedings. He held his hand over me. That is completely different, right? Particularly for those of us who stood on the edge, the Wehrmacht was something like a cover.[29]

One of the young Illegals in Hesse was Rudolf Weckerling, who was brought to trial before a *Sondergericht*. He was acquitted on one count, and his sentence was commuted to the time already served on the other. Weckerling, too, recalled that the Wehrmacht rescued him from further Nazi persecution. Warned by friends to leave Hesse after his trial, Weckerling went to Berlin:

> I was summoned to the Gestapo headquarters on May 6, 1940, here in Berlin, and there I was forbidden to speak [publicly] or work in the Reich. It was the substitution for a concentration camp, so to speak. It meant that I was utterly crippled and could do something for the Confessing Church only illegally.[30]

Through the intervention of Kurt Scharf and the Brandenburg Council of Brethren, Weckerling was placed in two rural parishes, despite Gestapo orders forbidding him to work. Scharf, as Weckerling recalled,

> knew people. There was someone in the Gestapo office, the son of a pastor, and Scharf had an unbelievable knack for negotiating openly and directly. . . . My first draft notice to the military came while I was in prison in Giessen. The second notice came while I was in these two parishes in Göbin. I had just had a small motorcycle accident; I arrived in the barracks, and the chief medical officer there held me back for a quarter year. I was finally drafted on June 6, 1941.[31]

For some in the Confessing Church, the Wehrmacht represented a haven from Gestapo harassment and even imprisonment. Through various contacts in military and government offices, as well as in the official church, a number of Confessing Church pastors were placed either in more benign sectors like the medical corps or in units commanded by officers sympathetic to the Confessing Church. Those assigned to civilian duty, like the women theologians in the Confessing Church, were sometimes able to negotiate their hours or receive assignments that enabled them to continue their church duties. In the official church consistory in Berlin, Elisabeth Schwarzhaupt mediated sometimes between the Illegals and government bureaucrats:

> They [the Confessing Church members] came sometimes, particularly to me or to Herr [Heinz] Brunotte. For example, the people from Burckardthaus [Note: a small church college in Berlin that trained women for church work; although part of the official church, it served as a refuge for many of the illegal women theologians in the Confessing Church] came to us when they had difficulties, and we helped a bit behind the scenes, as much as we could. We also had people in the ministry for church affairs who occasionally gave us advice.

I can give the following as an example. A teacher at Burckardthaus, Anna Paulsen, who was a well-known theologian then, was to be called up to civilian duty in the war. Now, of course, she had been drafted at the request of the Gestapo, to pull her away from her work. At that time, I went to the ministry for church affairs to complain about it. The official sat there on his swivel chair and told me that he couldn't do anything, but he could give me a piece of advice. In the ministry of employment there was a high government counsel who was the son of a pastor and who, with the minister's agreement, worked against turning the service obligation for war-related work into a political matter. On many occasions this man had already managed to rescind service obligations requested by the Gestapo.

With that I visited this man, who, with the help of his minister, did in fact achieve a principle that was somewhat followed: service obligations for war-related work only for real reasons, and not at the request of the Gestapo. In this way, we got Anna Paulsen and a number of other men and women vicars in the Confessing Church free again.[32]

At times, even the Wehrmacht was independent enough of Gestapo pressure to protect Confessing Church members under its jurisdiction. In 1969, Klara Hünsche, one of the Confessing Church's most active women theologians, wrote Wolfgang Gerlach that she had had no trouble continuing her illegal activities (which included work at a Christian school for "non-Aryan" children) during the war, although she had been called for wartime civilian duty:

Since the Wehrmacht protected us from the Gestapo, we could continue to work. I was not removed from my office on the Council of Brethren nor from my work at this school, although my "employer" was now the Wehrmacht.[33]

After the war, such recollections contributed to the widespread impression that the German Wehrmacht had consisted mainly of honorable military men, opposed to Hitler and innocent of any wartime atrocities. Nazi atrocities were blamed on the Waffen-SS (the fighting elite of the Nazi SS under the command of Heinrich Himmler).

Organizationally, the Wehrmacht and the Waffen-SS were separate until December 1941, when Hitler became commander-in-chief of the Wehrmacht. Throughout the war, some individual military officers in the Wehrmacht did indeed protect Confessing Church pastors in their units, even making special arrangements so that people like Ludwig Schlaich (see Chapter 6) could get leave to tend to their church duties. And, increasingly, some officers in the military became critical of the way Hitler ran the war; they formed the core of the July 20, 1944 attempt to assassinate the Führer and take command of the government.

Nationalistic Feeling and Private Conviction

But even the dissident voices within the military faced the dilemma that paralyzed Confessing Christians: the contradiction between national loyalties, Nazi goals, and private convictions. Although critical of Nazi leadership, they did not want to see Germany defeated in the war. On some level, subjugating oneself to command means aligning oneself with it; a soldier fighting on the front cannot maintain private opposition to what he is doing for very long. Helmut Gollwitzer described the crisis of conscience faced by those who fought in the war:

> I can still see a whole row of our young Confessing Church vicars who had been drafted, most not having enlisted voluntarily, and they planned to be witnesses for Christ in their companies. But they also planned to be respectable soldiers, and I intended to be that as well. When I became a soldier, the "Ten Commandments of the German Soldier" was still printed in the payment book. Those were respectable things from the Prussian tradition—not to plunder, for example, and that civilians and unarmed prisoners were no longer enemies, but were to be treated decently. At the beginning of the war against Russia, Hitler had that page torn out.
>
> I was protected and had been placed in the medical corps. But many Confessing Church pastors were in the front line troops and certainly did their duty as German soldiers, and shot. With the war against Russia, a psychological barrier fell. "Now we have to defend our homeland against the Bolshevists." This motive hadn't been there before, but then, in the military campaigns in the West, the war hadn't been so degenerate.[34]

Anti-Communism and racist attitudes toward the Slavs and other Eastern European peoples had helped bring the Nazis to power in 1933. Now these prejudices were used to legitimize German brutality in Poland, Russia, and other lands to the east of Germany. Martin Schröter, who fought in the East and in France, recalled that the war was almost a "crusade" for soldiers fighting on the eastern front.[35] Nazi propaganda inflamed border incidents and long-existent tensions between the Germans and Poles into horror stories. And, as Helmut Gollwitzer recalled, many Germans

> believed the propaganda about the atrocities, Hitler's fraudulent propaganda. The discomforts that the Germans endured there [in Poland] were inflated into a call to murder in the radio broadcasts here. "Bloody Sunday"[36] in Poland, where the Germans in Poland had been mistreated and some were killed—they held on to that throughout the entire war as the reason for the German treatment of the Poles.[37]

The German forces tried to reduce Russia and Poland to ashes, forcibly deporting millions from the eastern zones to the German Reich to work, mostly in war-related industries. By 1944, these seven million displaced persons, basically treated as slaves, made up 20 percent of the German labor force.[38] While the French, British, and Dutch were not spared German barbarity, the extent of the atrocities committed on the eastern front far exceeded what happened in the west. Colonel Hellmuth Stieff, who served on the Army General Staff, wrote to his wife describing the destruction in Poland and concluded his letter, "I am ashamed to be a German!"[39] Stieff was one of those whose war experiences gradually moved them toward resistance; he was executed after the July 20, 1944 attempt on Hitler's life.

As long as he served as pastor in Dahlem, Helmut Gollwitzer heard the confessions of some of the ministers and military officers who lived there:

> Some of them belonged to the Confessing Church. There were some occasions for confidential talks, and for those who were searching to lighten their consciences. Many knew, after the invasion of Poland had been won, how horrible the situation in Poland was, not only for the Jews but for the Poles as well. In [Nazi] party circles, I

heard the word "cortezization," which meant that we would treat the Poles just as Cortez had treated the Mexicans [Indians].

When the campaign against France began, I made a rather cynical wager with an important businessman who was unsympathetic to Hitler. He couldn't be convinced that Hitler would deal with the French exactly as he had done with the Poles. We bet a bottle of champagne, very cynically. But my prediction wasn't right; his was. Thank God, he was right. Hitler's reckoning with the French was totally different than with the Poles.[40]

One of the Confessing Church pastors who was in the troops invading Poland was Herbert Mochalski:

> I saw horrible things. . . . I'll never forget the scenes, how people dug ditches out on the land, and all around them the SS was standing, and it was perfectly clear what was happening. It's nonsense when a German soldier says—above all, concerning the invasion of the Soviet Union—that he never saw anything, that the soldiers didn't know anything. It's all simply not true! Rather, it was all so obvious. Or when we drove through the little towns, then one saw how the Jews were at the marketplace, and the SS men stood there and tore their beards out. Or how the Poles were loaded up. It's simply not true that we Germans didn't know what happened, where the soldiers had been.
>
> Thank God, I became sick, due to an ulcer, which isn't surprising . . . and came to the hospital. There was a series of officers, above all, the heads of the Military Action Headquarters, who belonged to the Confessing Church and now tried to do everything to get us out.[41]

Mochalski managed to stay out, and after Gollwitzer was sent to the front in 1941, took over Gollwitzer's duties as an illegal Confessing Church pastor in Dahlem. At the same time, Mochalski was drafted for civilian duty at a desk job in the munitions industry in Berlin; in 1944, he went to a small parish in Württemberg. But the scenes from Poland continued to haunt him:

> One saw it only driving by, you know? We sat on our trucks and saw it . . . so that we had no chance to learn what the SS was thinking. All right, we could, we should, have protested then, but how?. . . We wouldn't have changed anything. I mean, all that is no excuse. Indeed, we all failed in this respect, that things went that far at all, isn't that so? And that is the awful thing that weighs on all of us, up to today.[42]

Martin Schröter, son of a Confessing Church pastor in Breslau, was preparing to start his theological studies when the war began. Only after 1945 did he realize how much his conservative nationalist background had colored his attitudes toward the war. Schröter recalled how he and his fellow soldiers sarcastically referred to the SS troops as *Goldfasanen*—gold pheasants—because their uniforms were so ornate; yet, ideologically, he had been so prepared for war that he believed in a German victory right up to the end. He came from a home that, although patriotic, was anti-Nazi, but he saw the defeat of Germany and the defeat of Hitler as two different things:

> We were of the firm conviction that we had to win the war first, and then we would put an end to the brown rabble [the Nazis]. That we ourselves, from the top down, were essentially just chess figures for Hitler and his generals—that was unimaginable for us.[43]

Schröter and his fellow soldiers were not formally indoctrinated for the war against Russia. That had already occurred — in history lessons in school and in the "German National" sentiments so prevalent in Protestant homes. Formal indoctrination, commented Schröter,

> wasn't at all necessary anymore. It was anti-democratic propaganda, antiparliamentary propaganda, anticommunist — everything was thrown into one pot. Basically, that was what we had sworn to, politically. To that extent, as the war turned against the Soviet Union, that was tied up for us through and through with a crusade mentality. We were well armed ideologically for that. . . .
>
> When I think about the first major battle, the whole thing was expressed through the drumrolls. That was the great pathos, but it was basically only a symbolic concentration of this entire mixture of *Weltanschauungen* that had been stirred up within us. . . .
>
> The soldiers' oath to the flag didn't present any difficulties for me. "I swear, by God, this holy oath, that I will give unconditional obedience to the Führer and Reichskanzler of the German people, Adolf Hitler, etc." I still know the first two lines today. . . . Basically, I can say that I thought, right till the end, that we had to win the war. Even though, basically, it [defeat] was almost palpable. But, without any doubt, I successfully repressed the thought that we would lose it. . . . The idea that the war could be lost came very, very late.[44]

What were the real differences between the soldiers in the Wehrmacht and the more highly indoctrinated, committed Nazis in the SS units? If there was such a difference between them, why was the overall course of the war, and the behavior of the German army in the occupied countries, so brutal? Eberhard Bethge speculated:

> I would think that, initially, things were still developing. I think now specifically of General von Blaskovitz. He was named military commander in Poland, and thought that, as had previously been the case in wartime, he would be the one accountable. In the fall of 1939–1940, he realized that his power of command had been utterly reduced and limited by the SS units — that the SS troops in Poland played a role, and that he could not interfere, either through a military court or in any other way. Once he realized this, von Blaskovitz resigned.[45]
>
> For those of us in the Bonhoeffer family, this was naturally a very dreadful omen — to see that the army, with its so-called clean shield, couldn't stand up to this. There was a second army [the SS] that could appeal to Hitler and Himmler. . . .
>
> Shortly before the invasion of Russia, a so-called Commissar's Command came down from Hitler, which said that when we marched into Russia, every political commissar officer in the Russian army would be shot without a hearing.[46] The Commander-in-Chief von Brauchitsch[47] passed this command on to the army without hesitation, instead of saying that a German unit couldn't do something like that. I believe that, with that, the descent to a lower level was sealed, so that the difference between the army and the SS was greatly reduced.
>
> But to the question about the behavior of the army: First, they differentiated between whether they were defending Germany or whether they were really defending Hitler. Most of those from the Confessing Church said, "Now we have to defend Germany. It's no longer interesting how it came to this. We stand in deathly danger for our country. It's regrettable that our commander is Hitler, but that isn't the priority." With this belief, they carried on.[48]

Yet, many of these soldiers expressed despair in their letters home. One young theologian, Bengt Seeberg (who died in 1944), wrote,

> Sometimes I try to imagine our future existence, but then a mild horror always comes over me. . . . It will bring little joy to work on the reconstruction of the ruins, in the spiritual as well as in the external respect. . . . One thing is clear to me: Whatever the conclusion of this war, it will leave a massive wound. Fundamentally, no one is his own master anymore.[49]

Germany's defeat in Russia in the winter of 1941–1942, and at Stalingrad in 1942, was the turning point for Nazi fortunes in the war and a serious blow to the morale and convictions of German soldiers. (Between June and December 1941, the German military lost a quarter of its troops on the Russian front; only 6,000 of the 130,000 German soldiers at Stalingrad returned home after having been held in Russian prisoner of war camps.[50]) Among the men in his own unit, Helmut Gollwitzer said, feelings turned against Hitler only after the heavy losses in Stalingrad:

> Then things changed. I still remember the night before we left for Russia. Stalingrad had just fallen. We heard Göring's eulogy for the fallen German soldiers in Stalingrad on the radio. As he said, "Amen," we went to our trucks to drive to Russia. As we were lying that last time in our quarters, I remember how, after a somber silence, one soldier, of whom I would never have thought it, said, "Helmut, how can one criminal wage such a war, a war against his entire people?" That was the mood.
>
> But Goebbels said one true thing: "The gripes of a soldier are like gas pains; they're necessary." That's true. When a soldier goes through the mud and filth, such complaints can't be seen politically. The longer the war in Russia went on, the more people felt that it was a war of existence for Germany. . . .
>
> I must say one thing more to your question about the Confessing Church pastors as soldiers. . . . Whoever belonged to the Confessing Church was disqualified automatically for the military chaplaincy, and, in many cases, disqualified for officers' rank. I was a normal infantrist for one year. Only as I was about to be promoted to officer, I said, "I can't," and I signed up instead to be a medical orderly. The highest death rates in a normal war in the nineteenth and twentieth centuries have been among the infantry soldiers. But the death rate — I can't give figures, but only a general statement — the death rate among pastors and vicars of the Confessing Church was greater.[51]
>
> With that, you can see the qualitative losses that our people and our church suffered. During the Confessing Church years, we brought our best people together from the various regional churches, once or twice a year, for retreats. Of the 35 people that we had at a retreat in Coburg in 1938 or 1939, only 5 were still alive after 1945.[52]

Confessing Church Women during the War

The absence of the Confessing Church pastors and vicars was already felt by German parishes during the war. With half of the Protestant ministry and almost all of the theological candidates gone, church leaders searched for people to lead the newly orphaned congregations. After 1945, the memoirs of most Confessing Church pastors covered the war years cursorily, as if the Confessing Church had ceased to exist once the war began — as, in a sense, it had for those men whose memories of the war years would be of the battlefield, not of the pulpit.

But the Confessing Church did continue to function under the direction of the Councils of Brethren, and its skirmishes with the official consistories in various regions did not end. A main point of conflict was the illegal (under the Himmler Decree) collection of offerings during Confessing worship services. The Confessing Church and its pastors refused to give these collections to the consistories; instead, the money went to support illegal pastors and vicars and their families.[53] Moreover, some profound changes occurred during the war years. One was that, with so many men gone on the front, women assumed leadership of many parishes. Some were pastors' wives who simply took over their husbands' duties. There were also the women who had completed their theological studies in the 1920s and 1930s and attended the illegal seminaries of the Confessing Church, but who had not dreamed that they might be ordained, let alone be given pastorates.

After 1939, opportunities for these women suddenly increased. Doris Faulhaber had completed her doctorate in 1935. But for her and the nine other women in the Baden regional church who had completed theological studies, job possibilities within the church remained limited to working with parish women's groups or teaching religion to schoolchildren:

> But the war was our big chance, because almost all the men had to go, and the parishes, to a large extent, had been orphaned. Now there was a church councilman in the church administration who had been very conservative up to them, and very disdainful . . . and then, in the war, he apparently thought to himself: "Who do I still have [who could] take care of this or that parish?" And he thought of the nine women theologians. Apparently he thought something of us — that we were capable of something. And we were all put into pastorates, as substitutes, of course.[54]

Of necessity, Faulhaber and most other women in her situation were given not one but several positions. Faulhaber was made chaplain of a hospital in Mannheim, and, in addition, pastored a parish in a nearby village. But, although the church in Baden and other regions began entrusting women with parishes, church officials remained reluctant to ordain them. Most churchmen remained dubious that women pastors had much to offer male parishioners and believed that the ordination of women was not only inappropriate but even unhealthy for the German Evangelical Church. As one Confessing Church pastor wrote,

> The great danger exists that the transformation of the church to a "women's church" will be eased by the ordination of women. . . . Through this development, the church, eventually, would dissolve downright into a "women's club."[55]

At the beginning of the war, there were about 100 active *Vikarinnen* (women vicars) in the Berlin-Brandenburg church;[56] and there were several hundred women throughout Germany who had completed their theological education in the 1920s and 1930s.[57] They remained barred from many vocational opportunities, including the parish ministry. The rapidity with which the status of theologically trained women changed after 1939 illustrates how badly the church needed these women during the war years. As the number of wartime vacancies grew, the regional churches began

"ordaining" or "consecrating" lay elders, deaconesses, and women. These "ordinations," however, were seen as exceptions (in fact, they were performed under the
Notrecht clause), and those "ordained" were still barred, in most cases, from preaching and giving the sacraments.

In 1940, the *Vikarinnen* petitioned the national Council of Brethren for full ordination. "Experience has shown," they wrote,

> that *Vikarinnen* must now take over precisely those pastoral functions which have
> always been barred to them. . . . In parishes where there is either no Confessing pas-
> tor or no pastor at all, a Confessing *Vikarin* is either there or can be placed there.[58]

The petition was rejected, but the women continued to press their case, and some
influential men in the Confessing Church supported them — among them Kurt Scharf
(member of the Brandenburg Council of Brethren) and Martin Albertz, superintendent of the Berlin Confessing Church. Finally, in October 1942, the national Synod
of the Confessing Church approved the "emergency ordination" of its women theologians, granting them full rights to preach and administer the sacraments. In Baden
(which was not led by Confessing Christians), Faulhaber and the other women were
"consecrated" in 1944:

> We petitioned again and again that we wanted to be ordained, that we were already
> substitutes in these offices, and that we wanted to be admitted officially to the office
> of pastor. The church administration — here I'm speaking only of Baden — under-
> stood that, in part, and permitted us to have the *Talar* [the pastor's robes and col-
> lar]. . . . In 1944, we were "consecrated." That is, they avoided the term "ordained,"
> since that remained reserved for men. But it was basically the same thing, and the
> church counts it as such today. . . . I had taken my exams in 1930 and was "conse-
> crated" 14 years later; and the eldest of us had taken her exams in 1919 and was
> "consecrated" in 1944.[59]

In other circumstances, the fight for ordination might have consumed the
women's energies. But with the war and the continuing struggles of the Confessing
Church under Nazism, ordination, although important, was secondary to the more
pressing situations that confronted the women daily. Annemarie Grosch, who had
been one of the illegal students at the Confessing Church seminary in Berlin, was one
whose life and work were altered drastically by the war. Together with Götz Grosch
(her future husband, one of Dietrich Bonhoeffer's students), she worked as an illegal
Vikarin under Gerhard Jacobi, the Confessing Church pastor at the large Kaiser-Wilhelm-Memorial Church in downtown Berlin. Jacobi ministered to Confessing Church
members at that church privately, since the parish was not part of the Confessing
Church (the head pastor there was a "German Christian"). As Grosch recalled, the
Confessing Christians existed as a "foreign body" in the parish. Nevertheless, Grosch
described the head pastor as an "honorable" man who, despite his "German Christian" affiliation, allowed the Confessing Church Bible groups to meet in the church.

In the fall of 1939, Grosch had to replace Jacobi, who enlisted and was sent to the
front. (Gollwitzer recalled that the Berlin Council of Brethren met and approved
Jacobi's enlistment, because he had come under such pressure from the Gestapo in
Berlin.[60]) Shortly thereafter, Götz Grosch was drafted. At the same time, Annemarie

Grosch was drafted for civilian wartime duty by the Berlin air civil defense headquarters to stand night duty during air raids:

> Nevertheless, I continued my work at Kaiser-Wilhelm-Memorial at the same time. I started in the mornings, after being on watch all night at the civil defense headquarters in Berlin, and held the confirmation classes for Jacobi, with 80 confirmation girls. I didn't have any idea how I should do it; the discipline was terrible. I didn't have anyone who could advise me; moreover, I was wrecked from the nights.[61]

Grosch's application to be exempted from her nightly watch duty was successful; the "German Christian" pastor at Kaiser-Wilhelm-Memorial Church went to the employment office with his Nazi party insignia on his lapel to get Grosch released from her wartime duties.[62] After the arrest and trial of the Confessing Church seminary *(Kirchliche Hochschule)* examination committee in 1941, however, she and other illegal students were reassigned (or, in some cases, received additional assignments) to civilian war duties, like working in the munitions industry. It was a Gestapo tactic to place new pressures on the Illegals and make their work in the Confessing Church more difficult. Despite this, Grosch continued at Kaiser-Wilhelm-Memorial, where, after April 1940, she was the only Confessing Church worker there:

> Now the Confessing Church had connections everywhere, and tried to place us in the war factories in such a way that we could continue to carry out the work of the Confessing Church somehow. For example, I was placed in a practicum with a social worker at Siemens, at the conducting factory in Berlin-Spandau. I divided my work there so that I had time for parish work.[63]

She worked every day of the week and continued her parish work, often in the evenings. In the meantime, she became engaged to Götz Grosch; they were married during his one leave from the front, in the fall of 1942. Looking ahead, Grosch reasoned that if Hitler won the war, she would have to earn a living in some other way. Like many others in the Confessing Church, she expected that the Nazis would eliminate the Confessing Church eventually. In 1942, she began training as a physical therapist at a rehabilitation center, the Oskar-Helene-Heim, in Berlin.

> I was already 28, 10 years older than the other young students. Because they were short of physical therapists, I received some degree of responsibility very quickly. I was surprised to be elected the speaker of our group by the class. . . . They all knew that I was a trained theologian. I've always held it to have been more than just an election; there was certainly something behind it. . . . It had some kind of inner significance. In a class of 20 young women, some of whom belonged to the BDM [Bund Deutscher Mädel, the Nazi group for girls] it meant more.
>
> In the Oskar-Helene-Heim, you did well not to say too much at all. My fellow students would come to me privately and ask me this or that, because they sensed, somehow: There had to be something behind this theologian. You didn't talk politics with the patients. Most of them were soldiers who were very silent about their war experiences, just as my husband was.
>
> One of them remains unforgettable. She came and asked me whether she should marry a very high SS leader, who was one of Hitler's closest colleagues. . . . My God, what should I say? . . . This question burdened me greatly. But what should I say? She was an enchanting girl, head over heels in love. I only know that she must

have noticed my reservations. She asked me around 1943, shortly before I stopped there, when anyone who wasn't a totally mad Nazi could already figure out how the war would end. But one doesn't ask that when one is in love; then one naturally wants to go through thick and thin with the other person, and is blind.

I continued to do my parish work secretly. In February 1943, though, a great change came. My mother died of cancer. Now I was needed at home, and then in July 1943, my husband was killed and I stopped at once with my training, because now it had lost all meaning for me. As a war widow, I was freed for one year from civilian duty. I was never called up again, and continued my work for the church until the end of the war. . . .

At the same time that I was released from civilian duty through the death of my husband, the Confessing Church gave me a parish in Reinickendorf, in the north of Berlin, in addition to the work at Kaiser-Wilhelm-Memorial. This meant that I was on the road for every Bible study for eight hours: four hours going and four hours back with the streetcar, because the air raids always came. I crouched somewhere along the streetcar line, in a cellar or bunker. If anything had happened, I simply would have been gone, never again to surface. But these Bible studies were so intense that today, one can't even describe them, because they were so existential.[64]

Grosch recalled wryly that the Bible studies were the only Confessing Church activities officially permitted by Nazi authorities:

With that, the National Socialist state thought that they were pulling people away from us, so to speak, because in their eyes, the Bible was something boring and pious. Under this constraint, we discovered that the Bible can be dynamite when it's correctly interpreted. . . .

These war years in Berlin, in 1943, when these horrible air raids began, were apocalyptic, somehow. I remember the first big attack, in November 1943, shortly after the death of my husband, that is. Kaiser-Wilhelm-Memorial burned, too — that was the destruction [the church was completely destroyed except for the outer walls; the shell of the church was left standing after 1945 as a memorial]. I was in the parish. . . . Somewhere in the area there was a munitions depot, something from the military, anyhow — and that was always a target of attack. It caught fire, and there were also firebombs. Afterward, when I wanted to buy something — the people there didn't know me, I should add that, it's important — the owner of the shop was talking with another customer whom she knew and said, "This is the punishment for what we've done to the Jews." So, we did indeed know that much, that something wasn't right. And she dared to say that much, although I was a strange customer in her shop, and she didn't know me.[65]

In October 1943, Grosch and five other *Vikarinnen* in the Confessing Church were ordained: "We were to be ordained in the church to which I belonged, the Annenkirche [in Dahlem] in which I had married, in which the funeral for my mother and the memorial service for my husband had been held."[66] It had been Martin Niemöller's church, then Gollwitzer's. Two hours before the ceremony was to take place, the Gestapo surrounded the church. As Sieghild Jungklaus, one of the women ordained with Grosch, recalled, "The whole [Confessing] Church was nervous about it. The Gestapo, of course, didn't want any Confessing Church pastors, let alone women, ordained."[67] Last-minute arrangements were made to move the ordination to the nearby Confessing parish in Lichterfelde. Because it was dusk by the time the ceremony began, candles were lit throughout the church; the building had no air raid blinds. Jungklaus, who had brought her youth group along to the ordination, recalled that, emerging from the church, they saw the "Christmas trees" — the lights in the heavens above Berlin which showed that an air attack was approaching. As quickly as she could, she took them to the nearest shelter.

As Grosch's account shows, routine parish duties and ceremonies were often dangerous. Moreover, the Confessing Church worried about losing ground, because of the increasing number of vacancies, to conservative or even "German Christian" factions. This led to cross-regional exchanges, where a pastor from Berlin, for example, would be sent to a parish in Württemberg; in normal times, this was unusual in Germany's provincially bound church system. A number of Illegals took their exams or found temporary placements in Württemberg, with the approval of Bishop Wurm. As Sieghild Jungklaus, who took her second exam in Württemberg, recalled, this offered the protection of a "legal" exam to the candidates (an exam taken in the intact church of Württemberg was recognized both by the Confessing Church and by official church authorities[68]).

The Confessing Church had another influential friend in Württemberg — Hermann Diem, head of the "Society," the group of pastors in that intact church who had become members of the Confessing Church. In 1941, Diem asked Ilse Härter to work in his parish in Ebersbach, near Stuttgart. Härter, whom Kurt Scharf had moved to another parish after she had lost her position in Wannsee over the loyalty oath issue, accepted. She and Diem consciously decided to accustom the conservative parish gradually to the phenomenon of a woman pastor. In September 1943, when Diem was drafted, Härter remained:

> After he was drafted, it was completely taken for granted that I would do the entire work. . . . One day a letter arrived from a high church council official that it had come to his attention that, in Ebersbach, a woman was not only preaching in a *Talar* from the pulpit but was holding funerals as well. . . . It subsequently became clear that Diem and I hadn't known anything about a high church council order [in Württemberg] that practically forbade women from substituting in wartime vacancies. I personally don't know whether Diem really didn't know about it or whether he simply wanted, as usual, to get his own way with the church council — especially since he didn't want the replacement that the council wanted to send for him. He knew very well that the council would send someone who wouldn't work according to his [Diem's] beliefs.[69]

In Württemberg, only active or retired pastors could fill a wartime vacancy, although certain duties, like teaching confirmation classes, could be carried out by women. But with so many pastors gone, an enormous burden was put upon their replacements. Many were too old for military duty and, basically, too old to travel many kilometers each week, under the restrictions of wartime travel, to minister to village parishes. In addition, many of them had civilian wartime duties.

This was the case throughout Germany. In Brandenburg, Heinrich Vogel had continued, until his trial in 1941, to direct the Confessing Church seminary in Berlin and minister to his parish (whereby, as he noted, his wife took over many of his parish duties). In addition, he had to work nights as a radio transmitter for the military.

My age and my many children permitted me to be assigned here in my homeland, as a radio transmitter. So I could preach in my parishes on the side. They were a few miles from each other; that could be done by bicycle, through the meadows and fields of Brandenburg. After the night shift, I sat on my bicycle, drove through the meadows and fields, preached first at 9 a.m. and in my other village at 11 a.m. Then it was noon, and then I went to bed.[70]

Despite the number of pastors doing double duty, many parishes were left without a pastor. With these arguments, Ilse Härter and her Ebersbach parish negotiated with the church administration in Stuttgart; eventually she was allowed to replace Diem there until August 1944, when she was called back to Brandenburg to fill a vacancy there. Härter was ordained on January 12, 1943, together with another *Vikarin*, Hannelotte Reiffen. The ordination was almost canceled:

At the last minute, Dibelius put in his veto when he heard that we would be wearing the *Talar*. The evening before, Reiffen, Diem, and I went to Dibelius. We had worked out among ourselves that we would tell Dibelius that it would be liturgically disgraceful if one was there in a red dress and the other in green, and that, therefore, the *Talar* had to be worn. We laughed all the way to Dibelius. I can still see us going through Berlin; we walked arm in arm through the winter night. It was very slippery. We supported each other and amused ourselves royally about how we would teach Dibelius in this fashion. He swallowed it, too, since he agreed that it was liturgically impossible if the two *Vikarinnen* didn't have black dresses![71]

Church Nationalism and Impending Defeat

On the issue of the ordination of women (and on other questions that arose during the Nazi era), the Confessing Church's radicality was tempered by the Lutheran tradition in which many of its members had been raised. Yet, the political excesses of Nazism compelled some church leaders to re-examine their beliefs in a number of areas, particularly with respect to their nationalism and the theological underpinnings of that nationalism.

One of the most moving examples of this was Württemberg's Bishop Wurm, who, during the course of the war, began to speak more and more directly against the Nazi regime. At the height of the Allied bombing of German cities, Wurm recalled the churches' silence on November 9, 1938 and told a Stuttgart congregation that the Allied destruction of Germany was "God's revenge for that which was done to the Jews."[72] Because of Wurm's renown, Nazi authorities hesitated to arrest him (although he was warned by one friend in the government to be more guarded in his public statements). Other pastors who preached similar messages were executed, like Karl Friedrich Stellbrink in Lübeck.[73]

The contrast between Wurm and his colleague in Hannover, Bishop Marahrens, was striking. Both men were bishops of "intact" churches (undivided by the *Kirchenkampf*) and committed to a moderate course within the church. Both wanted to preserve the Protestant church against outside ideological influences, and both men viewed the more radical branch of the Confessing Church critically. Both were nationalists, but the course of the Third Reich and the war brought about a change of heart in Wurm that it did not in Marahrens. When Germany invaded Russia, the German Evangelical Church's Spiritual Confidential Council (chaired by Marahrens) sent a telegram to Hitler asking that God "give our hearts the ruthless decisiveness" to fight the war "free of all sentimentality."[74] Wurm—horrified—wrote to Marahrens in protest that the Germans had brought their suffering upon themselves:

> Christendom, too, must suffer, because it hasn't called injustice [by its name] more openly and more unanimously. Should it now be the Church that represses these thoughts in favor of an uninhibited passion for war?[75]

Even then, such criticism did not necessarily reflect the wish for German defeat, and the daily pressures of wartime life further hampered any genuine reduction in patriotic feelings. Christian Berg, at that time a pastor in Württemberg, described the mood among his parishioners during the course of the war:

> It was a gloomy slide into our fate. I believe that many people were not at all clear about what ship they were sitting on. In this parish, to the extent that they still held to the church, criticism, uneasiness, and rejection became sharper and stronger. Especially since in our area there was a place where Hitler had let the mentally ill die—the "unworthy life." That had gotten around. And there were naturally always some who listened to the BBC at night and had heard the reports about Auschwitz and the gassings of the Jews, and so on. That seeped through. And the numbness became more and more horrible. . . .
>
> It was hard to bear. The services for the fallen soldiers were hard, too. When the news of a fallen soldier came from Russia, it was customary to hold a service in his memory. I strictly refrained from using any nationalistic phrases in the homily. "For *Volk*, Fatherland and Führer____has fallen on the field of honor"—that's how many of the notices in the newspapers read.[76]

Instead, Berg stated, he said

> Nothing. Absolutely nothing . . . mostly, we held the picture of the fallen soldier before our eyes—what he had meant in the parish and what we had lost. That was dreadful. Above all as it became more frequent.[77]

As the war went on, the inevitability of defeat became clear. Martin Schröter's fiancée, Tüsnelda, realized this earlier than her future husband on the front. Her wartime duty was with the German occupation forces in France:

> I worked in the information service; I put through long distance calls for the officers. . . . We transmitted newspaper reports. From that, I knew what had happened in Stalingrad. It could be read very clearly and unadorned that, with this [Stalingrad], our chance to win the war had been wiped out. The shock in the German papers was so great that we could read that out of them. . . . I was denounced afterward to my chief, because I had told others how bad things were. I said, "It's all in the papers; read it yourself." But that didn't have any effect, and I was never allowed again to work on the newspaper reports. . . . I had many friends among the soldiers; we talked about these things a great deal.[78]

Particularly as the course of the war turned against Germany, enthusiasm for the war and for the Nazi leaders diminished. Those who recalled this the most, of course, were those who remained behind in parishes. Karl Steck, banished from Hesse, had found a small parish in the intact Lutheran church in Bavaria. After he was sent to the front, his new bride, Elsie Steck, assumed his duties there. The difference between the Bavarian parish and Dahlem stunned her. Although her new parishioners "weren't glowing National Socialists," they took it for granted that Nazism and Christianity could co-exist peacefully. Coming from the radical parish of Dahlem, Steck believed otherwise. The first time she entered the parish hall,

> I saw that a picture of Hitler hung on the wall in the meeting room. I said: "That has to go." I went over and took it down. With a matter-of-factness that showed, like in Dahlem, that we didn't know any other way. The people said, "Are you mad? That's terrible! We don't dare do that!" I said, "A portrait of Hitler can't hang in a church room."[79]
>
> They regarded me as a fully uncautious, somewhat corrupt being from Dahlem who was, however, nice enough—to whom one had to say, "Be a little quiet here." A cautious parish . . . they never suspected me, and they looked out for themselves. They had one high Nazi in the parish who, later, when the Americans came, shot at them. They were careful there, and they warned me to be careful. But I didn't really experience any basic enthusiasm there, not any Nazi enthusiasm. It was really different. One spoke about how to stay alive, and how one could best organize everything, and that was that.[80]

Luise M., the wife of another Confessing Church pastor away at the front, recalled the atmosphere in her Silesian parish, where "there were very many Nazis. There was hardly a man in the parish who didn't belong to the SA or one of the other Nazi organizations."[81] As the war went on, however,

> the criticism grew. They had long since lost some of their convictions. In our youth group, too. There we spoke openly with each other, particularly over such things. . . . We increasingly suffered under the realization that there were hardly any more Jews there. When people say today that they didn't know about it, I would say: It's not that simple. One sensed it.[82]

Once it was clear that Germany was losing the war, Luise M. remembered, many more people began coming to the Confessing Church gatherings:

> They simply noticed that things couldn't go on that way. But the courage wasn't present in S., or the occasion, either, to do anything public. . . . People simply had the feeling that, as individuals, they wouldn't have any effect. You could look for the people with whom you could have contact, with whom you could speak, and whom you could trust. That's still possible primarily within the realm of the church. That was true then, and it is also true now [Note: this woman spent the postwar period in East Germany; here she is referring directly to the situation there in the early 1980s.] Sometimes, it's not possible to distinguish: Is the primary thing the disappointment with the political system, or is it really the demand for the church? I believe that this was always the case in the Confessing Church. Which is more pressing? Which is more important to the people? The reaction against the state or really to be a Christian?[83]

It was a question that continued to preoccupy the Confessing Church: Were its members involved for the right reasons? Or did some come because they had discovered within the church one of the few ideologically free spaces within Nazi Germany? The favors that some Confessing pastors received from local Nazis — warnings instead of imprisonment, officials who ignored the Confessing Church's illegal activities — indicate that some Nazis found that they, too, needed the assurance of this space. Helmut Gollwitzer was not the only Confessing Church pastor to fill the role of confessor for some Nazi officials with heavy consciences. In his parish in Sachsenhausen, Kurt Scharf recalled:

> The mother-in-law of the Reich Employment Director came to a completely different opinion during the Nazi period. She, who in 1933 was a glowing advocate of National Socialism and the "German Christian" movement, who fought with me vehemently and attacked me, came to me in 1942, at the height of the war, and declared to me that she had been fooled by the Führer. She had recognized how dreadful National Socialism was, and what guilt we had taken upon ourselves through it.[84]

But the experiences of most people who tended parishes during the war years were less dramatic. Marta S., who had enthusiastically joined the Nazi party in 1933, had married a Confessing Church Illegal. After her husband was called to military service in August 1939, Marta S. was left alone in a rural parish and was expected to carry on his work:

> Four villages belonged to the parish: ours, with 20 houses; a second one a half kilometer away, a manor house with day workers, and one village two kilometers away, with a church and 30 houses. Three were farming villages. . . . As time passed, I had to do more and more condolence visits to the relatives of fallen soldiers — young women, old parents. . . . Coffee clubs, like all "worldly" things, were forbidden for all church circles. . . . I did Bible studies, with discussions. Only a few came; the most loyal were four to six women, sometimes more, depending on the weather. . . . The confirmation classes were held at first by the appropriate neighboring pastor or by another who substituted for him. The first was deaf, both were retired; for both it was a hard trip of four kilometers. After a while, then, they handed the classes over to me. . . . I took care of cleaning the church, put up the lists of hymns, decorated the altar on festival days. Occasionally, I played the organ when the organist, a farmer, couldn't make it. . . . Several times, I read sermons out of textbooks, but they were too long and difficult for our villages, and didn't address the situation during the war. It was simpler to write one myself. The pastors' wives I knew in the Confessing Church didn't have any reservations about this, but in the lectures at our college, the significance of the office [of preacher] had been so drummed into me that I didn't want to take the liberty of doing it without an official call. In the last year of the war, I received this call, but I preached a sermon only once or twice, shortly before the end of the war.[85]

In all parishes, the repercussions of the war were visible. In Marta S.'s region,

> many forced laborers from Poland worked for the farmers. How they did depended upon whom they were with. I didn't see any way to help them. . . . My husband hardly ever had leave and couldn't help me either. So I could only try to be friendly at the occasional encounter, as far as the language allowed. Once I was brought to a dying baby; unfortunately, I didn't know how to help, since there was no question of a hospital for them. . . . I was altogether too inexperienced.[86]

For Gerda Keller, the concerns of the people she cared for were so mundane as to seem ludicrous — yet they, too, were part of wartime. Keller, one of the first women theologians in Westphalia, had been sent by the church to villages in southern Germany, where women and children from the industrial town of Dortmund had been sent to escape the Allied bombings of the Ruhr Valley:

> I had to be three days in one village and then three days somewhere else. Everywhere I came, the mayors thought they'd gotten the scum of Dortmund, because our city women didn't know what to do in a village. When they arrived in these unscathed villages, the first question was "Where's the next cinema? Where's the next hairdresser?" Here they'd been bombed out, had lived through this misery, and now they believed, "Now we're safe; now we'll have a lovely time. The state has put us up."
>
> The people from the village didn't have any workers. The men had been drafted, and the women from Dortmund understood nothing about working the land, and didn't do anything, and couldn't do anything. It was difficult, then, to say to these women: "You have to work here. You must do something. It's not reasonable to expect that the people here will care for you, if you don't help with the harvest."
>
> It was very hard to make that clear to them. They said, "We've had enough of the war, and we've given everything up, we have our men in the war, too!" . . . a coal miner's wife, well, she can't go along on the hay harvest, or a shopkeeper — she can't do it, and doesn't want to. . . . It was mainly young women with their children.[87]

The daily ironies and tragedies of war left no one untouched. Dietrich Goldschmidt's Jewish father had emigrated to England 14 days before the war broke out. His wife hoped to move there to join her husband; after the war started, that was no longer possible. She never saw him again. As Goldschmidt related,

> He was used to riding his bicycle from Wimbledon to the British Museum, even during the war, even with his deafness. On November 6, 1940 he had played "*skat*" [a card game] with two other emigrants; the warning sirens began. He said, "My housekeeper is always worried when I'm not home during the alarms," took his bicycle, and drove down Wimbledon Road. His apartment wasn't far away. On the way, a bomb hit him, and there he was dead. So his fate met him there.[88]

The War Years in the Camps

With the onset of the war, the number of camps and prisoners increased dramatically. In 1939, there were six major concentration camps: Dachau, Sachsenhausen, Buchenwald, Flossenbürg, Mauthausen, and Ravensbrück, with a total of 21,400 inmates.[89] By 1944, there were 20 concentration camps and 165 work camps; when the total number of "feeder" camps and smaller work camps assigned to industry (for example, to the munitions factories) is included, the number of camps reaches more than 1,000.[90]

By 1945, 90 percent of the concentration camp population was non-German.[91] In addition to deporting the Jews in the occupied countries, the Nazis demanded "volunteers" to work in German factories and work camps. Eventually, almost five million Eastern Europeans — many of them women and children, and including prisoners of war — were deported forcibly to German work and concentration camps.[92] These Ukrainians, Lithuanians, Poles, and other Eastern European peoples were characterized in Nazi Germany as *Untermenschen* — subhumans; there are Germans today who recall walking past these work camps and peering through the fences, the way one might observe animals in a zoo, at the starving wraiths within. Given the barest of necessities, many prisoners succumbed to starvation, cold, and diseases like typhoid or were worked and, in some cases beaten, to death.

For Dietrich Goldschmidt and many others, the war years were especially grim, and the existential struggles in wartime life were intensified by Nazi persecution. The screws tightened incrementally on all those affected by the Nazi racial laws. For Goldschmidt, as a "half-Aryan," the call came in November 1944 when he was assigned to a forced labor camp in the Organization Todt (named after Fritz Todt, Minister of Armaments and Munitions, killed in a 1942 air crash). The people in these camps longed for Hitler's defeat, haunted by the real possibility that they might not survive the Third Reich. In 1988, Goldschmidt described the camp where he was:

> The members of the Organization Todt were divided into units, similar to the military, but their task was to construct military projects . . . At first, I was in a camp with 120 men. The men were either "first-degree mixtures," like myself, or they were the "Aryan" husbands of Jewish women. Since the majority of us came from Berlin, the men shuddered during the air attacks for their wives in Berlin. The women were forced laborers in factories in Berlin. These were so-called "protected"[93] marriages, and most of these women could still live in Berlin. . . .
>
> I can speak only for the camp where I was; I don't know how the other camps of the Organization Todt looked. From my experience, I wouldn't give a grim picture of the Organization Todt. But it should be greatly considered how it was felt, subjectively, by those who were affected. I stress emphatically that the camp where *I* was was no concentration camp. That is, we were housed indeed in a military barracks, where 24 people slept instead of 16. The room was overfilled. But we had an oven in the room, and we had as much wood as we could take from the forest to heat the oven. We received our board, and we even had the chance to steal sugarbeets or potatoes from the fields, whatever we wanted, so that we had enough to eat.
>
> We had a camp commandant who screamed like a starling, but he didn't touch anyone physically. And under the most threadbare pretenses, he gave individuals weekend leaves. I had such a leave myself once.
>
> In fact, we were under the control of the Gestapo in Magdeburg. We were threatened that if we didn't obey the camp rules, and above all, if we had sex with "Aryan" women, then we would come to Buchenwald. Where I still think today what a perverse idea that was. There were two or three people in civilian dress from the Gestapo who were in charge of us, and they didn't know anything else but to warn us not to have sex with "Aryan" women! . . .
>
> Our worries increased toward the end. First, it was a shock for many in the camp when the Ardennes offensive seemed to show that the war wasn't yet coming to an end. Because naturally it was clear to every man that he would be rescued only if the war came to an end quickly. So the victory of the Allies was longed for. The worry that I, and a man with whom I had become friends, had was only that too many would desert before the end — that they would leave the camp and not come back . . . because that could be dangerous for the rest who stayed behind. So we appealed again and again to the solidarity of the inmates. That held up, too, till around the end of March 1945.[94]

Their work in the camp consisted of felling trees, clearing a field, and then loading and transporting the earth to a nearby military air base to lengthen one of the runways:

> Our worry was that the work shouldn't take too long, because we said, if we're too lazy and do too little, something will happen. With that, you can see that the whole thing wasn't a concentration camp. We had only this camp leader and a few other people who guarded us. There weren't any others. If we had done too little, then the construction firm would have complained to the Todt commanders. So we had to do enough so that it always looked as though something were being done. There are stories about how often the window panes were washed, and so on.
>
> You see that, in retrospect, or even at the time, I didn't perceive all this as especially hard. The psychological pressure was hard, and the psychological pressure weighed more heavily on those who had families. In a sense, I was a bachelor. My wife — we weren't yet married, she wasn't allowed to marry — was in Berlin; we could see each other occasionally, she came out with the train . . . But we didn't have small children, and somehow, we were calm. We were young. I was 30 years old in 1944. Most of the men who were in the camp were 20 or 30 years older than I. They could take it with less composure.[95]

As Goldschmidt indicated, the fates of those put in the work camps (as well as their perception of that fate) varied. This was true throughout the Nazi camp system. Had the Nazis won the war, it is clear that the gas chambers would have been used for other groups. But at least some of the Confessing Church people who landed in the camps survived. Hebe Kohlbrugge, the young Dutch woman who had worked for the Confessing Church in Berlin, joined the Dutch underground after she was deported from Germany. She was arrested in the spring of 1944. In September 1944, she was sent to the women's concentration camp of Ravensbrück:

> We were 40,000 women. . . . They had taken whole villages, especially from Poland, so I can't say that they were all only resistance. . . . But the Dutch people were all from the resistance. Some of them just had had Jews at home and had not been in the active underground. Anyhow, that was active enough. . . .
>
> I was placed immediately as a nurse and, as a nurse, I came out of the Dutch group. I was with Czech girls and Polish girls and no longer with the Dutch group. . . . Two nurses always had one barrack, and one barrack had 1,200 to 1,500 people, and, well, nurse, there was nothing to nurse [with]. What did we do? We went in the morning into the barracks. We had eight trays of nothing, and then the people came, and when they were very, very, very, very ill, we were allowed to bring them to the hospital. When they were a little ill, we tried to give them these aspirins or to give a bandage . . . or to speak a kind word in the hope that that might help. In the afternoon, I had to sit and [write down] long rows of ciphers, but I don't know what they meant. I knew it at the time, but I don't know now.
>
> So, actually, to nurse, we had nothing. Later on, I was put into the baby barracks, and that was nursing; I had to nurse the babies. There were quite a lot of babies born, actually one or two every day, especially Polish babies, by those who had been taken out of the villages. Also Czech babies, for the same reason. . . . But on the whole, I had around 30 babies, and I always had the same number, because as many died as were born. So looking after the babies was quite a hard job.[96]

In the Ravensbrück concentration camp 92,000 women and children died. Recalling the women who guarded them, Kohlbrugge said that many were simple shop girls, rounded up by the Gestapo or the occupation forces, and taught to be guards in the camps:

> And then the difficulty was, if they were too kind, they were sent to Auschwitz. . . . Some really tried not to be nasty, as far as they weren't seen by others. Some, of course, were awful. But you can't say that they were all sadists, no. When I was in Holland in the camp [in Fürth, before her incarceration in Ravensbrück] just to give an example, there was *Aufseherin* [overseer] Jo, a Dutch girl. What had happened to Jo? She came from a very backward family; she fell in love with a German soldier. She wanted to marry the German soldier, an SS man. . . . Then they found out that she had an aunt who had epilepsy. That was no good for a German SS man; there was no chance of [having] good children. Then they said to her, a girl of 19. . . . "If you become a guard in Fürth, you will be allowed to marry him."
>
> Well, she became a guard. She didn't know what Fürth was. So she came in, and she was shocked, but saying "I want to go away" would mean the greatest difficulty for the boy, so she didn't dare to, and would mean the greatest difficulty for herself. She didn't have the background to be like that. What did she do? . . . Every time when she came, she walked bum bum bum bum bum, so we knew from afar *Aufseherin* Jo is coming, and everything was correct when she came into the hospital. She knew exactly that she did it. She never found anything that was not in order. We did lots of things in the hospital that were not in order. But *Aufseherin* Jo never saw anything at all. . . . She never talked about it, she never said anything, she could have easily denounced me. She didn't.
>
> So that when you read about the camps like Maidanek . . . I don't know if at Maidanek there were only dirty guards . . . who, of course, were terrible and frightful. . . . But it would be wrong to say that all these girls were mean. Of course, it was wrong to remain *Aufseherin*. Jo shouldn't have done so. But where should she go? . . . I don't know what happened to her after the war.[97]

Like Kohlbrugge, those who were not consigned into the death machinery and who lived for some time in the camps got an insight into the people who worked there — and they began to differentiate between the behavior of leaders and followers. Ernst Wilm, sent to Dachau for his protests against the euthanasia program, noted that the treatment he received there varied greatly:

> One has to differentiate between the camp SS, our guards, and the leaders. The leaders — the head of the camp, the commandant — to a great extent, they were evil people. They had started as little men in the SS and risen up. The camp staff of the SS, the simple SS people, grew milder and milder, in part because they were simply transferred to the SS from the air force. They weren't even asked. Now they were our guards, and they said to us: "I'm not here voluntarily. I can't come home to my wife in this uniform, either; she'll throw me out." They were ashamed of their SS uniforms. Those were old men.
>
> Then there were very many in these guard units — very many — from Bulgaria, from Rumania or Siebenbürgen, Slovakia — the so-called folk Germans. Every man who became a soldier in the occupied areas had to become an SS man.[98] They were all simply transferred into the SS "Prince Eugene" division, as it was called. One time, when I was in a labor commando, where we had to dig ditches, I saw something. We prisoners were standing around, and the SS unit leader had gathered the guard units around him. There were perhaps 10 men who watched us, either with guard dogs or loaded guns. Then he asked them: "Which of you understands Ger-

man?" Nobody. We were the enemies of the people, we old Westphalians, and those were the SS men. That was typical for the camp around 1943 and 1944. They were poor souls, these Croatians and Slovakians, because they couldn't stay in Germany, either. They couldn't become anything.

But one has to differentiate these people from those who were in one of the administrative SS offices outside the camp. For example, I worked for one period in the payment office of the Waffen-SS as a prisoner. There were about 120 of us clergymen, and we paid the entire SS. The entire SS. In this payment office, there was a young lieutenant who was put in charge of us, a splendid young man. We talked completely openly with him, although that was forbidden. He took all my secret letters to Munich, although that was extremely dangerous for him, putting his own life at risk. That was a fine fellow, and there were others, too.

You asked, where did they all come from? There is a very revealing encounter between a prison chaplain in Celle [after the war] and a farmer. The prison chaplain said, "I have SS people here in prison who loaded Jewish children onto a bus and said they were taking an outing with them, and they hanged them in the forest." The farmer said, "Oh, oh, what criminals they were." The pastor said, "Those were farm boys from Schleswig-Holstein. Before, they wouldn't have bent a hair on a dog or a horse or any animal. They hanged children."

That's how inoculated they were with the insane ideology of Nazism, racism, and all that went along with it.[99]

Asked about those who worked in the camps, Wilm, Kohlbrugge, and Goldschmidt attempted to explain and even forgive those who were too deluded, afraid, blind, or weak to resist Nazism. From their own experience, many Confessing Christians understood all too well how difficult it was for any German to stand up to Nazi pressure. But the widespread complicity in Germany—of people who knew what was happening and yet did nothing—troubled many in the Confessing Church, and haunted them even more after 1945.

The German Resistance

For those who weren't Nazis, the habit of complicity grew by degrees; its roots were in the tangled web of fear, nationalism, political naivete, and traditional subservience to the state. Resistance to Nazism developed gradually as well, but there were a few clearsighted Germans who realized from the outset that there could be no compromise with Nazism. At the beginning of the Third Reich, Klaus Bonhoeffer shared a law practice with two Jewish colleagues. His widow remembered that "one day he found a note on his desk: 'Break off from your Jewish associates. Someone who means well.' . . . My husband rolled the note up and lit his cigar with it."[100]

Even in the early days of Nazism, such scornful gestures of defiance were dangerous. Klaus Bonhoeffer had reacted automatically, without thinking about the reasons or possible consequences of that first step of resistance. One who did think deeply about this was Dietrich Bonhoeffer, Klaus's brother. As he wrote in his book *Ethics*,

Conscience comes from a depth which lies beyond a man's own will and his own reason and it makes itself heard as the call of human existence to unity with itself.

Conscience comes as an indictment of the loss of this unity and as a warning against the loss of one's self. . . . When the National Socialist says, "My conscience is Adolf Hitler," that, too, is an attempt to find a foundation for the unity of his own ego somewhere beyond himself. The consequence of this is the surrender of one's autonomy for the sake of an unconditional heteronomy, and this in turn is possible only if the other man, the man to whom I look for the unity of my life, fulfills the function of a redeemer for me. This, then, provides an extremely direct and significant parallel to the Christian truth, and at the same time an extremely direct and significant contrast with it.[101]

Within the Confessing Church, this call of conscience — based upon what Heinrich Vogel termed the "either/or" contradiction between Christianity and Nazism — led many to resist Nazism on some level. The repercussions of their acts of resistance varied, proving fatal for some and having no consequences for others. Ernst Wilm's sermons led him to Dachau; Helmut Gollwitzer's did not. Wilm survived Dachau; Ludwig Steil and Paul Schneider, two other parish pastors whose outspokenness landed them in concentration camps, died there.[102]

This is what makes it so hard to judge the Confessing Church. It was not a resistance organization, yet its very existence, of course, was based upon Christian opposition to the absolute demands of Nazism. The Nazis viewed this as a challenge to the regime, as the Himmler Decree (which forbade most Confessing Church activities) showed. Many Confessing Christians, though torn between the pull of their consciences and that of their national loyalty, still tried to do what they felt was right, privately and publicly.

The consequences of their actions are detailed in the Confessing Church's *Fürbittenliste* of those arrested and imprisoned. The ultimate price was paid by the Confessing Christians who died as the result of their resistance. The names of people like Ludwig Steil and Paul Schneider, Hildegard Jacoby, Werner Sylten, and Helmut Hesse are not widely known. Their actions — preaching, helping individual Jews, excommunicating (in Schneider's case) prominent Nazis from his parish — did not bring down Nazism. It is difficult to imagine what effect these Christians had during the Nazi nightmare other than that they preserved the integrity of their souls and comforted those whom they tried to help. Morally, of course, the rescue of each individual life was as important, and demanded as much courage of those involved, as a collective conspiracy.

This is the essence of the resistance within the Confessing Church. The Confessing Church sought neither to overthrow Nazism nor even, on the political level, to undermine it. It viewed its purpose, as a Christian church, as helping those (in Bonhoeffer's words) "under the wheel." Bonhoeffer decided that his duty was to go beyond this purposes, to political resistance — a position that makes him unique even among the martyrs of the Confessing Church.

But the actions of all Christians who spoke out against Nazism or tried to help its victims were exceptions, particularly by the time the war began. The Nazi regime had succeeded in persuading most Germans to keep considerable distance between themselves and the "enemies" of Nazi Germany. The success of this strategy probably rested as much upon the human tendency to withdraw from that which is morally troubling as upon any deliberate Nazi actions. As Emmi Bonhoeffer noted,

It was also the case that, when you reported atrocities, they would be denounced immediately as "horror stories." I can tell a story that is very characteristic of this period. It was 1942. I stood in a long line to buy vegetables and said to my friend, "Now they've started to gas and cremate the Jews in the concentration camps." The saleslady who heard that responded loudly, "Frau Bonhoeffer, if you don't stop spreading such horror stories, you'll end up in a concentration camp too, and then no one can help you." Everyone heard her. I said, "It's the truth. I think people should know it." We listened to the British radio.

But when I came home and told my husband rather proudly about my civil courage, he responded, "You are completely mad. Please understand that a dictatorship is a snake. If you step on its tail, it bites you in the leg. You have to crush its head. You can't do that, I can't do that, only the military can do that. Therefore, the only thing that makes sense is to convince the military to undertake a coup. Everything else is cold coffee." . . .

Only the military could do it. They had the weapons, the connections, and they could get to him. The ordinary citizen couldn't get close.[103]

As time went on, more and more radical Confessing Christians began to put their hopes in the military overthrow of the Nazi regime. With the exception of Dietrich Bonhoeffer, however, the position of Confessing Christians within the resistance groups that tried to overthrow Hitler was, to use Bethge's word, "marginal." None of these resistance groups emerged from the Confessing Church as such. There were individual members of the July 20 conspiracy to assassinate Hitler who were lay members of the Confessing Church, like Hans-Bernd von Haeften and Justus Perels (Perels' brother was a Confessing pastor) or who had close ties to the church, like Eugen Gerstenmaier; and there were church leaders who knew of the conspiracy, like Bishop Wurm.

Although the military's serious attempts to overthrow the Nazi regime occurred relatively late, discussions about ending the Nazi reign had begun before the war. Marion York von Wartenburg, widow of government lawyer Peter Yorck (a member of the July 20 conspiracy) commented that her husband had met with colleagues to discuss undermining the Nazi regime much earlier:

At first, they didn't think about how they could get rid of Hitler, because they were of the opinion that that was a matter for the military, for the people who had weapons. Later, Helmut Moltke had friends with whom he discussed this. Then Moltke and Peter Yorck came together, and that's how the Kreisau Circle was formed.[104]

Early in the war, the Kreisau Circle contacted members of the Allied governments to win support for an attempted coup in Germany. Like similar feelers put out by German military officers, these attempts were met with distrust. Most of the conspirators held high government positions and were Nazi party members. They used their positions to work against Hitler, but to outsiders their role appeared ambiguous. Marion Yorck von Wartenburg argued that such people

used their party membership to stay in their posts, in order to get information and see what was happening. If all these people had only operated in a vacuum, they would have lost touch with reality or never have had it. Von Trott, von Haeften, Albrecht

Kessel[105] they were all on the inside, and one could trust them completely, that they weren't Nazis.[106]

But another reason for the difficulties the German resistance met in winning sympathy abroad was that its members were at war, literally, with those whom they were soliciting for support. Many resistance members hoped that Hitler and the leading Nazis could be removed without an unconditional German surrender of the war. They feared that a German defeat would lead to Soviet claims on occupied German territories. Moreover, they were convinced that the German people would not support any new government that had "lost" the war. This put the resistance groups in an impossible situation. As Emmi Bonhoeffer contended,

> As long as Hitler was successful, his murder would only have led to a *Dolchstoß* ["knife in the back"] legend. People would have said, "If he hadn't been murdered, then today we would have a united Europe under German leadership." That was his dream. . . . This resistance was so unpopular and hard to understand; it had no echo whatsoever among the masses. I think that nowhere in the entire history of humanity has there been a resistance movement purely for moral reasons, when people are doing better from day to day. And, once things began to go downhill, German loyalty played a role.[107]

Eberhard Bethge said that the idea of murdering Hitler developed only gradually, as every other option failed or became irrelevant:

> As I recall, the first attempt to stop Hitler was in 1938, during the Sudeten crisis — but not yet to kill him. In the Dohnanyi circle [Bonhoeffer's brother-in-law] this was already under serious consideration in the fall of 1938. . . . There were attempts not to kill Hitler, but to stop him. In the summer of 1939, almost nothing in this tenor occurred, but, once Poland had fallen, the so-called *Sitzkrieg* ["sitting war"] began in the winter of 1940, during which Hitler hesitated to attack the West. Now there was the hope of doing something before the big war began. . . .
>
> Then came the big disappointment that Hitler successfully concluded the French campaign so gloriously. No one would have foreseen it. How could we now bring around those who had been decorated to cooperating in the resistance? Because it was already clear that, in this kind of dictatorship, a coup could be done only by those with weapons — that is, through the military. Therefore the bourgeoisie, the pacifists, the liberals, the left — all those who now wanted a coup had to do it with the military. From this time on, the major leftists — Reichwein, Haubach, Mierendorff, and so on[108] — cooperated with the resistance. This happened for the first time in German history.
>
> Hope grew anew when things in Russia didn't go as they had hoped. At Christmas 1941, when [Walter von] Brauchitsch was dismissed as commander-in-chief of the army, Hitler became not only the supreme war commander but commander of the army as well, and the problem emerged: Who would now give the command in Berlin to occupy the Reich chancellery? For von Brauchitsch, in whom we had placed certain hopes, was no longer there. Now Hitler had to be killed so that the head of command would be eliminated and, with that, the officers would be absolved of their oath. From that point on, there were still people who vacillated, but within the resistance groups . . . the matter was clear: It would work only if he were killed. Then come the two famous attempts, by Schlabrendorff in March 1943[109] . . .

and the 20 of July. As a matter of fact, it was much too late. The group to which I belonged had high hopes much earlier.[110]

The dreams and plans of the conspirators make the failure of the July 20 attempt more poignant. Although this conspiracy is known as the work of the Kreisau Circle, led by Helmut Moltke and Peter Yorck von Wartenburg, a number of groups were involved. The leftist members were in the Saefkow/Jacob Baestlein group, led by Social Democrat Julius Leber, and with ties to the Communist resistance groups. Leber was in touch with the Kreisau Circle, which in turn had connections to the Confessing Church, the Catholic Church, and Bishop Wurm. Dietrich Bonhoeffer was the contact between the Confessing Church and the military intelligence office, where several conspirators held important posts. The intelligence officers had ties with the other military conspirators, whose other connections within the German bureaucracy and with the foreign ministry completed the circle. This broad base was intentional; the leaders of the various groups wanted widespread support for the new government after the Nazi regime had been overthrown. The preparations for Hitler's assassination included detailed plans for stabilizing the situation immediately after Hitler's death and long-term plans for the restructuring of all levels of German society. The plans emphasized an ethical foundation for the new state, and the secret discussions that were held with Bonhoeffer, Wurm, and other leading church figures centered on the moral rehabilitation of Germany after the fall of Nazism.[111]

The attempt itself was carried out by Claus Graf von Stauffenberg. On the morning of July 20, 1944, von Stauffenberg placed a briefcase containing explosives under a table where Hitler and his staff were to hold a meeting. The bomb exploded during the meeting, its impact apparently reduced by the massive table. Although three of Hitler's staff died, Hitler suffered only superficial injuries. In Berlin, the various members of the conspiracy followed their planned timetable, not realizing that the attempt had failed. As soon as it became clear what had happened, the conspirators were trapped. Several were executed summarily on the evening of July 20; the others were imprisoned and tortured before being brought to trial before Judge Roland Freisler at the infamous *Volksgericht* (People's Court), where the trial was filmed for propaganda purposes.[112]

Six hundred people were arrested in direct connection to the July 20 attempt.[113] Only 160 to 200 of them had been directly involved in the conspiracy, but the Nazis used the occasion to wipe out every remaining trace of political opposition they could find. In August 1944, over 5,000 members of the former (now outlawed) political parties were arrested and imprisoned (although the Gestapo, according to Peter Hoffmann in his book on the German resistance, had planned this move before July 20).[114] Between July 20, 1944 and May 1945, 11,448 people were executed.[115] In addition, the Gestapo rounded up the families of the conspirators. Most of those arrested in this *Sippenhaft* ("kith and kin arrest") were released after several months, although von Stauffenberg's family (his children had been taken and placed in an orphanage under a different name) was reunited only after May 1945.

One wife who avoided imprisonment was Emmi Bonhoeffer. She had taken her children to a small village in Schleswig-Holstein and left them there with a relative. Bonhoeffer related the events that followed her husband's arrest:

They left my husband lying in his cell for 13 days with his hands tied behind his back. . . . Then I came to Berlin, 13 days after his arrest. From then on, the chains behind his back were removed and [his hands were] bound in front of him. I received permission to speak with him after the affair had been handed over from the Gestapo to the *Volksgericht*. There the state attorney, Gorisch, was responsible. A relatively honorable man; my father-in-law visited him once and said afterward: "That is a Pilate. He must do other than he wishes."

I visited my husband often, and we corresponded daily. . . . Once a week, I had permission to speak to him, in the presence of an official. The first time, he [Bonhoeffer] drew a circle with his finger on the table for me and cut a piece out of it, just as from a cake. I understood what was meant: "This is how many times I've been in, and this is how much they know." He still had the hope that he would get out.[116]

Klaus Bonhoeffer was sentenced to death on February 2, 1945:

Karl Friedrich, his brother, brought me the news of the death sentence. It was February 2, in the evening, at 10 P.M. I already lay in bed. My reaction was: I won't give up. I wrote to him in prison with this verse from Matthias Claudius: "What will become of him who risks the higher, eternal things? He will have his feet in the storm and his head in the radiance of the sun, and always be greater than that which he encounters."

Freisler handed down the death sentence on February 2, and on the 3rd I was together with my parents-in-law in town. We wanted to bring some cake to Dietrich [who was also imprisoned], whose birthday was on February 4, and we came into this very bad air raid. We were way underneath, in the Anhalter Station. It was very full, and then a bomb fell through. We fell on top of each other because of the air pressure, and the glass shards from the train standing next to us flew over us. My father-in-law said, "Breathe through your nose," but I already instinctively put my nose in the cradle of my arm.

At such times, you think entirely soberly. You think, basically, only "We'll see how long it takes before I suffocate." But it was a blind bomb that only tore a hole. The bomb didn't explode, and fresh air came through the shaft that it had torn open. The ambulance crews were there very quickly. We took our time, with the thousands of people who were pouring out of there. We came out last. We were driven on: "Faster! Faster! the roof is caving in!" Behind us, the roof began to collapse. In this atmosphere of panic, I learned that I was totally ruthless. I stepped on something soft. To this day, I don't know: Was it a backpack? a child? a dog? I didn't look behind me. I didn't bend down. I ran on.

We tried then to go through the streets on foot. Everything was flooded because of the broken pipes and water mains. I tried to stop a car for my parents-in-law, but all the top SS people were racing out of town, fully loaded down with their luggage. No one stopped. My mother-in-law went on, her arm in that of her husband, and looked neither right nor left. We came to the street where the *Volksgericht* was, and it was burning. I said to my father-in-law: "The *Volksgericht* is on fire!" with the thought, perhaps all the files were burned up. But he said only, "Quiet." Because, of course, there were spies everywhere.

We split up then at the Tiergarten Station. Both of them went home, and I went on to the Lehrter Station to see about my husband. Berlin is so huge. Already, in the streetcar on Lehrter Street, the people were clean and quiet, and they glanced at their watches to see how late they would be. And I among them, filthy! — another world between the Anhalter Station and the Tiergarten.

> I gave my husband a note, on which I had written a verse from the hymnbook:
> "You have the way of all ways; nothing will be lacking to you." The note came
> back: "Be completely at peace; I am as well."[117]

The nightmarish conditions in Berlin after the Allied bombings began, and the
irony of maintaining one's daily routine amid the serious work of resistance, made
the lives of those who resisted even more surreal. Gertrud Staewen, whose apartment
had become a transit point for Jews who were seeking hiding places, remembered,

> What my own children had to go through! Because they heard at every lunch time
> that their mother said something completely different from that which they learned
> in school. I can't thank God enough that he left me my children. They didn't betray
> me, neither inwardly nor outwardly, although Christoph [her son] was sometimes
> beside himself. . . . He was 15 years old. He was a flak helper — that means that he
> had to stand on the roofs at night to put out the fires, and then they would be sent
> through burning Berlin in the mornings, to reassure the parents that they were still
> alive. When the poor boy came in the door, the whole hallway lay filled with people.
> I had already calmed down the Jews and said, "My son will be coming afterward
> with a uniform on; don't be alarmed." But, of course, they were frightened, and
> Christoph was startled, too. Then he caught on quickly and went through.
>
> But one Sunday he appeared and said, "You have to leave Berlin now!" Helene
> was already arrested, and the others were to be picked up on that day. I would have
> been, too, if Christoph hadn't come and told me. I said, "Christoph, I can't leave
> now. You know what I'm doing." He was beside himself. He dragged me off to the
> train station, put himself with me in a train toward Leipzig, and we traveled to a
> friend.[118]

In 1943, the Gestapo had discovered the Kaufmann circle, to which both Helene
Jacobs and Gertrud Staewen belonged. The weak link in the circle had been a contact
man whom the Gestapo interrogated in order to find Franz Kaufmann's whereabouts.
The man panicked and telephoned Helene Jacobs from the Gestapo headquarters to ask
her for Kaufmann's address. Jacobs refused to give him the information over the telephone and arranged to meet him, not realizing that he was in the Gestapo's custody:

> He stood there at the kiosk. I still think of that scene, how he stood there. Two offi-
> cials stood far away from him so that I couldn't notice them. I told him that I had an
> appointment with Kaufmann at 10:30 at Breitenbachplatz, but that first I had to take
> care of something else, and he should wait there. The Gestapo thought, of course,
> that he had warned me, because I wanted to go off. Then they arrested me. They
> didn't want to know anything about me; they still only wanted to get Kaufmann.[119]

Jacobs led the officers on a wild-goose chase. Only after an air raid alarm sounded
did they take her to a police station, where she was imprisoned for the night. As she
led them through Berlin, ostensibly in search of Kaufmann, Jacobs managed to crum-
ple and tear up the lists of Jews and forged rationing cards in her pocket and drop
them along the way.

Despite her efforts, Kaufmann was found and shot immediately. By that time, the
Gestapo had enough incriminating evidence against Jacobs to keep her imprisoned.
She was in a Gestapo prison for two-and-a-half years. Shortly after her arrest, how-
ever, she had one strange day of freedom:

It was the first phosphorus bombing. I was in a barrack in Bessamerstrasse. These barracks, of course, were dangerous during these phosphorus bombings. All the women there, everything, tumbled over each other. . . . I didn't let myself get caught up in the panic. The guards weren't in a position where they could get things under control, but they had dogs. They had a room, and we were all supposed to go in there. I didn't go in. I let everyone go in before me, and remained standing. One guard still stood there. I had overheard earlier how someone in a neighboring cell had started a little flirtation with one of the guards, and I thought to myself, maybe he's the one.

I snuggled up to him. It looked really pretty, this burning phosphorus. I wouldn't have found my way out of the area. I looked around first, then I asked this guard, "What should we do now?" He said, "Try to put it out." Which was nonsense, of course. I did a bit, but thought, the guard will do something for himself. He can't stand here forever. He started moving, and went to the exit. I never would have found it, and I ran behind him. They had told us that we should take blankets; I had one over my arm. Otherwise, I didn't have any recognizable prison outfit . . . I ran behind him. Perhaps he really was a little good-hearted. He didn't bother any more with me. Through that, I got out. . . .

I sat still until the all clear came; that was in the early hours of the morning. First I went to Eva Bildt [Helmut Gollwitzer's fiancée], an actress. Her mother was Jewish, and she couldn't work anymore. . . . I had to get myself some money to telephone, and thought I could go there. She was up on her roof putting out the fires. I immediately saw that she was startled, as if [she thought] I expected her to protect me. That happened later the same day with Pastor Jannasch [in the Berlin Confessing Church]. She calmed down immediately when I said, "You don't need to be afraid, I only want to take care of some things. Give me just five marks." And with this fortune I took care of my business.[120]

What Jacobs did that day was cover the tracks of the Kaufmann Circle and its contacts as best she could. She concentrated on getting messages to people to destroy certain lists and other incriminating material. And in the evening, she returned voluntarily to the Gestapo prison:

I did that for the good reason that otherwise I would have pulled my wonderful aunt into it, and that would have been unbearable. She hadn't had anything to do with the thing. Moreover, I didn't have anyone who would have taken me in. If I couldn't find enough quarters for the Jews, how should I now look for one myself? I told Pastor Jannasch at once that I only had to tell him something. He had a piece of paper with names; someone could get pulled into it with that. On that day, I only had such things in my head. On that day, I felt myself totally above everything. I thought, I have to endure the prison . . . it was like an inner arrangement that I had made with God. I had already considered how long I could hold out. Of course, I was afraid, because at that point there was no verdict against me. That came only later. When these two-and-a-half years in prison were over and the Nazis were still around, they would have taken me to the concentration camp.

But on that day, I didn't think about all those things. It is astounding, the degree of inner concentration. I was so relaxed, and knew exactly what I had to do. I was never in such a situation again.

When I came back into the prison, naturally, the director couldn't comprehend why I had reported back there.[121]

The Last Days of the War

For the people of the Confessing Church, the Third Reich ended at different moments, in different places: in a parish, or on the road fleeing the Russian army, in a cellar, in a prisoner of war camp. The chaos and pathos of the *Zusammenbruch* — the collapse, as the end of the Third Reich was later called — were no different for Confessing Christians than for any other Germans. Their lives were dominated by the necessities of survival and seeing to it that those dependent upon them — from children to elderly relatives to parish members — survived as well. Yet, for Confessing Christians, there was another aspect to the *Zusammenbruch*. In the ruins of Nazi Germany they found hope, and their recollections of the final days of the war bear witness to this.

Annemarie Grosch, widowed only months after her marriage, ended the war taking care of her ailing father and shell-shocked brother and tending several parishes for the Confessing Church in Berlin:

> Basically, we waited only for the war to come to an end and that Hitler would fall. Nevertheless, I should add that we were very concentrated upon ourselves, on the immediate events of the war, the fear for family members who were there, and the worry: "Will we survive the next air raid? Will we have something to eat tomorrow?" That made you concentrate very strongly on yourself. . . .
>
> Spiritually seen, the war was very hard on us, because we couldn't wish that Germany would win. . . . On the other hand, when you listened to the BBC — and we did that — you knew what stood ahead for Germany, and to lose, too, was dreadful. So we were dreadfully torn, dreadfully torn. But nevertheless, for us personally — I think now of my family and of many who thought the way we did — the end of the war was a sigh of relief and somehow, although it was so terrible, a stroke of fortune. For we couldn't wish that things would go on with Hitler.
>
> The *Zusammenbruch* in 1945 made me happy, despite all the terrible things. Everything lay in ruins. My father didn't have a job, my brother couldn't study, but the next day I took my wandering stick and marched for 45 minutes on foot through my parish and simply carried on. And 10 days after the *Zusammenbruch* I had picked my entire youth group up out of the ruins, and we were together again like before. And now free again.[122]

Rudolf Weckerling, who had been on the Russian front, spent the final months of the war in retreat from the Russian army:

> We always came closer to the homeland. At the end, we were supposed to win back the city of Breslau. Then this command was altered to an order to retreat. At the time of surrender, we were in Czechoslovakia. Then some of us rode with horses over the mountains toward Silesia. There, the Poles who were forced laborers and now wanted to return to Poland took the horses from us, but Germans who were still there gave us bicycles. Somewhere these, too, were taken from us, and we had to make our way further on foot.
>
> The man who was with me went toward Berlin, and I wanted to go over the Oder River, because I knew, through a comrade that my wife had been evacuated from Berlin to Göbin. There, everything was already Polish, at first administered under the exiled government in London, and there I met my wife again. She had

been asked to serve there as a pastor. Before, while I was on the road, I had been a Russian prisoner of war for one month. They just let me run.

Then I did a little under the Poles there — had to hold a Catholic funeral and so — but then all of us Germans were deported because the change came; the Warsaw Poles had replaced the exile government. Then we went to Berlin on foot in the great trek of refugees.[123]

Hundreds of thousands of Germans fled toward the West during the final months of the war; eventually some 12 million Germans fled or were deported from the former German Reich in eastern Europe.[124] Their uncertainty and exhaustion were compounded by their terror of the Russian soldiers; stories of atrocities — particularly of the rapes of German women and girls — spread. In May 1945, Sieghild Jungklaus was in her parish in Pankow, a sector of Berlin, during the final street battles between Russian soldiers and the Nazis. She described some of the scenes she witnessed:

We did live through some horrible things. I recall that close to us at the Church of Hope, a house collapsed, and there were 60 people underneath in the cellar; they were buried alive and couldn't get out, and then the water pipes broke. They pulled out three alive from all those people. And they were very often parish members. . . . The final battles were very terrible when the Russian soldiers came. . . . One hardly knew at that point what was happening in the neighboring houses. In houses not at all far from the church and the parsonage, the SS had holed up in the cellars, and then the Russian tanks, came, and, of course, the SS didn't take any consideration. The Russian soldiers had pulled young women and girls out of the cellars and put them on their tanks, and thought that the SS wouldn't throw grenades then. Of course, they did throw them, and afterward all that young life just lay on the street. . . . Our church at that point was a mortuary. We laid the people out there until the relatives came and looked for them. But it was simply a war zone. There were terrible things. . . .

But we were protected somewhat against some things. As soon as we knew that a Russian commander's office had been set up in the City Hall [Pankow was in the eastern zone of Berlin], the superintendent and my father went there. We had a church warden who had come from Russia, who could speak Russian; he had fled at some time from there . . . he went along, and he knew, too, how to handle them . . . and so we obtained Russian protection signs. . . . That was put on the door, and when Russian soldiers came who wanted something, they slinked up to the door and then, Oh! they made sure they got out of there. Naturally, that was a very good thing for all the women who were staying down in our cellar.[125]

In Marta S.'s parish in Silesia, the parsonage was full of people who had been evacuated since the fall of 1944.[126] In September, shortly after she gave birth to her only child, the news came that her husband had been missing in action since 10 days before the birth:

My mother had been bombed out twice in Bremen and now was boarded with a farmer, and I went there with the child, too, since that house was healthier than the old damp parsonage. . . .

On January 26 [1945], the first treks from the east came past, in bitter cold. After that, I was always close to tears. The treks didn't stop, nor did the horror stories. . . . On April 19, the Russians broke through . . . barricades with panzers were built up, but the barricades only hampered those fleeing, not the Russians. We lived through all kinds of horrors, especially the women, from the children to the elderly. Our villages lay on the road toward Berlin. We lived in cellars and barns, with attacks day and night. . . .

When, after one month, those evacuated from the Rhineland wanted to go home, my mother wanted to join them, with me and the child. . . . We thought that we could survive better on the road than there. From May 18 till June 8, we went on foot to Bremen. . . . We learned for the first time on May 22, in Wittenberg, that the war was over! Since May 8! We got over the Mulde River, at that time the border, only under gunfire. Many died before our eyes.[127]

Those in the western part of Germany did not have to flee. But for them, too, the final months of the war were a time of horror. In Dortmund, Gerda Keller recalled,

I lived in the bunker from the end of October 1944 until May 1945. There you always had the occasional chance to be somewhere else, but in general, we lived in the underground bunker. It was hard, too, when there had been air raids. You were more or less safe in the bunker. But there was nothing to eat. And when the trucks came in from the villages with pea soup — that was the usual — they were shot at by low-flying bombers, and the soup lay on the street, and once again, we had nothing. That certainly was a bad time. At that point, things like the Confessing [Church] movement and so on — there was none of that. The only thing was to survive, and people tried to help each other, if possible.

There were some funny things. Right by the bunker (I was in the bunker near the train station) there was a storage warehouse of a wine trader. And they said, "Before we are defeated and the soldiers come in and get all our bottles and get drunk and don't know what they're doing — come and get as much wine as you want." Starving as we were, we filled our stomachs up with red wine. Can you imagine what came of that?

But perhaps it was the right thing. The day before Dortmund was occupied, they poured the last wine in the gutters. We didn't wash ourselves for weeks, because what little water we had — water ran down the walls of the bunker — we took that in our hands and let it run into containers, and had something to drink.[128]

In a village in Hesse, Friedemann M. witnessed the arrival of the Allies. (The Council of Brethren had assigned him to a Confessing parish there after Nazi pressure made it impossible for him to remain in Thuringia. Since childhood polio had left him with a bad limp, he had been exempted from military service.) Diehard Nazis in his village decided to fight back:

We were occupied on the evening of April 6 by Nazi soldiers — 17, 19 years old, under an SS commander. They took over every house and put machine guns in the upper windows. . . . The American infantry came through, and the firing broke out. We were all in the cellar and very afraid. Every house was taken; 21 farmhouses were burned.

Then it was still. I looked out of the cellar window and saw the green-trousered leg of a soldier. For me, that was the moment that the *Kirchenkampf* ended. I went out and asked, in my bad English, if he was English or American. "American," he said.

"Then I said, "I've been waiting for you for 12 years."[129]

The most genuine liberation, of course, was for those in the camps and who had actively resisted the Nazis. On the last day of the war, Gertrud Staewen managed to get to Weimar:

> I wanted to go to Weimar because my daughter was there. I had sent her to a friend there during the bad times. Now I wanted to be with my daughter when it came to an end. We didn't know in what form it would end.
>
> There we were in Weimar. I recall how I thought, then, can I do anything here? Across from us was a ruin, destroyed, and it was being cleared out by obscure figures. I said to myself, those are concentration camp people. They came through in the evenings, at night, and dragged themselves from hunger. I said to my friends, "Haven't you noticed, those are concentration camp people?" We gave them bread then. I can still see how they threw themselves upon it and ate. And now it was over.[130]

In many Gestapo prisons and work camps, the guards and directors simply fled. In Berlin, Helene Jacobs had been released from prison on April 13:

> The tendency was to empty the prisons before the Russians came. The director had three lists from the Gestapo. List 1 was released, List 2 as well, List 3 stayed there.
>
> One day, there was a very bad air raid. My aunt had bad bronchitis and was very weak. Still, on that day, she held a pillow over her chest and came to me in the prison. I just fell apart, because she had gone out on the street alone during the bombing. One of the July 20 women told the guard that I had collapsed, and the director then arranged with the state attorney that I be given leave from prison.[131]

Jacobs continued to live in the prison, however:

> My apartment was completely destroyed, I had absolutely nothing to eat, and for that reason I stayed there in my cell. The Russians came closer. Then, all at once, the guards were ordered to close the cells and simply leave. I said, "What about me?" "You do what you think is right." He left it, de facto, up to me, that I open up the prison, which he didn't feel capable of doing himself.
>
> I don't know how many there were. The commandant was gone; suddenly I was in charge at the prison. Then someone came and said, "Hitler is dead." I said, "Then we're going." We left together, a real caravan. We got to the Ku-damm [the Kürfürstendamm, the main boulevard in downtown Berlin] and there I saw the first Russians. Then I looked for my aunt. The Russians had ignited many houses; the house of my aunt was burning, too. It was all so macabre. Finally, I found her with relatives.[132]

In the work camp near Magdeburg, where Dietrich Goldschmidt was,

> the people simply ran away; the camp commandant also ran away. One day we were alone, and broke into the kitchen and got food for ourselves, and broke into the office and got our papers. Ursel [his fiancée] was already near Magdeburg with bicycles, and there we met. It was an adventuresome trip, until we finally reached Göttingen on April 30. Three weeks on a journey where we knew no one is waiting for us . . . the feeling of a genuine liberation.[133]

In spite of the horrors of the final months of war, he recalled that spring as "the loveliest spring I've ever experienced. It was warm, the cherry trees were in bloom. Everywhere, the green was stirring, the weather was pleasant; I can only rave about it."[134]

Goldschmidt and his wife-to-be survived the Third Reich. Marion Yorck von Warten-burg's husband died trying to overthrow it. The final days of the war brought a bitter-sweet gift for her, the final letter her husband had written before his execution:

> He had written it during the trial, right after the verdict was handed down. I ran to get it. Gestapo people had told me that he had written at least three pages. I couldn't get the letter; I went from Pontius to Pilate. There were at least six different Gestapo offices here; I went everywhere.
>
> Then, in April 1945, I was ordered to the Kaiserhof [where some Gestapo offices were located] by an SS department director. The man said, "Our Führer, in his humane greatness, has thought of giving the widows their portion, and you are among them." I said, "You know, I don't believe that my husband died so that I could receive a widow's portion from you." He hesitated for a minute, and looked at me, and said, "Do you want his letter?" I said, "I've been running after it for months." And so I had it.[135]

Klaus Bonhoeffer was executed on April 22, 1945 as the Russians approached Berlin; his brother Dietrich had been hanged on April 9, 1945 at the concentration camp in Flossenburg. Emmi Bonhoeffer had remained for most of the final months of war in Berlin, although her three children were in Schleswig-Holstein, north of Hamburg. Eberhard Bethge brought her the news of her husband's death. She decided to go to her children, over 300 kilometers away:

> At first, I went on bicycle; at the end, I swam. There were two other women who wanted to go north. Then, around the stronghold of Dömitz on the Elbe River (the village was Neukalis) we were arrested by Russian soldiers as we attempted to swim over the Elde [a small tributary of the Elbe], and locked up in a cellar. Of course, now we feared that the infamous call, "Woman, come" would come. Then the call came, and one of us was courageous. She went out, and after a short time she called, "Frau Bonhoeffer, you can come. We only have to put new collars on the soldiers' jackets."
>
> It was already cool, a bright summery evening. Under a blooming cherry tree outside, they had laid a stack of sweaty jackets, and then they had stolen a splendid damask tablecloth from some cupboard and had torn it into strips, about 10 centimeters wide. We had to take the old white strips out of these sweaty jackets and sew a new one in. All around us stood the Russian soldiers. We sewed and sang, stubbornly, to ourselves, German folk songs in harmony. The Russians are very musical. They enjoyed it, and they didn't touch us.
>
> In the meantime, the Russian commander had interrogated the wife of the mayor; we had been staying with her. She said that we hadn't wanted to swim across, but had only looked for work in the village. So they didn't shoot us, which we had reckoned with, but sent us back to Berlin. We were to be gone by the next morning, before 6 a.m. The two others turned back, but I said to myself, "What should I do in Berlin? My husband is dead, the house is destroyed, the children are in Holstein." I hid there in the cellar of a factory for five days and nights, and the mayor's 17-year-old nephew brought me soup and bread, and helped me to swim across.
>
> I swam over one evening. He had wrapped my backpack — some 40 pounds, everything that I had rescued — in a waterproof sack and tied it to a board, and hid the board under a bush by the river. Then he stood up above, on the bank, and I stayed down below on the cellar steps, where I had hid, so that I could see him. He told me that he would chat with the Russian guard when he came, and when the

guard went on, I should wait until he had made a fist with his hands behind his back. When he had made the fist, I should come down, untie the backpack, and swim, but as much under water as possible, because the guards on the bridge liked to shoot at the swimmers.

He stood and stood. The guard had long since moved on, and he still didn't make a fist, and I thought, "My God, did I misunderstand him?" Finally, he brought his hands together, and then I hustled down, untied the knots, and pushed the board with the backpack in front of me. We hadn't considered that, in the evenings, the water was very deep. I had to cross a small island, and I couldn't get up with the 40-pound backpack. But it was so sheltered — he had picked out this place very cleverly — that the place where I had to come up on the island couldn't be seen from the bridge.

In despair, unimagined strengths grow. The worst thing was pulling the heavy backpack up. It took me awhile before I finally came out and had pulled the backpack up. Then I crawled on my stomach through the nettles across the small island, dragging the board with the backpack behind me. On the other side, I still had to swim several meters, and on the other bank an English soldier was standing, and I thought, now he will arrest me. But he complimented me, applauded, and said he had watched the entire thing through his binoculars, and was very nice. He helped me immediately, took the backpack and led me into the village. There I had the address of the mayor's wife, Erika von Sell,[136] who was working as the secretary to the English colonel.

The house was closed up, and she wasn't there. I climbed in through a broken window, ate my fill in the pantry, pulled off my wet clothes, and lay in bed. After several hours, I suddenly heard a motor and whispering voices. She opened the door, and I sang out in my sweetest voice, "Please don't be alarmed! I swam over." She wasn't alarmed at all, sat down at once on the edge of the bed and said, "You'll have to be gone from here by six tomorrow morning. The Russians are moving on. See to it that you are in the English barracks before six and are taken along. I'm leaving already with the Colonel." She gathered a few things and then left.

Naturally, now, I couldn't think of sleeping. I went at dawn to the English barracks, and they took me with them to Hamburg. From Hamburg to Lübeck I went partly on foot, partly hitchhiking, and from Lübeck to Stawedder on foot.

The children were there with relatives. I looked through the little window in the house door and saw my three children, healthy, sitting around the table. I could go no further. They were 13, 10, and 6. Naturally, the question came at once: "Where's Papa?"

"Papa is far beyond us."

"Is he dead?"

Forty-one years later, Bonhoeffer's eyes grew misty, and she shook her head slowly as she remembered what she told them:

Sterben tun nur Körper.[137]
Only bodies die.

III

RESISTANCE
AND GUILT

✤ 9 ✤

Reflections on Resistance

Knowledge and Accountability

NAZI GERMANY'S REIGN OF TERROR was over; its purported glories had brought only tragedy. Once again Germans stood on the cusp of history, but this time it was no longer in their hands. That prospect was too much for the countries and peoples who had suffered under Nazism.

The victorious Allies took political and military control of defeated Germany during its transition from Nazism. The surviving Nazi leaders were brought to trial in Nuremberg. In the western zones, the Allies developed "denazification" and "re-education" programs, which attempted to weed remaining Nazis out of the public sphere and to train Germans in the rudiments of democracy. In the eastern sector—where there was no formal "denazification"—discovered Nazis were more likely to be summarily shot. Others tried to hide their pasts or to flee West or abroad.

But despite Allied efforts, only the Germans themselves could examine what had happened to them morally during the 12 years of Nazism. Only they could know the complicated truth of what had taken place. This soul searching, of course, was easily undermined by delusion and self-justification. The Allies had brought the Nazis to justice, and this underscored the moral significance of Germany's defeat: Why hadn't the German people themselves stopped Hitler?

The question haunted many people who had been in the Confessing Church. Annemarie Grosch, pondering it, replied,

> The difficult thing is that we neglected in 1933 and 1934 to fight Hitler. Afterward, it was difficult, because you can't demand that an entire people be full of heroes. And that would have been necessary later, because people risked so much with the smallest resistance. When people ask us now, "Why didn't you see to it, through a resistance movement, that Hitler disappeared?"—then I've often noticed that those abroad simply can't comprehend what it meant, under such surveillance, to have contacts with each other at all. The resistance groups worked individually, isolated and detached from one another, and you could have achieved something only if you had really been able to build up an entire network. And that was very difficult, somehow. The network was greater than we ourselves knew at the time; but still, there were just a few who were accountable, who knew what was happening.
>
> If you consider it all now—how the various attempts went—then, of course, it all fell short. I would say that von Stauffenberg should have sacrificed himself when he put the bomb in the Führer's headquarters. But who can demand that of someone else? He would have had to commit suicide; he shouldn't have put the briefcase

197

there and then gone. He would have had to have thrown the bomb in such a way that he himself would have been blown up.[1]

Marion Yorck von Wartenburg offered another insight into the dilemma of the German people:

> Only very few people knew what took place in the concentration camps in the final instance. Of the gassings and these things — we could have known more of them, perhaps, had we dug deeper. But people also sensed their helplessness against these things, and because of that, perhaps, they didn't want to pursue it as they should have.[2]

The difficulties facing persons who tried to resist the Nazis, and the general sense of helplessness, were certainly factors that made it difficult for any real or widespread resistance to Nazism to develop. But as Yorck von Wartenburg's comments indicate, postwar reflections about German resistance invariably raised the issue of German accountability — of what people could have known but did not want to know.

Resistance and the Institutional Church

The Confessing Church's record of opposition (and knowledge) on some points raised the troubling question of why it had compromised on others. At Treysa in August 1945, at the first national postwar meeting of German Protestant church leaders, Martin Niemöller, freed from Dachau only four months earlier, pointedly told his colleagues:

> Our present situation today is not primarily the fault of our people and the Nazis. How should they have proceeded on a path that they didn't know? They simply believed they were on the right path! No, the essential blame rests upon the church; because it alone knew that the road being taken would lead to ruin, and it didn't warn our people, it didn't unveil the injustice that had occurred or — only when it was too late.
>
> And here the Confessing Church bears a particularly large measure of the blame; for it saw most clearly what was developing; it even spoke out about it, but then became tired and stood more in fear of human beings than of the living God. . . . Through disobedience, we have neglected fundamentally the office with which we were charged, and, with that, we have become guilty.[3]

Niemöller's comments were to prove divisive and controversial within the church, because they went to the heart of the choices that both the German Evangelical Church and the Confessing Church had made during the Third Reich. "Should we go on as if nothing happened?" the Dahlem Confessing Christian Franz Kaufmann had asked after the deportations of Jews began. For a number of church leaders in the German Evangelical Church and even within the Confessing Church, the answer was yes. Moreover, they did not view this response as passive acquiescence to Nazi policies. On the contrary, many church leaders believed that the determination of the church to continue as a Christian church within a totalitarian system hellbent on destroying Christian values constituted a form of resistance. These church leaders simply believed that their task under Nazism was to preserve and protect the church.

Accordingly, for these church leaders their postwar notion of accountability was very different from that of Niemöller and others. In Treysa, Niemöller scathingly attacked the church's silence during the Third Reich. But the final statement issued at that conference by the newly established Evangelical Church of Germany offered a very different version of the church's behavior:

> Where the church took its responsibility seriously, it proclaimed the commandments of God, called by name crime and the breaking of laws, the guilt in the concentration camps, the mistreatment and murder of the Jews and the sick, and attempted to fight the seduction of the youth. But [Christians] were pushed back into the church rooms, as in a prison. Our people was separated from the church. Its word could no longer be heard in public; what it proclaimed was heard by no one.[4]

But it was not as simple as that. In all too many instances, cautious church leaders had tried dissuade Christians who wanted the church to publicly oppose Nazi atrocities. Whatever the arguments about "political" versus "religious" resistance, a key motive for most church leaders had been the importance of protecting the institutional church.

An exchange between Bavaria's Bishop Meiser and some more radical church members is an illustration in point. In 1943, a group of church members in southern Germany, including Hermann Diem and Gollwitzer's former "non-Aryan" vicar, Helmut Traub, had formed the Lempsschen Circle. In the name of the church, this group wrote a statement protesting the deportations of the Jews. It sent a copy to Meiser, asking that he sign it as well. "As Christians," they wrote,

> we can no longer bear that the church in Germany remains silent about the persecution of the Jews. . . . Every "non-Aryan," whether Jew or Christian, has "fallen among murderers" today in Germany, and we are asked whether we meet him like the priests and Levites or like the good Samaritan.[5]

Meiser's response, as a member of the Lempsschen Circle later recalled, was that he

> regretted, to be sure, the terrible things taking place in Poland and the concentration camps. But if he were to do something officially, he would only be arrested, and the Jews wouldn't have been helped; the persecution would become even more severe. In addition, he, Meiser, was responsible for a large regional church. If persecution broke loose, suffering and unhappiness would come over thousands of families; Meiser assured [us] as well that the church administration was doing much secretly and had already helped any number of Jews.[6]

The difference between Meiser's public caution and the more radical Confessing Christians who wanted to challenge Nazism openly had been there from the onset. As early as 1933, Dietrich Bonhoeffer had examined the options facing the church under Nazism in an essay, "Die Kirche vor der Judenfrage" ("The Church and the Jewish Question"). He concluded that there were three options: The first was to remind the state of its legitimate responsibilities; the second was to help the state's victims. The third course, which Bonhoeffer chose, was "to fall in the spokes of the wheel itself" in order to stop the wheel: to resist.

Bonhoeffer eventually concluded that resistance was not merely a legitimate option for the church but a *status confessionis*: a situation in which the precepts of the Christian faith demanded that Christians resist if they were to retain their confessional integrity.[7] The letters and documents from Bonhoeffer and other Confessing Christians imprisoned or killed by the Nazis for opposition activities show the extent to which their actions were based upon their faith. Yet, the consequences of their growing opposition to the state took them into the political realm and inevitably brought political retaliation upon the church. Nazi propagandists had used such instances from the beginning as proof that the Confessing Church was agitating politically. Moderate and conservative factions within the church tacitly agreed with this analysis. Attempting to distance themselves from such troublemakers, these factions questioned the sincerity of the religious motives of Christians who opposed Nazism. The distance between Meiser's and Bonhoeffer's positions remained profound, even after the war. Shortly after the war ended, Meiser refused an invitation to a memorial service for Bonhoeffer, commenting that the murdered theologian was not a Christian martyr but a political one.[8]

We can only speculate about the extent to which the responses of people like Meiser were influenced by fear, caution, pastoral nationalism, or the traditional Protestant subservience to the state. But these responses were certainly grounded as well in their very understanding of the duty of individual Christians and of the role of the Christian church. Meiser believed that Christian resistance to Nazism meant preserving the institutional church. Bonhoeffer arrived at the conviction that resistance meant risking all for the sake of the Christian confession of faith. "When Christ calls a man," wrote Bonhoeffer, "he calls him to come and die." The implications for the church, as well as for individual Christians, were clear.

Given the position of Meiser and other church leaders, resistance was left to be the option of individuals. But it should be noted that this was also the position of many Christians who were involved in the German resistance. Hans-Bernd von Haeften, for example, believed that the church's proper function was to minister and counsel people who had to make political decisions, not to become a politically active force itself.[9] Hebe Kohlbrugge, who had been active in the Berlin Confessing Church and then joined the Dutch resistance, believed that Christians could make such a decision only as individuals:

> I think, as a Christian, yes, but not as a church. So I quite agree with Bonhoeffer and von Trott, who did it from their viewpoints as Christians . . . But I don't think that the Council of Brethren should have been sitting around, saying, who can put the bomb under Hitler?[10]

At the same time, Kohlbrugge acknowledged that this view crippled the church's efforts to help the victims of Nazism:

> They made mistakes. We have made great mistakes . . . for instance, when people came to [Günther] Harder and asked for their *Ariernachweis* [racial proof for their "Aryan" identity cards], I had to look into the church books and give it to them. I did it without thinking . . . I didn't come to the idea that we should never have given any papers at all! . . . That we should have refused, right from the beginning. . . . It was, of course, a great mistake. That was a political mistake we made.[11]

As Kohlbrugge noted, similar mistakes were made by the Dutch churches, and for the same reason — the conformity of the church to its traditional role in society. After she returned to Holland, the German occupation forces demanded proof of "Aryan" identity from the Dutch people. As in Germany, people went to the churches for their genealogical records. Wiser for her experience in Germany, Kohlbrugge sought out a prominent Dutch churchman and argued that the churches should refuse:

> [I said] "We can't do it, it's impossible." K. said, "If they ask you a question, you must give an answer. If they do anything to the Jews, we'll help the Jews." But then it was too late . . . even in Holland, where we knew what the Germans were, where we knew what had happened to the Jews, we all brought it in. And so we did it in the Confessing Church. That was wrong, it was wrong in the Confessing Church, it was wrong in Holland, it's no question. . . .
>
> So — and to give no answer to this question would have been a political issue. But it wasn't refused because it was political. It was refused because you said, *"Wenn die Obrigkeit fragt, muß man doch antworten"* [When the authorities ask, one indeed has to answer]."[12]

In this context, the separation of religious and political obligations (or between religious and political "resistance") is related to the distinction between institutional and individual behavior. The two ethical questions that arise in any examination of the church's behavior are whether it consistently made this distinction throughout the Third Reich, and whether, in a system like that of Nazi Germany, this stand was tenable. On one level, of course, the institutional church was inconsistent: It did behave politically. It considered its public pronouncements selectively and carefully in order to avoid political confrontations with the Nazi state; it even admonished church members who publicly criticized the state. For some church leaders, this decision was certainly a tactical one, similar to that of the conspirators who remained in the Nazi party and in their government positions in order to remain in the resistance. But the church's own record of nationalism and early approval of the Nazi regime, as well as its critical lack of support for those who did engage in open political resistance, often make the line between conscious tactic and political conformity difficult to ascertain.

In short, the church followed an institutional pattern that, under democratic circumstances, could indeed have protected the institutional integrity of the church. But in Nazi Germany, this course only rendered part of the Confessing Church and most of the German Evangelical Church tragically passive. This stance also led church leaders to dissociate themselves from the political consequences of their positions. That these positions were religiously based, from the church's point of view, did not prevent their having political consequences and being interpreted by the Nazis as such. Nevertheless, after the war, it was almost easier for church leaders to deal with a straightforward political resister like von Stauffenberg than with someone like Dietrich Bonhoeffer.

The Resistance of Individuals

It is within the context of the "apoliticality" of the German Protestant church that the spiritual doubts and dilemmas of those who resisted should be understood. Individuals had many doubts — on Christian grounds, based upon their understanding, as Christians, of their obligations to society and to the church. For many Christians who became involved in the German resistance, particularly in the July 20 conspiracy, some of the most painful doubts concerned moral questions — particularly the question of whether the assassination of Hitler could be morally justified. In his biography of Bonhoeffer, Eberhard Bethge noted that

> the coup had to begin with the murder of Hitler. Given the backgrounds and manner of the conspirators, it cost a great deal to bring themselves to this conclusion; they were never entirely at peace on this point. . . . [Bonhoeffer] believed that, if it came to him to carry out the deed, he would be prepared; first, however, he would have to leave his church formally and on record, since it could not cover him and he would not want to make a claim on its protection.[13]

The difficult process through which such decisions were reached increased the isolation of those who resisted. As straightforward as the morality of their conclusions seems in retrospect, many resisters remained deeply troubled about the course they had chosen. In fact, the July 20 conspiracy was divided between those who believed it morally justifiable to kill Hitler in order to overthrow the Nazi regime and those who opposed murder as the means toward this goal. Helmut Moltke, the leader of the Kreisau Circle, agonized over the question. In part, he viewed it as a matter of justice. "Let Hitler live," argued Moltke in June 1943, "He and his party must bear responsibility to the end of the fatal destiny which they have prepared for the German people; only in this way can the National Socialist ideology be obliterated."[14]

But Moltke also wrestled with the question of murder on religious grounds. Emmi Bonhoeffer claimed that here the differences of opinion led not only to a practical division of labor between the Kreisau Circle and the Oster-Dohnanyi group (to which Klaus and Dietrich Bonhoeffer belonged) but to a mild estrangement between the two groups:

> [Moltke] was against the assassination on religious grounds. He said, too, the decisive thing was to fight this *spirit*. If he did that through murder, then that was capitulation — proof that he hadn't succeeded. With this view, we agreed between the Moltke group and the group around Dohnanyi and Oster that the Moltke group should concern itself with the aftermath, with the building of Germany later, particularly in the cultural realm, while the group around Oster should concern itself with the removal of Hitler. That was simply a sensible division of tasks. . . . Klaus and Dietrich were realistic enough to see that it was illusory to think that one could change the spirit spreading around us into another spirit, if one didn't extinguish or, in any case, drive out that class that embodied it at the time.[15]

There were others who brooded about whether, as Christians, they could participate in a murder. Peter Yorck "thought long and hard about this murder," recalled his widow, but concluded that killing Hitler was the only means of overthrowing the Nazi regime. This decision was like "a deliverance":

> For a person like him, so upright, it was very hard to bear. Always to receive the news of all the horrors that Hitler had perpetrated, and the dreadful things that were taking place in the Germans' name, in the rest of the world.[16]

Another who recalled discussing this question with one of the conspirators was Elsie Steck, parish secretary in Dahlem. Even before Steck left Dahlem for Bavaria, Hans-Bernd von Haeften was a member of one of the Bible study groups there. Von Haeften, an official in the foreign ministry, member of the Kreisau Circle and the Confessing Church, only reluctantly supported the assassination attempt on July 20; and in January 1944, he had used religious arguments to dissuade his brother Werner (who was Stauffenberg's lieutenant) from murdering Hitler.[17] Steck remembered that von Haeften arrived one evening with a Bible in his hand

> and said that he wanted to get to the bottom of it, whether the murder of a tyrant was in keeping with Luther. We spoke about it for a long time. He was shot after July 20. To a great extent, the people of the political resistance were among the people in Dahlem. In part, they lived there; in part, they attended the Bible studies and had close ties to Gollwitzer.[18]

But Steck believed that some conspirators were drawn to the Confessing Church mainly because it was sympathetic to their own concerns and convictions:

> I assume that very many of the men who stood there subordinated the church side of their political convictions—that they had political plans or, at the very least, feelings and thoughts of resistance, and that they could cultivate the church in this direction. [It was] not that they were intensive churchgoers and Christians who now thought that, from this standpoint, one had to fight Hitler. Rather, either because they were "non-Aryans," or had "non-Aryan" wives, or stood completely politically opposed to National Socialism—it was for that reason that they now held faster to the church than before. Because all these people had lived around us previously, and hadn't participated before so much in the church.[19]

Whichever came first—political convictions or religiously based motives—the faith of those conspirators who were Christians influenced how they viewed their choices. Even some of the most fanatical Nazis seemed to grasp this. During the trial of the July 20 conspirators, Judge Roland Freisler screamed at Helmut Moltke, "We and Christianity are the same in one thing only: We demand the entire person!"[20]As Moltke wrote his wife after the trial, the presiding judge of the infamous *Volksgericht* seemed to comprehend the crucial difference between the two:

> I stood before Freisler not as a landowner, not as a nobleman, not as a Prussian, not even indeed as a German—no, I stood before him as a Christian and as nothing else. . . . In any case, Freisler is the first National Socialist who grasped who I am.[21]

The July 20 conspirators faced harrowing decisions. But for all Confessing Christians who began to resist, ethical questions arose about what was right and wrong, about means and ends. In retrospect, some of these dilemmas seem absurd. When the Gestapo arrived at Günther Harder's parsonage to arrest Hebe Kohlbrugge, Harder admitted that she was there, telling Kohlbrugge later, "I had to say you were in my house; I'm not allowed to lie."[22] Annemarie Grosch confronted a similar dilemma after her ordination in 1943. The ordination was illegal, and the six Confessing Church pastors who had signed the ordination documents and performed the ceremony could have been arrested by the Gestapo. Soon after the ordination, Grosch said, she and the five other women who had been ordained were summoned,

> and, indeed, not directly by the Gestapo. They hid behind the church officials, the consistory, which was, so to speak, "neutral." We were summoned by consistory church councilor Dr. K., who had to find out whether the Confessing Church had undertaken an official church action in violation of the Himmler Decree.
>
> The criterion for whether it was an official action was the granting of the ordination certificate. This document is both a legal and religious document, which bestows upon the pastor the right to preach and distribute the sacraments. Now we were all asked, in turn, whether we had received these documents. I was the last one. I sat there with a heart that beat up into my throat. The five before me all told the truth. They could all deny it, because I had all the documents, since [Gerhard] Jacobi, my ordinator, had signed all the documents last.
>
> As the others were asked, I wavered: "Should you tell the truth or not?" As a theologian, you ask yourself that! Afterward, today, I think, how idiotic! But today, that's easy. Then I said, coolly, "No." I thought, "You're not putting them back into prison." Long after the war, I read the article by Dietrich Bonhoeffer, "What It Means to Tell 'the Truth.'"[23] He corroborated me. All the resistance fighters had this problem. Our problem was a small matter compared with the problems of the resistance fighters.[24]

These quandaries reflected both the era and the sector within German society that still placed a heavy emphasis on honor. Confessing Church lawyer Heinrich Schmidt explained it this way:

> I want to make clear how my parents viewed what I was doing. When I was imprisoned for the first time, my father wrote to my brothers and sisters. I found the letter later and was moved how my father wrote, "I am sure that Heinrich did not break any laws because he promised not to, before he left for Berlin." That was the world in which we lived. It's hard for the younger generation to understand.[25]

Postwar Attitudes toward Resistance

Some church leaders began to examine critically the distinction that had been made between the political and the religious realm after 1945. Others held this distinction to be as important doctrinally and institutionally as before. Initial postwar church attempts to deal with the consequences of the German political resistance were troubled and tentative, as this statement, issued by the Berlin-Brandenburg church government on the first anniversary (in July 1945) of the July 20 attempt illustrates:

> The Church of Jesus Christ can never approve an attack on the life of a human being, with whatever intentions it may be carried out. But among those who had to suffer were countless persons who never wanted such an assassination attempt; nevertheless, they were put to death. . . . Things would not have reached this extent had Christendom had more faith and more courage in its Confession, instead of allowing its convictions to be confused and Christian judgment to soften. Blame rests upon us all. . . . Of that which was preached to our people in the last 10 years, nothing was as fatal as the maxim that justice is that which is useful for the people. Justice is that

alone which corresponds to the will of God. . . . The individual Christian should certainly be able, for the sake of his Master, to bear confidently an injustice that befalls him; but the community of a people cannot stand unless law and justice are valid.[26]

The Berlin-Brandenburg church's statement pinpointed the heart of the question that troubled many Christians after 1945: Had the church more assertively proclaimed the Christian message to Germans in 1933, could it have resisted Nazism in a real "Christian" sense and avoided the political compromises that entangled it? Could it even have helped prevent the Nazi disaster, which the July 20 conspiracy attempted—futilely and so late—to stop?

This was the question that Martin Niemöller had raised in Treysa. But as the church's own reply in Treysa indicates, many church leaders were not aware, or did not want to recognize, that their own nationalism in 1933 had blinded them to what the Christian message in Nazi Germany really should have been. In 1933, many who proclaimed a nationalistic or "Aryan" Christianity very assertively believed that they *were* proclaiming the Gospel. So the question was not really one of proclamation but of recognizing the circumstances in which they, as Christians, were living. And it is significant that, when it acknowledged its guilt in the formal Stuttgart Declaration in 1945, the church saw its failure as not having confessed more clearly—not in not having resisted.

The churches' postwar discussion of the actual resistance groups was marked by a sense of missed opportunity, of unrecognized signals. In addition, many Christian attempts to grasp the significance of the attempted coup foundered because of the inability of many people to allow for exceptions to some of their traditional beliefs. Postwar arguments resurrected some of the debates that had torn the resistance groups—whether the murder of Hitler could be supported by Christians, for example. The title of one postwar booklet about the July 20 group, "Traitors or Patriots," echoed the tone of the debate between those who held the conspirators to have embodied the highest German ideals and others who saw them as traitors to the Fatherland.[27] In 1952, systematic theologian Hans Iwand even speculated that the failure of the July 20 attempt made it easier for some Christian Germans to respect it:

Perhaps one may see it as the providence of God that the failure allows their action to appear as pure sacrifice, which can have a greater significance in the spiritual and moral realms of our lives than if the assassination had been successful.[28]

In part, Iwand argued that had the July 20 attempt been successful, the Nazis would have succeeded in winning support for Hitler as a martyr, which would have undermined any new government that attempted to replace the Nazi regime. But there was certainly another level to Iwand's argument, because many of the adherents of the anti-Nazi resistance were left with a deep sense of moral failure. They had resisted, but too late and too little; and they now assumed the burden of guilt for their own sake, and for that of all Germans.

One who felt this way was Emmi Bonhoeffer's brother, Justus Delbruck. Delbruck had resigned his government post in Holstein in 1933 when Hitler came to power. "He didn't want to be a civil servant under Hitler," Bonhoeffer commented. Although the Russians freed him in late April 1945 from the Gestapo prison, they rearrested him four weeks later, supposedly to learn more about the July 20 group:

I believe that he made no effort to free himself. I later heard, from someone who had seen him there, that he sat by himself, utterly silent and withdrawn. I believe that he accepted the entire thing as a suffering of atonement. He gave this strange answer when I asked him, after the 20th of July, after the failed assassination: "Can you see any sense in it, that it had to go wrong?" He said, "I believe it was good that it was done, and perhaps good, too, that it failed."

I didn't ask him, "How was it good that it failed?" I knew him well enough to sense that he was thinking not only of the difficulties there would have been in establishing a working government as heterogenous as the resistance was. He was thinking, perhaps, that we would have gotten off too easily after all the crimes the Nazis had committed. Perhaps he didn't have the strength and the will anymore to resist inwardly. Physically weak, without medication, he died of diphtheria in October 1945.

Sometimes I think that perhaps he acquiesced inwardly to all that then came because he — just as my husband — was convinced of noblesse oblige. The noblesse had failed. It hadn't managed to realize its obligations. The educated bourgeois class didn't resist unanimously. Most of them ducked and conformed and tried to survive, and thought, "Oh, this is a storm that will blow over." Adenauer, for example, didn't open himself to the resistance and threw [Carl] Goerdeler out when he tried to win him over to the resistance. He never explained why. On the one hand, perhaps he didn't trust Goerdeler much. Many didn't; my husband was skeptical as well.[29] On the other hand, Adenauer probably thought like Talleyrand: "*J'ai vécu*" — I have survived. Stalin, too, said, "The Hitlers come and go, but the German people remain." But the people among whom I lived didn't think this way.[30]

The Significance of Faith for the Resistance

The people among whom Bonhoeffer lived were gone after 1945. Whatever doubts they had had, however tormented they had been before or after the assassination attempt, they achieved an astonishing clarity of moral vision, demonstrated in the letters and diaries that survive them.[31] The 11,448 Germans who were executed between July 20 and May 1945 were conspicuously absent from the postwar German scene. The Germans who survived to rebuild Germany and its Protestant church after 1945 had been shaped by their experiences under Hitler, which included whatever moral decisions and compromises they had made. Most of those who had concluded that political resistance was a moral necessity were gone. This included the Christians who had discovered the meaning of religious faith within the context of political resistance — people like Helmut Moltke, who wrote that he had once felt "that belief in God is not essential" for one to be a staunch opponent of Nazism:

> Today I know that I was wrong, completely wrong . . . the degree today to which we are demanded to endanger ourselves and be prepared to sacrifice ourselves presupposes more than good ethical principles.[32]

Emmi Bonhoeffer drew a similar conclusion, but commented,

> There is this very remarkable sentence in the memoirs of Margaret Boveri,[33] where Uwe Johnsson asks her, "How did it happen that, with your cultural level, you toyed

with the idea of joining the Nazi party?" To which she replies: "In my parents' house, much morality was taught, but no religion. In the extreme case, morality without religion doesn't stand up." A very remarkable sentence. . . . What does religion mean? Look at the many resistance fighters. Who was "religious" in the usual sense? Very many were in the active resistance for moral reasons and long-range political views.[34]

As Bonhoeffer noted, many of the conspirators were not religious. From her period in Dahlem, Elsie Steck concluded that even some of the people who became involved in the Confessing Church did so because they were seeking religious support for their political convictions. And many Germans who at least appeared to be deeply religious succumbed to the ideological traps of Nazism.

So what did their faith mean to the Protestants who resisted primarily for reason of religious conviction? As Moltke's statement indicates, it represented something "more than good ethical principles." But when we look at the doubts that haunted conspirators like von Haeften, it is clear that religion did not guarantee simple certainty or peace of mind. Dietrich Bonhoeffer wrestled with this question in prison. "One may ask," he wrote,

> whether there have ever before in human history been people with so little ground under their feet — people to whom every available alternative seemed equally intolerable, repugnant, and futile, who looked beyond all these existing alternatives for the source of their strength so entirely in the past or in the future, and who yet, without being dreamers, were able to await the success of their cause so quietly and confidently. Or perhaps one should rather ask whether the responsible thinking people of any generation that stood at a turning point in history did not feel much as we do, simply because something new was emerging that could not be seen in the existing alternatives.[35]

In the dark days of 1945, it took a true visionary to see the possibility of something new emerging. Some of the final letters from the members of the German resistance echoed the words of the father of the epileptic child in Mark 9:24: "Lord, I believe; help my unbelief!" Bonhoeffer's words suggest that it was possible for the act of resistance to help their unbelief. It opened the path to a vision of a new kind of faith. For some Germans, the July 20 attempt and other acts of resistance were proclamations of this faith. As Carl Goerdeler wrote before the July 20 attempt,

> It is a great error to assume that the strength of the soul of the German people is exhausted; frankly and intentionally, it has been merely buried alive. So the task of an act of rescue is to clear away the mass covering it, that is, the secrecy and terror, to restore law and decency, and with that, to liberate the immense growth in the power of the soul.[36]

[It is interesting that Goerdeler, of all people, described the purpose of the political conspiracy in this way, for he was not a religious man — although, in his despair before his execution, he searched for certainty in religion.[37]]

But for the Christian faith, the significance of the various acts of German resistance to Nazism depended upon the way in which Christians interpreted them — and on how they examined their own failure to resist. The Berlin-Brandenburg church's statement in July 1945 that "It would not have reached this extent had Christendom had more faith and more courage in its convictions" would be echoed in October 1945 in the Protestant church's Stuttgart Declaration of Guilt—in its tone that suggested risks not taken, responsibilities denied. And, as Martin Niemoller had stressed in Treysa, the questions of German guilt and resistance (or failure to resist) were closely related.

In 1945, the story of the Confessing Church was not a completed chapter in the history of German Protestantism. The behavior of the church during the Nazi era was an important new factor that influenced Protestant thinking and action on a number of issues. Part of Bonhoeffer's legacy was his writings about these issues, on Christian and political responsibility and accountability. These were questions that remained unresolved for a number of Christians. The Germans who faced the challenge of these problems after May 1945 had to examine the question of guilt. Guilt, like nationalism—or any phenomenon that concerns both individual conscience and the life of the larger society—is full of nuances. Guilt has its own dynamics; it can twist the soul, which, like a limb wasted by disease, may regain some function but never again its original perfection. Whatever their roles during the Nazi period, Confessing Christians now bore the marks of their experience within their souls.

Bismarck speaking, Bad Oeynhausen, Westphalia, 1895. *(Stadtarchiv Bielefeld)*

Demonstration by wounded war veterans, 1919, Berlin. *(Landesbildstelle Berlin)*

Crowds thronging onto Tempelhofer Feld, Berlin, May 1, 1933. *(Landesbildstelle Berlin)*

Facing page:
Top: Reich Bishop Ludwig Müller entering the Sportspalast, November 1933. *(Evangelisches Zentralarchiv, Berlin)*
Bottom: "German Christian" clergy following their flag to the Berlin Dom church, September 1934. *(Evangelisches Zentralarchiv, Berlin)*

Above: Pastor Fritz von Bodelschwingh speaking at the consecration of the World War I memorial before the Zion Church in Bethel, 1934. *(Hauptarchiv der von Bodelschwinghschen Anstalten Bethel)*
Below: Hitler Youth member standing at attention, ca. 1936. *(Stadtarchiv Bielefeld)*

"Illegal" theological students from the Berlin *Kirchlichen Hochschule,* ca. 1939. *(Photo courtesy Angelika Rutenborn, Berlin)*

Smoke rising from the crematorium in the village of Hadamar (photo taken secretly by village resident, ca. 1941) *(Stadtarchiv Hadamar)*

Pastor Fritz von Bodelschwingh with Bethel patient in the 1930s. *(Hauptarchiv der von Bodelschwinghschen Anstalten Bethel)*

Burning synagogue, November 9, 1938. *(Stadtarchiv Bielefeld)*

Jewish children awaiting deportation, 1941. *(Stadtarchiv Bielefeld)*

Jews being deported to the East, 1941. *(Stadtarchiv Bielefeld)*

Ukrainian woman and child during SS visit of "model" camp.
(Stadtarchiv Bielefeld)

Burning car at the Anhalter Bahnhof, Berlin, 1945. *(Ullstein Bilderdienst—Arthur Grimm)*

Soviet soldier raising the red flag on the Berlin Reichstag building, May 1945. *(Ullstein Bilderdienst, Berlin)*

Leonhardstplatz, downtown Stuttgart, 1946. *(Landesbildstelle Württemberg)*

Refugees, July 1945. *(Landesbildstelle Berlin)*

Women rebuilding Berlin, 1949. *(Landesbildstelle Berlin)*

Emergency housing, 1955. *(Stadtarchiv Bielefeld)*

Church of Reconciliation behind the Berlin Wall, 1980. The East Germans demolished the church, which was in the "dead zone" between the Wall and East Berlin, in 1983. *(Victoria Barnett)*

Some 2,000 East Germans in the Church of the Redeemer, East Berlin, October 6, 1989. *(Evangelische Pressedienst Bild/Schoelzel)*

✝ 10 ✝

"The Guilt of Others"

The Council of the Evangelical Church in Germany welcomes representatives of the World Council of Churches to its meeting on October 18–19, 1945, in Stuttgart.

We are all the more thankful for this visit, as we with our people know ourselves to be not only in a community of suffering, but also in a solidarity of guilt. With great anguish we state: Through us, inestimable suffering was inflicted on many peoples and lands. What we have often witnessed before our congregations we now declare in the name of the whole church: Indeed we have fought for long years in the name of Jesus Christ against the spirit that found horrible expression in the violent National Socialist regime, but we charge ourselves for not having confessed more courageously, prayed more conscientiously, believed more joyously, and loved more ardently.

Now a new beginning is to be made in our churches. Grounded in the Holy Spirit, founded with utter seriousness on the only Lord of the Church, they go about cleansing themselves of foreign influences and putting themselves in order. We hope to the God of mercy and compassion that he will use our churches as his tool and will grant them authority to proclaim his word and create obedience to his will among ourselves and our entire people.

That, in this new beginning, we may know ourselves bound with the other churches of the ecumenical community, fills us with deep joy.

We hope to God that, through the common service of the church, the spirit of might and retribution which wants to become powerful anew, will be avoided throughout the world, and [that] the spirit of freedom and love, through which alone tortured humanity can find solace, comes to rule.

Thus we pray to God, in an hour in which the entire world needs a new beginning: *Veni creator spiritus*!

(Signed by the members of the Council of the EKD)

Theophil Wurm, Bishop	Wilhelm Niesel, Pastor
Hans Asmussen, Pastor	Rudolf Smend, Professor
Hans Meiser, Bishop	Gustav Heinemann, lay member of the
Heinrich Held, Superintendent	Council
Hans Lilje, Pastor and Church Councilman	Otto Dibelius, Bishop
Hugo Hahn, Superintendent	Martin Niemöller, Pastor

The Stuttgart Declaration of Guilt

THE STUTTGART DECLARATION was one of the most important postwar statements of the Evangelical Church of Germany (hereafter referred to as EKD), this brief, hastily written statement presented to a small group of Dutch, Swiss, French, British, and U.S. church representatives. The arrival of these church leaders in Stuttgart took German church leaders by surprise. The visitors' purpose was to formally reestablish ties with the German Protestant church, but they also had another goal. As Swiss churchman Alphons Koechlin later said, they hoped,

> if possible, to demand a declaration from the German church that would delineate its relationship to other churches and the ecumenical world clearly, in such a way that a relationship of trust could be taken up at once. We hoped, however, not to have to demand such a declaration, but to receive it on the basis of the German church's own understanding.[1]

The foreign church leaders told the Germans it was crucial that they have such a statement to show to people in their churches at home, if the ties being re-established to the German church were not to unravel under the intense feelings of hatred and revenge in their countries toward the German people.

As the members of the EKD Council began to confer, it became evident that each viewed his church's behavior during the Third Reich very differently. The widest differences were on the question of who bore moral responsibility for the actions of Nazi Germany, as was illustrated by the preliminary drafts. Lutheran pastor Hans Asmussen wrote, "We know that it was our fellow citizens who brought inestimable suffering over all of Europe and to lands outside of Europe as well,"[2] thereby implying that the church and its members had not played a significant role in the course of Nazi Germany. This sentence was struck in the version submitted by Bishop Otto Dibelius (which was essentially the draft that the EKD accepted), with one important exception. Although Dibelius had penned the phrase "the solidarity of guilt," he wrote nothing claiming responsibility for the sins of the Nazis.[3] It was Martin Niemöller who insisted on the controversial sentence, "With great anguish we state: Through us, inestimable suffering was inflicted on many peoples and lands."[4]

"Through us." No one, in those postwar months, wanted to be held personally accountable for what had happened under Nazism. In their own eyes, the Germans had become a nation of victims — of refugees from the eastern territories, of prisoners in Allied prisoner of war camps, of humiliated civil servants who now were being summoned before Allied courts to explain their role in the Nazi bureaucracy. Far from being bound in a solidarity of guilt, Germans were rapidly closing ranks in a solidarity of silence about the past.

In this atmosphere, the Stuttgart Declaration of Guilt was seen widely in Germany as a capitulation to the political aims of the Allies and a betrayal of the German people. Anticipating this response, Hans Asmussen asked the ecumenical guests in Stuttgart not to publish the text. "Do what you can," he begged them, "that this declaration does not become misused politically."[5] But, of course, the Declaration was publicized; that had been the intention of the foreign church representatives. Inevitably, its text appeared in the press in Germany as well. Its signers found themselves, some very reluctantly, defending and explaining it to irate parishioners. The doctors at one institution run by the EKD's Inner Mission resigned en masse, announcing that they would not work for a church that betrayed its own people (it is worth noting that no such mass resignations occurred during Hitler's euthanasia program).[6]

Some members of the EKD Council, although they had signed the document, sympathized with these grievances. Now under attack, they gave various interpretations of the "solidarity of guilt." In Bavaria, Hans Meiser explained that the Stuttgart Declaration was purely an internal church document:

> For that reason, it does not speak in the name of the German people or its government. . . . . The Stuttgart Declaration does not take a position on the question of political guilt for the war as such.[7]

In Hannover, Hans Lilje replied to an irate church member,

> I myself, as a member of the Council of the EKD, have never signed a declaration, "the German people must confess itself guilty of this war and its atrocities". . . . . These phrases are not included in the Stuttgart Declaration. The Declaration mentioned is not a political but a church declaration. . . . . The men gathered there have done nothing for which they must be ashamed as Germans and Christians. Only those who hold the leadership of the Third Reich for utterly innocent could claim that.[8]

Hans Asmussen tried to remind church members that their current hardships could not legitimate the denial of what had happened in Nazi Germany:

> We are not traitors to the Fatherland. . . . . What does the injustice being done to our people today mean for the confession of our guilt? Firstly, it means nothing. It doesn't change in the least the evil that we Germans did in Poland, in Greece, in Holland. It in no way covers up our guilt toward the "non-Aryans." It in no way justifies our silence and cooperation in the evil 12 years.[9]

In his memoirs, Otto Dibelius, writing of the horrors of the Russian occupation in the East and of the deportations of Germans from Poland and Czechoslovakia, noted that, in Stuttgart, "it was not easy not to say one word about this and to limit ourselves to the account of the German's debts."[10] Moreover, many Confessing Christians believed "that they said and did what was possible in a totalitarian state, and will not need to accuse themselves," as one pastor in the Württemberg Society wrote Hermann Diem.[11]

Of all the signers, only Martin Niemöller chose to publicize the document and to draw political consequences from it as well. For the next two years, as he later wrote, "I did nothing else but preach the Declaration of Guilt to people."[12] It was one factor that rapidly turned the church hero who was freed from Dachau into one of the most controversial figures in postwar Germany.

"The German Passion"

Most Germans were outraged that their own postwar hardships were not mentioned in the words of the Stuttgart Declaration. If they were guilty of Nazi crimes, they reasoned, then the Allies, particularly the Russians, were guilty for German suffering after the *Zusammenbruch*. Memory operates selectively; immediate experience is the stage on which memory selects the dramas to be played and the principals to play them. The immediate experience of most Germans during the unusually cold winter of 1945–1946 was hardship. Food and fuel were scarce, and there was little intact housing, particularly in the bombed-out cities. Thousands of embittered German refugees arrived from the east every day. Most German soldiers were still in Allied prisoner of war camps; rumors of hard conditions in the camps spread throughout the civilian population, as did continuing reports of atrocities in the Russian zone.

It was easy to ignore the fact that the cause of all this suffering had been Nazi Germany. It was easy to forget the sufferings of the Jews and others in the concentration camps, which, significantly, were not mentioned in the Stuttgart Declaration. It was easy to lose sight of the fact that, in the cold winter of 1945–1946, the Dutch, British, French, Poles, and Russians were also suffering, shivering, and going hungry in the ruins of their cities.

Even when they remembered such things, few German politicians and church leaders dared to raise the question of German guilt in more than cursory form. Those who did took pains to qualify it, and this, inevitably, meant creating additional distance between postwar Germany and the Nazi past. Konrad Adenauer, addressing this first postwar meeting of the Cologne city council, listed the hardships of the residents of that severely bombed city and then noted,

> the blame for this nameless misery, this indescribable suffering, are those accursed people who came to power in the unholy year of 1933, those who have disgraced the name of Germany before the entire civilized world and who, as their own more than earned decline became certain, intentionally and consciously plunged our seduced and paralyzed people in deepest misery. . . . We, you and I, are not those guilty for this suffering. We, you and I, are condemned and forced, forced by the love for our people . . . to take this dreadful and heavy burden upon ourselves.[13]

With the consummate politician's sure aim, Adenauer had touched the misery of Germans, assuaged their guilt, and even made them feel noble — honorable figures in what the theologian Helmut Thielicke called "the German Passion."[14] In fact, Adenauer showed courage in blaming the Nazis instead of the Allied military authorities for the postwar hardships; as Helmut Gollwitzer recalled, many Germans did not even do that. Gollwitzer himself was a Russian prisoner of war until January 1950:

> I'll speak first about the situation among the prisoners of war. Hitler was gone. No one wanted to have been a Nazi, even the former Nazis among us. Among prisoners, there are three possibilities. Most of them become completely apolitical; they concern themselves with nothing more than survival and "I hope I'll get home." The second group adapts itself to its new situation. In this case, that meant to the Soviet point of view, either genuinely or out of opportunism. They became antifascists in the Soviet sense and cooperated with the antifascist committees there. In the third group, the reaction was defiant. They weren't just former SS men or particularly convinced Nazis. But all at once, in their imprisonment, their pride rose, and they took the side of the Nazis. The Russians took that very badly. These people had difficulties because of it. But if they didn't die, they did return home from their imprisonment.
>
> That's how it was there. Here, I only know what I've been told. My wife was in

Switzerland because her mother was Jewish, and she returned to Frankfurt in 1945 with an American military plane to become a parish helper among the ruins. [Note: Gollwitzer's Jewish fiancée, the actress Eva Bildt, had died, weakened and ill, after several years of forced labor in a munitions factory. He married Brigitte Freudenberg, the daughter of Adolf Freudenberg, who had worked for the Grüber office until his emigration to Switzerland in 1939]. She personally experienced how the dreadful misery of 1945–1946 held the Germans back from all remorse. Because — most people believed this — the occupation troops were responsible for the misery. "They're just as inhuman as we were," was how it was put. And, with that, everything was evened up.[15]

In Bremen, Marta S., widowed and with a small child, was one of the *Trümmerfrauen* — the war widows who now helped, with simple tools and their bare hands, to rebuild the ruined cities. She had been a Nazi, then the wife of a Confessing Church pastor and even in 1982 saw herself as both accountable for Nazism and a victim of it:

We couldn't laugh for years. If one heard laughter here on the streets in Bremen, it was almost always an American, not a German. I learned more and more, through books and so forth, and we heard from both sides, what we had done to the others and vice versa. Two years ago, I was in Warsaw. I wanted to see the area just once where my husband was missing — and, of course, with that I saw what the Germans had done in Poland as well.

When I reread the letters from that time, I see the hopelessness and doubt. In despair, both good and evil arise. Now, I've had years to think about the whole thing. Right after the war, there was no time to think because of the necessities of life. I had a small child, and the struggle to survive was very hard. . . . The bitterness was hard, and to deal with that was difficult.

In Bremen, we had an American enclave. Because I spoke English, I could speak with them, so they turned from "the enemy" into people. They were so optimistic; they believed that "re-education" could change us. But we had already had one "re-education" — to National Socialism. We thought, we've had so much re-education, how are we really going to find ourselves?

If the judges in Nuremberg had been Swiss, we would have been better able to accept the verdict. Since the victors were judges at the same time, it was hard to accept — and that the Russians, who had also committed crimes, could judge us.

The Stuttgart Declaration of Guilt impressed me deeply, and I passed it on, even to people who didn't want to accept that guilt. I had been in this conflict since 1933, and that has always made it hard for me. I was simultaneously a party member and a victim of fascism. I think it was much easier to be one or the other. We learned much too late that certain combinations simply aren't possible.[16]

Another woman, a theologian in the Confessing Church, admitted that she, too, was an early enthusiast of the Nazis and only gradually awakened. In 1945, she said,

I was this way — I wasn't happy that the Russians had marched in, I didn't say, "Now a new era has dawned!" Rather, for me, the developments in the war were a dreadful experience. . . . I was still in Berlin then. The British, the French — I thought, what kind of people are those, what do they want here? They were all marionettes, who didn't feel these things theologically, as we did. I always thought, "Is it really the case that we Germans — this sounds dreadfully arrogant now — that we are the only ones who must truly go through the filth and must think about what humane existence is?" That's how it appeared to me then.[17]

The recollections of one Confessing Church pastor who was in a U.S. prisoner of war camp in Italy for nine months after the war illustrate profoundly the extent to which personal suffering hardened some people to the moral catastrophe wrought by Nazism. Together with his fellow prisoners, he saw pictures of the Allied liberation of Auschwitz:

> They were projected on a screen; we had to look at them. Do you believe that a look at shocking pictures, by the average person who had perhaps five or six years of war behind him — that that aroused reflections about history? . . . No, the so-called "dealing with the past," I would say, had no significance, except, perhaps, for some individuals.[18]

But not all Germans were preoccupied with their own misery, and there were certainly some who began now to wrestle with the implications of their recent history. Kurt Scharf, distinguishing among the various moods in the German population in 1945, said:

> I believe that it is very difficult to pronounce a general judgment here. One must differentiate between the parish members who were residents in the region of the later Federal Republic and those banished from the eastern provinces. The refugees, as a matter of fact, did tend to even things up, even when they had been convinced members of the Confessing Church, and to say, "Yes, the injustice that occurred in the Nazi state was terrible, but through all that which happened to us in the East at the end of the war and during the final months of the war in general, the specific guilt of the Germans has now been balanced out." Among those who were affected by it, a kind of reckoning up took place. . . .
>
> It is true, too, that among the members of the Confessing Church, even among those who weren't banished, many could be found who rejected the methods of National Socialism — the terror, the duplicity, the dictatorial, totalitarian claims . . . who were, however, patriotically inclined, who fought conservatively and patriotically for their church in a Fatherland in which there should be justice and freedom, an inner and outward freedom.
>
> This group within the Confessing Church, too, felt bitter after 1945, that, in many cases, those who had actually resisted the National Socialists were now, again, the disadvantaged and grieving. That was even more the case in the German Democratic Republic than in the Federal Republic. But in the Federal Republic, too, it happened again and again, that people who had conformed to the Nazi *Zeitgeist* understood amazingly quickly how to curry favor with the military administration of the occupation forces. . . .
>
> So, with all that which happened in Berlin during the Russian incursion, in West Berlin as well, those affected were often precisely the previous opponents of the [Nazi] system — that is, the wrong people. Here in the Dahlem parish, there are still women alive who hid Jews, and through that, resisted National Socialism at the risk of their lives, and who, during the taking of Berlin, were raped, tortured, and beaten by the Russians because they owned villas. The occupation troops assumed that each person who had retained certain civil rights had to have been a party follower of the system in the National Socialist state.

This experience either reawakened or strengthened patriotic, even nationalistic, sentiments. But I don't believe that one can give a general judgment here. The mood varies greatly. I know many parish members, too, who take pains to acknowledge, without qualification, the unique, great guilt of the Germans during the Nazi era and during World War II, and recognize it truly as the basic cause of all the suffering that came upon the Germans afterward.[19]

Even for the best-intentioned Germans who had been in the Confessing Church, however, the task of wrestling with the moral questions raised by their own behavior under Nazism was daunting. Whatever their own record had been, they were now inextricably bound with Germany and its Nazi past. Many were hurt, even outraged, at the criticism they now heard from foreign Christians. One churchman with close contacts with the Swiss churches said that, even during the course of the war, he realized that he and his Swiss friends thought very differently about what was happening:

We couldn't talk at all about such things. After the war, it came out. Three of us had traveled to Switzerland again, in order to begin the dialogue in general. Those were unbelievably difficult talks. The accusation was that we had survived. The fact that we were still around, for them that was treachery. They didn't say it that way, but basically it could be felt. They couldn't understand that, under a totalitarian system, one has to make compromises, if one doesn't want to run directly into the open knife, and that one has to have a certain flexibility, and that one simply can't—oh, well, they couldn't understand any of that. Those were utterly exhausting discussions, lasting even into the nights. Thus, the tensions dissolved very gradually, until we came together again, came together completely. That happened finally in this way—that I was elected by the Swiss delegates to the governing council. . . . They elected me, as a German! That was a juncture that moved me greatly, that that was possible. With that, the bridge was truly there again.[20]

Despite the symbolic importance of the Stuttgart Declaration, the gulf between German Protestants and Christians in countries that had suffered under Nazism was not easily crossed. Hebe Kohlbrugge, the Dutch woman who had worked for both the Confessing Church in Germany and the resistance in Holland, experienced that first-hand. She had tuberculosis when she was liberated from the Ravensbrück concentration camp. After she recovered, she returned to Holland, where the Dutch church appointed her to help re-establish relations between Dutch and German parishes:

They said, "You know the Confessing Church and you know the 'other Germany,' and we look for someone who can take up contacts with Germany, to try to build a bridge against the hatred that has grown in Holland."[21]

But the success of her work depended not so much on her own efforts as on the Germans:

Well, of course, the Dutch people expected German people to say a word, to say, "We have done dreadful things." You know how Germans are; if they come inside, they say, "*Guten Tag!* How are you?" Well, that the Dutch people couldn't stand. But . . . if they just said, "I am happy that I can be here and what has happened can never happen again. . . . " Of course, there was sometimes bitterness, but it depended a great deal on the way the Germans acted.[22]

Breakthroughs of understanding did occur during this period. Martin Schröter, the son of a Confessing Church pastor, had fought in Hitler's army until the end with the belief that Germany had to win the war. He began his theological studies after his return home and attended an international meeting of theology students in Holland:

Well, we were invited, two students from each of the West German theological faculties, to an ecumenical meeting of theology students in Benfeld, near Haarlem. The idea was that representatives from those nations that were enemies during the war should come. Essentially, it consisted of the generation of those who had been soldiers. . . . The British were there, French, Swiss, Austrians. At first, we worked theologically, rather abstractly. But then a great deal occurred under the surface, or openly, as well. Of course, it was the period in Holland when there was still a strong air of animosity against the Germans, and our Dutch colleagues were roughed up by their own compatriots because they spoke German with us. To speak German in Holland was still — it was simply the language of the enemy, the occupiers.

It was on an evening that we had thought out very innocently; something cultural from every nation should be offered, songs or poems. And it went very well; it went smoothly, until it was the Dutch people's turn. The Dutch brought a poem from a Dutch poet who had been in a concentration camp and had been murdered by the Germans in the camp. All the Dutch knew who it concerned; we, of course, did not. We were utterly bewildered. When the poem had been read, all the Dutch stood up and sang their national anthem.

We sat there and felt, at first, ashamed, perplexed, as if we'd been slapped. We Germans didn't have a national anthem at that time. As a nation, we were the last piece of dirt, and now they stood before us suddenly with their pure honor, so to speak, and we as the murderers of this young Dutch poet. It was a very embarrassing atmosphere. All at once, we felt frightfully antagonistic.

I had a book of ballads along. Then I remembered a ballad by Konrad Ferdinand Meyer, *"Die Füsse im Feuer"* ("The Feet in the Fire"). The story comes from the Inquisition in France, that a wanderer in the night loses his way in the storm and rain and comes upon a dilapidated estate. And the lord of the estate gives him supper and a place for the night, and, on the next morning, the nobleman's hair, when he awakens his guest, has turned grey, for he has remembered in the night that this lost wanderer had been one of the king's hirelings who had tortured his wife, had held her feet in the hot coals of the fireplace because she hadn't admitted something.

So forgiveness, reconciliation, the renunciation of revenge — that was the theme. And the wanderer asks, "Why didn't you kill me?" For it was clear to him, too; they had recognized each other. Then the nobleman speaks, this is the last line: "Revenge is mine, so speaks God." Somewhat sentimental, but very moving.

In any case, that was the way for me to react to what had happened, and from the mood left by that, a long conversation developed for some of us, lasting the entire night. In this way, we tried to bring this very deep-seated conflict out into the daylight. It really got down to the emotional level, really like a good pietistic conversion, with tears and prayers.

For me, that was the hour of conversion from my entire previous political history and my political foundations. It became clear to me that this separation, of Nazism and fascism on the one side and the "Deutsch-National," nationalistic, soldierly, military, on the other side — that that didn't work, that they went together. And, suddenly, my entire participation during the war as a soldier came before my eyes in a completely new light. . . . For me, this was the beginning of my openness to socialistic thinking, toward my pacifist engagement. At first, I was a very militant pacifist, for a long time, until I balanced that out.[23]

The Church and Denazification

Such encounters with the victims of Nazism brought people like Schröter face to face with the issue of their own behavior during the Nazi era. But most Germans did not have this experience. On the contrary, their main encounters were with the victors, their former foes, since postwar governance of the German regions from 1945 to 1949 was regulated by the Allied military authorities in their respective regions.

This situation was as unavoidable as the postwar food and fuel shortages were, but Germans bridled under the Allied occupation policies. Nowhere did this become more evident than in Germans' reaction to the Allied denazification and re-education program. It was obvious to the Allied authorities that postwar Germany had to be built upon a clear moral foundation. Obvious, too, was the necessity of ensuring that Nazis did not gain a foothold in a new German government — not only for the sake of postwar Germany but as an act of accountability to the people throughout the world who had suffered under Nazism.

The Allied authorities counted upon the support of the churches in this endeavor — particularly because of their moral stature in the wake of Nazism. The international reputation of people like Martin Niemöller, and the public record of the conflicts that both Protestant and Catholic church members had had with the Nazis, led the Allied authorities to see the church "as one of the most important instruments for the reorientation of German society."[24] Initially, the Allies tried to enlist the support of Protestants like Dibelius and Wurm and Catholics like Münster's Bishop von Galen (who had openly attacked Hitler's euthanasia policies). In Württemberg, the U.S. military governor even asked Wurm to lead the provisional government there,[25] and the British asked von Galen to head the new Westphalian government. Both bishops refused, preferring to focus on rebuilding their churches.

This atmosphere of mutual respect deteriorated rapidly for reasons that lay on both sides. The Allies' problem, as Frederic Spotts noted in his astute study, *The Churches and Politics in Postwar Germany,* was that they expected the moral support of the churches for the "moral rehabilitation" of Germany but did not want the churches' opinion about the "political rehabilitation" of their country.[26] "The fact that the two cannot be out of step was largely ignored by the military in the rush to get Germany on her feet materially," noted Spotts,[27] and whatever their views on separating the political and religious realms, most German Protestant leaders now felt entitled to address both aspects publicly.

This conflict was intensified by the Allies' lack of knowledge about the traditional role of the Protestant church in Germany and about its recent history. Even military officers in the U.S. Religious Affairs Branch, which was responsible for the contacts with the churches, were hampered by their lack of knowledge and, in some cases, their lack of fluency in German (for example, several EKD statements were misunderstood or misinterpreted).[28]

Even if the Allied authorities did not have an extensive knowledge of the recent history of the German Protestant opposition, they seem to have grasped the source of the churches' antagonism toward them. One officer on Eisenhower's staff, after meeting with Wurm and Niemöller, reported back that

> Both are, I believe, ardent German patriots who have violently disagreed with policies of the National Socialist party in the past but who are also capable of similar violent disagreement with the Allied occupation authorities . . . there is doubt in the minds of some of our officers who have contacted them that the relations with them in the future will be entirely smooth and easy.[29]

This was an understatement. The EKD leaders were soon publicly criticizing Allied policies in terms that suggested the Allies were almost as dictatorial toward the churches as the Nazis had been.[30] Most Protestant church leaders, even if they had been utterly disillusioned with Nazism, remained patriotic and nationalistic. Newly freed from Nazism, they now rankled under the restrictions the Allied authorities imposed on them. Although the churches had more independence at this point than any other German institution, church leaders still had to receive clearance from the Allies to travel and speak publicly, for example. Martin Niemöller, as the U.S. officer who spoke with him reported, had

> rather elaborate plans for his future activities, which he contemplates will include extended visits to foreign countries. . . . Under our present policy, of course, foreign travel is prohibited to German nationals. I am sure that Pastor Niemöller will violently protest against such restriction on his movements. I feel, however, that for the present it would be in our interest to have Pastor Niemöller devote himself to internal affairs.[31]

From the Allied perspective, the most pressing internal affair facing the Protestant church and every other German institution was the establishment of ideological purity. Basic denazification guidelines were drawn up at the Potsdam Conference in July and August 1945; eventually, each Allied government set up its own procedures for its occupation zone. Denazification was strictest and most rigorously applied in the U.S. zone. For this reason, the U.S. forces came to be more identified with denazification than did the British and the French.[32]

Special courts — *Spruchkammer* — were established; here, Germans under suspicion had to appear and prove that they had not been Nazis (or if they had been party members, to present evidence exonerating them of anything more than nominal membership). There were five categories, ranging from party members whose high rank or activities made their removal from public positions mandatory to people who could offer proof of anti-Nazi activities.

The primary goal of denazification was to remove Nazis from positions of public influence — as teachers, civil servants, pastors, and journalists, for example. The program's failure was predestined, perhaps, by the numbers involved. In 1945, there were eight million Nazi party members and millions more in various party organizations.[33] By the end of September 1945, 120,000 people had been removed from their jobs, and 700 people a day were being arrested.[34]

Denazification united the Germans as had nothing else, even their own hardships.

It was condemned across the ideological spectrum. In 1986, Elisabeth Schwarzhaupt discussed her chief criticisms of the program. A lawyer in the official Protestant consistory in Berlin during the Third Reich, she was elected to the Bundestag in 1953 and in 1961 became the first woman minister in Adenauer's cabinet:

> I criticized the so-called denazification policy of the Americans. This policy of submitting every single person who had been a member of the NSDAP to a courtlike trial, in which he had to justify himself—I held that to be bad in light of the psychological effects on these people. The motives from which people joined the party—however, wherever, whenever—during the Third Reich are as diverse as people are different. Some succumbed to the suggestion, to this mood of embarking on something, in 1933. Others were anti-Semites from earlier. Others were coerced in order to retain their office, their job, or to obtain a position. It was so multifaceted, and that is so difficult to tease out in a courtlike trial, that these proceedings didn't have the effect of cleansing people of National Socialist ideas; instead, they tended to drive them more toward self-justification.
>
> I was in favor of holding court trials for the major criminals and punishing them severely. That is a different question. But the little fellow travelers, who were simply weak people or unpolitical people, or people who succumbed to suggestion—to compel them to such a legal self-justification—that wasn't very good. I understand it in light of the Americans and their totally different position. They have never lived in a totalitarian state and can't measure the pressure under which these people stood. I understand this error, but I believe it was an error.[35]

The Protestant church, too, had come under scrutiny in the denazification program. Eight to nine percent of the Protestant clergy had been party members at some point,[36] and when the U.S. military government began drawing up "mandatory removal lists" of persons whose Nazi background necessitated their removal from public life, 15 percent of the Protestant clergy in the U.S. sector (which included the regions of Bavaria, Bremen, Hesse, and Baden-Württemberg) were on the lists.[37]

EKD leaders viewed the eradication of Nazi influence from the churches as an internal church affair and saw Allied pressures as an attack on church sovereignty that paralleled Nazi attempts to "aryanize" the churches. In May 1946, after months of privately voicing its displeasure to the Allied authorities, the EKD established its own guidelines for the "self-cleansing of the church" and announced that German pastors should not have to appear in the Allied *Spruchkammer*. The church would take care of its own denazification.

This had been the tacit arrangement in the British and French zones anyway. U.S. strictness on this point varied; in some instances, the United States did press for the removal of pastors with party affiliations—although some churches circumvented this by simply moving the pastors to small rural churches until the storm blew over.[38] Eventually, the U.S. military authorities told the church that they would accept its denazification of clergy provided it was well grounded and documented.

There were a number of problems inherent in church attempts at denazification. The main problem was that, far from forcing the church to assess its own record honestly, denazification led to self-justifications and comfortable illusions about the actual record of the Protestant church under Nazism. "The vast majority of the pastorate," the EKD stated in a paper to U.S. military authorities, "stood, openly or hidden, in a continual war led against representatives of the party."[39] The EKD claimed that, since it had opposed Nazism anyway, it had practically conducted its own "denazification" during the course of the Third Reich.

The actual record, of course, looked different. Only about one third of all German pastors had ever been actual members of the PEL and the Confessing Church. In Württemberg, Bishop Wurm told U.S. officials that more than 800 Nazi party members had been removed from the ranks of pastors, deacons, and church board members in his church, many of them before 1945.[40] But Wurm's figures included Nazis who had left the church because the party (not the church) had demanded they leave.[41] Wurm also neglected to note that two of the most vocal critics of Nazism in the Württemberg church — Otto Mörike and Julius von Jan — had been successfully removed by the Nazis, and there had been virtually no open church support for them (although it should be noted that in von Jan's case, Wurm's private intervention probably kept him out of a concentration camp.)[42] In 1935, when Nazi officials accused the Württemberg church of removing "German Christian" pastors who were Nazi party members, the church even protested that "it is happy that there are National Socialist pastors in the ranks of the Confessing Church and among its own members, and it has never moved against a "German Christian" pastor just because he is a National Socialist."[43]

EKD claims that the Protestant church had always been anti-Nazi, then, were a whitewash of the church's past. But the EKD went further: It also attempted to qualify the guilt of party members, excusing party membership as an insignificant lapse in behavior that had not had any real political meaning. The EKD took this position not just on behalf of pastors but on general principle. In a statement to U.S. military authorities, the EKD argued that the "spiritual roots" of Nazism were so diverse that judgments were impossible in many cases and that many party members had been "totally apolitical and without the wish to work toward the *political* goals or ideas of the NSDAP."[44]

The EKD also used this argument to oppose the denazification of career soldiers. In the German military tradition, argued the EKD,

> the status of soldier was an unpolitical career rank that demanded the utmost discipline toward the commands of the superior officer and forced its members to keep their distance from political arguments outside their circle. [Note: One is reminded here of Martin Niemöller's remark that soldiers of his generation were not even allowed to vote; see Chapter 1.] Where the *moral* point lies at which the renunciation of his own political judgment is no longer bearable for an officer is a difficult question.[45]

In the public debate about denazification, then, the EKD (whose leaders, at that point, were the signers of the Stuttgart Declaration) argued for the most watered-down guidelines possible. It was the churches, both Catholic and Protestant, who asked "for an end to the internment and dismissal of nominal members of the Nazi party, which, in their view, hindered reconstruction by removing experts from vital positions."[46] It was the EKD governing council that argued for the principle of *nulla poena sine lege* — that individuals could not be punished for acts which were not illegal at the time they were committed; this principle, of course, was problematic because of what had been permitted legally under Nazi law.[47] It was the EKD which, in its 1946 statement about denazification, argued that moral sins had to be treated separately from political sins and that, since the essence of German guilt consisted of moral sins, these could neither be examined nor punished by a political institution like a court.[48]

The EKD's statements were not simply attempts to evade denazification or to exempt the church from its provisions. They reflected fears and prejudices widespread in Germany at the time, particularly the belief that wholescale denazification would lead to miscarriages of justice that could endanger the establishment of democracy in postwar Germany. Some people feared that Allied policies would lead to "renazification," not denazification (in the words of Pastor Hermann Diem, one of the few vocal supporters of the purpose of denazification), precisely because Allied mistakes in this area provoked such widespread resentment. One factor, of course, was the deep anti-Communism and anti-Soviet feeling of most church leaders, who believed that Soviet behavior in the eastern zone had stripped it of any right to judge German behavior. This was tied to fears that postwar Germany would become Communist; indeed, church leaders feared that if the ranks of German civil servants were thoroughly denazified, only Social Democrats or Communists, who had been thrown out by the Nazis in 1933, would be left—a prospect that, as Frederic Spotts noted, "fairly terrified" Catholic bishops (and Protestants as well!).[49]

Other qualms about denazification procedures arose from widespread reports of beatings, mock trials, and other miscarriages of justice. In 1949, the EKD distributed a lengthy memorandum, consisting both of church statements and of numerous affidavits collected by church leaders on injustices in the denazification program.[50] To prevent "a new wave of nationalism in the German people," the memorandum was printed only in English and in a limited number. The EKD noted that it had no way of checking the reliability of the reports; some of them were secondhand, while others related incidents that, compared with what had happened in the Nazi courts, seemed more inconvenient than unjust. Many of the complaints, however, were serious enough to warrant legitimate concern.

Inevitably, church efforts to address what it viewed as new injustices were sometimes used by former Nazis to regain their positions.[51] Because the Protestant church was seen as a "resistance organization" (and recognized as such by the courts in Bavaria[52]), it was now in particular demand as a reference for individuals summoned before the *Spruchkammer*. Just as pastors in 1933 had helped Germans obtain proof of "Aryan" identity from the church ledgers, they were now besieged by people requesting character references to present to the *Spruchkammer*. These forms, which could also be filled out by documented victims of the Nazi regime, were called *Persilscheine* ("Persil" was the brand name of a laundry detergent).

Even high-ranking Nazis now scurried to obtain *Persilscheine*—in some cases from the very people they had persecuted. Hitler's chancellery assistant, Viktor Brack, was on trial in Nuremberg. As Berta Braune, whose husband had gone to Gestapo prison for his opposition to the euthanasia measures, related,

> One day, a letter from Brack's attorney arrived for my husband: Could he write a statement exonerating [Brack]. . . . I only know that my husband spent three sleepless nights before he answered the letter. He wrote the lawyer that, unfortunately, this would be impossible. For Brack was informed about the matter in every respect. He had even been particularly involved in silencing [Braune] through the arrest, and [Braune] could not write any exonerating testimony here.[53]

Such instances showed that denazification was a problematic means of confronting the Nazi past. Instead, as Dietrich Goldschmidt believed, it often led to denial:

> The denazification procedure was that now everyone had to prove, "I wasn't a Nazi." That is as false psychologically as it is understandable. For it compelled each person to show that he hadn't been a Nazi at all. . . . Then people wrote the so-called *Persilscheine* for each other. For example, I was in Göttingen, and one of the directors of the firm for which I had worked in the camp wrote to me, whether I couldn't write a *Persilschein* for him . . . that he hadn't done anything to me. To which I wrote him back, "How was that, please? Indeed, you didn't do anything to me, but do you hold that to have been a service, the basis of which you could now, so to speak, contribute to the reconstruction of this land?" So he didn't receive that from me. My wife's former boss showed up in Göttingen, too, and wanted to have a certificate from her. . . . She belittled him, because he had been a party member.[54]

Helene Jacobs, too, was asked for *Persilscheine*. She filled out only one. In the apartment building where she had lived and hidden the artist who forged false papers for Jews,

> there was a man who had to train us in civil defense or something like that. He sensed, he knew my inner perspective, simply intuitively. . . . I was the first who could have done this civil defense. But he noticed that I didn't want to; I refused. He let me completely alone. He is the only person for whom, afterward, in the denazification, I spoke up. For he knew exactly.[55]

One purpose of denazification, of course, had been to compel Germans to confront the issues of guilt and complicity, and many agreed that it failed in this respect. Was this because the Germans, supported by their church, found ways of getting around it? Or because of a flaw inherent in the program itself? One of the few pastors to publicly support denazification, and to attack the EKD's position on it, was Hermann Diem, head of the Confessing Church-linked Society in the Württemberg church. In the Society's view, the EKD was behaving not like a Christian church but like "any business owner" who defends his employees in order to keep the business going.[56] Instead of seeking exemptions from denazification procedures, Diem argued, the EKD should submit to them and establish a religious procedure to examine Christians who had fallen prey to Nazi ideology.[57]

But the Württemberg Society's position was an isolated one, and Diem himself, by 1947, believed that the Allied military government had wasted an important chance. "It is unfortunately true that the occupation forces have further brought democracy into miscredit," he wrote.[58] As outspoken as he was about German guilt, Martin Niemöller published a scathing attack on the Allied denazification procedures in February 1947. Even those Confessing Church veterans who shared the Society's criticisms of the EKD believed, ultimately, that denazification had been a mistake. In 1986, Rudolf and Helga Weckerling, who had both worked as pastors in the Confessing Church, spoke about it. Rudolf Weckerling began,

> Denazification was only counterproductive. Because, above all, the presupposition for conversion and repentance is naturally present only among Christians, but most of the "neutral" Christians, like the entire people (which was only superficially

Christian), all said: "It was terrible, but we really couldn't do anything." Everyone has an alibi story that he can tell.

The church demanded that its officials, from the pastors on up, be denazified within their own ranks. They didn't have to go before the *Spruchkammer* that had been set up by the Allies. That was a new privilege the church had obtained for itself with the lie that it had been anti-fascist, with the exception . . .

Helga Weckerling interrupted, "That was not a conscious lie; they were convinced. They simply saw themselves, after 1945, a large part of the church, as 'the better Germany.' I believe that. It wasn't a conscious lie." Rudolf Weckerling recalled his encounter with denazification outside the church:

> My dentist, who had denounced me, had been in the party, and he wanted a so-called *Persilschein* from me — that he had been only a fellow traveler and had gone into the party out of consideration for his family and that his son had fallen in the war, and so on. He didn't admit that he had denounced me, but wanted me to fill out this untruthful certificate. . . . Later, he spread it around Giessen that I was a very un-Christian pastor, that I wasn't prepared to forgive and work for reconciliation.
>
> The idea of the Allies for us was "re-education." This was an instrument of that, and so there were dreadful self-justifications and denunciations. From the church, too, because the church had broken solidarity with the people. Pastor B., for example, wasn't a "German Christian" but was a party member. In the parish there would be an organist, or a warden. They had to come before the *Spruchkammer*; they would be punished harder. The church made it soft for its own people, for the understandable reason I mentioned before: "How can I stand judgment over my colleagues who erred?" The bad conscience that they had because of that was expressed in this way: that they began, on the part of the church, to make open criticisms of the Allies. . . . as Böll said, people turned from Nazis into democrats in five minutes after 1945. Through that, there was no real coming to our senses.[59]

The real question, of course, was whether the ideology and prejudices behind Nazism lingered. Critics were correct when they asserted that no legal procedure could exorcise that. In a report submitted to the U.S. Army in September 1945, Karl Barth said that no German still really believed in Nazism; the Nazis had become too discredited during the course of the war.[60] But was that true? Or were Nazism's roots so deep that one needed a conversion experience, like that Martin Schröter underwent in Holland, to really confront one's own role in this history? Only an intentional examination of all the beliefs that people had thought were "innocuous" — the patriotism, nationalism, loyalty to the Fatherland, anti-Semitism, or anti-Communism — could bring the role of these factors in encouraging Nazism into a new light. Only then could they be seen not as a series of extenuating factors that explained away Nazism but as a way to gain insight into the moral and political implications of personal belief and prejudice.

The problem was that feelings like nationalism, which had so blinded the Germans to Hitler, were precisely those that, in the wake of Germany's defeat, ran highest. The Protestant church, which had never during the Third Reich successfully confronted its own nationalism or anti-Semitism, was even less able now to do so.

Many persons called to account for their pasts probably felt the way Wilhelm

Niemöller did. Niemöller, an early party member and Confessing Church pastor, was briefly interned in a British detention camp with SS members and prisoners of war suspected of Nazi party affiliations. He expressed his bewilderment 36 years later:

> The British examined me hard after the war. I tried to explain it to them, but they didn't understand it. Who can imagine such things, anyway? One way or another, a dictatorship is more or less a great matter of coincidence. You don't know what's genuine; you don't know whether they're setting a trap for you.[61]

The Württemberg Society argued that the EKD's behavior under Allied occupation only repeated the church's tactic under Nazism — of seeking and maintaining a protected status for itself. With that, argued Hermann Diem, the church had broken solidarity with ordinary Germans. Such solidarity did not mean following the masses in their prejudices, but lay in defining a clear moral position and committing the church to it. The German people had not had that kind of moral leadership during the Third Reich, argued the Society, and the church was failing to offer it now as well.

The Allied denazification program was finished by the fall of 1948, and it was widely seen as an utter failure. Of the 3,600,648 Germans summoned before the *Spruchkammer*, only 1,667 were removed permanently from public office (23,060 were "conditionally" removed and eventually reinstated). And 1,156,299, although party members, were exonerated as having been low-ranking or provisional members. Acquitted altogether were 1,213,873. Some of the latter had actually resisted; others benefited from a *Persilschein*. Proceedings were dropped against 1,265,749 Germans (for example, against minors and German soldiers returning from the front).[62]

Denazification, then, did not bring about a change of heart in Germans, nor did it remove many Nazis from public office. The Allied military government, remarked Spotts critically, had failed to work cooperatively with the churches, and the churches, for their part, "failed to make it clear that they honestly wanted genuine Nazis out of public life."[63]

The Effects of Denazification on Political Attitudes

One disturbing outcome of the denazification debate was that the discussion of German guilt became politically polarized, thereby ensuring that when "guilt" was discussed, a host of other themes arose. The various positions taken rapidly acquired certain political connotations. Helmut Gollwitzer, who moved toward the left, recalled,

> At this time, the community of those who had come from the Confessing Church was still there. Then it fell apart. We had rediscovered the public political responsibility of the church, the significance of the church, in the opposite sense of what had happened in 1933. That is, no longer the power of a right-wing politicized church, but that of a church engaged for the possibilities that we have today, for a democratic state. There we have to cooperate, as a Christian party within the confines of parliamentary democracy. The Catholics supported that, and some Protestants joined in. That was one group.
> The other concluded, from what we had learned and gone through, that the

church was a living substance within society. Hans Iwand, one of our most important members, said, "A confessing church is always in the opposition, in every party, in every system, in every government." Then the foreign policy questions came in. . . . Should the new Germany, this new western German state, orient itself toward the West, or should we remain neutral? On that point, the Confessing Church split. Those who came out of the emphatically Lutheran tradition almost predictably became pro-Adenauer and pro-West. But one couldn't predict with those who had gone through the Dahlem experience and who had been influenced by Barth, because Barthianism had opposed the identification of the Gospel with a specific political direction. There were very painful divisions among us.

If I try to be objective, I would say that the political consequences of the *Kirchenkampf* occurred in two forms. First, in the conservative form, the CDU — a CDU leaning toward liberal democracy, as represented by people like Hermann Ehlers or Eugen Gerstenmaier. The second form was the strengthening of oppositional, nonconformist elements in German Protestantism.[64]

The "oppositional, nonconformist elements" would be led by people like Gollwitzer, Martin Niemöller, Hermann Diem, and Kurt Scharf, their politics roughly that of the German Social Democratic left. The conservative group, which generally supported the pro-West, anti-Communist course taken by West Germany under Konrad Adenauer, included Otto Dibelius anal Helmut Thielicke (and, among the Barthians, Hans Asmussen).

The dividing line was not necessarily between those who advocated a clear church commitment to specific political positions and those who believed the church should stay out of politics — although church conservatives frequently accused church members with leftist sympathies of politicizing the church. Such charges, however, ignored the fact that the German Protestant church had always been a presence within the German political sphere, beginning with the tradition of "throne and altar."

In fact, during the Nazi era, the strategies used by the different church factions evolved from their respective positions within the political realm. The more conservative pastors like Dibelius and Wurm worked through the system because that was where they had their contacts; more important, they believed that they, and their purportedly well-intentioned contacts in the Nazi bureaucracy, continued to share a common purpose. After the war, both the Catholic and Protestant churches established offices in Bonn to generate public discussion (and support) on certain issues, and to work with the political parties. In Bavaria, Bishop Meiser assigned a deacon to help establish the conservative CDU party there; in Hannover, Bishop Marahrens helped found the regional CDU.[65]

Whether a Christian was motivated by religious or political beliefs remained in the eye of the beholder. A fine example was a spirited exchange of letters between Helmut Thielicke and Hermann Diem, provoked by Thielicke's Good Friday sermon in 1947, in which he attacked the Allied denazification policies as "faith murder and soul murder."[66] On a deeper level, the debate between the two pastors, both of whom had been in the church opposition to Nazism, focused on their antithetical conceptions of Christian responsibility and guilt. The church's responsibility, Thielicke argued, was to address people where they were, not where they should be; and the German people, in 1947, were tired of hearing about their guilt and hearing nothing about "the guilt of others."[67] In Thielicke's words, the "so-called" Christian motives of the Allies

> goes hand-in-hand with a rather extensive Morgenthau praxis [Henry Morgenthau, President Franklin D. Roosevelt's minister of finance, who was viewed in Germany as anti-German and revanchist] and, rightly or wrongly, the propaganda slogans of Nazism haunt people's thoughts just as before, due to the hypocrisy of certain nations. . . . Now the church blows the same horn as the Allies . . . for [the church] has made a deal with everyone. . . . It's never done better; no person possesses such freedom, no person receives so many CARE packages, thanks to its thawed-out international connections.[68]

It was a litany of the points of resentment felt by many Germans against the EKD, whom, they believed, got "special treatment" from the Allies (and this, of course, was tied to the EKD's decision to exempt pastors from denazification). Resentment invariably returned to the Stuttgart Declaration, in which, by not mentioning "the guilt of others," the EKD had betrayed the German people.

In reply, Diem told Thielicke that his sermon had given the congregation "stones, not bread." While Thielicke might have comforted his listeners by voicing the anger they felt, he had not told them "how, through Christ, they should come clear with their own guilt and that of others."[69] Thielicke's tone, said Diem, had left his listeners with no other recourse than "national self-assertion," which threatened to drive "the future . . . into the arms of political reaction."[70]

The Diem-Thielicke correspondence, published jointly, revealed the contrasting ways in which the two church factions that emerged from the *Kirchenkampf* concretely addressed the issue of guilt during the crucial immediate postwar period. Here a pattern developed that did not always follow ideological lines or even theological ones. Most Confessing Church pastors, after all, had been nationalistic and, as Gollwitzer noted, Barth's students went in different political directions after 1945. But in terms of actual behavior, the dividing line was not between those who remained "unpolitical" and those who became political activists in the name of the church. Rather, the division was between church traditionalists committed to preserving stability and tradition (both political and ecclesiastical) and those elements in the church that were more iconoclastic in their attitudes toward both church and state. That was where the line had been in the church opposition during the Third Reich, and that was where it remained, more or less, after 1945. Church members who had been more openly critical of the Nazi regime were subsequently more critical of the postwar governments; those who had worked through the system during the Third Reich continued to do so after 1945. This pattern was also true for internal church questions, like that of the ordination of women. Although the women who had been ordained during the Third Reich remained so, after the war they were once again barred from pastorates by church traditionalists. In many regions, postwar women theology students had to fight again for the right to ordination.

The postwar situation, moreover, was complicated by the creation of two German states whose respective systems were based upon fundamentally different political visions. Church leaders and pastors of all persuasions began taking sides. Otto

Dibelius, a staunch supporter of the Adenauer government in the west, had no trouble criticizing the eastern German Democratic Republic; Martin Niemöller pleaded for tolerating church-state compromises in the east that he found intolerable in the west. These ideological biases began to influence postwar political attitudes toward church-state questions in east and west. It is not surprising, then, that the discussion of the nature of German guilt became politicized to the extent it did, or that people justified their political sentiments on the moral grounds of how they judged the Nazi era.

Others pushed the Nazi past even further away and "demonized" Nazism, seeing Hitler as an almost magical evil figure who had mesmerized the German people against its will. These people saw the Third Reich as an act of fate, which led them to the conclusion that the German people were exonerated of any significant political role in creating the Nazi system.[71] Such views, though extreme, fundamentally denied any political participation in Nazi Germany and reflected many Germans' feelings of utter powerlessness, of having been victims to fate. All decisions and compromises appeared to have been forced; both personal and collective paths appeared to have been inevitable. For Christians, these feelings were intensified by the absence of any clear turning point to which the church could look back and say with certainty: Here it would have made a difference had we acted differently. A host of unresolvable questions, tossed back and forth in a volley of self-accusation and self-justification, haunted individuals' attempts to come to terms with their own history. Hans Thimme, who had been the assistant to Westphalia's church president Koch, himself became president of the Westphalian church in 1968. In 1988, he mused about the question of guilt:

Well then, Martin Niemöller occasionally said that if 10,000 pastors, in response to something like the *Kristallnacht*, had publicly and radically protested, then perhaps 10,000 pastors would have been executed and 10 million Jews rescued. But that is just a formal declaration, which is unrealistic, basically, for one can't say whether it would have been that way.

In any case, it really is the case, when you look at the Stuttgart Declaration of Guilt, that what is pronounced there is pronounced for those of us who were conscientiously the Confessing Church: We did *not* do that which we should have done. We concerned ourselves more, so to speak, with the defense of the church than with the defense of human beings. . . . To that extent, the Declaration of Guilt is really not only a formality toward the ecumenical world, so to speak . . . but a genuine declaration of our own self-knowledge. . . .

On the other hand, one must understand the situation, and this situation was basically the same, more or less, among the different directions [that is, within the church].

My liberal father saw through National Socialism from the very beginning, much more than I did. He was always against it, and was arrested in 1935. Why? Because the Gestapo had opened a letter he had written a Jewish woman. It was a letter in which he had written only that he wanted to comfort her, she should persevere . . . this system had no promise, it would go to ruin, she should be brave and hold up . . . because of that, he was arrested. He came into prison . . . and after several weeks, he was released. . . .

That was the one direction, which said clearly, we stand up for the Jews. . . . In the newspapers, we didn't learn anything [about the persecution of the Jews], but we learned it, somehow. I remember how it shocked me, my wife, too, but somehow we didn't have the courage or didn't find the strength, or we thought, too, "That can't go well, but they have to realize that themselves," and so on, but, in any case, we didn't undertake any loud protests on this point. . . . You have to understand this, too; there was a shroud of silence spread out over the entire German people; one almost couldn't get through it. One didn't hear anything. . . .

All of us were compromisers, somehow, one almost has to say that, even those who were consistent opponents. . . . Only in retrospect does one notice how one existed somewhat schizophrenically. . . . I was a pastor of the Confessing Church, and I never made any secret of that . . . but I always said, I am not against the state; I'm against this ideology. But basically one couldn't separate the ideology from the state, since this ideology was the official state. And here one made compromises, and — it's hard to say. I don't know if I could do differently, if the situation repeated itself.[72]

The more time passed, the harder it became to uncover the truth of what had really happened to the German people under Hitler, and all indications were that that was the way most people wanted it. Hitler had been evil, but Hitler was gone. His millions of followers wanted nothing more than to put the past behind them and resume normal lives. Gradually, this became possible. In the early 1950s, the regional governments in the Federal Republic passed legislation limiting or ending some of the punishments meted out under denazification; and most of the former Nazis who had actually lost their jobs were able to re-enter the sphere of public service.[73]

For some survivors of the *Kirchenkampf* and the resistance, this increased their distrust of the postwar political parties, particularly the Christian Democratic Union (Adenauer's party). In Holstein, Emmi Bonhoeffer was elected to the local city council and recalled her political experience there:

At that time, I joined the CDU [Christian Democratic Union, Adenauer's party] because Theodor Steltzer, the first minister president in Schleswig-Holstein after 1945, who had been in the same prison as my husband, told me, "The bourgeoisie has to reconstitute itself, otherwise the British people will get the wrong impression." The Social Democrats had already become organized. I was rather naive. I knew Lukaschek, one of the co-founders — also a comrade from the prison. He and Steltzer were both people of integrity who had survived the resistance. Thus I came into the CDU. But I left it very quickly. There were too many old Nazis in it for me.[74]

In Baden, where Martin Schröter and his wife Tüsnelda had a parish, he helped establish the local CDU. (Like Gustav Heinemann, Schröter eventually left the CDU for the SPD [Social Democrats] over the rearmament controversy). In their village, a former Nazi was elected mayor. As Tüsnelda Schröter remarked,

At first, they were very quiet, the Third Reich people. . . . But then they started up again. At first, they "hadn't heard anything, hadn't seen anything" . . . but ever so slowly they came back in, and one became the mayor again.

Her husband added,

The great majority of our generation had basically repressed the confrontation with the 1930s. And the first to raise their heads again were the old Nazis. They pushed their way back into the leading positions on the local level.

Tüsnelda Schröter added, "That was the problem, they were more capable . . . " "Organizationally as well," Martin Schröter continued. "The others didn't see through that." Asked if the village people didn't know that these leaders were former Nazis, Martin Schröter replied,

> You know, on the local level, it's difficult. There, people say, "The main thing is that he's a competent administrator. It's of secondary importance what ideological foundation he has, whether he's a Nazi or a socialist or a Green. In any case, he has to have ideas for the community, has to bring in industry." . . . Those are the visions that people have.[75]

It took years before the scope of the history of Nazi Germany was publicly examined. Only during the 1980s, really, did German towns begin to open their archives and collect oral histories; areas previously covered up began to be examined openly. Dietrich Goldschmidt asked,

> Why . . . did it take 40 years for people to ask more pointedly? That says, basically, that the number of millions of party members wasn't a fiction. It says, basically, that there are millions of people who don't want to be reminded of this era. They took off their brown uniforms from one day to the next, and they can't get over it, that they fought for the wrong thing. That is the situation today. . . .
>
> One could draw a line, to a certain extent, at the year 1925. All who are older, who were born before 1925, basically have to ask themselves, "What did we know, essentially, and what did we do?" That failure to act is guilt, too, even when one didn't do anything, so to speak. That's how I would see it.
>
> That is also denied emphatically, as if there were no collective guilt. That deserves to be discussed more closely. There is such a thing, you will know that too, the term, "socialization." People grow into a certain human society, assume its values, assume its *Weltanschauung*, orientation, and assume, with that, to some extent, the disorientations of this society. . . . Guilt originates in the fact that this bias isn't investigated. That is what Giordano terms "the second guilt."[76] We absolve people of "guilt," at best, when they have really tried, even if they were children, to account for what happened previously.[77]

The concept of collective guilt, however, never became politically acceptable in Germany, although, as Bishop Wurm noted in December 1945, it was a biblically valid concept that fit the postwar German situation very well:

> the idea of a collectivity of guilt is a biblical one from A to Z. The Bible views sin not simply in isolation but always in connection with something; it affixes responsibility in an overall context, in all directions. "The fathers have eaten grapes and the children's teeth are set on edge; I will visit the sins of the fathers upon the children unto the third and fourth generations." That is one of the rules of life, a divine law we recognize again and again. People cannot survive without this comprehensive obligation.[78]

There were some people within the churches (often, notably, the very individuals who had been more active in working against Nazism) who did examine their own role during the Nazi era. Helga Weckerling, who had worked in the Confessing Bible circles with Jewish Christians, described how she dealt with this herself:

> During the Hitler era, I was of a completely different opinion, but I never joined an active political resistance. We broke off completely from my brother, who was a

convinced National Socialist, and from the Germans who were anti-Semites. But we, too, had to learn what it means to be with Jews in a church. That didn't come automatically, and we learned that first during the Hitler era, and only later did we reflect upon it. Those were spontaneous decisions and automatic reactions against that which Hitler and the "German Christians" did. Through being in the Confessing Church, we rejected what the Germans did at that time.

But we have never felt ourselves to be free of guilt, because we simply didn't go into the resistance, as Bonhoeffer did. I would never speak of "the" Confessing Church, either, but of some few in the Confessing Church who acted clearly. We were driven by our failure, even after 1945, as it stands in the Stuttgart Declaration of Guilt, why we "didn't love more ardently" and didn't cry out for the Jews more clearly. The fact that we failed the Jews is not even in the Stuttgart Declaration of Guilt, unfortunately. One has to consider that. It became clear only much later how we had failed. . . .

I can say only that the entire German people failed. But I can't say that we did any better. . . . I still think that we had far too little courage, and also that our awareness here wasn't clear enough. That the men could have refused to fight the war, or that we automatically could have gone with the Jews into the concentration camps, as some Catholics did. . . . So to distance ourselves from the Germans' guilt in some way, or to deny it. . . only after 1945 did [we] see what really should have been done.[79]

The Reparations Provisions

Officially and politically, the issue of German guilt was resolved by the reparations act of 1953, which provided for the payment of reparations to the state of Israel for the sufferings incurred by Jews under Nazi Germany. Additional laws eventually provided for damages to other European countries that had suffered under the Nazis and for individuals who wished to bring claims for injustices they had suffered. The *Wiedergutmachung* — literally, making good again — left many who had suffered under the Nazis dissatisfied. Some, like Gertrud S. (see Chapter 8), were too proud to make claims. She chose to return to Germany in 1947 out of a sense of mission:

I said to myself, where I can work now, I want to work in Germany, simply to get back on my feet and also to help young people come to their senses. It was an idealistic vision.

I returned in January 1947. I came to Heidelberg, to my foster mother who was still alive, and stayed in Heidelberg. I had hardly arrived when I received a message from the employment office to present myself, and was welcomed as an emigrant. What do you think they offered me? I was to remain in Heidelberg, where the American occupation forces were, and they had a position for me in the *Spruchkammer*. Imagine that! That was the legal body at that time that had to judge the Nazis and fellow travelers. It was as if I'd fallen out of the clouds. How can I sit in judgment over things I could judge only from the files? I got out of Heidelberg soon after. . . .

The ways in which I was taken back in by my acquaintances — it was a resumption without complications. But then, perhaps I wasn't a person who ran herself ragged to look here and there if I could get something out of it. With the reparations, too, I just couldn't shrug it off — all that one had to fill out for it. I refused. I demanded only that my social security be resumed, and I received that. But all the other I found repugnant. I have two hands, and I can work.[80]

For individuals, the process of obtaining reparations from the German government was wearing and often demeaning. Dietrich Goldschmidt was summoned to court as a witness by three other men who had been in the work camp near Magdeburg with him. Under questioning, Goldschmidt found himself contradicting their version and gained insight into how relatively unscathed he had emerged from the Third Reich:

> Basically, they emerged from this war as little people. They were little people when they came into the camp, and they remained little people when they came back out of the camp. Their dreams of what they could become in life were broken by the Nazis. First, they couldn't become anything before they came into the camp. In the camp, they suffered. After the camp, nothing more came of them. When, now, after the camp, nothing more could come of them — then the Nazis were guilty. I mean, I had it easy. For me, this period in the camp and the persecution is an episode. For these people, so to speak, it was the defeat of their lives. . . .
>
> For each month that I sat in the camp, I myself received 150 marks. That means 750 marks in all. . . . I put in a claim for personal damage to my education, in the sense that I hadn't been permitted [under Nazi law] to work on a required doctorate. . . . But this wasn't recognized. I took it to court and lost the case on the final appeal. But, in the end, I've been able to make my way, and it doesn't pain me particularly.
>
> But many things went badly. Take the so-called *Wiedergutmachung*. I hate the expression. What can one make good again? Absolutely nothing. One can pay damages. There is only one area in which the reparations are generous; that is the reparations for all those who were already in public service, that is, who were civil servants. My brother, since he was in the service of the state for five months as a junior barrister, has received a pension as a court councilor for his entire life since 1951 or 1952. . . . He has received that up to the present day. There is nothing comparable to the reparations of those who were in public service. . . .
>
> In retrospect, when I see the standard of living the Federal Republic has achieved, I find that a scandal. . . . I find it a particular scandal that an entire group of special cases have not yet received damages . . . whether it's the Mengele twins [Note: the twins on which the notorious Nazi doctor, Josef Mengele, experimented] or the socially persecuted, whether it's the gypsies or the Jews in Israel, who, according to the regional principle, haven't received anything — the Polish Jews who were in Auschwitz or Theresienstadt receive no reparations. . . .[81]
>
> One can best compare reparations for the war victims with the pensions of former career soldiers. The pensions of former career soldiers, including the SS, increase very regularly, just as all pensions increase.[82]

Helene Jacobs, who had worked underground to help the Jews, spent from 1952 until her retirement in 1971 in the reparations office in Berlin:

> I was one of the few who had proven themselves. I had taken my papers from the files in the prison and went to a lawyer. He was a Jew and wanted to rebuild his practice and asked whether I would be his head secretary. I wanted to study law; I saw that I understood something of it. My main reason was that I wanted to make reparations for the injustice of the state.

In the meantime, the reparations office had been founded. . . . It handled mainly land and firms that had been confiscated by the Nazis. I did only subordinate work there, because I didn't have a completed degree. [Note: the reason was that Jacobs, when she refused to obtain an "Aryan pass," was not able to continue her studies.]

In 1952, the reparations office was founded. It concerned the individuals who had been persecuted because of their political or racial affiliation. I applied there. I thought, one can't make it good again to these people, but we should endeavor, as far as possible, to show people that it was in the German interest to work through this entire injustice that had been carried out in our name and to pay damages to people.

I stood fairly alone among my colleagues. I tried to do everything for the benefit of the persecuted. Their tendency was more to reject all claims — that was also easier, according to the law, and they wanted to act only according to the law.. . . .

The people who had claims on the money had to prove that they were Jewish. That was relatively easy, and when someone was Jewish, one could assume that they had suffered under the Reich. But then they also had to prove that they had not done anything against the laws of the government, which was nonsense. A former NSDAP member could become president of the Bundestag [Note: Jacobs is referring to CDU member Karl Carstens, Bundestag president from 1979 to 1983; another prominent politician, Kurt Kiesinger, chancellor from 1966 to 1969, had been a Nazi party member from 1933 to 1945.], but a Jew who had been punished by the powers of this party still had to suffer for that. I did everything I could, and I was able to do a little good. It ended when I became 65. I filled in my last day as unobtrusively as possible. I saw most of my colleagues there as my enemies.[83]

The Consequences of the Guilt Debate for Church and State

The shortcomings of the reparations program, like those of denazification, revealed the inherent limitations of any political attempt to redress the injustices done by Nazi Germany. While necessary and important, these programs could not be expected to achieve a moral or religious resolution of the Nazi past. As Dietrich Goldschmidt commented, there could be no real *Wiedergutmachung*. Denazification and the payment of reparations meant that a part of the past had been "settled," in a bureaucratic sense — but the feeling lingered that nothing, really, had been settled at all. Eberhard Bethge was not the only Confessing Christian critical of the church's postwar attempts to address the question of guilt:

> It doesn't even know what it should say. Look at this article on guilt in this new church lexicon. Here they treat guilt feelings, that is, the psychological side of guilt, and the juristic liability of guilt. Period. Cardinal Höffner and Bishop Lohse speak on May 8 in the cathedral [Note: the respective heads of the German Catholic and Protestant churches in 1985; they spoke on the anniversary of the war's end in the cathedral in Cologne.] and don't teach the people what guilt is, either.
>
> To that extent, Stuttgart is better than its text. The experience of Stuttgart (that is, the Declaration of Guilt) is better than what they left us as sentences. These sentences, coming out of the ruins of Stuttgart, from these 12 men, were without precedent in the history of the German church. There was nothing like this after World War I.[84]

In 1982, Heinrich Vogel, who had led the Berlin Confessing Church's *Kirchliche Hochschule* during the Nazi years, said something similar to Bethge when asked about the legacy of the Stuttgart Declaration:

> Well, if you ask me about the Stuttgart Declaration: necessary and good, unfortunately somewhat weak. But it was enough. You know, we don't want to talk so much about the weak part. It was good, that it stands there clearly, and I would say, if I had formulated it, it would have turned out differently. But sometimes it is even a good thing when the radicals don't formulate it, but those who say the minimum, at least. Among our particularly lovely verses in the hymnal is a stanza: "Give us the minimum of heroism." Isn't that enchanting? That is realistic. Even a man like Martin Niemöller did have hours of the deepest temptation in the concentration camp. Only those who have no experience in religious decisions, in temptation, maintain that this is a matter of egotism.[85]

What, in Vogel's opinion, was the weakness of the Confessing Church? His answer focused on the way Confessing Christians after 1945 dealt with their history:

> Particularly in the historical catastrophe that broke over us, there could have been an unbelievable chance to rethink, a conversion toward great repentance, political repentance as well, a genuine Reformation. But the Reformation — the entire *Kirchenkampf* had been for its sake! — didn't happen. But perhaps there is more there, I don't know in what area, than we think.[86]

The most remarkable aspect of the Stuttgart Declaration may be something that its signers (and readers) took for granted — it was a statement by the institutional Evangelical Church of Germany made to the international Christian community. It was an acknowledgment that the German church had failed as a church to counter the moral evil of Nazism. As such, it indeed raised the issue of collective guilt for Christians, even if it could not resolve it; and the debate that the Declaration provoked showed that its words touched a deep nerve in postwar Germany.

In the brief period before 1950, other church statements addressed the issue of guilt and repentance. The synods of most regional churches eventually voted to approve the Stuttgart Declaration. In 1948, the members of the Confessing Church's Council of Brethren issued the controversial Darmstadt Statement of Guilt, which attacked more critically the political silence of the Protestant church during the Nazi years. It called upon Germans to reject "all the false and evil ways in which we as Germans went astray in our political wishes and actions."[87] This affronted some conservative church members; the real controversy, however, concerned the political conclusions drawn in the document — particularly in light of the political atmosphere in Germany in 1948. In 1947, the United Socialist Party (SED), which would soon lead the government in the German Democratic Republic, had been founded. The cold war was beginning. With this in the background, Confessing Church veterans who met at Darmstadt made their political views clear:

> The alliance of the Church with the old and traditional conservative powers has taken its heavy revenge upon us. . . . We denied the right to revolution, but tolerated and approved the development of an absolute dictatorship. . . . We went astray when we overlooked that the economic materialism of Marxist teachings should have

reminded the Church of the task and the promise of the parish toward the life, and life together, of human beings in this world.[88]

In 1948, it seemed to the signers at Darmstadt that the emerging government in the Democratic Republic was led by Communists who had opposed and suffered under Nazism and who now made a point of their antifascism. In contrast, the government in the west seemed increasingly eager to put the past behind it and willing to tolerate the presence of former Nazis in its ranks. In reality, an honest examination of the Nazi past would be as problematic in the Democratic Republic as in the west, but at the time, some Christians began to distinguish between the "idealism" of the east and the "materialism" of the west.

Both in terms of the people involved and the divisions between them, the differences between the Stuttgart and the Darmstadt declarations paralleled the divisions between the Confessing Church synods that had been held in Barmen in 1934 and in Dahlem in 1935. At both Barmen and Stuttgart, the entire spectrum of the church opposition to Nazism had been represented. The differences in viewpoint between them resulted, in both instances, in statements that were more ambiguous, but were signed by all factions present. The church statements that emerged from Dahlem and Darmstadt were far more direct in their political rejection of Nazism and were able, therefore, to draw more specific connections between their theological positions and the political commitments they believed the church should make. But because of their controversial conclusions, the Dahlem and Darmstadt statements spoke for a relatively small group of Christians. Like most minority reports, they have tended to get lost in church history.

Neither the Stuttgart nor the Darmstadt document, however, referred directly to Nazi Germany's crimes against the Jews, which showed how difficult it was for Germans even to begin to address this issue. In 1950, the EKD broke its silence officially to acknowledge its guilt toward the Jewish people. The EKD synod in Berlin-Weissensee was the first time that German Protestant leaders had critically discussed their theological anti-Semitism in light of the Holocaust.

Heinrich Vogel had written the text to be voted on by the synod, and an intense debate arose, particularly over Vogel's third thesis: "We believe that God's loyalty toward his elected people of Israel remains in effect even after the crucifixion of Christ." These words challenged not only the foundation of Christian anti-Semitism but the fundamental supercessionist assumption of much Christian theology that the Christian church had replaced Israel as God's chosen people.

In the synodal discussions that followed, German church leaders not only debated theological points but began to speak openly about their own experiences during the Third Reich. A Württemberg delegate shared Bishop Wurm's message (Wurm did not attend the synod): "If there's one thing that doesn't let me sleep peacefully, it's the fact that, in the years before 1945, we were silent on the question of the Jews."[89]

Synod member Judge Lothar Kreyssig had been forced to retire in 1940 after he issued a court order forbidding the transfer of patients to euthanasia institutions and filed a warrant against Hitler's chancellery chief Philip Bouhler. But in Weissensee, Kreyssig stood before the synod and, in a moving statement of remorse, wished that in each train that drove east, where they were to be gassed, a Christian would have ridden along in the discipleship of Jesus Christ because it would have left him no inner peace and he'd been compelled by God to do it. . . .One time, God showed me a sign. . . . At that moment where he showed me, I was joyful to do it, and the next morning I had lost this obedience and the person it concerned went east, and today he is dead, and I stand here.[90]

The theological and personal discussions in Weissensee ended with the synod's unanimous approval of a statement of guilt toward the Jewish people. Heinrich Vogel's theological claim that God's promise to Israel remained valid was included, as was his appeal "to all Christians to renounce all anti-Semitism and, where it rises anew, to resist it earnestly, and to meet Jews and Jewish Christians in the spirit of brotherhood."[91]

As Kreyssig's and Wurm's words indicate, these were not empty statements. It is the fate of many church statements to be relegated to obscurity almost as soon as they are issued. For those who took it seriously, however, the Weissensee Synod statement provided the foundation for the further examination of the Christian church's contribution to anti-Semitism.

The engagement of Confessing Christians in their church and society did not end in 1945. However they chose to resolve the past for themselves—whether it was to move politically toward the socialism they had condemned in the 1930s or to move in the opposite direction, upholding church tradition and aligning it with the goals of the new Federal Republic—their decisions would play a crucial role, in east and west, in the ongoing reorientation of German moral and political values.

❧ IV ❧

"THE INABILITY
TO MOURN"

❦ 11 ❦

Postwar Germans and Their Church: Rebirth or Restoration?

IN 1967, THE NEUROLOGIST Alexander Mitscherlich and his wife, the psychoanalyst Margarete Mitscherlich, wrote a book, *Die Unfähigkeit zu Trauern (The Inability to Mourn*[1]), in which they examined the ways in which Germans' unresolved and denied guilt about the Nazi past had influenced the course of postwar German society. One of the Mitscherlichs' theories was that, in effect, Nazism had destroyed the parts of the German cultural, religious, and political tradition it had used. For many Germans, particularly for the generation born after 1945, it was easier to break entirely with certain traditions than to attempt to reconstruct them in the postwar, post-Holocaust era. This break created an emotional distance to the past that the Mitscherlichs described as "the inability to mourn."

The Mitscherlichs were not the first to observe the phenomenon. The philosopher Hannah Arendt, returning in 1949 to the land she had fled in 1933, described the widespread destruction and suffering she found in Europe, and then noted the Germans' reaction:

> But nowhere is this nightmare of destruction and horror less felt and less talked about than in Germany itself. A lack of response is evident everywhere, and it is difficult to say whether this signifies a half-conscious refusal to yield to grief or a genuine inability to feel . . . busyness has become their chief defense against reality. And one wants to cry out: But this is not real—real are the ruins, real are the past horrors, real are the dead whom you have forgotten. But they are living ghosts, whom speech and argument, the glance of human eyes and the mourning of human hearts, no longer touch.[2]

Postwar Germans became famous for their "busyness," for the long hours they spent rebuilding their ruined cities. Recalling those years, Germans often said later that they had neither the time nor the strength to mourn. And with their rapid emergence from the ruins and the "economic miracle" of the 1950s, Germans seemed to have put the past behind them.

But this was an illusion that avoided the crucial postwar tasks of confronting the past and of mourning. During the Third Reich, Germans believed that the Nazi worldview was the fulfillment of a Germanic "tradition," and they based their national identity upon this tradition. In 1945, the Germanic illusion was shattered, and the role of German institutions in the Third Reich made them a problematic burden. Germany was a stigmatized nation, its churches, cultural bodies, civil service, and financial and educational institutions all marked, in varying degrees, by their past association with Nazism.

The Mitscherlichs' book generated controversy when it appeared in Germany. But whether or not people agreed with their conclusions about the national and personal disorientation of postwar Germans, the difficulties of returning to pre-1933 traditions and institutions had become obvious. In the most extreme reaction to this dilemma, the terrorists of the 1970s and 1980s rejected West German social and political structures as irrevocably immoral. Most Germans, however, searched for a less radical political resolution of the problem of the past. On the left, Germans examined those aspects of their culture — anti-Semitism, for example — that had supported the rise of Nazism. Having uncovered the historical roots of German prejudice and nationalism, these Germans measured postwar attitudes and policies according to the political standards of anti-Nazism. On questions ranging from the treatment of foreign workers to school curriculum, they viewed a conscious break with the Nazi past as a moral necessity. For these Germans, the Third Reich remained a postwar reality, at least symbolically. They integrated the lessons they had learned under Hitler into the postwar political debate and raised the banner of "anti-Nazism" above their postwar causes.

More moderate and conservative Germans, less prone to critical self-examination, chose simply to repudiate the 12 years of Nazism. But this was not the complete break with the past that more radical Germans held to be necessary but only the excision of the 12 years under Hitler. "In 1945, we began anew, there, where we had had to stop in 1933," said Otto Dibelius.[3] He was referring to the restoration of the German Evangelical Church, but could have been describing the course chosen by a number of German conservatives who viewed the Third Reich as an interruption — the distortion, but not the irrevocable contamination, of their traditions.

Within the church opposition to Nazism, there was disagreement about the extent to which German Protestant anti-Semitism and nationalism had legitimated and fostered Nazism. The more radical wing of the Confessing Church viewed its church's tradition critically, both in the political and the religious sense. These Christians saw Protestant nationalism, with its coupling of throne and altar, as the main factor that had blinded the church in its dealings with the Nazis. Accordingly, after 1945, they viewed the repudiation of this part of Protestant tradition as a morally necessary act. Opposing this viewpoint were the leaders of the intact churches and people like Dibelius, who distinguished between Protestant nationalism and Nazism, and who maintained, furthermore, that their very loyalty to German Protestant traditions had constituted the core of the church's resistance to Nazism's attempted politicization of the churches.

Rebuilding the Church

The differences among these factions, although evident in the first church meetings after the war, were overshadowed initially by the immediate demands of coping with the chaos left by the war. Like all Germans, church leaders had to deal with the destruction of their homes, cities, and churches. Allied bombings had leveled many churches and church-owned properties. One report, from December 1944, only begins to show the extent of the destruction:

> In Berlin, in the inner city and in the suburbs around the ring [the road circling the central city], ⅔ of all churches have been completely destroyed, ⅖ more so strongly damaged that they can be used, at most, in the warm season. Only ⅕ is structurally intact, but owing to the restriction on heating can't be used in the winter.
> ⅔ of the parish halls have been destroyed. . . .
> In Essen, there is 1 church left for 200,000 Protestants. Cologne has no Protestant church left, for 150,000. . . .
> In Stuttgart, too, the inner city is now without a church.[4]

Most church-owned hospitals, institutions, and kindergartens had been demolished. The church's Inner Mission reported that 329 residential institutions (with a total bed capacity of 20,171) had been destroyed in the western zones. In the east, of the 690 Inner Mission institutions that had existed in 1933, only 65 were still structurally intact.[5]

The human needs of the millions of refugees from the east and those who had been bombed out in the west were even more urgent. In 1947, for example, the Protestant church's *Hilfswerk* (aid committee) estimated that 12 million of the 15 million German children were undernourished, and 7.5 million were homeless.[6] The *Hilfswerk* began to coordinate aid efforts and distribute the food and clothing sent from overseas. By October 1948, the *Hilfswerk* had distributed almost 1½ million aid packages from various foreign charities.[7]

Brigitte Möckel had been a theology student in the Confessing Church. Her family had come from Siebenbürgen, the Rumanian region settled by ethnic Germans. Now she found a job at the *Hilfswerk*:

> In the meantime, the whole wave of refugees from the east had begun. At first, not really from Rumania and Siebenbürgen; they weren't banished and didn't have to leave. The *Hilfswerk* put an office at the service of all these different peoples from the east. The pastors who came out of those regions could be active for their people. A position was opened up, too, for those from Siebenbürgen. I took that over until 1948. At first, it was very important indeed. The people could get advice there, look for work, and meet. Then it became even more important, because in Rumania, once the war was over, the Russians came in and told the government, "You will have to consider what you will do with the Germans. Most of them went along with it"[Nazism].[8]

Now the migration of ethnic Germans — both those who had always lived in Rumania and those who, encouraged by the Nazis, had moved there — began anew. Many were deported to Soviet labor camps. By the end of 1946, these refugees began trickling into Germany:

> They didn't return to Siebenbürgen, but to Frankfurt/Oder [the city of Frankfurt on the Oder River, in the east] to the releasing centers. These people were in very bad condition, in poor health, came into a country where they had never been before, where they had no relatives, no friends, knew no one — and for that, this aid committee was twice as important. That was in 1946, 1947.[9]

Emmi Bonhoeffer, too, was busy helping refugees. An American pastor had told his parish about the "other Germany," about people like the Bonhoeffer brothers, who had died fighting Nazism. Soon Bonhoeffer was receiving CARE packages of food and clothing from the United States. In Germany itself, as a "victim of fascism," she received doubled food rations:

> So for us, going hungry had come to an end. But I used this opportunity to receive the packages to describe to the Americans what the circumstances here were. The people lived off stolen beets and potatoes, or they ate from the empty food cans on garbage heaps, often slept four people crossed over two beds, sometimes three generations in a room. In one community, with around 10 villages, we had 6,000 refugees, in addition to 5,000 residents. The trains of refugees from the northeast were all dumped in Holstein because the French zone didn't take any refugees.
>
> In the beginning, I just passed everything on, right at the door. Then, one day, the village schoolteacher came to me and said, "Frau Bonhoeffer, it's not good to do it the way you do. The people are getting used to it. Recently, on the street, I heard how one woman said to another, "Now I have a coat, dress, and shoes; I lack only underwear. I'll go to Frau Bonhoeffer and she'll write a letter to America. I'll have my underwear in six weeks at the very latest."
>
> Then came a package with a beautiful black coat, with a silk lining and fur trimming. On it stood: "For Mrs. Bonhoeffer personally." A woman came who asked, "Frau Bonhoeffer, don't you have a coat for me?" I still had the conversation with the teacher in my ears, and so I hesitated. She wasn't used to this hesitation, and offered to work for me. I thought, working isn't a bad idea.[10]

Bonhoeffer organized a system in her village to give refugees work — helping war widows, doing necessary rebuilding, eventually even repairing the main road from one village to another. In return for a certain number of hours worked, the refugees received clothing and food from Bonhoeffer's CARE packages. She wrote to the American parish and told them about it:

> The Americans liked that very well. They called it, "There's a chance to receive charity without losing self-respect." That was very American. The result was that I no longer received packages, but crates of clothing.[11]

In the biggest project, a group of men cleared off and built a sports field for village children:

> Then I found someone who could paint, and had him paint a sign, once it was done: "This sports field was built in 1952 by 22 refugees and residents for clothes from America." I was back there recently. The sign is gone, and the whole school has been torn down. Now there are little cottages where the school stood, and where the sports field was, there are now little enclosures with benches. No one has any inkling now of what took place there.[12]

But Emmi Bonhoeffer never forgot. In 1986, she was still wearing a coat from that era — not the one from America, but another one:

> My children had learned to spin wool. We exchanged American cigarettes for five pounds of raw wool from a shepherd. A friend of mine had a spinning wheel, and another friend could sew. After I had gone for two years without a coat — naturally, I

couldn't take any coat when I swam over—this coat was completed. I'll wear it to the grave, because it is a piece of history. I don't need any other coat. It is as warm as fur. I never want to wear another coat.[13]

Surely Emmi Bonhoeffer was not the only German to retain something from the postwar era as a reminder of the blessings that came in the period of hardship. "I believe that things went well again for us too quickly," she reflected in 1986. It was an attitude shared by many in the churches. The painful task of rebuilding Germany embittered some Germans, but led many others to reflect on the grace of history. Whatever their hardships, they had been rescued from Nazism; and those who had defeated Germany were helping rebuild it with a generosity that moved many Germans. In London, the Jewish publisher Viktor Gollancz organized an aid effort that sent 60,000 packages. In the words of Karl Silex from the *Hilfswerk*, "After all the Jewish suffering that has happened, what this Englishman and Jew has done and is doing, in a unique gesture of reconciliation, can only fill us with gratitude and shame."[14]

This gratitude and a sense of deliverance were present in postwar Germany, too. Despite the sorry state of most church buildings, worship services were filled. As Hans Thimme recalled,

> It was a creative time, this first period. The gratitude to have come out of it one more time, the astonishment that we were emerging from this void at all, this affirming joy, was something very special. And, despite the unbelievable primitiveness of the conditions, there was this joy that the loving God was giving us one more chance. The "merciful judgment of God"—Edmund Schlinck wrote that then as a pamphlet—that was what we felt, very strongly, and attendance at the worship services was overfilled. It was truly a genuine new beginning.[15]

Many of the young pastors who had been illegal in the *Kirchenkampf* now embarked on a new beginning in a double sense, for they were now part of the official church, received salaries, and could work without Gestapo harassment. But, although they were now freed for the more routine aspects of ministry, some parts of their work remained extraordinarily difficult. Foremost was the question of how to minister to parish members who had not shared the convictions of the Confessing Church during the Third Reich (the majority, in most parishes). Some were church "neutrals" who had steered clear of the *Kirchenkampf*; others were Nazi party members who had left the church. One reason that the EKD had opposed strict denazification had been its pastoral commitment to such people. The church would turn no one away, and many of those who now filled the church pews depended on this. Gerda Keller (one of the first women theologians, who after the war became a parish worker in Dortmund) recalled,

> The church—that was the place which still was most trusted by the people. There they were prepared to join in again quickly. Basically, we expected more from this revival in the church after the war. In this first effervescence—"The church stood for something"—that pulled the people into the church, also because we didn't now conjure up a trial against all those who had belonged to the party. Instead, well, we tried to pull them in, because they now had things hard. The relatives of the Gestapo people, they were very badly off. Very badly.[16]

For the Illegals, of course, dealing with these people as parish members was a radical departure from the tasks they had faced during the Third Reich. Ministers who had held official pastorates had had the experience, at least, of dealing with a broader spectrum of parishioners; even the Dahlem parish had had its Nazi party members. Many of the official ministers had engaged Illegals to work exclusively with the Confessing Christians in their parishes, where the Confessing Church had existed, de facto, as a separate parish group. The ministry experience of these Illegals had been limited to working with these small groups of ardently convinced Confessing Christians. After 1945, these Illegals, now fully recognized pastors, served in parishes whose members may have had no ties to the Confessing Church. One young pastor returned in 1947, at the age of 36, from an Allied prisoner of war camp and was assigned to a parish in Berlin:

> The parish was "neutral." They had no inkling whatsoever. There had been a number of withdrawals from the church during the Third Reich, and I can recall that they soaked it up like a sponge, how Niemöller and the others had been repressed. They hadn't known all that. . . .
>
> I have all my sermons from 1947 to 1969. All of them. I had to preach every Sunday, sometimes twice when we had a sermon exchange, and every two weeks at vespers. . . . It was a bit like spring then, a spiritual spring, in 1947, 1948, 1949. . . . When we had a communion service at 11 P.M. on New Year's Eve, in the half-destroyed church, with 60, 80, 100 people coming to communion . . . they knew why they were coming out of their cold apartments through the snow for a half hour in 1948 and 1949. Or our youth work in those days. They knew, indeed. Pardon me— but today you would reach something like that only by holding a disco in the parish.[17]

For this pastor, addressing the spiritual needs of postwar Germans meant telling them about the Confessing Church. "They hadn't known all that," he recalled. Had they? Could they have known? What else hadn't they known? Each pastor now had to decide how to confront these issues with parishioners.

In downtown Berlin, Annemarie Grosch was still working at the Kaiser-Wilhelm Memorial Church, now a bombed-out hull. She gathered her women's groups in homes and parish halls:

> The picture in my parish changed after 1945. Just as, before 1945, I had had these totally incriminated women ["incriminated" under the "Aryan" laws] who had suffered as "non-Aryans" under Hitler's policies, after the end of the war, the women who had been Nazis under Hitler came suddenly to my circles. The leaf turned. Now they were in need of help, looking for support and protection and, somewhere, for a relationship in which they could come to their senses and rebuild— which happened among them only in part, but in part genuinely. The tensions in the women's groups and youth groups now really began between those who had suffered under Hitler and those who had been Nazis. I didn't throw the former Nazis out; I tried to talk with them, but that was very difficult. . . .
>
> When those of us who had been together before 1945 made some kind of allusion to jokes under Hitler, many grinned and knew what was happening. Among those who were newcomers, some of them grinned along, but some did not. With

that, I could discern their political attitude before the *Zusammenbruch*. Namely, one hadn't told such jokes to those who had been National Socialists. They always asked, "What is going on?" They didn't know the jokes. Whereas others, who had also come in new, who had been opponents, understood everything immediately.[18]

Some Confessing pastors took pity on former Nazis and absorbed them, without judgment, into the parish community. Others rankled under the situation. Rudolf Weckerling was one of the former Illegals who feared that the precepts he had upheld in the Confessing Church were being watered down in the postwar church now emerging:

> Of course, we noticed right after 1945 that the *Kirchenkampf* of the Confessing Church hadn't been won. We had survived as a church because of the Allies, for it was clear to everyone that, after the extermination of the Jews, the extermination of the Christians stood on the bill—in any case, the extermination of Confessing Christians. We made that clear to ourselves, on the one hand, but on the other hand, we didn't know right away what that would mean concretely for our work after the liberation.
>
> Suddenly, I was pastor in a parish in which, according to the records, the pastor who had been there before was a friend of Reich bishop Müller and a convinced "German Christian," and that was obvious too. There were swastikas in the church at the entrance and on the altar. I was alone there. . . .
>
> It was an unbelievable situation. Now, the new orientation among the people was this: Suddenly, the church, which hadn't been worth anything in the Third Reich, was very important somehow. The people came in huge numbers to the church and searched for comfort and support and an orientation. Others, who had left the church because their party membership required it, now they wanted to join again. . . . During this period, some of us who had belonged to the Confessing Church met every Thursday. For us, that was simply the place to "retank," an oasis of orientation for how we could be Christians and pastors after 1945. That was the so-called *Unterwegs* circle.[19]

The *Unterwegs* circle (literally, "on the road") was a group of Confessing Christians who sought to integrate their experiences in the postwar church. They met regularly and published (from 1947 to 1954) a magazine, *Unterwegs*, that discussed political and religious questions. Its editor was Wolf-Dieter Zimmermann, a former Bonhoeffer student. Among those who wrote articles for the magazine were Gertrud Staewen, Helene Jacobs, Gustav Heinemann, Heinrich Vogel, Karl Barth, and Eberhard Bethge, who published some of Dietrich Bonhoeffer's writings there for the first time.

In the lead editorial in the first issue, the *Unterwegs* group committed itself not just to keeping the cause of the *Kirchenkampf* alive but to changing the very structure of the Protestant church:

> We seek fellowship with people from all camps. . . . For that reason, amidst all the rigidity and restoration of the church, we are striving for a renewal of its teachings, proclamation and law in the sense of the Barmen Theological Declaration of May 1934, and for the sake of fellowship with Christians in other peoples and lands.[20]

Restoration or Renewal?

The *Unterwegs* group wanted the EKD to be rebuilt as a confessing church, not as the tradition-bound, nationalistic church that, they believed, had so compromised itself under Nazism. It was one thing to work toward this goal in individual parishes; it was far more difficult to create new structures for the institutional church as a whole. The *Unterwegs* group and those who shared their commitment faced several formidable obstacles. The first was that most regional church leaders simply wished to rebuild their churches and organize their administrations as quickly as possible. Preoccupied by the immediate problems of bombed-out church buildings and the unceasing influx of refugees, EKD leaders were hardly inclined to take a break to re-evaluate the church's institutional structure — which most of them saw nothing wrong with. Dibelius' remark about resuming church operations where they had stopped in 1933 was typical; in fact, Dibelius believed that only this would prevent a revival of Nazism. As he told Allied commanders, only the Protestant church offered "traditional ideology" that could "fill the vacuum left by the collapse of the Hitler movement."[21]

This point of view was the diametrical opposite of one expressed by Martin Niemöller:

> On absolutely no account may a church restoration on the foundation of the conditions before 1933 be the outcome, if the entire struggle, suffering and sacrifices of the past 12 years are not to be in vain.[22]

The difference between these two viewpoints was clear; a viable alternative to the EKD was not. Those who sought such an alternative were a minority, even within the Confessing Church. Their experience — as Bonhoeffer students or as Illegals working outside the official church system during the Third Reich — had been one that very few pastors, and even fewer church administrators, had had. Their entire education, exams, and ministry had been an unorthodox departure from the way in which Germans usually trained for professional careers. They had studied illegally, taught by professors who had left the official (Nazi-regulated) theological faculties. When they had passed their exams, which were held secretly in student apartments or professors' homes, they were given unofficial assignments in parishes in which the majority of parishioners were unaware of what they were doing. (Annemarie Grosch said that this was her situation at Kaiser-Wilhelm-Memorial, for example.) They had been paid not by the official church consistory but by the voluntary donations of Confessing Christians and those official pastors willing to help support them.

It had been an uncertain existence, often hand-to-mouth, but one that, they believed, reflected a more serious and committed Christianity. Now these Confessing pastors did not wish to return to a *Volkskirche*, a concept that had evolved from Martin Luther's radical assertion of the "priesthood of all believers" and had represented various alliances throughout German church history. In the nineteenth century, the religious socialists and the founders of the Protestant Inner Mission had used the term to declare the church's independence from the German upper classes. In the 1930s, the "German Christians" reconceived the *Volkskirche* as the "Aryan" church required for an "Aryan" people.

Institutionally, the position of the *Volkskirche* within German society was between the people and the state. Supported by a state-levied church tax, but with the right to govern its own affairs, the *Volkskirche* was neither a free church nor a state church. Throughout its history, this situation intensified many of the church-state problems it was meant to resolve, for the church constantly had to redefine its position toward the state. The very notion of a *Volkskirche*, based upon the premise that lay members should be part of the governance of their church, encouraged many Germans to believe that the church's public positions should reflect popular opinion.

Confessing Christians had witnessed the extremes of this attitude in the "German Christian" movement. After the war, they feared that the *Volkskirche*, with its comfortable place in German society, would bow too quickly to the expectations of bourgeois German taxpayers who attended church twice a year and expected their church to uphold their own personal convictions and avoid controversy. For this reason, many former Illegals, although working in the official German Evangelical Church, viewed their institutional church with distrust. This shaped the relationship of some pastors to their church for the rest of their careers. As one woman pastor recalled in 1982,

> I went completely to the radical other side, to Bonhoeffer and these people. From that point on, I was disenfranchised, and that has been very dangerous for me, naturally, because, through that, I never learned to assume responsibility in public. From the beginning, I was in the cellar, do you understand that? I never got used to it, and it has been very difficult for me, because—this plagues me up to today—I never learned to claim my rights. It was always the case that, as the Confessing Church, we were the minority, the ones they put up with. We were indeed of the opinion that we represented that which was right—but we simply weren't the *Volkskirche* anymore. That is very dangerous now, when I express it this way. I simply can't express it differently. Basically, from this time on, it has remained the case that I can't come to terms with the problem of the official church.[23]

From this standpoint, the restoration of the official *Volkskirche* represented the defeat of the Confessing Church epitomized by Dietrich Bonhoeffer. Rudolf Weckerling believed that the re-establishment of the EKD as a *Volkskirche* was a denial of the *Kirchenkampf*:

> They structurally liquidated the Confessing Church. And resumed here: that each person who has been baptized as a baby is to be seen as a Christian. The clarifications and differences of these 12 years were covered up with the "cloak of love." It certainly wasn't the love of Christ, but rather a laissez-faire love, because one didn't see any perspective in a free-church structure for the church.
>
> Pragmatically, perhaps they were right. Percentagewise, among those who had been engaged in the Confessing Church, there were far too many pastors and far too few lay people, so that an entirely new form would have had to have been found during this postwar period. . . .
>
> Perhaps the development had to go the way it did, but it is very ominous and fatal nevertheless, because the voices of Niemöller and others remained so much in the minority.[24]

Weckerling and others opposed the resumption of the Protestant church's traditional ties to the state and distrusted the *Behördenkirche*, a church governed primarily by its bureaucracy, not by the active lay community of believers. Both factors, which had weakened Protestant opposition to Nazism, tend to make church independence in any era contingent upon the courage of individual leaders. Heinrich Albertz, a Confessing Church Illegal who entered politics after the war, noted that, after 1945,

> Almost all the elder [pastors] went back to their desks. The first step was the return to this church tax system. I believe that we would have had a totally different church if it hadn't gone this way. The strongest example is Berlin. With Dibelius, Scharf, and others, a new church administration was founded, but the consistory remained. When there is no strong bishop there, nothing remains but a bureaucratic administration.[25]

Those who believed that the church had been paralyzed by its bureaucracy during the Third Reich put their postwar hopes in a more engaged laity — the ordinary Christians who had filled the illegal Confessing Church collection baskets and braved Gestapo surveillance to attend Bible studies. The *Kirchenkampf* did encourage the growth of an active and motivated Protestant laity. One postwar sign of this was the *Kirchentag*, a biennial week-long national church meeting at which lay, clergy, and politicians worshipped and discussed current issues. There were other, more subtle signs of change. Albrecht Schönherr recalled how some of these affected Christians at the parish level:

> The parishes now participate in a special way — for example, that one says the creed and the Our Father together today. That is only since the *Kirchenkampf*. Previously, that had never occurred. The pastor said all that alone. Many don't know that. The Eucharist, too, is conducted much more strongly as an experience of community; that, too, stems from this period.[26]

Nevertheless, there was the sense that the Confessing Church had consisted, as Weckerling said, of "too many pastors, too few lay people." Elsie Steck recalled that in 1945, once the churches were no longer under Gestapo pressure, "there was bickering, and, in the parishes, there hadn't been nearly as much going on as the Confessing Church had imagined."[27]

As in 1933 and 1934, conflicting visions of the church's identity and proper role in society divided those who had been in the church opposition to Nazism. Even persons committed to making the postwar Protestant church a "confessing" church differed on what that really meant. For the *Unterwegs* group, it meant a free church (as opposed to a *Volkskirche*), supported only by committed Christians and making no attempt to placate nominal Christians — a church prepared to take clear stands on social and political issues. For people like Hans Thimme in Westphalia, a "confessing" church meant something else:

> In Westphalia, at that time, we represented the opinion: We were the Confessing Church, but we were *the* church. We weren't a group in the church, we weren't a party in the church, we weren't a direction, rather, we were the church. . . . That means that our understanding of ourselves, from the beginning, prevented us from forming a political church group. . . .
> In that respect, the position of the Council of Brethren is interesting. In fact, it continued to exist after 1945, although, in some individual church administrations

and churches, the church leadership consisted of the Confessing Church — but there was still this Council of Brethren in addition. And that is the problem, somewhat.[28]

The Council of Brethren represented the radical sector of the Confessing Church, and Thimme's remarks reveal the difference between traditionalists who wanted to restore the church and radicals who wanted to change it. Because of Allied pressure, and pressures within the churches themselves, most regional churches after 1945 were led by people who had stood somewhere in the church opposition to Nazism (although it must be noted that the rapidity with which some people now claimed to have been Confessing Christians was matched only by the rapidity with which they had welcomed Nazism in 1933).[29] But there were certainly those, like Hans Thimme, who had viewed the Confessing Church as the true church during the Third Reich and now believed, in turn, that *the* postwar Protestant church was a confessing church. But the continued existence of the Confessing Church's national Council of Brethren (until the 1960s) proved that an important sector of the Confessing Church, although it remained within the German Evangelical Church, often differed from its direction. Indeed, the postwar Council of Brethren described itself as a "counter-movement" to traditionalist tendencies within the EKD:

> For the Confessing Church did not originate as a resistance movement against the "German Christians" and National Socialism, but from a new understanding of the word of God and Reformed theology. . . . Besides its official organs, the EKD needs those, too, that are not bound to the set paths of the institution, but that can seize a spiritual/theological/church-related initiative with greater freedom and independence.[30]

The pre-1945 circumstances of the various regional churches now influenced how they absorbed Confessing Church Illegals and parish members as well as how they viewed the Council of Brethren. In Westphalia, for example, the church was led until 1985 by men who had been in the Confessing Church.[31] But the Westphalian church had remained somewhat intact during the *Kirchenkampf*, led by Confessing Christian Karl Koch, despite the presence of an administration dominated by "German Christians."[32] In other parts of the Old Prussian Union Church, particularly in Berlin-Brandenburg, the Confessing Church had been forced farther from the mainstream and had broken off to establish its own church government. In other regional churches, including the intact churches, whose bishops had straddled the line between the church opposition and conservatives, the Confessing Church had existed only as scattered groups of loyal pastors and parishes.

Their different situations during the Third Reich now affected how church leaders adapted the legacy of the Confessing Church for their own churches — in particular, what version of the *Kirchenkampf* they adopted. Hans Thimme, for example, believed that only those Confessing churches which had broken off from the official church could afford to adopt, in his words, "a gruff radicality." Thimme differentiated between the Confessing Church as "movement" and as "institution," and he supported the institution:

> We had to resume with that which was given, the *Volkskirche*, for we were a people which consisted of baptized people, even after 1945. . . . I believe it would be important that you make clear that what happened here after 1945 wasn't restoration, basi-

cally. That came afterward. But what was carried out in 1945 was, at first, simply the grateful resumption of an affirmed tradition.[33]

There was considerable rancor between those who saw the re-establishment of the German Evangelical Church as "the grateful resumption of an affirmed tradition" and those who viewed it as a compromise of the Confessing Church's principles. Nevertheless, all these groups did remain within the EKD, including the Council of Brethren. Otto Dibelius became bishop of Berlin, but Council of Brethren member Kurt Scharf was given jurisdiction over East Berlin and succeeded Dibelius as bishop. Even Martin Niemöller became head of a regional church (in Hesse) and headed the EKD's foreign office until 1956.

The Rehabilitation of the "German Christians"

The EKD successfully united the different factions that had made up the church opposition to Nazism. But the most problematic group was not the Confessing Church radicals or the intact churches but the "German Christians," who had pressed for an "Aryan" church and accommodated their theology to Nazi ideology. Now they, too, sought to regain their place in the *Volkskirche*. Most regional churches held heresy proceedings — hearings and seminars in which "German Christians" were "debriefed" and in which they had to admit they had succumbed to false teachings. Hans Thimme was in charge of this task in Westphalia:

> No "German Christian" could automatically re-enter the parish, but all "German Christians" were run through obligatory departments of testing, controlling, and heresy hearings. Either they didn't come back into their office at all, or they came back in a limited fashion — that is, only in assistanceships — or they then came into seminars. I myself had to hold such seminars. . . .
>
> These courses were rehabilitation courses, if you will. . . . I got more the compromisers. The most striking thing about it was that they "had never been 'German Christians.'" They trivialized it. Basically, they tried to make clear that they had always been good Christians and loyal citizens, and so on. That is, on the whole, the "new beginning" among them didn't come through a very explicit repentance. They shrugged their shoulders and went on.[34]

It is difficult to establish exactly the number of "German Christians" who retained or regained positions in their churches. Frederic Spotts estimated that 8 to 9 percent of the Protestant pastorate remained active "German Christians" up to 1945 and that most regional churches voluntarily cleaned their ranks of these pastors.[35] Cleaning the ranks, however, did not mean barring "German Christians" from the ministry. Both Thimme and Kurt Scharf recalled that most "German Christians" were simply removed from parish positions to ones less prestigious in the church's eyes — positions as chaplains in deaconical institutions or hospitals, for example. Joachim Hossenfelder, the fanatical "German Christian" leader who had called for the merger of "heroic, manly" Christian ideals and "Aryan" precepts, was demoted from his pulpit in a prominent Potsdam church to a parish in a remote village in Brandenburg; after 1951, he became a chaplain in an East Berlin hospital.[36]

There were apparently instances in which former "German Christians" retained pastorates or even positions as superintendents, from which, according to Hans Iwand, they continued to harass Confessing pastors.[37] Some former "German Christians" even atempted to pass themselves off as Confessing Christians. As Martin Fischer recalled, this situation made many Confessing pastors cautious around new colleagues:

> More "German Christians" had remained in Germany during the war. They sent more Confessing pastors to the front. That's why, in 1945, there were so few of us. All of us were very insecure in those years. We didn't know at all who had belonged to us and who had been a "German Christian."[38]

The church decided to base its policies toward former "German Christians" on Christian teachings of forgiveness. Wilhelm Niemöller, a former "German Christian" himself, viewed the reinstallation of the "German Christians" into church offices this way:

> Where it concerned the "German Christian" pastors, I always spoke up for the charitable way. If Jesus can convert Paul, then a parish (which names itself for Christ, not for Paul) should be in the position to pardon, to forgive and take someone under its wing. . . . When a Christian parish no longer has the capability to forgive . . . then it has lost its readiness and ability to offer shelter. And its credibility. Naturally, I have to ask the person who has taken such a false path, "Have you come away from that, or can I help you? Can we count on you?" But one doesn't do that with a hammer.[39]

Kurt Scharf, too, defended the church's general treatment of former "German Christians":

> In the church, we viewed these [heresy] proceedings as an act of counseling and as a confrontation with the teachings of those fallen or errant brothers who, in our opinion, had misused their office during the National Socialist era. To a great extent, those affected were removed from their parishes or lost leading positions like the office of superintendent. They took over especially difficult pastorates on probation, pastorates that were isolated or difficult to administer. Seen as a whole, I believe that, through these proceedings, the past has really been cleaned. An untroubled brotherly relation was achieved between those who had belonged to the Confessing Church and those who had been "German Christians" and also to the largest group, the so-called neutral pastors.[40]

Postwar Policies toward the Women Theologians

But the rehabilitation of former "German Christians" was difficult for some Confessing Christians to accept. It was particularly hard for the women pastors who had led parishes, because, with the reconstruction of the church, even ordained women who had led parishes were now pushed back into traditional women's positions. In fact, here the status of the different callings within the church became apparent. The German Protestant church had always seen proclamation of the scripture as the central purpose of its existence. Accordingly, the vocation of preacher and the parish ministry carried greater prestige than did deaconical work, counseling, and religious education. After 1945, like the "German Christians," although for a different reason, the women who had preached and served parishes for the Confessing Church were moved into "less important" positions. For the "German Christians," demotion served as a punishment. Few people seem to have considered what this meant for the women who had served the Confessing Church. During the Third Reich, particularly during the war, the churches had needed the women. Now, as Doris Faulhaber and other women discovered, things had changed:

> Everything became totally reactionary again. The new bishop told me, for example, that all the children whom I had baptized, in the hospital and in this parish [that the baptisms] were "illegitimate" — that hopefully I knew that. . . . The children weren't rebaptized. But he had still said it; that was his opinion. Moreover, he told me: "You can't remain here in the City Hospital. This is a job for men." Yes, the men all came back from the front and from the prisons, from the Sudetenland, and so on. And what did they do with us? Sent us back to giving lessons! With one difference: We all came now to the *Gymnasiums* [which prepared students for university study]. Earlier, that was impossible.[41]

Although the women's wartime ordinations were recognized, it soon became clear that most of the men leading the EKD considered the ordinations and the women's parish ministry as exceptions made necessary by the war. Some women were able to remain in parishes, but most were pushed out. Annemarie Grosch, for example, was unable to find a parish in Berlin. She finally moved to Schleswig-Holstein, where she became director of the women's groups of the church in that region. Moreover, restrictions that had been ignored during the war were now reapplied; one was the requirement that women pastors remain unmarried. Thus, Helga Weckerling and Brigitte Möckel had to leave the pastorate when they married after the war.

For women entering the ministry after 1945, the practical gains won by the women during the *Kirchenkampf* did not set a precedent in church law. Although Ilse Härter continued her work as a pastor after 1945, for example, her church in Rhineland continued — until 1963 — to ordain postwar women as vicars, not as pastors, and women were not entitled to perform the full range of pastoral duties. Full equality for ordained women in Rhineland came in 1975; in some other regional churches — for example, in Lübeck, Hessen-Nassau, and Brunswick — women were not allowed to be ordained at all until the 1960s.

In many cases it seemed easier for church leaders to forgive the theological heresies of the "German Christians" than to support the full ordination and employment of women who had been serving their church conscientiously. Before she left for Schleswig-Holstein, Annemarie Grosch was summoned to the Berlin church consistory. There she was greeted by the same official who, at the Gestapo's behest, had interrogated her and the other women after their ordination in 1943:

> And then, suddenly, [he gave me] my certificate of ordination. At my retirement here, in December 1977, it became clear to me how carefully the church leadership of the Confessing Church had attended to everything that belongs to administration. The regional bishop of Schleswig read from my files, for example, from my examination in 1939, from all the reports of my teachers — things that I myself had never seen. . . . In the chaos of the war, my own safe at the Commerzbank was bombed

out. So I have no more record of my second theological exams. The only thing I possess is the certificate of ordination. . . . The Confessing Church, then, had really figured that it would later have to account officially for all of its official church actions. That was our security! I always thought, when I moved to Schleswig-Holstein, "Funny, you don't have any papers that you can produce except for the ordination certificate. What will happen if things become critical?" Because, as women, we were still very insecure.[42]

Although some churchmen viewed the women's postwar work as less significant than that of parish pastors, the social contribution of postwar religion teachers and other church workers was, in its own way, an act of proclamation. Doris Faulhaber, initially bitter at her removal from the parish and her position as chaplain, came to see her job of teaching religion to adolescent girls in a *Gymnasium* as her contribution to the postwar rebuilding of Germany. She told her pupils about what had happened in the churches during the Third Reich:

They sat there as quiet as mice, these smart girls, breathless, with their mouths opened wide. You could have heard a pin drop, they were listening so. And then I said, "Yes, well, that's enough — haven't you heard of these things?" No. "Haven't your parents ever told you about them?" No. That will have been 1956, 1958, perhaps — some years after the war, then. Knew nothing about it! . . . The parents had been younger then, were probably in the Hitler Youth and the SA, and had kept silent about it. There is much here that was simply kept silent about. . . .

Sometimes I have thought to myself, that if I had it to do over again, I would become more politically engaged, as a Protestant theologian, with my convictions and with all that I know. It would be worth it. One can't turn back the wheel of time. But to some extent, I made such a decision when I applied for the school position in 1946. Earlier, I had always pushed that far away from myself . . . but in 1946, I thought to myself: join in on the rebuilding of Germany. It had to do with Germany. We weren't divided yet. And the rebuilding of Germany is a political matter, a political engagement. For my part as a religion teacher, I wanted that, as someone who had something to do with German youth. The youth of today are the people of tomorrow. I wanted that, particularly because of all that I had behind me.[43]

Deepened Political Commitment

Most Confessing Christians viewed the rebuilding of their church and society not just as a political task but as a moral one. In Berlin, Marion Yorck von Wartenburg carried the legacy of her resistance against Hitler into the judicial sphere. Although she had a doctorate in law and had passed her first legal exams, she was not sure what she could do after the war. In Berlin, the Soviet command was vetoing the appointments of all judges who had been in party organizations or had served in the German military. Just as the absence of male pastors during the war had increased opportunities for Confessing Church women, the absence of judges with unblemished pasts enabled Yorck von Wartenburg to be appointed a judge, first in East Berlin and then as presiding judge of the juvenile court in West Berlin. Yorck von Wartenburg recalled how her experience under Nazism influenced her work:

It was always written, and the psychiatrists who were active as expert witnesses always said, that I treated the defendants as human beings. I didn't address them as "the accused," as was still the custom then, but always by their names. . . . After all these experiences, one does strive to make reparations for what has happened. I believed that I could do that through my manner of conducting a trial.

For example, we had one trial—here in Berlin, there was a black market. Those were real gangs; they killed each other, too, or tried to, in any case. I had a Polish Jew. He had shot another, had hardly hit him, thank God, and was charged with attempted murder. . . . In this trial against these people, I said afterward in my verdict that the fact that the accused was still alive, despite the German occupation and German misdeeds, had to be considered. They had lived for years only in the underground. They had never learned what justice was, what law was. Then I couldn't simply intone all the violations of law they had committed. Of course, they were sentenced. You can't prevent that, when one man has shot someone else with a gun. But, in my verdict, I did allow these mediating factors to have their say.

Afterward, the defense lawyer came to my chambers and said, "The accused said, 'the woman was decent to me; I will be decent to her. I accept the verdict.'" Six judges before me had adjourned this trial, because they were afraid of the Allies. In this case, all the defendants were Jews. It was very difficult, and the defendant had also said that he didn't understand anything, that he needed a Jewish, Polish, and Yiddish translator. Before, we had had five translators sitting there. Then I talked with him. I spoke to him, asked what his name was, where he had grown up, where his family was. After we had spoken about all that, I said, "Should I have a translator translate that?" "No," he said, "we understand each other." I could send all the translators home.[44]

For some Germans, then, their postwar work was a means of reconciling the pain of the past, an attempt to create a different kind of Germany. They sought not only to overturn the mentality that had dominated Nazi Germany but even to redress, as far as was possible, some of the damage that had been done. As soon as the war ended, Gertrud Staewen went to Buchenwald to see if her friends had survived. The Allied forces were barring Germans from the camp, and her only means of entering was to join a group of former Nazis who had been ordered to work in the camp kitchen and perform menial tasks:

Then I had to do this bitter thing and appear with all the Nazis, to peel potatoes. A whole group was still living in the concentration camp. Mostly it was Jews, Polish Jewish working-class people. I would have thought to myself that they would have spit on us and everything else. Not a trace. One showed me how to peel potatoes better; I had peeled them too thick. Then I began, naturally, to talk with some of them, and that was something completely wonderful. It's hard to believe. They had gone through everything. Nevertheless, they were grateful. . . .

For a long time, I did what I could in Weimar. I rolled away debris for people. First under the Amis, and then they left, the idiots, and then under the Russians. Now the Russians were my commanders. Once I found a German child with a toy panzer—a Russian officer had given it to him; at that point they could still live in private housing. I looked more closely at the panzer and saw that it was painted very superficially red, and that the swastika showed through. I took it away from the poor child; I will be sorry forever, he cried so terribly that he had lost his only toy—but I couldn't stand it. I went to the Russians, and said, "Herr Commander" — he sat there with his cap on his head — "Look here, Herr Commander, child-loving like you are, you give a German child this panzer. Look at this panzer closely, please. Do you see the swastika here?" Then he tore the cap from his head, threw the panzer away, and screamed, "No stars for children! No Nazi star and no Soviet star! See that you get out of here and buy something else for the children!" I said, "Herr Commander, what should I buy, there aren't any things to buy." "You think out! You the right woman! You will be leader of women's group!"

Ooooh. Then I said, "No." "What?" He became terribly angry. And yelled at me, "You dare say no? High honor, you, leader of Democratic Women's Organization." I said, "My dear Herr Commander, I have gone through enough in my life. I am joining no more associations."[45]

In her postwar career, Marion Yorck von Wartenburg continued to live according to the principles she had followed in resisting Hitler; Gertrud Staewen ended the Third Reich as she had begun, as a nonconformist. Both women continued the patterns of political behavior that had guided them even before 1933. But an active political awareness of the consequences of their decisions and of those of their government had become necessities in the postwar world. For Germans deeply troubled about the Nazi past, being apolitical like the "good Germans" who had followed the Nazis blindly was impossible. And even if the past hadn't brought them to this conclusion, the German situation after 1945 would have.

12

Political Developments and the East German Church

The Politicization of *Vergangenheitsbewältigung*

THE REBUILDING OF POSTWAR German society and its churches was a political and moral task, and the division of Germany into radically different political systems magnified the complexity of the undertaking. From the beginning, church developments in each country were closely related to political developments. Postwar Germans had to define themselves with respect to the past and in relation to the two new German governments as well. Moreover, the way in which Germans dealt with the moral questions raised by the Nazi past was influenced not only by their immediate political *Sitz-im-Leben* but by how they judged both new systems.

In the German Democratic Republic, the Soviet occupation forces dealt far more ruthlessly with former Nazis than did the Allies in the Federal Republic. The full extent of this difference became clear only after the fall of East Germany's socialist government in 1989, when mass graves were excavated outside the boundaries of the Sachsenhausen and Buchenwald concentration camps. After 1945, the camps served as detention centers for suspected Nazis, members of Nazi organizations, and persons who had been denounced. As many as 85,000 people who died of starvation or sickness were buried in the forests beyond the camps.

The atmosphere of fear and distrust that had permeated Nazi Germany continued, after 1945, in East Germany. Former Nazis and their sympathizers did everything possible to cover their pasts. Luise M., who had worked with youth groups in a Confessing parish lived with her husband in a small farming village, where he served as the pastor. She later recalled an incident "typical" of that early postwar period:

> Among these farmers were some who were probably "German National," basically, and had never become Nazis. They did what was necessary, and their work was accepted. One of them had joined the SA; he had a large number of children. When the Russians came, he hid his uniform. Then one man was shot while he went through the village on his horse, because he hadn't understood the call to halt . . . he was shot through a misunderstanding on the Russians' part. Now the funeral came. Our warden didn't dare to ring the bells. At that time, I still had a lot of courage. The fear came only later. I rang the bells, but didn't go to the funeral, for my husband said, "Disappear back in the house."
>
> Then this farmer came in his SA boots, in order to take part worthily at this

funeral. In working clothes, but he put these SA boots on. The people had buried all their good things, and my husband had said, "It doesn't matter how you come; come in working clothes." This man came in SA boots, and was taken directly away from the funeral. That will have been the end of May 1945.

As an SA man, he had left the church. His children weren't baptized or confirmed. He came back after several months. I know that my husband always kept in touch with his wife and gave her good advice. Then he came to us on his own and told my husband: "I'd like to rejoin the church." My husband replied, "That pleases me, but we don't do that automatically; one doesn't change his faith like a shirt." Then we held family Christian studies in his home for a long time.

After that, they all joined the church again. With that, they were seen as having overcome National Socialism, in the village as well. No one denounced him later, because he had paid for it, somehow. . . .

It is true that the Nazis who had something to hide got out. They went to the West, or maybe even further abroad. They couldn't have stayed here any longer. . . . But there were many who came from the east, of whom we didn't know what they'd done there. If no one came later who denounced them, then that wasn't discovered at all.

I'm thinking of people who were on the eastern front as soldiers. Their families had fled the eastern regions or had been deported and now lived in the region of the GDR. There they found their families again. I mean, now and then it came out that they had been Nazis, if someone else recognized them. Things didn't go well for them then.[1]

In part, the Russians' actions may have reflected their feelings of revenge for all they had suffered at the hands of the Nazis. But their behavior was also tied to the Communists' sense of justification regarding how they had conducted themselves under the Nazis: Communists, after all, had been among the first victims of Nazism. Now the names of Communist martyrs were resurrected—like that of Ernst Thälmann, head of the German Communist party, who was imprisoned from March 1933 until his murder in Buchenwald in 1944. Communists who had survived the Nazi era now rose rapidly in the ranks of the leadership of the German Democratic Republic (GDR). One of the most prominent was Erich Honecker, who led the GDR from 1961 to 1989; Honecker had spent 10 years in Gestapo prisons.

While the Soviet approach to denazification was different from that taken in the west, the results were strikingly similar. By the 1950s, the new postwar governments in East and West Germany, supported by their respective allies, had effectively severed the link between the Nazi past and their postwar states. In the western Federal Republic, democracy became a "cure" for Nazism, so that former Nazis could rehabilitate themselves as they established their commitment to democratic values—all the while (with few exceptions) continuing the civil service careers they had begun during the Third Reich. In the Democratic Republic, it was safer to hide all signs of having been a Nazi; and the new GDR leaders denied any ties whatsoever to Nazism, not only for themselves but for their new socialist nation. Nazism, the GDR leaders claimed, had been the offspring of capitalism.

The record of broad public complicity in Nazi Germany was forgotten; the policies toward the past, in east and west, thwarted a genuine, deep public examination of what had happened to Germans under Nazism. More significantly, the official attitudes of both the East and West German governments reflected the main characteristic, in both countries, of *Vergangenheitsbewältigung*—the use of postwar political positions to symbolize moral judgment of the Nazi past. *Vergangenheitsbewältitung* could be defined as the attempt to come to terms with what had happened morally during the Third Reich. But there was no way, of course, to morally fathom, let alone resolve, the reality of the concentration camps, the murder of the European Jews, and the atrocities that had occurred throughout Europe.

The conclusion drawn by many Germans, particularly Confessing Christians, was that Christian precepts of repentance and forgiveness did not suffice, either as moves toward reconciliation with the victims of the Nazis or as attempts to reconcile the past within one's own conscience. The only real response to the past, they decided, was to act differently—that is, to act politically. This meant that many Germans justified their political decisions and alliances by viewing these as repudiations of the Nazi past. Accordingly, these Germans charged their political opponents with continuing some aspect of Nazism.

In many cases, this process of self-justification was very open. In the GDR, Luise M. recalled the schoolbooks her children brought home in the 1950s, in which the Nazi era

> was, in some respects, equated with conditions in the Federal Republic. . . . There was a friend/foe mentality built up, very systematically: "Where are the Nazis? They're in the West." . . . It's true that the Communists, a large part of them, who returned from exile, came to the GDR, and that there are people living there who really were persecuted by the Nazis.[2]

Within the churches, opinions on the relation of the new GDR state to the Nazi past differed. Those who viewed the socialist state with abhorrence were cynical. One woman pastor felt that the only difference between the Nazis and the Communists was the different insignia on the flag:

> I came back to Leipzig and saw the same thing there that I had to live through during the Nazi era. There were the red flags again. That gave me a direct shock. I saw that, and couldn't comprehend how that was possible. That the same people, who had lived through everything before—maybe they were all dead and these were already new people!—that they did the same thing. Basically, that has remained my opinion. This new division in Germany which appeared was very painful for me, because now one really had no more freedom.[3]

In 1986, Albrecht Schönherr, a Bonhoeffer student who subsequently became the first leader of the East German church, was asked if Christians in the GDR had repressed the past. He responded,

> In a certain sense, one can speak of a repression of it among us. Officially, nothing was repressed. Rather, one must say that for our government—it continued to see the fight against fascism as its main task. Naturally, that has a justifiable self-vindication there. One can speak of repression only to the extent that there was, and is, an entire group in the parishes with whom one simply can't speak about it, where, among themselves, the people simply shut up about it. . . .
>
> Naturally, there was a group from the Confessing Church that immediately

adjusted to a very positive attitude toward the state, and others who felt more resistance against this state. This group with the positive perspective was relatively small . . . and was denounced, of course. There were many people who said, naturally, that they had gotten too close to the state.[4]

Early Common Church-State Interests

In the GDR, the history of the Communist resistance against Nazism and that of the Confessing Church's struggles with Nazism led to what both sides perceived initially as a sharing of past interests, and, with that as a basis, the potential for future cooperation. Another factor played a part in early church openness to the new socialist state, at least among Confessing Christians who wanted a change in some of the traditional attitudes of their church. In the Federal Republic, the EKD had quickly resumed its powerful place in society, in what some critics charged was a continuation of the traditional unity of throne and altar. In the fledgling Democratic Republic, although church and socialist leaders expressed a willingness to tolerate each other, the constitution of the GDR made it clear that the church would have no institutional ties to the socialist state, which, in its turn, had no commitment to the long-term interests of the Protestant church.

With that, the Protestant church in the GDR became the "free church" that some Confessing Christians had hoped for in the Federal Republic. In 1950, Gustav Heinemann — a Confessing Church member and postwar member of the EKD Synod, as well as a prominent politician (beginning with his short term as Konrad Adenauer's interior minister in 1950) — welcomed the postwar changes in both churches, but particularly the clear-cut situation of the church in the GDR. "With the liberation from state-church bonds," he said, "our churches have finally won a liberation from political and social bonds as well."[5] The church's earlier link with the upper classes had blinded it, Heinemann continued, to the needs of the working classes, driving them to Marxism. Now the church was freed to preach the Gospel, unswayed by social pressures to curry favor with a Kaiser or Führer.[6]

But as became clear, the new situation in the GDR did not ensure freedom from state pressure. One Confessing Church pastor who recalled the difficulties in church-state relations during the period from 1945 to 1961 was Kurt Scharf, pastor of the church in Sachsenhausen during the Third Reich and member of the Confessing Church Council of Brethren. In October 1945, Berlin bishop Otto Dibelius appointed Scharf head of the eastern portion of the church provinces of Brandenburg and Berlin — the part of Dibelius' district that was under Soviet control. From the very beginning, Scharf helped lead negotiations between the church and the state in the GDR. As he recalled in 1981,

the church was a kind of foreign body in the socialist state that was consolidating itself in the German Democratic Republic. . . . In the first period after 1945, the negotiations with the functionaries of the Communist state were relatively tolerant. Frequently, they had suffered together in the concentration camps with Christians, and because of that, felt respect for us and a special fellowship with us.[7]

The fact that the church in the east was represented by men like Scharf and Heinrich Grüber (the former head of the office that had helped the Jews) helped considerably. Hans Seigewasser, the GDR minister for church affairs, had been in the concentration camp in Sachsenhausen and learned to respect the Christians imprisoned there. Later, he told Scharf how he had waited every evening to hear the bells ringing from Scharf's church.[8]

In contrast, Scharf said, the Communist functionaries who had survived the Third Reich by going into exile in the Soviet Union were far more dogmatic and less sympathetic to church concerns. Nevertheless, he recalled that "it was possible to speak openly, in the early period, with the Communist functionaries."[9]

By the beginning of the 1950s, however, ideological hard-liners in east and west were gaining control. In the GDR, the issue of the state's opposition to the church's youth work was as volatile as it had been during the Third Reich. Like the Nazi regime, the socialist state saw the ideological indoctrination of youth as a crucial instrument for building a new kind of society. As Scharf recalled later, the church's arguments with the socialist authorities over this issue paralleled the confrontations the Confessing Church had had with Nazi authorities over the church's youth work. And the tactics of the GDR leaders were often identical to those of the Nazis—penalizing youth who did not join a Communist youth organization, for example, and scheduling state-sponsored youth events at times when they inevitably conflicted with church programs.

The church's conflict with the East German state over the student and youth parish work occurred within the broader context of the Stalinist era and the intensifying cold war. But it also took place against the historical context of the institutional support that the German state, before 1933, had offered the church. In the Federal Republic, after 1945, the Protestant and Catholic *Volkskirchen* regained their right to teach confessional religion in the public schools. Such a right, in countries with a stricter separation of church and state (like the United States), was not viewed as an inherent right of the church. But East German Christians compared their situation not with that of other "free churches" but with that of Protestants in the Federal Republic. They viewed these restrictions as attacks on their rights as a church and believed that their church was under attack by the socialist government. In Kurt Scharf's words, the controversy over the church's youth work erupted because

> We were pushed out of the schools. Religion classes were no longer allowed to take place in GDR schools. We didn't want confessional schools. We wanted the general schools, the overall school organizations, to be open for the message of the Gospel. . . . From 1951 to the early summer of 1953, the fight for the youth parishes burned very strongly. Youth pastors, student pastors, and deacons were arrested in large numbers and treated very badly, during their imprisonment, by state and police officials.[10]

Scharf, Heinrich Grüber, and the East Berlin church superintendent, Friedrich-Wilhelm Krummacher, continued to negotiate with state authorities. Even during this difficult period, Scharf said, it was possible to talk with some people in the state bureaucracy:

> It was possible with Grotewohl, the minister president, and with Otto Nuschke, the head of the east CDU. Again and again, I was at the Ministry for State Security in

the Normanenstraße, to speak up for those imprisoned. In the period between 1950 and 1953, I could fight for the release of some of those imprisoned. . . .

The fight for the youth parishes was suddenly broken off, from the side of the state, on June 10, 1953. The bishops were summoned to the government, and Minister President Grotewohl gave a declaration about a "new course" of the state. It was similar to the Leninist era in the Soviet Union, in which a period of very hard repression of the church was suddenly replaced by a new course, a course of liberality and tolerance. This occurred on June 10, 1953, and helped bring about June 16–17, 1953. [Note: the date of the workers' uprising in the GDR]. On June 9, an amnesty had been proclaimed, through which all of our imprisoned church people became free. The youth parishes could work again; other political prisoners, too, came under the amnesty. When the release of prisoners didn't take place quickly enough, it came to demonstrations in many places in the GDR between June 10 and 17, in front of the prisons and local government offices.[11]

The events of June 1953 were the first in a pattern that would recur in the GDR for the duration of its existence as a separate socialist state — a pattern in which a specific church-state conflict coincided with public unrest on other points, its effects rippling throughout the entire society. In May 1953, the GDR government had ordered a 10 percent increase in factory productivity, but had refused to raise workers' wages. This demand, together with overall economic pressures and a sinking standard of living, led to strikes and protests throughout the country. Although the governing SED (Sozialistische Einheitspartei Deutschlands) party announced its "new course" on June 9, the productivity requirement remained in effect. On June 16–17, thousands of workers marched through Berlin and other cities. On June 17, Soviet tanks put down the uprising. Twenty-one people were killed, 187 injured, and some 1,200 jailed.

One East Berlin pastor recalled how the events of June 17 affected her parishioners:

Naturally, a group of our men from the parish were with those who marched and believed that now, somehow, the rudder could be turned around. . . . They simply weren't happy with the kind of government. . . . Then they wanted to form a strike government, at the big square, and the Russian panzers were already there. . . .

I was told that the Russian panzers drove ruthlessly into the crowd. You have to imagine, where thousands have gathered, and now, suddenly, the panzers come in from several sides — where should they have gone? There was a whole group killed then. . . .

For some, that brought things to the point that they emigrated to the west, because they became afraid. The border was still open; it wasn't hard at all. I know of one very active, respected church elder, who had carried the flag — a red flag! — in front of the strikers' group from his factory. Now he rode in the Underground to work, and someone with a party badge said, "I have very disagreeable memories of you from June 17." For this man, that meant that he immediately rode back along a different route to his house, took his wife and children, and crossed over. Because, of course, he had to reckon with imprisonment.[12]

GDR leaders viewed the June 17 uprising as an attempt to overthrow the government. As Kurt Scharf recalled, the concessions the church won for its youth parishes turned out to be of brief duration:

Now the sudden, apparently positive relations between church and state became more difficult again. With respect to the youth parishes, we found that they never entirely recovered from the phase between 1951 and 1953. Participation in the life of the youth parishes was reduced about 40 percent by the state's persecution. . . .

During that period, I was at an entire series of universities, in Rostock, Greifwald, Leipzig, and, of course, repeatedly at Humboldt University [in East Berlin]. I publicly debated in the main auditoriums with social scientists, before huge numbers of students. I sensed that even those students who belonged neither to the church nor to the student parish had come for the special reason of supporting the demands of the church for the freedom of the spirit. Applause always came on behalf of the church speaker, not on behalf of the social scientists who recited their regimented socialist philosophy and interpretation.[13]

The EKD and East-West Issues

In the GDR, the 1950s were emotionally charged for those in and out of the churches. But the growing tension between the church and state in the east affected Protestants in the west as well, since the EKD was the one German institution that transcended the border between the two Germanys.

The EKD had been formally established in 1948 (at a meeting in the GDR town of Eisenach, the birthplace of Martin Luther) as a federation of 27 regional churches. Initially, the EKD included churches in the east. Only in 1969 did the eight regional churches in the GDR formally withdraw from the EKD — and even then the special relationship that existed between the churches in the GDR and the Federal Republic continued. This relationship was borne not only by the institutional and material support the wealthier western churches were able to give churches in the east but by the conviction of some people that the churches in the Federal Republic could learn from the experiences of the Christians who lived under socialism in the Democratic Republic.

The Protestant experience under Nazism had increased awareness of how easily the church could become compromised. Now the Protestant church in the Federal Republic enjoyed a comfortable, unharassed place in society. As the EKD began to benefit from the general postwar prosperity there, some veterans of the *Kirchenkampf* worried that the church would quickly forget the risks of social and political conformity. "The favorable treatment of the church can be a specific form of persecution," warned Rhineland's culture minister Paul Mikat in 1963,[14] a sentiment echoed by East German bishop Schönherr in 1977, when he preached in a West German church for the first time and spoke of what GDR Christians had learned under socialism: "A church never does as well as in the times when it has things tough."[15] One lesson of the *Kirchenkampf* was that a politically persecuted church sometimes arrived at a more vibrant Christianity than the politically comfortable one.

But the special relationship meant more than close ties between churches in east and west. It also meant that the EKD was deeply affected by the course of the cold war. One of those involved in building contacts between East and West German Christians was Martin Fischer:

In July 1945, we decided to reopen the *Kirchliche Hochschule* [in Berlin]. Dibelius didn't want to; he wanted a state theological faculty. We could have made a new start in the GDR, but the costs were too high. Our work in Zehlendorf [in West Berlin] went very quickly, and in this destroyed city, we had a lot to do. It was very difficult; people can't imagine it anymore. In Zehlendorf, a widow invited us to hold our first lecture in her home. At this first meeting, we had more students there than chairs. . . .

Out of 400 students, 250 came from the GDR. They had no western money; we had to provide everything for them. In addition, we wanted to keep our contacts with the church in the GDR in good shape. After 1945, the student parishes in the GDR did everything over here — ordinations, and so on. . . . Heinemann strongly supported the idea of holding the church together, and we invested a lot of energy in this direction.[16]

The GDR border was still permeable; the Wall, the armed guards, and barbed wire had not yet sealed off the border between east and west. In the 1950s, East Germans traveled to visit friends and relatives — in the idiom of the time, *schwarz über die grüne Grenze* (illegally crossing the "green border"). Inevitably, as conditions in the GDR became more repressive and the Federal Republic grew wealthier, people came over and stayed. From 1949 to 1961, between 100,000 and 200,000 crossed over each year; in 1953 — the peak year — 331,000 left the GDR.[17]

The official position of the EKD was that people should stay and work for a better society where they were. This conviction was reached gradually and painfully, as Albrecht Schönherr recalled, for he himself was strongly opposed to socialism at the beginning. After the war, he had been a parish minister, then a church superintendent, in the Brandenburg church. At the time, as he said,

I was very much in opposition. I was always a greatly feared conversation partner when I was superintendent in Brandenburg. In those days, it was still the case that the people were visited before the elections, and [the candidates] spoke with them. No one came to me anymore, because they were afraid to.

At a certain point in my life, it must have been 1957, I simply asked myself whether I really believed in God, in a God who was still God in the GDR. It really had to do with the first commandment. At that time, I went to the government representative in Potsdam, and said, "I want to be a Christian here. I stand here with both feet, but I want to be a *Christian* here, and nothing else." For me, that was the point, the period, in which I tried to consider theologically what it meant to be a Christian in the GDR.[18]

Schönherr's transformation did not lead him to an uncritical affirmation of socialism; those who chose to remain as Christians in the GDR continued to come into conflict with the state there. Nonetheless, Schönherr and others began to see their position as Christians in a socialist state in a new light. While acknowledging the restrictions placed upon them, they became aware of their unique freedom as Christians. For many, this understanding of freedom was based upon their experiences as Confessing Christians under Nazism. Looking west, East German Christians were often more aware of the seductive power of wealth and conformity than were their colleagues in the west. As Friedemann M., a Confessing Church pastor who subsequently became a national councilman in the East German church, reflected,

I have learned that the important thing for the church is not to have leaders and parish buildings, but to have Christians in the individual parishes who take the Gospel and the sacraments seriously — and to do this without buildings, without government support, without money. This was a lesson for us. We had always had the church as an institution. The pastor was a civil servant, and when it rained, the pastor would go to the mayor and ask for money to fix the roof. The pastor got his money and had a lifelong job; he could lose it only for reasons of immorality. Otherwise, he was completely insured, and if his wife were widowed at age 24, she had money for the rest of her life.

In the Confessing Church, we learned to give all this up — and to learn this in only 12 years is a great gift. It has done much for church life today in the GDR.[19]

Ideological pressures on the Protestant church continued. As Kurt Scharf said, the church was a "foreign body" within the socialist system, and conflicts were inevitable. For this reason, those who chose to remain as "Christians in socialism" were very critical of those who left. Socially, of course, the exodus of skilled labor, professionals, and medical workers created serious hardships. Luise M. recalls how discouraged her husband became over the mass emigrations in the 1950s:

Overnight, I would say, an entire family was gone from our village. Among them, two church elders — people who had opened their mouths sometimes. My husband had spoken about everything in the parish with one of them. They fled, very secretly. In those days, you could come to West Berlin with no problem. You were controlled, but if you didn't have anything suspicious on you, then you were let through. Over a period, they had taken their most valuable things over, so that one day, they weren't there anymore.

I'm critical here, too. With the farmers, it hit my husband very hard. In order not to endanger us, they didn't say anything about it. We should have noticed; my husband had been there a few days previously, and they had shown him an album with pictures of the entire farm. Everything had been photographed. My husband found it beautiful, but didn't think that they wanted to leave.

One should have spoken with these farmers. One should have told them, I think, that particularly people like them had a very great task here. . . . Regarding the doctors and the pastors — there are pastors who left, who we didn't think had a valid reason. Some were worked up by their wives; some said politically unwise things and unguarded things, which wasn't their job. As a pastor, it's not one's duty to incite against the GDR.

There are other people of whom I would say, I wouldn't want to cast stones at them . . . I mean, I left, too, but somehow I see that as a different situation. We left only when there really was no task left for my husband there [after he retired]. A good friend said to me then: "We're sad that you're leaving, but we understand it. When you make this decision now, you may never ask yourself: Should I have done differently?"

For that reason, when someone asks me now, "Are you sorry about it?" then I say, "I just don't think about it anymore."[20]

As Luise M.'s words illustrate, many Christians who chose to remain in the GDR were not necessarily choosing to do battle with socialism ("it's not one's duty to incite against the GDR") but deciding to carry out a Christian witness there that was politically cautious, and in some cases supportive of the GDR government. The official church, in East and West Germany, worked actively to discourage emigration. As Martin Fischer recalled,

> We couldn't wish that the population would flee. We said, at the very least the doctors shouldn't leave their patients. Then the people here said that we were Communists. . . . The general mood was: One goes west, it's better there. We said, "No," for reasons of integrity. One doesn't desert his people when they are in need. So, in the east, we attempted to establish this consciousness, and to strengthen people in that. . . .
>
> One pastor wrote me a letter. He had five children and wanted to know whether he should come to the west. I said, "If you ask me, I would say 'no.' Your church must remain, even if you go. And the church has received enough wrath."
>
> He stayed there. Later, he wrote me again and thanked me. He said that he had come into a personal crisis, out of which my letter had helped him. He stood fairly alone in the parish; many of his parish members had fled. But then he had come into contact with a group of young people. They had tried to move to the west, and, because of that, their families and friends had turned against them. The youths told him that if the church couldn't be their home, they were completely lost. They were prepared, too, to be baptized. So he took them in, and that was the beginning of a new parish. This pastor was trustworthy for those who had problems with the government.[21]

Kurt Scharf continued to live and work in East Berlin until he was expelled in 1961. In 1982, Scharf explained the EKD's policy to discourage people from leaving the GDR:

> We wanted to be a "church in socialism." We wanted to offer the witness of the Gospel in the GDR right then and there. That's why we never spoke up for fleeing from the GDR. On the contrary, we were opposed on principle to fleeing the GDR. We wanted precisely the Christians to remain in the GDR, so that they could work there as Christians, in an explicit affirmation of the social duties a church has in every kind of state.
>
> Before the construction of the Berlin Wall there were pastors, too, who came west from the GDR. The entire church administration, not just the West Berlin department and our Berlin-Brandenburg church, did not take those concerned on as pastors, but reproached them: "You have become fugitives. You have left your office and your parishes in the lurch." We did not install them as pastors. They had to endure a long period of probation in the west, either in a purely administrative position or in nonchurch jobs. Mostly, they were helpers in the deaconical services before they were permitted to assume a pastorate again. They could do this only when the GDR church leadership, in that region from which the pastor concerned had left, didn't put in a veto against it.[22]

Because of these factors, not many pastors fled. But the exodus from the GDR weakened the society there and, inevitably, led to tensions between the two Germanys. By 1957, 1.7 million citizens — 15 percent of the population of the GDR — had fled to the west.[23] In the early months of 1960, Kurt Scharf began negotiations with GDR state authorities to see if the 1961 *Kirchentag* — the week-long lay meeting of German Protestants, which drew hundreds of thousands of church people from all over Germany—could be held in both East and West Berlin. The GDR government tried to block this. As Scharf remembered:

> The state wanted to permit only a limited number of participants from the Federal Republic, and had isolated certain prominent church representatives and speakers, from the onset, as "undesired."
>
> The result was that we carried out the *Kirchentag* in both parts of Berlin, against the will of the state. It was in July, three weeks before the Wall went up. East Berlin was blocked off to those traveling in from the rest of the GDR. Nevertheless, thousands from the GDR, particularly from Lutheran Saxony, came to Berlin for the *Kirchentag*. When they had been turned away at three places, they tried at a fourth to get in to East Berlin, over the fields and through the forests. Once they were in East Berlin, they could participate without hindrance in the programs in West Berlin.
>
> It was an unheard-of demonstration of church freedom and church unity, this *Kirchentag* in 1961. But the state reacted to it with the construction of the Wall.[24]

Scharf believed that the Berlin Wall, built only days after the end of the *Kirchentag*, was directly related to the threat the GDR saw in the churches, although the number of defectors among *Kirchentag* participants had been small. But the events of the *Kirchentag* had dramatized the general dissatisfaction in the GDR. During the days immediately before and after the *Kirchentag*, 1,000 to 2,000 East Germans fled daily to the west.

The shock of the Berlin Wall was great. Martin Fischer recalled his feelings at the time:

> Of course, we hadn't held that to be possible. But I can understand the standpoint of the GDR. We didn't sit there and cry; we couldn't disappear and desert our friends. Suddenly politics was there again, in a thing that, in reality, could not be comprehended politically in any way.[25]

Politically, the Berlin Wall represented the GDR's desperate attempt to survive by halting the emigration of its skilled workers. For those who had lived through the Third Reich, the building of the Berlin Wall raised the specter of something else—a spiritual blow that, as Fischer said, was incomprehensible merely on a political level.

Now, Christians' decisions to remain in the GDR had new implications. Liselotte Lawerenz, a Confessing Church pastor who worked as a hospital chaplain in Potsdam, recalled August 13, 1961:

> It belongs to the most horrible days of my life. We had been to the Berlin *Kirchentag* with people from the GDR. We weren't supposed to go to the *Kirchentag*, but we sneaked around and got through somewhere. . . . It was a marvelously exciting atmosphere . . . and then during the night of August 12–13, it was a Saturday-Sunday, there were noticably many tanks on the road, and everything drove past our house. I remember that I woke up screaming. Usually I don't dream; when I sleep, I sleep well. It was just this agitation . . . and then they told us that morning. It was an insane shock for the people. Previously, they had always lived with the thought that those [in the west] would surely do something for us, they wouldn't leave us to the Russians. . . . But the wall through Berlin, through a living city, that was really the most ghastly thing I've experienced. Suddenly, most families were separated . . . the parents suddenly lived in East Berlin, the children were married and lived on the

other side, or vice versa. Of the old people who died of it, we just said, "They have the Wall sickness," simply because there was no more connection there. It was desolate and, in a way, ghastly.

But if the GDR wanted to endure, it had no other recourse.[26]

The "Church in Socialism" and Its Consequences

Despite the personal desperation created by the events of August 1961, the church's resolve to remain as a liberating force within socialist society strengthened. Inevitably, however, this led to certain political decisions by those who had chosen to remain and by the West Germans who supported them. The Wall itself, for the 28 years of its existence, became a political reality whose international implications often obscured the tragedies of the families it divided. Given the postwar existence of two Germanys, each bound to an opposing alliance, many Germans believed that the GDR had no choice but to exist — that the Wall was a necessary evil, ultimately created by tensions between the United States and the Soviet Union.

Within this context, the decision to work as "Christians in socialism" was not a decision to undermine that system but to search for possibilities within it. In the long run, this probably enabled the Protestant church to exist the way it did in the GDR, as a "free space" for Christians and others whose beliefs brought them into conflict with authorities there. But, of course, this was what many church moderates had attempted to do during the Third Reich — to maintain the integrity of the institutional church's existence and hinder state interference in church affairs. In the GDR, the culmination of the church's efforts in this respect was the church-state agreement signed in 1978 by Albrecht Schönherr and Erich Honecker. This agreement, in which the church recognized the legitimacy of the socialist government and the GDR government, in turn, recognized the German Protestant church as a legitimate institution, was without precedent. [Note: This agreement did not affect the small "free churches" that existed in the GDR, like the Baptist church. These churches were not recognized by the government and continued to suffer harassment by the state.]

The broader ramifications of the course chosen by the "church in socialism" are still not completely known, even after the collapse of the GDR. After the East German secret police (Stasi) files were opened to the public in January 1992, the full extent of the church's contacts, not just with government but with the Stasi itself, became clear. Some church leaders were attacked as informers; and the East German church leadership in general was accused of having conformed more to government demands than to the needs of individual Christians and dissidents.

It is difficult to evaluate the Stasi records on its meetings with church members and pastors objectively. Church leaders summoned to the Stasi had no choice but to meet with them, and the church's interpretation of such meetings was often different from what can be found in Stasi files. The Stasi naturally interpreted events and meetings to serve the state's purposes, and much of the information it received from informers was based on innuendo, not fact.

Nevertheless, the achievements of the "church in socialism" put it in a problematic position: By trying to establish a "middle ground" between the socialist state and individual East Germans, it ran the constant risk of either compromising too much or too little — of either betraying or endangering the people it hoped to help.

The position that it attained within socialist society and the commitment of some (if not all) of its pastors and laity to work as "Christians in socialism" naturally reflected their hopes that the socialist system was both worthy and capable of reform. To some extent, the church's course of creating a "free space" for dissidents in GDR society, while working within the system there for reform, evolved from the experience of its leaders in the Confessing Church. This course, and its roots in the Confessing Church's history (particularly the writings of Dietrich Bonhoeffer), influenced theologians throughout the world, particularly those in the Third World who developed the "theology of liberation," which examined the church's role as a political force in society. The history of the German Protestant church's failure to resist Nazism was interpreted by liberation theologians as an example of how churches could be compromised in a dictatorship by their ties to the ruling classes. Bonhoeffer and the Confessing Church were seen as examples of Christians who had examined these ties critically and broken them. Now, the church in the GDR seemed to offer an example of a "third way," one in which the traditional Christian distrust of socialism had apparently been overcome.

In essence, this "third way," with its hopes for a reformable socialism, was based upon the conviction that the economic controls of socialism did not have to include social and cultural repression, including repression of the churches. In the GDR, Christians were relinquishing their old fears that socialism was an inherently repressive system; and the GDR government's reciprocation, represented by the 1978 agreement, seemed a sign that this was indeed the case.

The hope with which many Christians greeted these developments obscured the fact that the risks for the GDR church remained very similar to those that the Confessing Church had faced: of knowing which concessions to government authorities compromised the beliefs or the freedom of the church. The practical consequences of the 1978 agreement, as Kurt Scharf saw them, were that

> the state no longer sees the church, when it is active and alive and its work very effective, as a direct disturbance. Just as before, there are differences in *Weltanschauung* that have an effect. There are continuing intrusions [by the state]; for Christian parents, or even for professors at the universities who very consciously stand by the church, there are daily bureaucratic, career, or ideological kinds of difficulties. But, on principle, the work of the church is respected by the state today and is recognized as a stabilizing factor in society. Since 1978, a change really has taken place.[27]

Asked about how the church-state agreement had affected the lives of Christians in the GDR, Albrecht Schönherr replied,

> In many respects, of course, it's totally different than in the FRG. If I've just spoken about facilitations and such things, then that refers primarily to the relations between the state and the church. The individual Christian has it harder, for naturally he is also wooed by the Marxist party, particularly when he is intelligent. Here, it's been

shown that those who profess their Christianity most openly and clearly have it the easiest. When one says, from the beginning, "I am a Christian, please take me as such," then that is accepted, too, and one doesn't try to alienate him from that or otherwise to get him. It becomes difficult only when he doesn't do that, but when he tries to talk his way around it somewhat. Then, of course, he remains under fire.

One difficulty is that the young academics who denote themselves as Christians and are active have scarcely a chance of achieving leading positions. Of course, that is connected to the planned economy, because in leading positions one likes to have the kind who are absolutely reliable, who do what the people above say. And one does credit Christians with too much individual initiative and, perhaps, too much rebelliousness if difficulties come. For that reason, there are few who have been able to bring themselves into decisive positions.[28]

The Protestant church in the GDR created an unusual place for itself in socialist society: one in which it was recognized officially by the state and, at the same time, was used by dissidents within that system as an ideologically free space.

Was this arrangement — essentially, a recognition of mutual integrity by the church and state — consistent with the legacy of the Confessing Church? Asked in 1986 about the Confessing Church's legacy in the GDR, former Bonhoeffer student Albrecht Schönherr replied that, for him, it concerned "truth and freedom":

> Truth means that the church is not simply the church because it exists, but because it has to stand for the truth of the message of Jesus Christ. The church is the church of Jesus Christ only as long at it is the church of *Jesus Christ*. That is important to emphasize, again and again, because every church, like any other institution, wants to preserve itself, and thinks it does that through renewing itself, through the fact that more people come in — and that, because of that, it has a certain right to exist. But I think that what Barmen and the Confessing Church made clear is how the church is dependent upon whether it meets this [other] commitment. Otherwise, it doesn't deserve to be the church, or, one could say, otherwise it is dead. . . .
>
> I think that that does play a role here; particularly as a weak institution in terms of power, the church must ask itself repeatedly: Why do we exist, basically? There are many things of which we could be relieved. That is, the social things that we do in the church — naturally, the state could take those over. Perhaps not as well, but it could. Again and again, what concerns us is this message [of Christ] and nothing else.
>
> The second thing is the word "Freedom." It appears to me that here the *Kirchenkampf* truly had a visible consequence for us. When we founded the Federation of Evangelical Churches [Note: in 1969, when the GDR churches broke away from the EKD] those in the west told us: "It won't last long, with the developing strength of socialism, before you become a socialist church." This fear accompanied us permanently, so that we always had it before our eyes. And, because of that, we were especially conscious not to yield one bit of the freedom that we believed we needed. Naturally, not a freedom of general kind but the freedom of proclamation. Whenever it concerned proclamation, we insisted on principle. . . .
>
> We opposed state influence, in whatever form, on church synods, laws, on the filling of offices. . . . Of course, the state tried that occasionally, and, indeed, from behind the scenes. . . . But except for one single case, it never worked. When the synods noticed that the state was manipulating somewhere, then they did exactly the opposite.[29]

The Protestant church in the GDR maintained this delicate balancing act throughout the separate life of the GDR as a state. Travel restrictions for pastors, high church officials, and synodal members were certainly not as strict as for ordinary citizens. The GDR government distrusted the growth of the peace movement and the ecological movement in the GDR during the 1980s and the ties of these groups to their counterparts in the west and to GDR churches. The result was the arrest and deportation of some prominent GDR critics in the fall and winter of 1988–1989 and in the increased harassment of some individual churches that had served as meeting places for these groups.

Initially, the Protestant church in the GDR preserved credibility in both its official and unofficial functions to an impressive degree. After November 1989, the church served as mediator and consultant for the different political factions, and several pastors eventually served in the new GDR government after the March 1990 elections. Often the only location where all parties could agree to hold the town meetings that convened throughout the country was the local churches.

In the months after the fall of the Berlin Wall, the opposition that had brought down the socialist government broke up into different political factions. Those divisions, which had been there all along, were between those who had hoped to reform socialism from within — and who, for the most part, opposed the unification of East and West Germany — and those who had sought socialism's complete downfall — and who now put their economic and political hopes in the GDR's rapid absorption by the west.

Present within the Protestant church as well, these divisions moved some Christians to re-examine the history of their church and its place within socialist society. The church's re-examination of its role intensified after the Stasi files were made public. Within the churches, many maintained that the church had no other option than to work out some arrangement with the state. But the question remained: Was the arrangement it reached the right one? What purpose had the "church in socialism" served?

After November 1989, many East German Christians asked this question. In the final days of the GDR, thousands of citizens had ignored the church's pleas to stay in order to change the GDR from within and had fled to the west. Thousands of others had gathered in the churches before taking their protests against the government into the streets. Most of these people, whatever their persuasion, had had little previous contact with the church. Yet, in the final days before the Wall fell, they joined in church demonstrations and filled the churches for special prayer services. As one GDR pastor later wrote,

> Why did many come into the churches? They weren't invited, basically. And the churches, basically, weren't prepared for them. Those who came simply took the general ideology of the "openness" of the church literally . . . in a society that otherwise offered no free space, the groups used this openness. . . . That the church offered this free space, in which grass-roots democracy could be practiced, which promoted a consciousness and articulation of problems, prepared activities and offered protection — all that certainly speaks for the church, and for its spiritual power as well (as does the nonviolence of the revolution!); but it simply can't be attributed uncritically to its spiritual power.[30]

This pastor concluded, rather cynically, that the church's independence in the GDR had been purchased, in effect, by the material support given it by West German churches, and that this

> prevented the GDR churches and many of their members from standing *as a church* with both feet in their social environment. It remained a "foreign body" in "real existing socialism."[31]

For this pastor, the East German church wasn't socialist enough; he was among those who had hoped to reform socialism and retain a political (and national) identity separate from the Federal Republic. As the March 1990 elections showed, it was a minority opinion. Yet, it is interesting how this pastor's criticism of his church echoed that of the Confessing Church radicals' criticism 40 years before of the EKD. In the GDR, he charged, the church's "inclination toward restoration is once again greater than that toward revolution or, at the very least, toward social evolution."[32]

The Protestant church in the GDR faced a task very similar to that it had faced in Nazi Germany — of balancing institutional survival against the more radical demands of religious and moral conviction. The questions that arose from this situation were just as important for the Protestant church in the Federal Republic. In fact, despite the radically different postwar histories of the two Germanys, the churches in east and west were as torn by the question of political witness and the meaning of the Christian faith as they had been at the end of the Third Reich. The question was not which political system was more inherently "Christian," or even which system provided a more conducive environment for the practice of the Christian faith. The issue was the same one that had confronted the Confessing Church: What should the church be? For what should it stand?

13

Political Issues and the West German Church

AFTER 1945, IT WAS UNDERSTANDABLE that many Confessing Christians, confronted by the question, "What should the church be?" responded by demanding new moral standards of the German political realm. The constitution of the Federal Republic, which guaranteed basic civil liberties that Germans in 1933 had not even seen as necessary, was an important step in repudiating Nazism. Many postwar regulations, such as those permitting members of the West German military and police forces to refuse orders they believed were immoral, or those stringently controlling the sterilization of the mentally ill and disabled, were the direct result of the Germans' experience under Nazism. So was the commitment of many Germans to building a relationship with Israel and paying reparations to the Jews who had suffered in the concentration camps.

In light of its experience under Nazism, it is likely that the postwar German Protestant church would have become more politically active even if the country had remained united. But the EKD's experience in uniting Christians in East and West Germany impelled both individual Christians and their institutional church to examine their religious attitudes toward their political reality. Their political judgments, in turn, influenced their view as to what the church should be.

For those who believed that the church should speak prophetically on the moral implications of political questions, this meant moving into the turbulent arena of German political debate — not merely commenting on domestic German affairs but on the larger questions of the cold war. The United States and the Soviet Union loomed behind all internal dealings between the two German states; and some Germans held the superpowers responsible not just for the postwar division of Germany but for all tensions that emanated from this arrangement. These Germans saw themselves and their countries as victims, not protagonists, of the cold war. Critics of the GDR viewed the Wall and the Soviet soldiers, tanks, missiles, and other weaponry stationed there and maintained that the GDR government, whatever its claims of sovereignty, was merely Moscow's puppet regime. Critics of the Federal Republic pointed to the thousands of square miles of West German territory reserved for use by NATO, areas that were exempt from German military and government regulation. They stressed that these areas were dotted with mines and with chemical and nuclear weapons, so that, the critics maintained, the Federal Republic had no more genuine independence than the GDR.

The opportunity for public debate between these two opposing viewpoints was limited in the GDR. These issues were argued that much more vehemently in the Federal Republic. In the EKD, dissent was already simmering at the time of the Darmstadt Declaration in 1947, which stated that blind anti-Communism had impaired the church during the Nazi era and was threatening to do the same in the postwar period. Furious debate erupted in 1950 with Konrad Adenauer's request for additional Allied troops to be stationed on West German territory and with his determination to re-establish a German army. The controversy continued for the following 40 years over related topics: West German membership in NATO, the deployment of NATO nuclear warheads, the establishment of mandatory conscription in the German army, and regulations for conscientious objectors.

Confessing Christians' Perspectives on the Cold War

As the one institution that represented Germans on both sides of the border, the EKD was in an unusual position. Institutionally, it continued to unite Christians in East and West Germany. In the early 1950s, its leaders, from Dibelius to Niemöller, made their hopes for political unification clear as well. The EKD's goal of reconciliation of Christians in east and west was based upon Christian teachings and was reinforced by the widespread horror at the prospect of another war. The 1950 rearmament controversy came at a time when another European war seemed possible; in one pamphlet the Württemberg Society distributed in 1950, Confessing Christians based their postwar pacifism on their recent experience under Hitler and called upon Christians to:

> Reject every summons or permission for the rearmament of Germany. Resist all public or secret preparation for it. Renounce today all soldiers' privileges. Refuse service in the armies in every form.[1]

Martin Schröter recalled how his parishioners in a village in Pfalz saw the rearmament controversy:

> Those from our generation who had themselves been in the war, it was very important for them. We noticed suddenly that they had a great need to catch up on working through their own experiences in the war as soldiers. . . . Basically, if I'm judging correctly in retrospect, there was no real enthusiasm, no fundamental agreement that a real young man must also be a soldier. There wasn't that. There was more submission: "Yes, if that's the way it is, then one has to do it." It was particularly the wartime generation who were against rearmament and military service, but it didn't affect them directly anymore, and their own sons, they weren't that far yet.[2]

The exploration of the new possibilities for the Christian churches in socialist societies had not yet begun in Eastern Europe. But in the Federal Republic it now started within one group of former Confessing Christians. They based their hopes on two premises: first, that the church's anti-Communism in 1933 had contributed to its blindness concerning Hitler's true intentions, and second, that postwar Germany must become solidly pacifist if it were finally to break with the tradition of German militarism. Those within the churches who hoped for reunification and reconciliation with the east as a means of avoiding war began to search for a "third way," in the words of Karl Barth—a middle ground between east and west, one in which the dialogue between Christians, despite the altered European landscape, would promote understanding between those living under conflicting ideological systems.[3]

But most Protestant leaders, while wishing for reconciliation, disagreed strongly about the political and moral legitimacy of the two Germanys and the real intentions of their respective allies. There were those like Martin Niemöller, who believed that a united Germany under Soviet leadership was preferable to a divided Germany under two superpowers.[4] Others, like Hans Asmussen, viewed Communism and Nazism as "godless religions" of the same stripe and rejected any reunification concept that would give the Soviets more control over Germany's destiny.[5]

The two viewpoints were fundamentally irreconcilable, and they finalized the ideological—although not the institutional—split between the church factions that had stood so uneasily united throughout the *Kirchenkampf.* Herbert Mochalski, a radical member of the Confessing Church's postwar Council of Brethren and a drafter of the 1947 Darmstadt Statement, represented one point of view:

> We always rebelled against the division of Germany and, indeed, not for nationalistic reasons but because we say that both parts, as we have them today, are the occupied colonial lands of the respective victors. One must say that very clearly. We aren't a sovereign state in the Federal Republic, but a colony of the Americans. Don't be shocked. Just as the others are a colony within the entire Soviet empire. . . . We are the spear's end of the western superpowers against the East.[6]

At the other end of the spectrum stood Elisabeth Schwarzhaupt, the moderate who had worked as a lawyer in the official church consistory during the Third Reich and who joined the Adenauer government in the 1950s. Convinced that postwar democracy in the Federal Republic was made possible by the Allied powers and subsequently by NATO, she viewed the Soviet presence in eastern Europe not as a stabilizing factor but as a potentially expansionist one:

> I was convinced that the western orientation of the western occupied zones was the only possible and correct policy. There were too many major dangers hidden in the concept of holding the four occupied zones [the three western zones combined with the eastern one] together. The Russians, with their very penetrating policies, probably would have achieved superiority.[7]

Arguments about the moral questions arising from the cold war were complicated further by the Germans' wish for stable relations between the two German states. Whatever their own judgments about the two systems of government, Germans personally affected by the east-west border longed for periods of détente in which contacts with relatives could be increased. Accordingly, West German politicians in both major parties were committed to improving the relations with the east, even when this objective occasionally conflicted with wider European or NATO interests. To non-Germans, this aim made German behavior appear enigmatic and at times unpredictable. Among Germans—particularly in times of increased East-West tension—

anxiety about and even distrust of the underlying intentions of the United States and the Soviet Union spread.

The recollections of Luise M., the pastor's wife who lived in the GDR, illustrate how the course of East-West relations affected the lives of individual Germans:

> In the first years after the war, I came over here 7 times, "black across the green border," as they said. That was the adventure of my life. . . . Then, later, we received passes a few times to travel over here with the whole family. . . . With the construction of the Wall in 1961, it was all over. My parents [in the west] became ill and didn't come over later, for they had the feeling, "When we come to you, it's only harder for you to visit us. When we're old and no longer able to travel, perhaps it'll be easier for you to get permission." [Note: Various regulations enabled West Germans to visit relatives in the east; regulations permitting East Germans to visit West Germany were more stringent and evolved more slowly.]
>
> From then on, I always tried to come over for every "round" birthday of my parents and for their silver anniversary. I wasn't allowed to come for any occasion.[8]

After her husband retired in 1968, the couple applied for permission to move to the Federal Republic. By the time permission was granted in 1975, her husband had died and Luise M. left the country alone. Her two daughters remained with their families in the east; her son had emigrated to the west in 1974. When interviewed in 1982, she requested anonymity, even regarding the name of the village where her husband had been the parish minister: She worried about possible repercussions for her daughters and their families in the GDR.

For Luise M., then, the easing of political tensions, as well as the working relationship the church carved out with the GDR state, were crucial:

> In 1970, my father had a stroke and was paralyzed on one side, and my mother sat here alone. Then I tried very hard, because I knew that my father was waiting, always calling for me, and I wasn't allowed to come. One rejection after another came from Berlin. They said, "When the FRG recognizes the GDR, or when it meets this or that demand."
>
> Then, in 1972, came the *Verkehrsvertrag*. [Note: the Travel Treaty, which greatly eased the restrictions on East German travel in the west]. . . . The treaty was personally so important for me, because I was one of the very first who could travel. . . . And when the first regulations were there, I was one of the first to make use of them. I was here for 14 days and saw my father alive, and that was very, very lovely. A half year later, he died; I was able to come to the funeral, and I could stay with my mother for 14 days, to help her get going again.
>
> From that standpoint, of our personal experience, we said at the time: How good that they continue and try to make small things easier. Things went better for me then, too. I had become physically ill from this feeling of being absolutely cut off. I must say that because of this, I have been shaped in my entire attitude toward these things, and perhaps can't see it entirely objectively.
>
> Now I live here. I was able to stand by my elderly mother in her last years. But my daughters are not allowed to come to me. They may come only when I become terminally ill, or perhaps when my son marries. But then only my daughters themselves — not the others [their families]. Do you understand that I see the matter completely differently, then?[9]

The *Kirchenkamp's* Legacy on East-West Issues

Inevitably, the way the Wall personally affected Germans influenced their political judgments. But for Confessing Christians, there was another factor. Their experience under Nazism moved them to seek, and to see as necessary, in east and west, a morally defensible role for their church and for themselves as individual Christians. Their years under Hitler had established a moral criterion for their postwar political judgments and actions: Did they stand for that which had compromised itself under Nazism or for that which had resisted Nazism?

Within this context, a number of questions linked the Nazi past and the postwar present. How did Germans see the issue of guilt? Did they believe that the postwar sufferings of ethinic Germans in eastern Europe had somehow "atoned" for what Germany had done to the Jews? How did they view German nationalism? as a fundamental cause of Nazism or as an innocent national loyalty that Hitler had misused? How did they view the postwar division of Germany? as an understandable response to what Nazi Germany had done to the rest of Europe or as the unfair destruction of their Fatherland by other nations, who once again had made Germans the victims of history? Who had truly resisted the Nazis? the Communists, rounded up and driven out in 1933, or the July 20 conspirators, most of whom had hoped to save Germany not only from Nazism but from Communism as well? Did postwar Germans have a moral obligation to repudiate all forms of militarism and nationalism, or had Hitler's downfall robbed these of any inherent threat?

All political judgments are value judgments, but as these questions illustrate, the postwar political values of Confessing Christians were founded on their evaluation of their own moral behavior under Nazism, and the conclusions the different factions in the church reached were politically at odds with each other. The various groups differed profoundly on which postwar government and policies best embodied the lessons of the *Kirchenkampf* and offered the clearest repudiation of the Nazi past and on where the church was freer to develop as a "confessing" church.

These differences deeply affected the nature of political debate in the Federal Republic, because they brought the specter of the Nazi past into the discussion of the solution of problems in the political present. For individuals who had taken part in the church's opposition to Nazism, the postwar political scene in the Federal Republic became a moral battleground on which two practical questions had to be settled: the proper church-state relationship in the west and the role of the churches in relations between East and West Germany.

On the one side were the more radical members of the Confessing Church, who continued the "Dahlemite" tradition. Soon after the establishment of the Federal Republic, these people explicitly linked their experience under Nazism to their growing political opposition to the postwar course charted by Konrad Adenauer. Armed with the 1947 Darmstadt Declaration, these Confessing Christians rejected the anti-Communism of the 1950s and called upon their fellow Germans to atone for the enormity of the suffering of the Russians under the Nazis. The postwar task facing Germany, they announced, was reconciliation with the peoples of Eastern Europe, not an anti-Communist crusade that threatened to unleash a new European war.

This group was an outspoken minority within the EKD whose influence extended beyond its numbers. Throughout the postwar decades, these Christians helped to create a broad forum within the EKD for the airing of political controversies. The authority of these Confessing Christians came from their record during the Third Reich of having more consistently opposed the Nazis than anyone else in the EKD. Martin Niemöller, Hermann Diem, Kurt Scharf, Helmut Gollwitzer, and Ernst Wilm were among those who gravitated toward postwar pacifism. Most, although not all (Hermann Diem, for example), came out of the Church of the Old Prussian Union, not the intact churches. Their church ties certainly influenced their postwar position within the church and within larger German society. "A confessing church is always in the opposition, in every party, in every system, to every government," Hans Iwand had said.[10] Confessing Church radicals sought their place in the opposition—not only within the EKD (through the continuation of the Council of Brethren, for example) but within the political sphere as well.

In many cases, their presence as "the opposition" influenced the very nature of their political activities. As outsiders, these Christians could and did avoid compromise. There had been so many compromises made during the Third Reich that many believed that compromise itself reflected moral uncertainty, if not failure. Now, on issues like nuclear disarmament, the group felt compelled to speak out with the clarity it had lacked in the early years of Nazism. The unequivocal political witness of Christians had become a moral imperative. As Eberhard Bethge frankly acknowledged in 1985,

> Today, all the left-leaning circles, among which I count myself, do indeed have a great inclination toward the world—to be frank, toward the political world—after we made such fools of ourselves being "apolitical."[11]

The most outspoken and acerbic personality within this group was Martin Niemöller. Like most church leaders, he had welcomed the beginning of the Third Reich; unlike them, he rapidly became one of its most articulate public foes. His seven years in concentration camps gave him a stature in many circles that Dibelius and others did not have, and his persistence in raising the issue of German guilt was discomforting for those who had made compromises with the Nazis. Niemöller was a formidable, uncomfortable presence in the Federal Republic, and Konrad Adenauer viewed him as a personal nemesis (an "enemy of the state," in Adenauer's words).[12]

By the mid-1950s, however, Niemöller was far to the left of both the political and ecclesiastical mainstream in the Federal Republic. Although their priority of reconciliation with Christians in East Germany made them critical of cold war hard-liners, most EKD leaders shared Adenauer's anti-Communism. More important, they were committed to the pluralistic *Volkskirche* that they had re-established. As a consequence, they had to avoid extreme positions that would antagonize any large group of church members. The division within the EKD paralleled that within the church opposition during the *Kirchenkampf*; it even involved the same people. As at the Dahlem Synod in 1934, one side wanted to preserve church unity while the other side was committed to establishing a clear position as a church.[13]

After 1945, Christians who sought to live "in opposition" helped create a broad base, unbound to any political party. They came together at the *Kirchentag* gatherings or in grass-roots political groups, leading protest marches and speaking at political demonstrations. People like Niemöller became freelance political prophets, listened to on the strength of their record of opposing Nazism. Because of their position as outsiders, they were often able to address controversy with a candor that was not possible within the political mainstream. They were committed, as well, to reminding Germans of the Nazi past. These Christians, in their open disdain for the nationalistic throne and altar tradition within German Protestantism, formed a new basis for Christian-based political activism against the throne — that is, against political authority.

The insistence of this group that this position represented a moral repudiation of the Nazi past embittered people who had been part of the church's opposition to Nazism and who continued to see the tradition of the German Protestant church as intact and German national feelings as legitimate. These leaders — among them Hans Asmussen, Lilje, Dibelius, and Wurm — now felt that their own role in the *Kirchenkampf* was being questioned and, indeed, on political grounds. All that seemed to matter now was the political failure of the church during the Third Reich, although the churches' fight against Nazism, as Rudolf von Thadden put it, had been to fight evil, not to consider alternative forms of government.[14]

The course of moderation chosen by so many church leaders during the Nazi era came under attack. Not only was Niemöller's insistence on admitting the church's failure under Hitler a reminder of the failures of the Protestant mainstream, it also sought to question the moral basis of the postwar political convictions of conservative Christians. "Why is not the Niemöller who is anti-Adenauer confronted by a Niemöller who is pro-Adenauer?" Karl Barth asked pointedly.[15] Conservative church leaders based their reply upon what they saw as the inherent legitimacy of Protestant support for states that upheld Christian values. Patriotism, they claimed, was a virtue, and they continued to distinguish between national and Nazi loyalties. In their view, loyalty to the Fatherland might have blinded them to the true nature of Nazism, but it also led them ultimately to stand up to the Nazis. Niemöller's attempt to draw parallels between some aspects of Nazi ideology (such as its anti-Communism) and postwar West German policies were rejected by church conservatives as half-cocked, dangerous attempts to put the moral imprimatur of the Confessing Church on positions that not all Protestants held.

Indeed, more radical Confessing Christians claimed that these conservatives (Meiser, Wurm, and Dibelius in the older generation and Helmut Thielicke and Eugen Gerstenmaier in the younger) had not been actual members of the real Confessing Church at all. To the extent that many of these church leaders came out of intact churches or had retained their positions in the official church, this claim was literally true. It was also true, in general, that the individuals who had pursued the *Kirchenkampf* as an internal church affair also sought to keep the church out of political controversy in the postwar period.

On the other hand, the role of these conservatives in the *Kirchenkampf*, however ambigous their actions had been at times, could not be denied. People like Wurm and Dibelius genuinely believed that they, too, drew upon a moral legacy of opposition to

Nazism. They believed, as Christians, that their duty was to minister in spiritual matters; as citizens, they saw their responsibility as supporting authority and speaking out on public issues in a manner consistent with Christian values. They welcomed the Federal Republic as a parliamentary democracy whose constitution guaranteed the rights of the church that the Nazis had sought to eradicate. And, with respect to the main international issue confronting postwar Germans, Dibelius and others viewed the fight against Communism as consistent with Christian values.

Marta S., who had joined the Nazi party and had married an illegal Confessing Church pastor, shared this view. She recalled the ways in which her experiences during the Third Reich influenced her postwar political attitudes:

> Ever since then, I am distrustful of all mass movements and demagogues. I am not in any party. Before every election, I think about it, then I vote, mostly CDU. Some acquaintances from earlier times ask me today how it is possible to be a Christian and not be in the SPD [Social Democrat party]. But you know, back then the Confessing Church fought the *Zeitgeist* of the 1930s. Today, the *Zeitgeist* in our city is red — in the church as well — and I ask myself, are they really concerned about the independence of the church . . . or are they going along now with this *Zeitgeist*? . . .
>
> In the GDR, too, many in the churches go along with the system there. I think that a dictatorship is a dictatorship. In retrospect, I am more tolerant of the "neutral" pastors than I was back then. Then, we had no ties to them. Later, I experienced some people from these neutral circles in the GDR, and saw how valiantly they stood against the government. I think back then we sometimes had the wrong fronts. It's not the Red Card [the Confessing Church's membership card] that determines who is a Christian! . . . Then, the doors of the church were often too narrow; today, they're often too wide. It is difficult to know where the limits of tolerance are.[16]

Although Stefanie von Mackensen, like Marta S., had been an early member of the Nazi party, she took a very different political direction after 1945. Asked in 1984 about her postwar political attitudes, von Mackensen replied,

> For years now, I've voted SPD [Social Democrat], since Brandt was chancellor. I'm strongly interested now in social questions, in questions concerning youth. I try to understand them. I would almost say that I'm a pacifist. But I don't belong to any party, and I am against nuclear weapons, 100 percent. I believe, too, that here we must acknowledge that this will be a confessional battle.[17]

The Question of "Christian" Politics

The differences between the political affinities of the two women represent a more fundamental difference that became important in the debate between Confessing Christians who moved toward the right after 1945 and those whose sympathies became more left-oriented: the differences in how Germans viewed the concept of "Christian" politics and the question of a "Christian" mission for postwar Germany. In Social Democrat and more left-leaning circles, Germans categorically rejected the notion of any kind of national mission as a continuation of German nationalism. Within the cold war context, the CDU and groups further to the right viewed a German role in the fight against Communism as a legitimate and necessary mission, and as a "Christian" one. When in 1960 Konrad Adenauer told Pope John XXIII that God had given the German nation a "special mission" to fight Communism, former Confessing Christians on the left loudly protested Adenauer's words. Speaking in the Bundestag, Gustav Heinemann even linked Adenauer's remarks to a concurrent outbreak of anti-Semitic activity in the Federal Republic.[18]

Both sides, of course, claimed to be practicing "Christian" politics, but the opposition of the left to Adenauer's course implicitly rejected the thesis that West German democracy embodied "Christian" values. For CDU people, however, it did; the very title of Adenauer's party, the Christian Democratic Union, expressed this idea of unity between Christian and democratic values. This name kept some veterans of the *Kirchenkampf* out of the party, while attracting others to it. Heinrich Albertz, when he entered politics, avoided the CDU:

> I was skeptical about what "Christian politics" meant. For that reason, I never joined the CDU, because of the "C." And I was skeptical about the power of the state, and so on, but I don't know if that is the influence of the Confessing Church, or more that of the Reformed tradition.[19]

Elisabeth Schwarzhaupt, initially a supporter of Martin Niemöller's religious views in the EKD, moved gradually toward the CDU:

> Politically, I wasn't on Niemöller's side. I still tried, at that time, to separate the two, and perhaps I underestimated the political motivation of Niemöller. In 1949, I refused to enter the Bundestag, or to join the CDU, either. At that time, I was generally against the "C" in the name of the CDU. I had reservations about the concept of a "Christian" party. That changed somewhat during the first four years of consolidation, under the impression of Adenauer's politics.[20]

Like Schwarzhaupt, some conservatives were cautious about designating one political direction as "Christian." Others, like Eugen Gerstenmaier, who had a doctorate in theology and had been active in the Württemberg church (not, however, in the Württemberg *Sozietät*), held this to be legitimate and saw a fundamental relation between the Federal Republic and Christian values. Gerstenmaier had been a Nazi supporter until 1939; during the war, he had become critical of the regime, finally joining the Kreisau circle. After the July 20 attempt on Hitler's life, he was sentenced to seven years' imprisonment (he was freed from the Gestapo prison by the Americans). Gerstenmaier's views on Christianity and German patriotism were representative of one sector within the CDU. Citing both Bismarck and the July 20 group as examples, he wrote,

> German national sentiments have been influenced, for many generations, by the Christian faith. . . . The Christian faith, up to today, has set critical norms and limits for German national consciousness. . . . National sentiments and national consciousness . . . must have the stuff and the power to move the members of a people beyond the rational, in the depths of their heart and being, to bring their spontaneity and love into movement, and very certainly to influence their conduct. One will tell me that— since Hitler!— this is, quite simply, unlimitedly dangerous. To that, I can reply only

that the vacuum that dried-up national feelings . . . and a wasted-away national consciousness leave in a people is even more dangerous.[21]

Like Dibelius, Gerstenmaier was convinced that a sense of national identity (in and outside the churches) had to fill the "vacuum" in Germany after 1945, and he believed that the legacy of the July 20 conspiracy lived on in the postwar patriotism of Adenauer's party.

Protestants who moved toward the left claimed that such sentiments led to the creation of a "mythology" about Protestant "resistance" to Nazism — and, moreover, that this mythology was encouraged by the Western Allies. As one observer wrote, "the ideology of the cold war during the 1950s dominated the field with slogans about the 'Christian west' against the 'godless east.'"[22] At the same time, he noted,

> a scenario was painted how the flag-bearers of Christendom, the churches, had resisted brown totalitarianism just as bravely as they now stood up to red totalitarianism. Certainly, there were also voices at the time that contradicted such glorification, but they didn't fit into the spiritual and political landscape of those years.[23]

There was some truth to the charge. During the 1950s, the picture of the entire church opposition to Nazism (that is, not just the Confessing Church, but the intact churches as well) that emerged emphasized the confrontations that church leaders had had with the Nazis and played down the numerous compromises that had been made. These portrayals ignored altogether uncomfortable truths like the anti-Semitism of many church leaders and members[24] and the churches' mixed record in fighting the euthanasia program.

During this period, those *Kirchenkampf* veterans who were most outspoken about their failures during the Nazi era did indeed gravitate toward the political left, like Martin Niemöller. For church leaders who agreed with Adenauer, the Evangelical Church's integration in, and support for, the Federal Republic represented the moral repudiation of the Third Reich. For those who vehemently opposed Adenauer's course, the only genuine repudiation of the Third Reich was to unmask the moral hypocrisy of the Federal Republic and those who supported it.

On all sides of the political spectrum, Germans justified (and often absolutized) their political positions on the basis of *Vergangenheitsbewältigung* — on how they approached the Nazi past. As Hebe Kohlbrugge (the Dutch woman in the Confessing Church who subsequently joined the resistance in Holland and was imprisoned in the Ravensbruck concentration camp) observed, this sometimes blinded people to new injustice:

> I don't know what happened to West Germany. I never understood and I shall never understand. . . . I can't tell you why the Confessing Church has so little influence on the German church. I have never understood it. I always thought that the Confessing Church had really meant a new way of church. And why, after the war, this was gone with the wind, I don't know. . . .
>
> I've never understood why a church falls down like that. Even Niemöller. I admire and love this Niemöller from the Confessing Church. . . . I think Niemöller, when he became church president in Hesse . . . [that] he was ridiculous in the way he dealt with people in the east. . . .

Just one example. Niemöller was in the [Prague] Christian Peace Conference; I was too. We were in Hungary. Then—I traveled through Hungary before, visited people. Then a young pastor came and said, "I want to talk to Niemöller. I want to tell him our difficulties. I want to see him." Well, I said, come. "No," he said, "we are not allowed to enter the hall where the conference is." . . . I knew that they were really not allowed to enter the hall. Which I found out very easily—you see people even if they have no uniform.

So I went to Niemöller. I said, "Listen, Lieber Bruder Niemöller, there are these two or three nice young pastors, would you mind making an arrangement one afternoon, maybe, when we have free time, to see them, walking along the bridge or something like that." "Nein! They can come to me!" I said, "Dear brother Niemöller, that won't work, they're not allowed here in the hall." "Nonsense! They can come here. There's a door." All this sort, and we knew each other, he was always very kind and nice when we met. I said, "No, honestly, they can't." "I won't go to them; they can come to me. I will receive them, but here."

Well, they couldn't. What then? Is that a pastor? Or is that a U-boat captain? . . . He just didn't believe it, he didn't want anything to be wrong in a socialist country. . . . The difficulty is, and I understand it, that many people can't bear to think that life all over the world is dreadful. So they want either America to be nice and good or Russia to be nice and good. And to live in a world where both sides are horrible is difficult. But we have to live in that world, and the church should help to show you that it's like that.[25]

The church's role in transcending the East-West conflict led many Christians to become moral advocates for one side or the other, and not just in Germany. The so-called legends of resistance covered the compromises made in the past, but the lessons drawn from the past often clouded the complexities of the present. Given the political polarization of the postwar era, this was not surprising, but it was not inevitable. The *Kirchenkampf* experience enabled some Confessing Christians to rise above ideology. In 1982, Heinrich Vogel, who had been arrested and imprisoned by the Gestapo for his activities in the Berlin Confessing Church seminary, mused about his political path during the Nazi years and afterward. Throughout the years, he said, his political course had been dictated by his opposition to any "synthesis" of Christian faith and political ideology. In 1957, he was one of the founders of the Prague Christian Peace Conference (one of whose meetings Niemöller and Kohlbrugge had attended), along with Czech theologian Josef Hromádka. Many Christians initially welcomed the Prague Conference as a chance to promote understanding between Christians in East and West. After the brutal end of the "Prague Spring" in 1968, the Conference was criticized for its failure to condemn the Soviet actions in Czechoslovakia. As Vogel recalled,

At first, it was wonderful. It was like a confessional spring at the first conference, the sign of which was a wonderful brotherhood, all the more wonderful since a whole sector of the participants experienced, for the first and only time, the possibility within the Communist realm to be outside their countries together with other brothers.

I left this Conference later in protest against this synthesis of socialism, the *Gleichschaltung* of Communist propaganda and the responsibility for peace. I left the Conference during the period after the so-called Czech crisis, where the Russians raped their satellite Czechoslovakia (in 1968). I don't tell you that here to show what a hero I am, that's not how it was, but only to tell you that there were situations after the war where the protest against the synthesis had to be practiced from the other side.[26]

Vogel had learned that, while the blows of history can be constricting, the course of history can be redemptive. As painful as the division of Germany and Europe was, it forced some people to seek human solutions that transcended the ideological blinders on both sides; and what enabled some Germans to do this was their experience under Hitler. Marion Yorck von Wartenburg, as presiding judge of the juvenile court in Berlin after the war, joined the CDU. But in 1986, she reflected,

I let myself be classified in today's party-political schema only with difficulty. By nature, I am conservative. But I can be just as anarchistic, and so unprejudiced in judgment that I am not at all confined within conservative corsets.

But I always say that the power of my life, even today, naturally comes from the time together with my husband, and from the period of the fight against Hitler and for — what did my husband write — for freedom, the worth of humanity, and justice. I am a very unhappy rebel for freedom, the worth of humanity, and justice. Naturally, that shapes a person.[27]

❧ 14 ❧

Christian Faith and Political Vision in Germany

THERE IS ONE ASPECT of religious belief that invariably sets it apart from the rest of society: The human soul, however bound it becomes by worldly powers, ultimately possesses the capacity to free itself. However religious institutions may affirm and participate in the political systems in which they find themselves, religion remains an inherently revolutionary force (this is what Iwand meant by a *confessing* church being "in opposition in every system"). This is why religious groups pose such a threat in totalitarian societies, which either persecute religious groups or try to coopt them ideologically (perhaps Hitler failed to transform the Protestant church into a Reich church because he tried to do both). It is why one measure of a free society is the extent to which it protects the freedom of different religious groups.

Under Nazi persecution, Confessing Christians had discovered the freedom within their faith; they had been confronted with the question of how religious faith should be actively lived and proclaimed. The question retained its immediacy in the postwar era. What did their Christian faith mean now? For some, the initial question was whether they could continue as Christians at all. Martin Fischer, who had worked illegally in the Berlin Confessing Church, began to work with university students in Berlin. In the first postwar years, he and his students wrestled with these challenges:

> For some, the question was, "How will God still allow the Germans to live, how is that possible?" For us, there was a more important question: Do we have a work that God can affirm, or should we quit completely? What does God's promise mean for us? For that reason, the [Stuttgart] Declaration of Guilt was very important for us younger people, much more so than for the older ones.[1]

In examining the relevance of their belief in the postwar German context, Confessing Christians were influenced by the degree to which their faith had been politicized by the experience of Nazism. Many now viewed their Christian identity, and Christian faith itself, as "political." For Brigitte Möckel, who had been a member of the Württemberg Society, the Confessing Church was the "compass" that she followed throughout her life:

> My direction hasn't changed. . . . Basically, I didn't study theology so much in pursuit of a career as toward an orientation in this political environment, in this strange

National Socialist world with which I couldn't come to terms. I just tried to find something that would bring clarity. Perhaps that is something, too, which was very important later: that in this fashion, we understood from the very beginning what not very many in the church knew then—that the political and the church go together in faith and theology, that they are very connected, and that you need the one for the other.[2]

In 1982, Martin Schröter, the Confessing pastor's son and soldier whose theological studies had been postponed by the war, elaborated on this understanding of faith. Asked what it meant to him to be a Christian, he responded:

In any case, it means praxis and not dogmatic theory. . . . The love of God is there for all, but that is only one sentence. When I examine the love of God as it was revealed through the life of Jesus, then it is a highly differentiated matter. The practice of God's love is the advocacy for the oppressed and a kind of resistance against the oppressor as well, for the sake of the oppressor. Love also bears the face of resistance.

This, I believe, is the false teaching of the *Volkskirche:* the love of God is for everyone, for the rich, the poor, just like a big bell jar over everything. That is a misunderstanding of the Gospel. Here we have made a doctrine of the love of God, and essentially have taken it out of the context of its being, out of the praxis of God's love, which took form on this earth for us . . . the question is: On which side do I stand? Advocacy means resistance.[3]

For people like Schröter, the recognition that the churches should have done far more to resist Nazism led them to define Christian faith as active engagement on behalf of the oppressed. Their political viewpoints became fused with a certain view of the church and the Christian faith. As Helmut Gollwitzer observed, in the Nazi era the "Dahlemites"

had learned that the church is not an auditorium where every religious interpretation has the same rights . . . In the Protestant church, too, there is a line between correct teaching and false teaching, and one has to draw that line.[4]

Ideally, the line was drawn by the Gospel itself. Hermann Diem, addressing an early postwar CDU meeting, declared, "The real political relevance of our presence as a church rests decisively in our proclamation (of the Gospel), which crosses through all political decisions."[5]

Christians from all points on the political spectrum probably could have agreed with Diem's words. Nevertheless, they arrived at very different political conclusions, and politically conservative Christians remained more explicit in their separation of faith and politics. During the Third Reich, this attitude led many to pursue a moderate course that avoided open confrontations with the Nazi state. Unlike more radical Christians, these church moderates did not see this tactic as the source of the church's failures during the Nazi era, and they continued to defend the distinction between faith and politics in the postwar period. The parallels between their attitudes during the Third Reich and after 1945 are illustrated by Erika Dalichow's recollections. She had worked in Burckhardthaus, a Protestant church college for women entering church service; many of the women in the Confessing Church participated in Burckhardthaus' programs during the 1930s. In Burckhardthaus, Dalichow recalled, there was a "conscious decision not to speak about politics":

That was forbidden for us. We had to package it; we had to cover up whatever we wanted to speak about, when it went in this direction, in such a way that it couldn't be attached. . . . But I must tell you that it was very difficult. If you wanted to remain in office, then you had to proclaim the Gospel skillfully. . . .

It was completely different than it is today. Back then, we were identically theologically prepared. And, if I may say so, we still knew that we had something to say. Today, when I think of theology, I greatly regret that it is open to pluralistic possibilities . . . and that the theological work has been pushed somewhere to the outskirts. . . . That goes along with the pluralistic situation of our theology today. You know what comes of it—numerous people leave the church, I would say, because we are too politically engaged and no longer have a clear foundation.[6]

The way in which Dalichow and others saw the active role of faith in society was illustrated in a sermon preached by Otto Dibelius in East Berlin in 1955 (entitled "The Power of Silence"). "We should love the masses, but look undissuaded beyond them toward God," Dibelius said, continuing:

We cannot say no to the masses. For these masses consist merely of individual human beings, and when our Lord Jesus Christ loved them . . . then we must love them too. . . . But: because we also know the demonic power of the masses, it is our task as Christians not to be carried away by the masses, but rather to move among them just as Jesus Christ rode through the masses on Palm Sunday: with his gaze upon God. For, dear friends, the masses can only be rescued from the curse hanging over them through an unbelievably immense love that meets them.[7]

Dibelius' words echoed the command of the apostle Paul to first-century Christians to be "in the world, but not of it": not to be carried along by movements, but to live with one's gaze upon higher truths. Radical Confessing Christians interpreted faith as the liberating force that had prevented their total submission to Nazi ideology. But for more conservative Christians, Paul's words implicitly upheld the separation of faith and politics, and separated the convictions of individuals from the institutional role of their church. Elisabeth Schwarzhaupt, who shared this view, elaborated upon it in 1986:

Today, in my opinion, the EKD is in a critical phase regarding its relationship to politics. I would wish that our pastors would concentrate more strongly on the Christianity of the people in their personal lives, in their own attitudes of faith, in order to help them understand the Gospel of Jesus as a help for a personal position of faith. I would wish that they not draw the political consequences, which naturally everyone has to draw somewhere, for their parishioners. Because the rational question simply belongs there; what does one bring about when one demands, for example, unilateral disarmament in the West? What consequences does that have? Does it really have a consequence of peace, or more of war?

The church can't solve this rational question: What do I achieve with my political behavior? At least, not so easily . . . one can't say, as the church, "*The* Christian position is this." Certainly, it's the church's position to want peace. Certainly, it's the church's position not to want a war of aggression. But whether we serve peace or war, today or tomorrow, with this or that political step—certain rational political considerations are preliminary to that. It's not a church affair, but a political one.[8]

For Schwarzhaupt, the lessons learned from the Third Reich did not necessarily offer a blueprint for postwar Christians:

> I believe that one can't so easily transfer experiences from the Confessing Church during the Third Reich to the political life of a people in which each can freely express his opinion.[9]

Because of the postwar prominence and political standing of many who had been in the church opposition to Nazism, their perspectives on the significance of Christian faith for political ethics influenced German public discussion of important political issues. Schwarzhaupt's cautious perspective was typical of the more conservative sector of those who had been involved in the *Kirchenkampf*. Like Schwarzhaupt, many of these church members remained engaged, politically and theologically, after 1945; and many of them continued to wrestle with the questions raised by the past. But they did not explicitly define their Christian identity in terms of their postwar political views, or posit both as forms of moral *Vergangenheitsbewältigung*.

But for the sector of the Confessing Church that wished to carry on the tradition of the "Dahlemites" and that viewed itself after 1945 as more radical Christians, a conscious commitment to *Vergangenheitsbewältigung* was a central part of their postwar politics and Christian identity. The thinking and activism of this group had a great influence upon the development of the postwar German left.

The Consequences of the *Kirchenkampf* for the Postwar German Left

In the postwar decades, many who had been involved in the church opposition to Nazism found themselves in the position of mediator between their contemporaries and the postwar generation of Germans. The problems inherent in this role arose most dramatically for the radical sector of the Confessing Church, which chose, as Heinrich Albertz said in 1968, "to stand between the fortresses . . . we take it upon ourselves to be shot at from both sides."[10]

Among those Confessing Christians who moved toward the political left, the lessons of the *Kirchenkampf* led them to base their political thinking strongly upon moral analogies — to search for parallels between postwar problems and the issues the church had confronted in the Third Reich. To some extent, veterans of the *Kirchenkampf* from all points of the political spectrum drew analogies between their experiences under Nazism and their postwar politics. But it was predominately on the left that people like Martin Niemöller and Heinrich Albertz began to discuss the failures of the Germans under Hitler as failures of collective political morality, and to believe that the political ethics of individual Germans should necessarily be founded upon a sense of accountability for the behavior of their nation.

There was a vast difference between this perspective and that (held by many conservatives) which tended to view the failures of the Germans under Hitler as lapses in individual morality or judgment, and to demand public accountability only from those who had held public positions. In the more radical sector of the church, the symbolic moral importance of political choices became paramount — and political compromises on important issues were viewed not just as necessary evils but as morally inexcusable.

This, in turn, shaped both the political ideology and practices of the German left and had a profound effect upon many young Germans, particularly those who became politically involved in the 1960s. The importance of the 1960s, which marked the end of the Adenauer era and the beginning of the Brandt one, has been noted by many German scholars. With respect to the church, historian Martin Greschat has written:

> The decisive caesura in German Protestantism in the 20th century was not, in all probability, after 1945 or 1918, but the 1960s. Only then did wider circles manifestly understand what had been set into play in the first half of this century.[11]

In many countries, the student protests of the 1960s dramatized the clash between generations; in Germany, this conflict was deeper, for it reflected the distance not only between parents and children or teachers and students but between those who had lived in Nazi Germany and those who, born later, bitterly rejected the values of the older generation.

In this conflict, the radical Confessing Christians — most prominently Kurt Scharf, Helmut Gollwitzer, and Heinrich Albertz (after he resigned as mayor of Berlin) — supported the legitimacy of young Germans' criticism of their elders. [For Albertz, who had succeeded Willy Brandt as Berlin's mayor in 1967, the transition was most painful. In June 1967, during protests against a visit by the Shah of Iran, a young student, Benno Ohnesorg, was killed by Berlin police officers. Albertz, who had received the Shah and initially accepted the police version of Ohnesorg's death, subsequently resigned, after conversations with Scharf, Gollwitzer, and student leaders. The experience initiated Albertz' move toward the left; he eventually resigned his various SPD responsibilities. In 1971, he returned to the parish ministry.] On the other side, many conservatives feared, in the students' revolt, what became reality in the German terrorist groups — an outright attack on democratic institutions. As a result, debate arose within the churches about former Confessing Christians who joined the various extraparliamentary political movements in the Federal Republic from the 1960s through the 1980s; some church conservatives denounced them as traitors or terrorist sympathizers.

Scharf, Gollwitzer, and Albertz viewed themselves as mediators — in the case of Albertz, risking his life to carry out this role (after the 1975 kidnapping of Berlin CDU leader Peter Lorenz, Albertz flew voluntarily as a hostage with five released terrorists to South Yemen to obtain Lorenz' release). These Confessing Christians sought to intercede in the leftist debate about whether working "extraparliamentarily" or staying within the political party system was the more moral option. The violence of the terrorists, of course, fell completely outside the realm of this debate, and Gollwitzer warned young Germans in 1976 against becoming deluded into false solidarity with the terrorists.[12]

But the postwar pacifism and antinationalism of these Confessing Christians made them the natural allies of those young Germans who wanted to become different kinds of Germans than their parents had been in Nazi Germany. These Confessing Christians had a record of protest during the Nazi era, and they continued to search for links between the German past and present, instead of merely denying the past. For many younger Germans, then, these Confessing Christians seemed to embody this "other" kind of German.

Albertz and others saw their activism as part of the postwar responsibility that they bore as Germans. They felt a particular responsibility to those who were outsiders—because of what had been done to outsiders in the Third Reich. In Albertz' 1976 sermon after the death of terrorist Ulrike Meinhof, the analogy was clear:

> these are all our sons and daughters; it is the burden of our older generation, it is the burden of this state, that it wasn't open and prepared enough to carry out certain overdue reforms. And it rests, just as obviously on us Christians as well, who apparently still often forget—although the picture hangs in all churches . . . that our Lord Jesus Christ died as a criminal among criminals, and that his last words to a human being were directed toward a criminal, and to no one else.[13]

As Albertz' words show, his experience in the Confessing Church led him to reflect anew about politics and about Christology and the purpose of the church. For many radical Christians in Germany, the very essence of their post-Holocaust faith was that they held themselves morally accountable for the political events around them. The legacy of the *Kirchenkampf* was an ongoing dialogue between Christian faith and the political sphere.

Within the Confessing Church, this process began during the Third Reich. Before his death in 1945, Dietrich Bonhoeffer wrote scores of poems, essays, and letters examining the spiritual and political challenges that Confessing Christians faced. Yet, asked about what happened to Bonhoeffer's conception of the Confessing Church after 1945, his biographer Eberhard Bethge replied bluntly that it was "kaputt":

> The very thought drives me mad. It's not just negative. In one sense, things are being dealt with now, which didn't take place before. But that shows, too, that the era is past and dead; it can't be brought back to life. . . .
>
> It's not at all easy and can't be answered in black and white. It's clear that our basic convictions, which then had a naive form, couldn't continue to be held so simplistically. But the conviction in itself: that that which we did was absolutely important, and that the other was absolutely evil—that's completely unchanged. I'm just disappointed, unfortunately, or have become more skeptical, because our view, Bonhoeffer's view of things, basically, isn't understood. After it appeared in the first decades as though Bonhoeffer were right—with the self-criticism, the Stuttgart Declaration of Guilt, etc.—now it's evident that we are a minority. . . .
>
> To that extent, I am sometimes "very down." I wonder, are we a psychological type that can exist only as a minority? in protest? That could be. There are those who say, "Who were the 'Dahlemites,' the resistance fighters? The ordinary people who half went along with it, half not—*those* were the resisters." Today, some smart young historians see it that way.
>
> I can't live at all without retaining my identity from that era, even today. I'm too old, too; I won't change anymore. But to make myself understood—I don't have that much hope anymore. Perhaps that is too negative. So, it goes "up and down."[14]

In Bonhoeffer, Bethge and others saw a certain kind of faith—one in which the morality of certain political decisions became a *status confessionis,* a viewpoint so fundamentally derived from Christian teachings that acceptance of it is implicit in the

Christian confessions. This understanding of faith led to a basic commitment to political activism. In turn, the political lessons that Confessing Christians drew from their
experiences in the Third Reich profoundly shaped their religious faith after 1945.
"When I was police senator [in Berlin]," Albertz recalled in 1980, "I thought about
what I had done during the Third Reich. One has a different perspective when he
himself has been in prison."[15]

Albertz had been briefly in a Gestapo prison. What he and other radical Christians saw as the Confessing Church's specific failure was that the Gestapo's prisons
had not been filled with Christians who had resisted Nazism. Remorseful about the
church's silence during the Third Reich, they spoke out that much more forcefully
after 1945. If the church had been silent about the Jews, it would now align itself
vocally and actively with those oppressed in the postwar world. These Christians
became committed to broadening West German democracy to include minority
points of view. It was not enough, they believed, that these critical voices be free
from harassment; they had to have a say in the course of German society. Indeed,
postwar political activism of these Christians helped create an atmosphere in which
critical groups (like the Green party in the 1980s) achieved a political status and
degree of influence unique in Western democracies.

For Christians who moved in this direction, the moral clarity of their political
vision became an outward sign of their Christian faith. This concept—of political
vision as a symbol of a transformed Christian faith—was one of the most important
legacies of the Confessing Church, and not only in Germany. It is very influential, for
example, in much liberation theology. For Germans, however, one area in which it
played a crucial and problematic role was with respect to how, as Christians and Germans, they wrestled with their relationship to Judaism and the people of Israel after
the Holocaust.

After the Holocaust: Theological and Political Responses

The Holocaust—the murders of six million Jews by a purportedly "Christian" people—posed a direct challenge to Christians throughout the world. They were confronted with the consequences of the anti-Semitism that had been supported by
Christian churches for centuries, and which made the Holocaust possible. More
crucially, Christians had to acknowledge the churches' failure (and, in most cases,
the lack of any attempt) to stop the Nazi persecution of the Jews. The postwar
attempts of some German church leaders to differentiate between "Christian" anti-
Semitism and Nazi "racial" anti-Semitism obscured the fact that, whatever their
historical differences, these two streams had emptied, finally, into the same murderous river.

The Holocaust challenged parts of Christian doctrine and tradition that had not
just gone unquestioned but virtually unnoticed. For that reason, any examination of
the church's anti-Semitism required both a critical look at the churches' behavior
during the Third Reich and a serious re-examination of their Christology and theology. As Helmut Gollwitzer reflected in 1980,

> The Jews are truly the key. That is the essential point with the Jews, theologically
> and biblically: How do we go about unlearning this part of the Christian tradition?
> That remains one of the most provocative questions in German Christianity today.[16]

The examination of Christianity's ties to Judaism and the Jewish-Christian dialogue that began after 1945 were arduous attempts to undo the damage of centuries.
For Gollwitzer and some others, the starting point was to reconnect Christianity, historically and theologically, with its roots in the Judaic tradition—to acknowledge that
Jesus of Nazarath was, as Gollwitzer put it, "indivisibly a member of this [Jewish]
people."[17] Jesus had emerged from the Jewish tradition, and his ministry and message
were firmly rooted in Jewish scripture and tradition.

The early Church's break with that tradition and its supercessionist claim to be
the new chosen people of God were based upon the belief that Jesus was the Messiah, the fulfillment of God's promises to the people of Israel. But this break and the
subsequent centuries of anti-Semitism did not just oppose the Jewish belief that
Christ was not the promised Messiah, although Christian anti-Semitism focused on
this and on the accusation that the Jews had "murdered" Christ. It led to the move of
Christianity from being a sect within Judaism (as it had been during Jesus' life) to
being a religion of the Gentiles, finally evolving into the Christian empire. With the
dawning of the "Christian era" and its literal unity of throne and altar, the notions of
Christian culture and civilization became definitive for the politics of Christian
Europe. From the Crusades to the Inquisition to the Holocaust, these politics were
influenced by a Christian doctrine that based its Christological doctrine not just on
the facts of Christ's life and death but on "the political realization of Christ's messianic kingdom in the Christian imperium," as German theologian Jürgen Moltmann
noted.[18] The consequences, Moltmann observed, are that:

> If the church exists in a chiliastically interpreted Christian empire of this kind, then it
> is bound to interiorize salvation and leave everything external to the Christian
> emperors: the church looks after people's souls and their salvation; the emperor
> claims their bodies, and provides for the welfare of the empire . . . The Christologies
> that are developed in theocracies like this are anti-Jewish, because these political
> theologies themselves are anti-Jewish.[19]

Christian and Jewish scholars who sought to redefine the Christian-Jewish relationship after the Holocaust faced two theological tasks. One was the examination of
the roots of Jesus' ministry in the Judaic tradition. The second, just as important, was
far more difficult: to define the genuine differences between the two traditions and to
distinguish these from ignorant prejudice. Historical ignorance was a major problem,
as U.S. theologian Rosemary Radford Reuther noted in her book on the subject,
Faith and Fratricide:

> Learning history is, first of all, a rite of collective identity. Christians learn who they
> are by learning the story of Jesus, and through Jesus, carrying down a history created
> by the Christian Church and society. The history of the Jews disappears at the time
> of Jesus. This testifies to the Christian claim that it is the true Israel which alone car-
> ries on the biblical legacy. This Christian way of learning history negates ongoing
> Jewish existence. If we learned not only New Testament, but rabbinic Midrash . . . if

we read Talmud side by side with the Church Fathers; if we read the Jewish experience of Christendom side by side with Christian self-interpretation, this Christian view of history would fall into jeopardy. . . . For Christians to incorporate the Jewish tradition after Jesus into their theological and historical education would involve ultimately the dismantling of the Christian concept of history and the demythologizing of the myth of the Christian era.[20]

As Reuther indicated, ignorance not only affected Christian attitudes toward Judaism; it skewed Christian self-knowledge and an understanding of the Christian relationship to God. The Christian church had come to see itself as the people of the new covenant, in effect replacing the people of Israel. The theological recognition that God's covenant with the people of Israel was still binding, and that the new covenant did not supplant the old, required a radical revision of Christian thinking. This could not occur, however, until Christians tried to understand what the covenant at Sinai signified, not only for the Jews but for the rest of the world. Because of the shared tradition, that is, Christians can understand their relationship to God only if they understand — and acknowledge the difference of — Israel's relation to God.

The difficulties that such issues presented for Christians were evident at the 1950 EKD synod in Weissensee. The transcripts of the synod show that a number of the church leaders who met there were shaken profoundly by Auschwitz and genuinely wished to make some statement of repentance to the Jewish people. But the transcripts also show how deeply embedded anti-Semitism remained in the theological beliefs of the synodal members, and the extent to which their understanding of the Christian faith hampered any acknowledgment of the validity of the Judaic tradition. The theological point stressed by Heinrich Vogel (that the Jews continued as the people of the covenant after the death of Christ) was debated heatedly at the synod, for it went against most members' understanding of Christian salvation and redemption.

The realization of the continuing validity and importance of the Jews' role in humanity's relationship with God became particularly crucial for those who had been in the Confessing Church.[21] It not only gave them a new understanding of both religions but new insights into their experiences as Confessing Christians under Nazism. The recognition at Barmen of the importance of the first commandment, and the necessity, in Heinrich Vogel's words, of breaking away from "all false syntheses" of God and country, had indeed been milestones in the German Evangelical Church, as had the establishment of the Pastor's Emergency League in 1934. In the "Aryan" paragraph and the "German Christian" attempt to remove the Old Testament from the Bible, these Confessing Christians saw that the selective incorporation of Christian dogma into political ideology, tacitly accepted for centuries in the unity of throne and altar, had reached an unacceptable extreme in "German Christian" doctrine and the Nazi worldview.

But, as the Stuttgart Declaration admitted, the Confessing Church had not gone far enough. It had failed to establish a theological and ecclesiastical foundation for Christian resistance to Nazism. Because the Holocaust challenged Christians in Germany both theologically and politically, it compelled them to move from their previous understanding of their religious identity as being bound to some kind of "Christian empire," and to look at their own historical responsibilities. While these challenges emphasized the connection between theology and the moral and political life of Christians, they also revealed an uncomfortable truth about their civilization. Christian values, while they had indeed shaped German culture and politics, had long ceased to define them. In fact, the Holocaust revealed the extent to which the process had become reversed: the extent to which dominant cultural and political biases had determined Christian thinking and the institutional behavior of the church. It was understandable that many Protestants, after 1945, desired nothing more than to return to their pre-1933 church traditions. But these no longer existed, and the world in which they had flourished had changed. The old modes of belief could survive only at the expense of ignoring the historical and theological reality of the Holocaust.

For those Confessing Christians who recognized this, and who linked their post-war faith with the establishment of a relationship to Judaism, this was not merely a theological task. It meant building personal relationships with the Jewish community, particularly to those who had survived the Third Reich. The relationships that ensued are described poignantly by Albrecht Goes, a Württemberg pastor whose parsonage served as a hiding place for Jews trying to escape Nazi Germany. In a 1985 essay (Goes was 77 at the time), he wrote,

> I want to say: uninhibited speech, after all that has happened, is not possible. A dou-ble-edged pain forces its way into all expressions of affection: the pain of the one who gives, the pain of the one who receives. Margarete Susman, [Martin] Buber's assistant in earlier days, wrote about this "between us" late in her life: "He was our neighbour. We lived with him and loved him. How can we make amends for this dreadful transformation? Forgiveness is His who will judge; ours is only the limit-less, inextinguishable grief."[22]

In the years after 1945, various groups in Germany fostered German interest in dialogue with Jews. Jewish-Christian groups were founded in many cities. In 1958, Aktion Sühnezeichen (Action for Reconciliation) was founded by church leaders in East and West Germany; many of the organization's supporters (and two directors, Kurt Scharf and Dietrich Goldschmidt) came from the ranks of the Confessing Church. Aktion Sühnezeichen's purpose was not only to help countries that had suf-fered under the Nazis but to teach young Germans about what had happened and bring them into contact with the people of other countries. It began with construction projects to repair damaged churches and synagogues in Britain, France, Holland, and Norway; in 1961 (the year of the Eichmann trial), the first group of young Germans was sent to work in a kibbutz in Israel. In East Germany, young East Germans were assigned to repair Jewish cemeteries and serve as guides in the memorials at former concentration camp sites.

Some Confessing Christians eventually visited Israel. Annemarie Grosch recalled her experience there:

> I believe that we will never rid our history of this. We can't come free of it. And should not come free of it. And don't want to, either; in any case, I don't wish to. In 1966, I went to Israel with one of the first adult groups. The Israelis said to us then, "We can handle the youth from Germany, but you—how do we know that you weren't perhaps guards in a concentration camp?" I can understand that very well.
>   The institute at Yad Vashem made the greatest impression on me. Yad Vashem

is this house where the entire documentation about the persecution of the Jews during the Third Reich is, and there is a huge memorial building, where the names of Maidenek, Bergen-Belsen, and all the other concentration camps are engraved in the floor. In Yad Vashem there is a statement, in English and Hebrew, that says: "Forgetfulness prolongs the exile. Remembrance is the secret of redemption." That is a wonderful statement. Forgetfulness prolongs the exile. Remembrance is the secret of redemption. Don't forget, don't repress, but remember.[23]

For Christians, remembering the Holocaust meant becoming conscious of the link between what had happened to the Jews and what had happened to them; their theological concerns could not be addressed separately from their own experiences in Nazi Germany. Perhaps this is another reason that it took the EKD so long to issue a statement on the Holocaust to the Jewish community (that is, the Weissensee statement in 1950). The question of anti-Semitism remained difficult, even for Christians prepared to discuss it. There were many, like Bishop Wurm, who spoke of sleepless nights, haunted by remorse that they had not spoken out publicly to defend the Jews. There were others, like Hannover's Bishop Marahrens, whose grudgingly worded postwar statement only proved how deeply engrained anti-Semitism remained in some church leaders:

> However greatly we may still differ in our faith from the Jews, and although they have brought a series of serious harm [*schweres Unheil*] upon our people, they still shouldn't be attacked in an inhumane fashion.[24]

Despite such viewpoints, the theological confrontation with Protestant anti-Semitism had begun and was continued by a small group of theologians. They and other Germans began to examine the political implications of anti-Semitism as well. It is striking to see how rapidly the church discussion about the Holocaust did move to the political level, both in terms of the German relationship to Israel and to the consequences that Germans drew from the Holocaust. This may simply illustrate how difficult the theological questions posed by the Holocaust remained for Christians; but it also reflected the widespread tendency among Confessing Christians to translate the lessons of their experience under Nazism into political consequences.

But determining the political "lessons" was, if anything, even more difficult than the theological task of understanding Judaism and unlearning anti-Semitism. For Christians, these lessons ideally needed to be grounded in new theological insights into the Jewish-Christian relationship. In practice, there were relatively few German Protestants who fundamentally revised their beliefs. And for many Germans (including many Confessing Christians), the lessons drawn from the Holocaust were based upon the perception that the murder of the Jews, while a terrible part of the history of Nazi Germany, was not the definitive event in that history.

The reasons for this are fairly straightforward. The Germans' understanding of their history under Nazism depended not only on how they morally or theologically confronted that history but also on what had actually happened to them personally. Ordinary Germans experienced the war and its consequences far more immediately than they did the murders in the concentration camps. Even for Germans who felt a strong responsibility to atone for the Holocaust, the fact remained that their experience of the Third Reich differed drastically from the Jewish experience of the Holocaust.

For many conscientious Germans, the Holocaust became a symbol of political injustice and evil. For Jews, it was not just a symbol but a reality that lived on in the broken lives of the survivors and the new awareness, in every Jew, of what was possible. Many Germans' lives, too, were broken—but by events that took place at the same time as the Holocaust—most significantly, by the war.

In this respect, the German experience of Nazism was lived out on the edge of the Jewish experience. Ironically, Hitler's attempt to exclude the Jews had been successful; they and the Germans ended the Third Reich in two separate worlds. Up to May 1945, Germans' lives retained the possibility of a kind of normalcy that Jews living under Nazi rule had lost, step by step, from the beginning. For Germans and Jews alike, this normalcy was illusory, a masquerade. But it was perceived differently, particularly after 1945. Both groups had tried to cling to the normal routines of their lives during the Third Reich, as a way of maintaining sanity and of continuing their private lives. But for every Jew, this attempt at normalcy was doomed.

It was different for Germans, and, after 1945, this fact influenced many Germans' attempts to understand what had happened. Rationalization is the principle risk of books (including this one) that portray the ordinariness of German life under Hitler; and yet it is important to understand that the way in which people lived affected how they later remembered the era, and the conclusions they drew in their memories. It does not excuse or explain away the Third Reich; rather, it helps explain why *Vergangenheitsbewältigung* took the forms it did.[25]

Above all, it explains why, despite attempts at Jewish-Christian dialogue in Germany, the estrangement between Germans and Jews could never be bridged completely. Normalcy, having proven such an illusion in the Third Reich, remained so for many Jews. What remained most real were not their postwar lives but the aftermath of the evil they had suffered and the awareness that a Holocaust was a possibility. To many Jews, the emphasis by some Germans on the Holocaust as a symbol of political evil in general seemed to diminish the full horror of what they had experienced. "Never again," said the Jews, and they meant one thing only. "Never again," said many Germans, and they meant different things: never again dictatorship, never again war. They meant taking clear political positions that symbolically represented anti-Nazism.

The difference between these two perceptions illustrated a fundamental problem with the process of *Vergangenheitsbewältigung* as it occurred even among those who genuinely wanted to make amends for what Nazi Germany had done. The problem was that political conversion—the commitment to live differently after the Holocaust, to be a different kind of German— was not enough. It was possible for Germans to alter their political behavior, for example, and still avoid the issue of anti-Semitism entirely. To many Jewish victims of the Holocaust, the use of the Holocaust as a symbol from which moral lessons could be drawn for other situations appeared to relativize what had happened—precisely because such analogies no longer differentiated between the Jews and other victims of Nazism. When the Holocaust was viewed solely as an example of political oppression, the Jews who died in the camps could symbolize victims of oppression everywhere.

Observing the postwar discrimination that Turks and other guest workers suffered in West Germany, for example, some Germans drew the parallel that the "Turks are the Jews of today." The recognition of the problems of racism and discrimination in postwar Germany was important and necessary. The problem was that viewing the Jewish experience under Nazism in this symbolic fashion removed it from the larger context of the Holocaust and changed many Germans' perceptions of the Holocaust itself. It evaded the historical fact that anti-Semitism has existed in all kinds of political and economic systems—in other words, that it is not merely a political problem but has its roots in the dynamics of prejudice, on another level. Moreover, it obscured the theological meaning of the Holocaust for Christians—which goes beyond the question of Christians' political accountability for the evil that was done.

In this area, those who had been in the Confessing Church had a great opportunity and responsibility, for on the basis of their unique experience in Nazi Germany, they had insights into both the theological and political consequences of the Holocaust. They could join the legitimate ethical conclusion that Christians are called to defend the value of each human life against all forms of oppression with the necessary theological examination of the destruction that the Holocaust had wrought, not only upon its victims but in the souls of all who had been part of this history.

For many Jews, the theological, political, and moral consequences of the Holocaust were part of a congruent whole, embodied by the state of Israel. In this respect, Israel was not just a political state but stood for the ongoing relationship of the Jewish people to God. Even many nonobservant Jews feel a deep sense of unity with Israel—that their fates are bound to its fate. In contrast to this, the Germans' experience existed in fragments, full of conflicting feelings and conclusions. *Vergangenheitsbewältigung* pitted Germans against each other, against their past, their culture, their religion, and their sense of national identity.

Thus, the political experience of many Germans drew upon the memory of the Holocaust, and certainly took it seriously; nevertheless, it remained profoundly distant to the Jewish experience. Most people interviewed for this book had difficulty discussing, or even recalling, what had happened during the Third Reich to the Jews they knew. This difficulty was mirrored by the continuing estrangement of many Jews from German society, even Jews who chose to live in Germany after 1945.[26]

The entire problem shows the extent to which the dialogue among Christians, Germans, and Jews has been affected by the nature of their respective experiences. Yet the Holocaust, for all that it destroyed, did not end the relationship between Germans and Jews or Christians and Jews. Instead, it took this tragic relationship onto a new level, on which some Christians acknowledged those parts of their tradition that had had such murderous consequences for the Jewish people, and searched for ways to alter this.

Some Germans emerged from the Third Reich with new insights into what had happened to them and to the Jews. Helene Jacobs, who had refused to cooperate with Nazism from the beginning, made an important distinction as she reflected on this issue:

> Today, they talk about the "exclusion" of the Jews—I can't express it so well, because it's so frightful for me—as if the Jews were only a minority. . . . But it was our world that was destroyed then. I have to explain that better. When young people come to me, I can explain it sometimes to them. But those who are as old as I am

don't understand it at all. . . . I stood *for* something, for a part of myself, not against something. It was my cause. In that moment where we became part of this discrimination, we destroyed ourselves. I was part of the persecuted. We belonged together. . . . My whole theme was always collective responsibility, which we must all preserve. You see that I have always been an outsider in my surroundings.[27]

Many Germans interviewed for this book shared Helene Jacobs' sense of alienation from their own country, even when they were convinced that the nation that developed in the decades following the Third Reich was very different from the nation that brought Hitler to power in 1933. But throughout German history, political vision has been bound to a deeply felt sense of national identity as well as to religious faith.

The German nation was the site where Germans sought to realize their political vision and where they wrestled with questions of national and religious identity. Historically, such questions have been settled by the establishment of political or ideological boundaries that determined who belonged and who was excluded. The early Christian church, in defining its doctrine, denied the validity of Judaism. Nazi Germany found the answer to these questions in its notion of an "Aryan" soul and a racially, nationally defined Fatherland. Hitler succeeded in part because these notions, particularly that of the Fatherland, were meaningful for most Germans.

After 1945, there were many Germans for whom the question of national and religious identity was highly problematic. For many, particularly for those who had been in the Confessing Church, their Christian identity was now merged with a strong antinationalism. After 1945, they remained bound to their ignominious Fatherland. What did it mean to them now?

✧ 15 ✧

Faith and the Fatherland

S INCE 1945, GERMAN NATIONAL IDENTITY has been bound inseparably with the process of *Vergangenheitsbewältigung*. The kind of "Germanness" that people claim for themselves and wish for their country is one indicator of how they have chosen to examine their past. Many of those who most explicitly wish to atone for Germany's Nazi past also deliberately reject any continued claim on a territorial or symbolic Fatherland.

Because it was impossible to extricate entirely from its use in Nazi propaganda, "Fatherland" became one of the symbols and phrases whose postwar political potential could not be separated easily from the way in which they had been used during the Third Reich. The German national anthem, "Deutschland, Deutschland über alles," for example, was banned for a period in East Germany (although the East Germans tried to "denazify" the term "Fatherland" by speaking of a new "Socialist Fatherland"). In West Germany, the Haydn melody was retained as the national anthem, but the first two stanzas, because of their association with the Nazi era, were not sung at state functions.

From the 1950s through the 1980s, public references to a German Fatherland became the preserve of the political right wing, particularly that sector which represented those who had fled the eastern provinces after 1945. Among these refugees, loyalty to the Fatherland was part of their ongoing claim to the eastern provinces of Pomerania and Silesia, which after 1945 had become part of Polish territory. For many (though not all) of these Germans, the Fatherland continued to exist regardless of postwar realities, and they viewed the regions east of the Oder/Neisse rivers (the East German-Polish border) as German territory.

At the annual meetings of these refugee groups, native costumes were donned and traditional folk dances performed, but the real purpose of the "homeland reunions" became evident when some prominent CDU politician rose to speak. The political centerpiece of such gatherings was fundamental opposition to West German recognition of the Oder-Neisse border. Talk of a return to the Fatherland often inflamed deeper, even uglier passions in Germany. In the mid-1960s, for example, the EKD published a paper recognizing the postwar borders as permanent; after this, right-wing arsonists set the Berlin homes of former Confessing Christians Heinrich Vogel and Dietrich Goldschmidt, both of whom had spoken out in favor of the paper (Vogel had helped write it), on fire.

The insistence of some Germans on reclaiming their lost Fatherland represented a claim on the actual land, but, as the emotionally charged tone of such discussions showed, the Fatherland was more than mere territory. Although some Confessing

Christians rejected the notion of a Fatherland after 1945, it had become like German history itself; one could repudiate it, but not erase it. For those Germans who had grown up under the Kaiser, who had been raised with certain ideals and values that they described as *vaterländisch*, the real and symbolic loss of their Fatherland was like a death, leaving a permanent void in their lives and shaking the foundation of much in which they had believed. In the introduction to his memoirs, Otto Dibelius wrote, "What one feels at the deathbed of loved ones, or in the face of the collapse of his Fatherland—others may describe that: I cannot."[1]

This tragic sense was magnified by the personal losses suffered in the war, made even more bitter because those who had fallen as soldiers for their Fatherland had also fallen for Hitler's Germany. Marta S., once an enthusiastic Nazi, had had to flee Pomerania, and her husband had died on the Polish front. She never became reconciled to these losses:

> For me, to be German is simply a sorrow. I have wept so many tears for Germany as well as for my husband. I can't hear the German anthem today without crying. Because there is no more Germany. We have become a people without a history. After the war, many of my students were disposed to be "European," against German nationalism. But I hold a vacuum here to be dangerous, for a new Goebbels could rise again to fill it in a false manner.
>
> One must always consider where the line is between nationalism and national consciousness. I always tried, with my students in the schools, that they think about things, and not simply fall for slogans. . . . They should see: All things have two sides, and most have more.[2]

Marta S. continued to hold onto a German national consciousness. But it was undeniable that such national feelings seldom inspired the fervor that the Fatherland once had. As Stefanie von Mackensen reflected,

> My son fell in the war. Can you imagine how I've blamed myself, that I voted for this man Hitler, who unleashed this war in which my son was killed? As a mother, I can't absolve myself of all that. . . . To be German—it's hard for me, now, to say the word "Fatherland." I am shocked myself. What that idea, "Fatherland," once meant to me.[3]

Most particularly for those who had been in the Protestant church, estrangement from the Fatherland signified the loss of other political ideals. As the theologian Elisabeth Grauer explained,

> We had always seen the church and the Fatherland as tied to each other. Through Nazism, we learned that we had almost made a God out of it. Therefore we now see it differently, relativized. There are no more absolute values, Godlike values, in that sense. It's a major change. The ideal of *Volk*, Fatherland, Freedom, that these were ultimate values—that's gone. That naturally alters one's entire political perspective. . . . For me, much was simply destroyed.[4]

For many Confessing Christians, the Fatherland lost its place as a dominant, governing ideal in their lives after 1945 (for some, this had happened in 1933). For others, however, this did not occur. Hans Thimme, asked if he had felt estranged from Germany after 1945, replied,

No. No, I didn't. Perhaps that is somewhat related to the fact that I was a soldier in Russia. The confrontation with Russia was such that, somehow, the feeling was there — we knew that Germany had started the war, and we were clearly against it. But if there was a front, then there was a considerable difference whether the front was in the west or in the east. For we distanced ourselves from Russia, not just from Communism, but from Russian imperialism, too, which had already threatened Germany during World War I in a significant manner. It was very much so that I always had the feeling that if I had to be a soldier at all, then this was basically the front on which one could justify it a little, so to speak, before his own conscience.

Afterward, in the Declaration of Repentance in 1946 [a statement by the Westphalian church] . . . at that time we unanimously voted, as a regional synod: We are bound with the German people in guilt, but this guilt, this accountability, must now be borne together, and because of that, is a basis for our attempt now to make a new beginning together. I always distinguished between National Socialism and being German. For me, my German identity never came into question.[5]

In the fall of 1989, the term "Fatherland" reappeared in speeches and on banners and posters. After the opening of the Berlin Wall, most Germans rejoiced; certainly, no one who had ever crossed that grim border could be unmoved by the suddenness with which it became irrelevant. Many Germans, too, commented with relief that, finally, their country had done something commendable in the eyes of the world. Yet this itself revealed the extent to which the shadow of the Fatherland's past continued to lurk over Germany's present. There was little evidence, after November 1989, that many Germans wanted to reflect on how the resolution of the Nazi past could influence the latest turn in their history. If anything, many spoke as if the past could — finally — legitimately be buried. Didn't the Germans have the same right to patriotic feelings as any other people?

Yet there were occasional disturbing signs that the past had not really been put to rest. When Ilse Härter, a retired Confessing Church pastor, publicly expressed her misgivings about German reunification, she was accused in a letter from a middle-aged colleague of *Vaterlandsverrat* — treason — in a tone that disturbed her deeply:

I haven't read something like that since the 1930s. . . . Now, we simply have this history. It won't go away, and we can't behave as if we were a normal nation, without this past. . . . But that some people still think this way — that is what is so unbelievable for me, and that has so upset me.[6]

The extent to which Germans continue to feel drawn together toward some collective destiny as a Fatherland, or are moved simply by normal national feelings, is influenced by the nature of national feelings themselves as well as by how Germans have dealt with their history. National feelings can lay dormant, still powerful, for years. The disintegration of Soviet dominance in Eastern Europe, and the reemergence, as a political force, of long-standing tensions among different ethnic groups in Rumania, Yugoslavia, and the former Soviet Union, show that this is a universal phenomenon, which reveals as much about the essence of national or ethnic feelings as it does about the history of such sentiments among the Germans.

The intensity of national feelings is heightened when these merge with religious ideals (and the extent to which many religions, throughout the world, adapt themselves to cultural and national traditions illustrates how this process works both ways). When this happens, religion lends nationalistic notions, like that of Fatherland, an aura of absolutism, divine empowerment, even inevitability. Historically, the German Fatherland was always more than a political slogan or even territory; it was a domain where political and religious ideals merged and, in the Third Reich, became demonically distorted.

For Eugen Gerstenmaier and one sector of German conservatism, the Fatherland transcended the political entity of the state; it was the force that moved Germans' souls. From their perspective, the Fatherland was the meeting ground of Luther's two kingdoms—the realm of the world and that of the divine. But *Vaterlandsliebe* had helped create and empower Nazism, and, after 1945, it hindered Germans' attempts to confront the Nazi past. The "legends of resistance" that sprang up after 1945 about the Confessing Church, the Communists, and the other groups who had had conflicts with the Nazis all had some foundation in fact. But on some level they served as rationalizations and ignored the fact that most Germans who lived during the Third Reich were, indeed, loyal to their Fatherland and were bitter, after 1945, that they had lost it.

The primary dilemma of *Vergangenheitsbewältigung* is that, for most Germans, the past exists only in pieces. There are so many groups of Germans; each has its part of history and its victims. There are the refugees from the East, who mourn the loss of their homelands, of their Fatherland, and grieve for the millions who died fleeing Eastern Europe. There are the Jews and gypsies, singled out by the Nazis for eradication, for whom the German Fatherland became the site of the Holocaust. There are the political opponents of Nazism, both those who turned against it very late and those who opposed it from the beginning. There is the largest group, the ordinary Germans, some of whom took risks, trying to help a Jewish neighbor, perhaps, and others who took none, and looked the other way as the Jews were taken away by the Gestapo. And there are some, of course, who agreed with it all, who believe that Hitler was a great statesman and who mourn not just the loss of a Fatherland but of Nazi Germany itself. Then there are the children and grandchildren of all these people, and all have their version of what really happened in Germany between 1933 and 1945.

This is one reason for the polarization in some parts of the German political sphere, for the fundamental reluctance of some groups to make compromises, even when it becomes necessary for their political survival (the West German Greens suffer from this, and the East German New Forum fell apart after November 1989 because its numerous members could not unite on a platform.) This problem reflects the unspoken belief that a compromise of moral ideals in the political sphere represents a betrayal of those who died at the hands of Nazi Germany.

There are so many dead. Germany is covered with graves and memorials, from the heathered mounds in Bergen-Belsen that cover the remains of thousands of Jews to the military cemeteries of Allied soldiers to the still undiscovered and unmarked graves that undoubtedly exist in some forests and fields. The scale of death wrought by Nazi Germany is so enormous that perhaps it is bearable only if broken up, and yet this diminishes the value of each of those lives claimed by one group or another with almost vicious possessiveness. It is almost as if the Germans believe that revering one group of victims belittles the memory of the rest of them.

The emotional weight of these dead, however, is felt in its entirety, even if many individuals are too bewildered, grieving, or ideologically blind to view the history of Nazi Germany as a whole. In 1985, West German President Richard von Weiszäcker noted in Jerusalem,

> Every German bears the inheritance of the history of [his] people — the legacy of the entire history with its bright and dark chapters. It is not up to him to refuse the dark parts. Honest remembrance gives us Germans the freedom to do justice to our present responsibility. Only in this way can we master the future, after a past which no one can undo and from which no one can dissociate himself.[7]

Confessing Christians and the Fatherland

The notion of a German Fatherland will always be accompanied, in the shadows, by the specter of its one-time Führer. The immense burden of the past haunted many Confessing Christians, even those who had risked their lives to fight Nazism, to the end of their lives. Ernst Wilm, asked what it meant to him to be German, replied,

> Well, Germany is my Fatherland and remains my Fatherland. When I went to other countries after the war, then I essentially lived off the fact that I was a former concentration camp inmate. That I could document, through that, that I hadn't been among the Nazis. . . . But I placed myself among the guilty, just as Martin Niemöller, in all his speeches on the question of guilt, repeatedly did. . . .
>
> Now, when I look at the overall mood among our German people . . . when I see how little they are prepared to repent, how little they wish to learn from what happened, how little they confess that we are all guilty — then I've thought to myself, sometimes, if only you were no longer in Germany. If only you were, perhaps, in Switzerland.[8]

Wilm was not the only one to feel a stark sense of separation from his compatriots. Dietrich Goldschmidt, asked whether he viewed himself specifically as a German, replied bluntly,

> No. No notion for me. I am here because I believe that my task is here. I am not here because I especially love this land. . . . No, I have a very distanced relation. I could settle effortlessly tomorrow in England or in the U.S. . . .
>
> There's something else. In the meantime, I've been around the world a great deal because of my career . . . the worst experience I had was right after the war. In 1947, I was in England for the first time after the war. We arrived at the Hook of Holland on land and had to wait a while until the train drove on to Germany. I went into the restaurant and wanted to try to buy a cigar for my father-in-law, who liked to smoke. Since I don't smoke, I didn't know what to buy, and I was confused, accordingly, and stuttered it out in English. Then, in a booming voice, another passenger said, [in German] "Buy Ritmeester! We always had that during the war; that is the best." I would have liked to sink into the ground.
>
> I feel something similar today. Two weeks ago I was at a burial ground, a memorial for 2.2 million Russians. There was a school class from Saxony there, which I find very commendable and very proper. Still, I thought to myself, how

must these people feel, when a group goes through here, not even particularly striking, but who are speaking German loudly. We can't get away from it.[9]

Eberhard Bethge was another who came to see his land differently from abroad,
but, unlike Goldschmidt, he remained close to his German roots:

I believe that the lesson for us, even if we belonged to the resistance and could basically say, "We weren't guilty," is that we are Germans and remain so. Abroad, it
seals our lips, and we can't run away from it. Today, I see a certain hope in Richard
von Weiszäcker, that he is capable of saying, "There is no escape. A door will open
only by going right through it." After the war, we thought that the world would not
accept us for decades. Then the cold war began, and suddenly we were insanely
important again, and the lie began.

But I found, even very soon after in England, that if I stand by the fact that I am
a member of this people, in which I don't only have Goethe and Beethoven, but in
which I have Goethe, Beethoven, and Hitler — as soon as I say that, then the others
begin to listen to us again and be interested in us. But with the excuse, "It was only
Hitler," the matter only becomes worse. There are Germans in Washington, for
example, who say, whenever Elie Wiesel does something, "Oh, now things will
become so difficult for us again." My wife and I have never had this experience.
More than ever, when we have accepted Elie Wiesel and then reported how it was
for us, then the doors didn't close, but opened. . . .

In 1957–1958 we were at Harvard for one year. The question came whether we
didn't want to stay longer. But the separation from our kind of German culture, German liberalism, German theology as well — I never wanted that, or could do it, and
never seriously considered it.[10]

The act of simultaneously acknowledging German identity while remaining critical of it was described by Marion Yorck von Wartenburg in 1986:

It is difficult even today. It is difficult even today. I am very easily critical. Today, when
I see things again that they do wrong — it is all difficult. I have to work at it. I envy how
the Americans have such a natural and patriotic feeling for their successes. . . .

But I think that the Germans have it hard; they are situated in the middle of
Europe. They aren't on the Atlantic or the Mediterranean. They have always had
their best periods and best people when everything was open, when all the forces, all
the influences, passed through from right to left, north, west, east, south. They found
their own statehood very late, and the reign of Bismarck wasn't the right form,
either. Bismarck was certainly a great man, but it didn't hold. The way it is now,
with this division — I know, indeed, that we are easier to bear in a divided condition,
for our neighbors and for the rest of the world. But it is hard for the Germans.[11]

The task of examining the Nazi past and their own identity was probably easier
for people like Bethge and Yorck, who had been involved in the resistance against
Nazism, and for Goldschmidt, who had been among its "non-Aryan" victims. For
those who spent the Third Reich in the middle — neither as convinced Nazis nor as
resisters — the process was more difficult. For those who wished to acknowledge it,
this task raised the question of their own guilt. Elisabeth Schwarzhaupt, who had
been a lawyer in the official church consistory in Berlin, had tried to work within the
system, as a moderate. Asked how she had dealt with the issue of guilt, she replied,

I must say, I am still not finished dealing with it. I believe that we Germans can't resolve it completely. Naturally, I think about whether I shouldn't have behaved more radically, that is, to have withdrawn from the consistory after the Reich church council withdrew [in 1936]. But as far as I remember, that didn't play a considerable role for me at the time. For it all happened so slowly, little by little, that I basically never had a concrete occasion to say, suddenly, "I won't go along with this anymore."

But, aside from that, I would have been faced with the question of existence. I wouldn't have found another job and wouldn't have known what I should live from. For, as a woman lawyer, I wouldn't have gotten in anywhere else. . . .

That I am nevertheless a German, and that these horrible crimes — which I first learned about, for the most part, afterward — were committed in the German name, that I feel accountable there, and that in every conversation with foreigners I stand under a certain pressure — that is another question. I don't like to be judged by people who have never lived under a regime of terror themselves. But I do feel accountable for that which happened in the Germans' name.[12]

There were different ways in which people felt bound by what Nazi Germany had done. Those who became alienated from all notions of Fatherland often became estranged from their own contemporaries as well. It appeared to many former Confessing Christians as though they simply did not belong to their generation. Rudolf Weckerling, speaking of the other elderly Germans who shared his apartment building in Berlin, mused,

When we tell these things, for whom are we speaking? In this building, we don't speak for a single other person who lived through all these things, too. These are older people who see it utterly differently, only evasively — above all, one doesn't speak about politics or religion. . . . I believe that this behavior is highly developed among us, that is, it shows this mechanism of denial. One doesn't want to be reminded.[13]

Herbert Mochalski, who as a "Dahlemite" and outspoken opponent of the Adenauer government became isolated in postwar Germany and within the EKD, remained cynical about his own generation, and about his compatriots in general:

I believe that the sector that is politically aware has become larger. . . . But the overwhelming majority, even today, poses a latent potential for right-wing developments. That is no question for me. Only the outright materialism and our high standard of living have covered that up today. If it would come to a crisis, I don't know which way the German people would lean. Until now, it's always tended toward the right.

The younger generation today have just begun to ask, "Well, how was it then?" Because they never received an answer at home. After the war, nothing really changed. Once again, we had no revolution. The judicial system has remained the same, the civil service has remained the same, the teachers have stayed the same. We can only hope for the next generation.[14]

Martin Schröter, too, felt alienated from his generation and his country. After his retirement from the ministry, Schröter moved into an alternative commune with Germans of all ages:

Basically, I always have felt rather isolated on political questions among the colleagues of my generation. That is the peculiar thing. We do have friends from our student days, but, on political questions, we're very, very far apart. Up to today, we basically have no kindred spirits among people our age in political questions, or very few, and in any case, none from student days.[15]

What does it mean for him, then, to be German?

To be a stranger in my land. Whereby I will probably always have difficulty, as a result of this whole process, to develop anything like a national feeling. Basically, I have no national consciousness, unless it comes through the language. . . . I ask myself sometimes, what it means to me to be German. I don't know. . . . The [50-year-old] colleague who lives here in the commune is much more "German," I believe.[16]

Schröter, who became active in the movement against NATO missiles in the 1980s, explained that one reason for his involvement was his lack of national feeling for West Germany: "My feelings say: What is that supposed to mean, 'our own country?' People, that is so provincial. I can't see any sense in the Federal Republic as something that we should defend."[17]

Emmi Bonhoeffer, who lived in an apartment in a senior citizens' building in Düsseldorf, echoed Schröter's sense of isolation. Her feeling toward Germany itself was, she said,

A critical love. Here in this building I count as terribly leftist, but for these people, everything left of center is terribly leftist. I am rather alone. The basic position is, "We don't wish to be reminded. It was all so terrible!" There were two women with whom I got along well. One was a Jew from Prague; she has died. The other was a teacher who was unequivocably anti-Nazi. . . . But it doesn't matter to me. I have books, my violin and viola, have the radio, have my children, friends, my grandchildren; I don't feel lonely.[18]

Berta Braune, who lived in a senior citizens' home until her death in 1987, spoke about the silence of her neighbors about the past:

My suspicion is that the people who close their eyes were perhaps real National Socialists. They say, "We don't want to hear any more about it," and, through that, keep themselves completely out of the question of dealing with the past. I don't think that's good. I believe there must be a release for everyone somehow, simply to talk about it, even if that is in a counseling situation. Our judgment doesn't play a role, but the liberation of the other plays a role. This liberation won't come to those who say, "I can't hear about it anymore; I don't wish to speak about it."

Recently, I encountered an example, a ministerial civil servant who played a major role as a party member during the Third Reich. And it was his daughter who told me, "No, my brother and I have said to ourselves, we don't want to give our opinion in any way on these matters anymore. It doesn't achieve anything. At some point, it has to end."

That is what I call a "lazy peace." . . . For me, that wouldn't be the way.[19]

For Helene Jacobs, the Fatherland died in 1933; she was one of the few who never cooperated with Nazism. She was an outsider in Nazi Germany and remained one after 1945 in West Germany. In 1986, she reflected on her relationship to her country:

> Back then, I said, I must defend my world. That was my point of departure. Today, I tell young people, you have to defend your world. When one tries to understand every extreme offshoot and to give it the benefit of the doubt, then one repeats it all. For these young people whom Hitler won over, they weren't all evil. Just like today, with the extremists. Today, I read in the newspaper that there was a meeting of sympathizers for these right-wing extremist groups. I ask myself, am I living in the same world as other people?[20]

Many Germans, including politicians, dreamed that a European consciousness would not only replace the void left by Nazism but would serve to prevent the dangers of selfish nationalism. At the same time East and West Germany were reunited, the European Community was moving toward economic unity. But while European unity defused the significance of a united Germany on one level, the feelings of many Germans focused not only on economic and diplomatic realities but on their land itself.

Of course, many of those interviewed for this book did not live to see the fall of the Berlin Wall. Toward the ends of their lives, some had said their farewells to the lost part of their Fatherland, like Stefanie von Mackensen, who had grown up and lived in Pomerania. She recalled,

> I have been back three times to Poland, to my Pomeranian homeland. I am deeply impressed by this amiable people, the Poles. When I read about the atrocities that happened there, it upsets me. But I have no hatred toward the Poles, that this land has been taken from me. I can travel through this land, can even feel homesick, but I don't have any antipathy toward the people who live there . . . and I've had the experience that it's not the people, but the land. When I traveled through this countryside, I was back home. It didn't matter to me that the people weren't there anymore. . . . Perhaps there will come a time when there are no more nations, but only people.[21]

Marion Yorck von Wartenburg's last memory of Silesia was from the summer of 1945 when, as she said, "I had been torn away from all the roots of my life up to then, so that the best thing for me was to travel like a vagabond, to wander." Illegally, with her sister-in-law and the widow of Helmut Moltke, she made her way on foot to the Yorck estate, which was surrounded by Soviet soldiers and under Polish rule:

> I had always thought that I would find Kauern just as I had left it. But it was completely destroyed. I remember how books lay around and my sister-in-law picked one up, by Hamsum, *The Last Chapter*. Everything, the house, it was so horrible. The way it looks after a war, right? . . . The land hadn't been cultivated in the fall of 1944, and in the spring of 1945 wasn't tilled either, and, as a result, it was a meadow full of red blossoms and blue cornflowers. You could only see where the roads had been by the rows of trees. Everything was overgrown with camelias, and we saw marvelous fields of pheasants. It happens so quickly. I never would have thought that such cultivated earth, when there is a warm spring and summer, after a half year, is like a wonderful wilderness.[22]

That was when Yorck released her claim on the land. She never went back: "When I see the Poles there, then I say to myself, 'Now the Poles live there.' And I hope that they are just as happy there as we were. It is a beautiful land."[23]

Perhaps it is easier to relinquish something when one has been able to take leave of it, literally — to return, see what is left and what connections remain; perhaps that was what enabled some people to accept the finality of the postwar borders in a way that others could not. Some Germans, like Heinrich Vogel, sought a postwar national identity that bridged the borders between east and west.

> You know, basically, for my entire life, at least for the decisive decades of my life, for over 30 years, I have been committed to serving as a bridge between east and west. I was professor for systematic theology at Humboldt University in East Berlin and, at the same time, at the *Kirchliche Hochschule* in the west. . . . Today, I would still stand up for this bridging function, with the goal — I won't live to see it — that we live together again as one people in one state. [Vogel died in December 1989.] We would have to disown our fathers if we were to disown our Fatherland. I can't imagine how it might be. I could say, God grant that it happens, if it does happen, neither according to the eastern nor to the western form. Not like the west, either, do you understand? But who wants, today, to say anything concrete about that? . . .
>
> I am the holder of the *Bundesverdienstkreuz* and of the *Vaterlandsverdienstorden* [the highest medals of honor granted by West and East Germany, respectively]. Imagine that, on the same hero's breast! And even the Vladimir Medal of the Russian Orthodox Church. You'll understand when I tell you that with a smile. My friend Gustav Heinemann probably meant well when he handed me that great cross, but — think it over — the people over there did, too. . . .
>
> So when I smile about these honors, it doesn't mean that I despise them. I have staked my entire life on serving as a bridge, as a professor of theology. You see how difficult it is, in the present age, to practice freedom. Very difficult. One doesn't get out of it without misinterpretations and misunderstandings. . . . For it is not at all always clear that this or that decision concerns freedom — that it concerns genuine freedom.[24]

Was it easier in other centuries?

> There have been times when it wasn't so difficult as in this century! But now we have this century, and must practice it in this century. I don't believe it was ever easy. True freedom was never easy.[25]

The question of freedom concerns the freedom of the conscience, ultimately of the soul. For many Confessing Christians, the hardest step they took in their opposition to Nazism was the first one, that of realizing they had an obligation to something greater than their Fatherland. As Martin Niemöller recalled,

> That was the breaking point with the "German Christians": From the very beginning, they put the Fatherland above the discipleship to Christ, the national interest above their belief.[26]

Although the course of Niemöller's own life showed how torn he remained by patriotic loyalties, he and other Confessing Christians tried to distinguish between national loyalties and their religious faith. It was only that which gave them the freedom to oppose Nazism at all.

The price they paid was painful to the end of their lives, for they had to uproot themselves from the world in which they had been raised. Shortly before he turned 90, Martin Niemöller reflected,

Today, no one knows anymore what the Fatherland is. I don't know anymore, either. I have a homeland. But this homeland is the region of Tecklenburg. My parents came from there; that's where I have the feeling of being at home. . . . I took my matriculation examinations in March 1910, and 14 days later, I joined the Kaiser's Marines. After that, I had no home at all, basically. . . . I became homeless as a young person.[27]

Throughout their lives, many Germans remain bound to the region where they were born and where their families have come from. Martin Niemöller had returned briefly to the region of Tecklenburg in the 1920s before he began his theological studies. Although he spent the following years in Berlin and, after his release from Dachau, in Hesse, he chose to be buried in the village in Tecklenburg where he had been born 92 years before. He had rediscovered the region in the bitter period after World War I and came to love the rolling hills there.

The love that Niemöller felt for Tecklenburg, like that Stefanie von Mackensen and others felt for their native provinces in the east, was not quite the same as their love for the Fatherland. The land from which one comes remains mere land, marked by the loveliness and particularities of its landscape, free on some level from political burdens.

In 1982, a group of citizens in the region petitioned the town government of Wersen, where Niemöller had been born, to declare him an honorary citizen of the town. The uproar that resulted revealed that the old "Dahlemite" could still arouse controversy at the age of 90, but it also showed how the people on the town council had dealt with German history — for the council, after much argument, denied him the honor. The official reason was that Niemöller hadn't performed any service specifically for the town, but, as the debate that had taken place among members of the town council became public, it became obvious that the real reason was the controversial positions Niemöller had taken throughout his life. Council members criticized his postwar pacifism, his trips to Moscow, his role as elderly prophet for the peace movement. But what made headlines was that one town council member charged that Niemöller had brought discredit to Germany by signing the Stuttgart Declaration of Guilt in 1945.

It is one more piece of evidence that the conflict which plagued Germans during the Third Reich, between loyalty to Germany and loyalty to their consciences, is still unsettled. Eberhard Bethge believes that it is a conflict that has faced the Germans for ages:

It is an old German story that national solidarity toward the outside world has first place, and it was taken for granted that inner freedom — every form of emancipation in the last century — had to retreat in the face of freedom for foreign policy. In the name of this freedom for foreign policy, internal political freedom is destroyed or restricted. That's why we were not a democratic people up to [the Weimar Republic]. "Freedom" was a very great German word in the nineteenth century — but in terms of foreign policy. Not in domestic politics. . . . That's why Bismarck is much more important than Marx.[28]

Germany may someday shed the disgrace that Nazism brought upon it. But many of the changes that Nazism wrought, in the eyes of the world and in the hearts of the

German people, are irreversible. This has to do not only with the emotions aroused by the memory of Nazi Germany but with the facts that it left the world to face: the millions dead and the countries broken and altered by the war.

The corruption of the once idealized German Fatherland only symbolizes a greater, universal loss. Nazi Germany changed the way people think. It left many with a more cynical view of the human race and a diminished or utterly destroyed belief in God. It offered horrific proof of how quickly the most civilized society can degenerate into bestiality; it reminded the world that even those values that humans hold to be most durable, even eternal, are, in fact, unbearably fragile. For many, the Holocaust crippled religious belief. For centuries, human faith has relied upon traces of the divine in earthly life, for evidence of a link between human existence and the transcendent. Auschwitz appeared to break that link, for it seemed to offer proof of God's failure, indifference, or outright nonexistence.

Yet the link remains. The experience of the Confessing Church during the Third Reich showed how entangled the political life of a people and their religious life can be. But, while the earthly and divine realms should never be fused, they can never be separated entirely, either. Human religious faith, its dreams, philosophy, and morality, all the edifices of mind and spirit, cannot be mastered by any nation. Earthly rulers have always been tempted to try. Poets and priests have idealized their homelands throughout the centuries, and demagogues have sought to use these ideals for their own purposes; Hitler mesmerized even educated Germans with his talk of "blood and earth." Yet, even under the worst dictatorship, a nation holds its inhabitants in thrall only to the extent that they lack or abandon the spiritual independence to keep themselves from submitting totally.

That is the lesson of what happened to Confessing Christians during the course of their lives. Between the moments of birth and death, whatever changes were wrought within their souls depended on where they rendered allegiance during their brief period on earth—to the powers that ruled Germany or to the principles of faith that brought them into conflict with the Nazi regime. Ultimately, their conflict with Nazism pitted them against themselves; it was a struggle not just for but within their own souls. Martin Luther believed that there were two kingdoms—the dominion of earthly powers and the divine realm of spiritual might. Whether or not we agree that these kingdoms are separate, the truth is that we all walk their grounds. Throughout our lives, we are torn between them, and who can be certain, finally, which terrain is more treacherous?

Notes

Abbreviations

EZA   Evangelisches Zentralarchiv, Berlin

LKA, EKW   Landeskirchlichen Archiv der Evangelischen Kirche, Westfalen, Bielefeld

All translations from published, archival, and interview material are mine unless otherwise noted. In citing works in the notes, short titles have generally been used.

Introduction

1. Between 1945 and 1953, around 12 million Germans fled or were banished from Eastern Europe; some two and a half million of them died of starvation, exposure, or diseases like typhoid.

2. LKA, EKvW, 5,1: 100a:2, "Pfarrernotbund."

Chapter 1. The Lost Empire

1. Alan Palmer, *The Kaiser* (London, 1978), 9.

2. Interview, Martin Niemöller, Wiesbaden, December 9, 1981.

3. Karl-Wilhelm Dahm, *Pfarrer und Politik: Soziale Position und politische Mentalität des deutschen evangelischen Pfarrerstandes zwischen 1918 und 1933* (Cologne, 1965), 79–81 and 97–121. A number of pastors interviewed for this book recalled growing up with such attitudes.

4. Interview, Kurt Scharf, Berlin, August 6, 1981. Scharf wrote more about the societal atmosphere in which he grew up in *Für ein politisches Gewissen der Kirche* (Stuttgart, 1971), 25–27.

5. Interview, Wilhelm Niemöller, Bielefeld, March 9, 1982.

6. Holy Bible, Revised Standard Version (London, 1946), 894.

7. A. S. Duncan-Jones, *The Struggle for Religious Freedom in Germany* (London, 1938), 43. This book, written by a British clergyman whose visits to Germany began before World War I, is particularly interesting in light of his eyewitness accounts of events between 1933 and 1938.

8. Otto Dibelius, *Ein Christ ist immer im Dienst* (Stuttgart, 1961), 146.

9. See Chapters 1 and 3 in Dahm, *Pfarrer und Politik.* See, too, the introduction to Martin Greiffenhagen, *Pfarrerskinder* (Stuttgart, 1982).

10. Interview, Rudolf Weckerling, Berlin, February 5, 1986.

11. Interview, Ernst Wilm, Espelkamp, March 11, 1982.

12. Ibid.

13. Interview, Sieghild Jungklaus, Berlin, February 6, 1986.

14. Dahm, *Pfarrer und Politik,* 9ff.

15. Johannes Schneider, ed., *Kirchliches Jahrbuch* (1907, 1915, 1920, 1930). Between 1910 and 1915, 36,290 people left the church for "atheistic" reasons. This trend was reduced during the war years; then, in 1920, 305,584 left the church, again for "atheistic" reasons. Schneider, and many other conservative church leaders, saw this as an alarming sign of increasing Social Democratic and Communist influence. (*Jahrbuch,* 1915, p. 466; 1930, p. 101.)

16. Eberhard Bethge, "Adolf Stoecker und der kirchliche Antisemitismus," in Bethge, *Am gegebenen Ort* (Munich, 1979), 207.

17. In 1932, 43 theologians, pastors, and church leaders were asked to contribute to Leopold Klotz, ed., *Die Kirche und das Dritte Reich, Fragen und Forderungen deutscher Theologen* (Gotha, 1932). Nineteen were critical of the new National Socialist ideology, 12 approved of it, and 12 declared themselves neutral or undecided. In these latter 24 contributions, the "Jewish question" emerged as a clear factor in the authors' openness to National Socialism. See, too, Robert P. Ericksen, *Theologians under Hitler: Gerhard Kittel, Paul Althaus and Emanuel Hirsch* (New Haven, CT, 1985).

18. Interview, Helmut Gollwitzer, Berlin, November 6, 1980.

19. For an analysis of the role this played, see Fritz Stern, *The Politics of German Despair* (Berkeley, CA, 1961).

20. Joachim Kreppel, *Juden und Judentum von Heute* (Zurich, 1925), 258ff.

21. Ibid., 132.

22. See Gordon Craig, *Germany 1866–1945* (New York, 1978), 506ff.

23. Dahm, *Pfarrer und Politik,* 147–48.

24. Ibid.

25. Günther Dehn, *Die alte Zeit, die vorigen Jahre* (Munich, 1962), 212.

Chapter 2. The Weimar Years

1. Interview, Stefanie von Mackensen, Iserlohn, April 1, 1984.

2. Dahm, *Pfarrer und Politik,* 177.

3. Ibid.

4. Ibid., 159–65. See also Ernst Christian Helmreich, *The German Churches under Hitler* (Detroit, MI, 1979), 63–66 and 121ff.

5. Craig, *Germany,* 415.

6. Ibid., 450.

7. Ibid.

8. Ibid., 454.

9. Interview, Helmut Gollwitzer.

10. Interview, Emmi Bonhoeffer, Düsseldorf, May 16, 1986.

11. Interview, Dietrich Goldschmidt, Berlin, November 1, 1988.

12. Interview, Doris Faulhaber, Mannheim, January 25, 1984.

13. Golo Mann, *Deutsche Geschichte des XX Jahrhunderts* (Frankfurt, 1958), 6.

14. Interview, Gertrud Staewen, Berlin, January 27, 1982.

15. See Claudia Koontz, *Mothers in the Fatherland* (New York, 1988).

16. Interview, Gertrud Staewen.

17. Interview, Martin Schröter, Warburg, February 8, 1982.

18. Klaus Scholder, *Die Kirche und das Dritte Reich*, Band 1: *Vorgeschichte und Zeit der Illusionen, 1918–1934* (Stuttgart, 1972), 25.

19. Interview, "Matthias K.," Frankfurt, December 6, 1981. Speaker wished to remain anonymous.

20. Bodo Harenberg, ed., *Chronik des 20. Jahrhunderts* (Dortmund, 1990), 422.

21. Interview, "Marta S.," Bremen, March 18, 1982. Speaker wished to remain anonymous.

22. Ibid.

23. Interview, Emmi Bonhoeffer.

24. Interview, Stefanie von Mackensen.

25. Interview, Wilhelm Niemöller. In his book, *Kampf und Zeugnis der Bekennenden Kirche* (Bielefeld, 1948), Niemöller contrasted the tradition of nominal church membership in regions that became heavily "German Christian" with the more actively devout laity in the Prussian churches (p. 17).

26. Duncan-Jones, *Religious Freedom*, 30.

27. Ibid., 34.

28. Interview, "Marta S."

29. Interview, Wilhelm Niemöller.

30. Quoted in Günther van Norden, *Der deutsche Protestantismus im Jahr der national-sozialistische Machtergreifung* (Gütersloh, 1979), 54.

31. Interview, Gertrud Staewen.

Chapter 3. Nationalism, Nazism, and the Churches

1. Heinz Bergschicker, ed., *Deutsche Chronik 1933–1945: Alltag im Faschismus* (Berlin, 1983), 52.

2. For a detailed study of this aspect of Nazi Germany, see Martin Broszat, *Der Staat Hitlers: Grundlegung und Entwicklung seiner inneren Verfassung*, 8th ed. (Munich, 1979), particularly Chapters 7 and 10. See, too, Craig, *Germany*, 591ff. for his view of the *Gleichschaltung* of the various ministries and the bureaucracy. Whereas Broszat interprets the situation as the result of confusion, Craig believes that there was an "element of design" in the confusion that resulted. "During the Kampfzeit," writes Craig, "Hitler had learned the old lesson of divide and rule and had become adroit in devising checks and balances that protected his own position by making the contenders dependent upon his arbitrament of their disputes" (pp. 595–96).

3. Bergschicker, *Deutsche Chronik*, 52.

4. Interview, Helene Jacobs, Berlin, February 3, 1986.

5. Bernd Hey, *Die Kirchenprovinz Westfalen, 1933–1945* (Bielefeld, 1974), 31. Hey quotes Hans Buchheim, *Glaubenskrise im Dritten Reich* (Stuttgart, 1953), 10–11.

6. See Helmreich, *German Churches*, 128–29. The figures are from EZA, B19/131.

7. LKA, EKvW, 5, 1: 294:2, "Deutsche Christen."

8. Translation from Helmreich, *German Churches*, 123.

9. Interview, Stefanie von Mackensen.

10. LKA, EKvW, 5, 1: 292:2.

11. Scholder, *Kirche und das Dritte Reich*, Band 1, 419–20.

12. Leonore Siegele-Wenschkewitz, *Nationalsozialismus und Kirchen: Religionspolitik von Partei und Staat bis 1935* (Düsseldorf, 1974), 87.

13. Duncan-Jones, *Religious Freedom*, 43–51.

14. Wolfgang Gerlach, *Als die Zeugen schwiegen: Bekennende Kirche und die Juden* (Berlin, 1987), 40.

15. Helmreich, *German Churches*, 148.

16. Ibid., 147.

17. LKA, EKvW, 328: Fasc 1, "Leitsätze zur judenchristliche Frage".

18. LKA, EKvW, 328: Letter, 5.7.33.

19. Siegele-Wenschkewitz, *Nationalsozialismus und Kirchen*, 138.

20. LKA, EKvW, 5, 1: 294:1, 30.1.38.

21. LKA, EKvW, 5,1: 294:1, October 1937.

22. Siegele-Wenschkewitz, *Nationalsozialismus und Kirchen*, 138.

23. Ibid., 142.

24. Klaus Scholder, *Die Kirche und das Dritte Reich*, Band 2: *Das Jahr der Ernüchterung: 1934 Barmen und Rom.* (Berlin, 1985), 60–61.

25. Ibid., 160.

26. Eberhard Klügel, *Die lutherische landeskirche Hannovers und ihr Bischof 1933–1945* (Berlin/Hamburg, 1964), 71.

27. Interview, Ernst Wilm, Espelkamp, March 11, 1982.

28. Scholder, *Kirche und das Dritte Reich*, Band 2, 19. Scholder's discussion of how this affected the Protestant church, on pages 17–32, is very helpful. See, too, Broszat, *Staat Hitlers*, Chapter 10.

29. Broszat, *Staat Hitlers*, 408.

30. Interview, Heinrich Schmidt, Dortmund, July 16, 1979, trans. Ulrich Wolf-Barnett.

31. Hey, *Kirchenprovinz Westfalen*, 61.

32. Quoted in Scholder, *Kirche und das Dritte Reich*, Band 2, 42–43.

33. Ibid.

34. EZA, KKA, Nr. 35d/518, Memorandum, (Humburg to Fiedler), 30.1.35.

35. Interview, Eberhard Bethge, Bad Godesberg, November 12, 1985.

36. Ibid.

37. Interview, Herbert Mochalski, Bad Homburg, December 10, 1981.

38. Throughout the Third Reich, those pastors who hoped for a clearer stand remained extermely cautious. When Berlin theologian Wilhelm Jannasch was asked, in 1937, for his opinion as to whether party members could remain in the Confessing Church, he made his views clear, between the lines: "I expressed my personal view neither recently nor will I express it in this letter . . . nor do I consider myself entitled to force my conscience's view upon the church when it is not inwardly yet ripe for it." (EZA, 249, VKL, 10 (11.5.37).

39. Broszat, *Staat Hitlers*, 294–97.

40. Interview, "Marta S." Records from the Berlin Document Center confirm her version.

41. Interview, Wilhelm Niemöller.

42. Ibid.

43. This has been confirmed by records from the Berlin Document Center.

44. Interview, Eberhard Bethge.

45. Interview, Stefanie von Mackensen.

46. See Scholder, *Kirche und das Dritte Reich*, Band 2, 183.

47. Interview, Stefanie von Mackensen.

48. Ibid.

49. John Conway, *The Nazi Persecution of the Churches 1933–1945* (London, 1968), 103.

Chapter 4. Convictions and Conflicts

1. Interview, Helmut Gollwitzer.
2. Scholder, *Kirche und das Dritte Reich*, Band 2, 71.
3. Klügel, *Landeskirche Hannovers*, 37.
4. Ibid.
5. Scholder, *Kirche und das Dritte Reich*, Band 2, 330.
6. Ibid., 57.
7. Klügel, *Landeskirche Hannovers*, 223.
8. Ibid.
9. Interview, Martin Niemöller.
10. Interview, Helmut Gollwitzer.
11. Scholder, *Kirche und das Dritte Reich*, Band 2, 34–35.
12. Among those present were Heinrich Held from the Rhineland Confessing Church, Hans Lauerer and Bishop Meiser from the Bavarian Lutheran Church, Martin Niemöller, and Pastor Karl Lücking from Westphalia. The theologians present were Friedrich Gogarten, Karl Fezer, Gerhard Kittel, and Ernst Haenchen. Karl Barth's appearance was unexpected. (Scholder, *Kirche und das Dritte Reich*, Band 2, 53ff.)
13. Ibid., 56.
14. Ibid., 95.
15. Ibid., 283.
16. Ibid., 61ff.
17. Ibid., 378 (Note 104).
18. Ibid., 62.
19. Ibid.
20. LKA, EKvW, 5,1:100a: 1, "Pfarrernotbond," letter, 31.1.34.
21. As Meiser wrote to Müller on January 28, 1934, he was prepared to support Müller's authority, but only if that were legitimate under church law. Meiser noted that since this was not the case he stood "on the side of the pastors of the PEL." (LKA, EKvW, 5, 1: 100a: letter, 28.1.34).
22. Wilhelm Niemöller, *Der Pfarrernotbund: Geschichte einer kämpfenden Bruderschaft* (Hamburg, 1973), 58.
23. Ibid.
24. The March 2, 1934 decree by which he attempted to do this was declared "legally inapplicable" by the courts, and in any case, he failed due to resistance in the regional churches. See Scholder, Band 2, 9.
25. Ibid., 113.
26. Ibid., 85.
27. Interview, Hans Thimme, Babenhausen, May 26, 1988.
28. Ibid.
29. Interview, Stefanie von Mackensen.
30. Interview, Hans Thimme.
31. Scholder, *Kirche und das Dritte Reich*, Band 2, 217.
32. Interview, Helmut Gollwitzer.
33. Klügel, *Landeskirche Hannovers*, 170 (italics are his).
34. After 1945, these churches (Rhineland, Westphalia, and Berlin) adopted it formally as a full confession.
35. Interview, Hans Thimme.
36. Interview, Günther Keusch, Berlin, January 15, 1982.

37. Ibid.

38. Ibid.

39. See the chapter on Althaus in Ericksen, *Theologians under Hitler*. At that time Althaus' stature as a theologian gave his criticism of the Barmen Declaration considerable weight in the churches, particularly the Lutheran ones.

40. EZA, Kirchenkampfarchiv, Nr. 35d:508, "Entwurf" (draft of statement sent to Hitler).

41. LKA, EKvW, 5,1: 100a:1, "Pfarrernotbund Rundschreiben" 10.

42. LKA, EKvW, Best. 5,1: 100a, "Pfarrernotbund," 26.1.34

43. Hans Prolingheuer, *Kleine politische Kirchengeschichte* (Cologne, 1987), 78.

44. Ibid.

45. Scholder, *Kirche und das Dritte Reich*, Band 2, 75.

46. Klügel, *Landeskirche Hannovers*, 7. See, too, Jonathan Wright, *"Above Parties:" The Political Attitudes of the German Protestant Church Leadership 1918–1933* (Oxford, 1974).

47. Interview, Helmut Gollwitzer.

48. Ibid.

49. Interview, Gerda Keller, Dortmund, February 20, 1980.

50. Interview, Helmut Gollwitzer.

51. Interview, Gerda Keller.

52. Interview, Martin Schröter.

53. Klügel, *Landeskirche Hannovers*, 54.

54. Jochen Klepper, *Unter dem Schatten deiner Flügel* (Stuttgart, 1956), 99.

55. Dibelius, *Ein Christ*, 183–84.

56. Ibid., 167.

57. This was confirmed in my interview with Doris Faulhaber. Anna Paulsen, a leading woman theologian in the Confessing Church, also confirmed it in her book *Amt und Auftrag der theologin* (Burckhardthaus, 1963).

58. Interview, Elisabeth Schwarzhaupt, Frankfurt, June 6, 1986.

59. Interview, Ilse Härter, Goch, December 3, 1981.

60. Interview, Martin Schröter.

61. Interview, Herbert Mochalski.

62. Interview, Hans Thimme.

63. Interview, Kurt Scharf.

64. Niemöller, *Der Pfarrernotbund*, 58–59.

65. Hey, *Kirchenprovinz Westfalen*, 92.

66. Ibid.

67. Niemöller, *Der Pfarrernotbund*, 58. Twenty-two members were left in Hannover, 29 in Bavaria, and 442 in Württemberg.

68. LKA, EKvW, 5,1: 100a, "Pfarrernotbund, Rundschreiben," 7.12.33.

69. Interview, Heinrich Schmidt.

70. Scholder, *Kirche und das Dritte Reich*, Band 2, 331–32.

71. Ibid.

72. Duncan-Jones, *Religious Freedom*, 86.

73. Klügel, *Landeskirche Hannovers*, 144.

74. The information on Jäger is from Scholder, *Kirche und das Dritte Reich*, Band 2, 353–54. The information on Müller is from Bosl, K., G. Franz, and H. H. Hofmann, eds., *Biographisches Wörterbuch zur Deutsche Geschichte*, Vol. 2 (Munich, 1974), p. 1960.

75. Scholder, *Kirche und das Dritte Reich*, Band 2, 340.

76. Interview, Hans Thimme.

77. Ibid. See Hey, *Kirchenprovinz Westfalen*, 61ff.

78. Klügel, *Landeskirche Hannovers*, 172.

79. Ibid., 47.

80. Scholder, *Kirche und das Dritte Reich*, Band 2, 342.

81. Dibelius, *Ein Christ*, 185.

82. Ibid., 199.

83. Interview, "Matthias K."

84. From a memo, "Die Lage in der protestantischen Kirche und in der verschiedenen Sekten und deren staatsfeindliche Auswirkung: Sonderbericht des Chefs des Sicherheitshauptamtes des Reichsführers SS, Feb:März 1935," in Heinz Boberach, ed., *NS und Kirche: Berichte des SD und der Gestapo über Kirchen und Kirchenvolk in Deutschland, 1933–1944* (Mainz, 1971), 63–64.

85. Ibid., 71–72.

86. Interview, Helmut Gollwitzer.

87. In 1935, for example, Bishop Wurm wrote, "Had the German Christians not tried from the beginning to hinder the formal recognition of the Provisional Church Government, the Kirchenkampf could have been ended already at the beginning of this year. . . . As long as no truly independent church government exists, a church like the Confessing Church and, with it, the regional churches tied to it, cannot do without a purely church administration." EZA, 17: 77–78, ("Die Stellung der Württ. Landeskirche zur Vorläufige Kirchenleitung und zur Deutsche Evangelische Kirche," 6.11.35.)

88. In 1988, Hans Thimme, who knew Zöllner, described him as "over 70 years of age, a proven Lutheran church leader in Westphalia. He had a rare sense of mission. He believed that, on the basis of his truly unsurpassed achievements, he would be in the position of uniting the church on the one hand and leading it to a compromise with the state on the other. Behind that, naturally, stood the Lutheran-influenced loyalty to the state and simply poor judgment of the situation. He did not see through it, and he did not see through the satanic nature of National Socialism." (Interview, Hans Thimme.)

89. One of the main points of contention was whether to take a stand of support for Karl Barth (EZA, 35d, Vorläufige Kirchenleitung, Protokoll 35/423).

90. Interview, Hans Thimme.

91. EZA 399 19, 6.10.37.

92. Klügel, *Landeskirche Hannovers*, 215.

93. Ibid., 190.

94. Interview, Martin Fischer, Berlin, November 5, 1980.

95. Interview, Christian Berg, Berlin, January 13, 1982.

96. Interview, Martin Niemöller.

97. Interview, Elsie Steck, Bad Homburg, December 8, 1981.

98. Ibid.

99. Interview, Elisabeth Schwarzhaupt.

100. Interview, Kurt Scharf.

101. Dibelius, *Ein Christ*, 142.

Chapter 5. Daily Life and Work

1. Klepper, *Unter dem Schatten*, 41.

2. From Schneider, *Kirchliches Jahrbuch*, 1931, 183–90.

3. EZA, Best. KKA, Nr. 615/424, 19.12.39. Paragraph 23 of the 1927 law (the so-called *Vikarinnengesetz*) stipulated that a beginning woman was to receive 70 percent of a beginning

male pastor's salary. According to the women themselves, their salaries varied even within the same regional church. As the women complained in one memo, "Only very rarely are the guidelines of the *Vikarinnengesetz* observed." (EZA, KKA, Nr. 503/81–4).

4. Interview, Annemarie (Schilling) Grosch, Neumünster, December 31, 1980. Although Annemarie Schilling did not marry until 1941, I use her married name (Grosch) throughout this work to avoid confusion, as I do with all the women whose names changed with marriage. In the original archival documents, of course, their unmarried names appear.

5. Werner Hilgemann, *Atlas zur deutschen Zeitgeschichte 1918–1968* (Munich, 1984), 81.

6. Interview, "L. M."

7. Hilgemann, *Atlas*, 11.

8. Interview, Elisabeth Schwarzhaupt.

9. Interview, Ilse Härter.

10. Interview, Annemarie Grosch.

11. Interview, Elsie Steck.

12. Interview, Hans Thimme.

13. Interview, "Anton L.," Berlin, January 15, 1982. Speaker wished to remain anonymous.

14. Interview, Ilse Härter.

15. LKA, EKvW, 0,3: 54:123, "Seelsorge mit Studenten, 1937–47," letter 12.1.38.

16. Ibid.

17. Ibid., letter dated 8.6.37.

18. Interview, "Matthias K."

19. Interview, "L. M."

20. Interview, Heinrich Vogel, Berlin, January 15, 1982.

21. Ibid.

22. Interview, Rudolf and Helga Weckerling.

23. LKA, EKvW, 5,1: 111:2, Fürbitte I, 30.12.36.

24. LKA, EKvW, 5,a,112:F2, Fürbittenliste, 4.11.37.

25. EZA, KKA 105–6, "Bericht über die kirchenpolitische Lage," letter from Ortsgruppenleiter to district NSDAP office, dated 21.11.35.

26. Interview, "Friedemann M.," East Berlin, August 4, 1980.

27. Ibid.

28. Ibid.

29. Between 1933 and 1936, the PEL collected around 433,000 Reichsmarks to support pastors who had lost their jobs. (Niemöller, *Der Pfarrernotbund*, 63.)

30. LKA, EKvW, 5,1, 111:2, Fürbitte 2, "Merkblatt für die Angehörige."

31. EZA, KKA 405/46–47, letter dated 31.10.35.

32. LKA, EKvW, 5,1: 112:Fasc. 2, Fürbittenliste.

33. Helmreich, *German Churches*, 200.

34. Interview, Heinrich Schmidt.

35. Ibid. See, too, Broszat, *Staat Hitlers*, 260, in which he notes that "numerous SS leaders" were sentenced in April 1934 to lengthy prison terms for mistreating concentration camp inmates. Although certainly an isolated case, the incident described by Broszat illustrates Schmidt's point.

36. Interview, Werner Koch, Emlichheim, May 15–16, 1981.

37. Interview, Hebe Kohlbrugge, Utrecht, February 24, 1982.

38. Interview, Annemarie Grosch.

39. Interview, Heinrich Vogel.

40. Ibid.

41. EZA, KKA, Nr. 19/15, "Der Präses der Bekennenden Kirche von Berlin: Betr. Verordnung der Staatspolizei Berlin vom 28. August 1937."

42. Vogel is in error here on the date. According to the *Fürbittenliste* from January 1, 1939, Vogel and 14 other pastors in Brandenburg and Berlin stopped receiving their salaries at the beginning of November 1938. This disciplinary measure, taken by the church consistory in Berlin, was because they had supported the Provisional Church Government on the prayer liturgy issue. (LKA, EKvW, 5,1: 112:Fasc. 1, Fürbittenliste.)

43. Interview, Heinrich Vogel.

44. As quoted in Joachim Beckmann, ed., *Kirchliches Jahrbuch für die Evangelische Kirche in Deutschland, 1933–44* (Gütersloh, 1945), 265.

45. Interview, Heinrich Vogel.

46. Interview, Annemarie Grosch.

47. Interview, Heinrich Schmidt.

48. Klügel, *Landeskirche Hannovers*, 230.

49. LKA, EKvW, 5,1: 112:Fasc 2, Fürbittenliste, letter dated 1.9.52.

50. LKA, EKvW, 5,1: 112:Fasc. 2, Fürbittenliste, letter from Koch's brother to Wilhelm Niemöller, dated 19.6.48. This is confirmed by Eberhard Bethge in *Dietrich Bonhoeffer: Eine Biographie* (Munich, 1978), 613.

51. Debate about this issue became especially heated during the war. Several statements (pro and con) about the political purposes of the *Fürbittenliste* are to be found in LKA, EKvW, 5,1: 112:Fasc. 2.

52. Ibid., "Zür Fürbitte der Gemeinde für ihre bedrängten Brüder."

53. Statement from Liselotte Lawerenz.

54. LKA, EKvW, 5,1: 111:Fasc. 2, Fürbittenliste I (8.8.37).

55. Helmreich, *German Churches*, 214.

56. Holstein defended Confessing Church pastors on a number of occasions. Like other lawyers who went to court for the Confessing Church, he strategically emphasized the patriotism of his clients. We can only speculate the extent to which this was merely a tactic to win judicial leniency or actually reflected the sentiments of those on trial; but it did haunt some Confessing Christians later. At his trial, Niemöller even testified to his personal dislike of the Jews. See James Bentley, *Martin Niemöller: Eine Biographie* (Munich, 1985), 171–72.

57. EZA, KKA, Nr. 389/90–91, letter dated April 1939.

58. Interview, Christian Berg.

59. EZA, VKL, Nr. 8. Notes made by Günther Harder, 22.12.41, "Urteil des Sondergerichts gegen Albertz et al."

60. Ibid., 3.

61. Ibid., 2.

62. Interview, Heinrich Vogel.

63. Interview, Elisabeth Grauer, Göttingen, February 9, 1982; additional information from Isle Härter, January 4, 1989. The survivor was Charlotte Friedenthal, who, with Dietrich Bonhoeffer's help, escaped to Switzerland in 1941.

64. EZA, VKL, Nr. 8, p. 4.

65. Ibid.

66. Interview, Heinrich Vogel.

67. Helmreich, *German Churches*, 306–7.

68. Bethge, *Bonhoeffer*, 776.

69. Interview, Hans Thimme.

70. EZA, KKA, Nr. 94B, "Abschrift, Pfingsten 1939."

71. LKA, EKvW, 5,1: 238, "Iserlohn, Februar 1940."

72. Bethge, *Bonhoeffer*, 690. In the Rhineland, 60 Confessing pastors already serving in the Wehrmacht were legalized in 1942–1943.

73. Quoted from the English translation of Bethge's Bonhoeffer biography: *Dietrich Bonhoeffer, Man of Vision, Man of Courage.* Translated from the German by Eric Mosbacher (and others) under the editorship of Edwin Robertson (New York, 1970), 518.

74. Interview, "Anton L.," January 15, 1982. Speaker wished to remain anonymous.

75. Ibid.

76. Ibid.

77. Ibid.

78. Interview, "L. M."

79. Interview, Doris Faulhaber, Mannheim, January 25, 1984.

80. Interview, Hans Thimme.

81. Interview, Doris Faulhaber.

82. LKA, EKvW, 5,1: 111:2, Fürbittenliste.

83. EZA, KKA, Nr. 179.

84. Werner Koch, *Heinemann im Dritten Reich* (Wuppertal, 1972), 209.

85. EZA, KKA, Nr. 385/38, "Urteil, 27.1.39."

86 EZA, KKA, Nr. 385/50–63, July 1940.

87. Ibid., 52 and 54.

88. Ibid., 57.

89. Ibid., 59.

90. Ibid., 61.

91. Interview, Kurt Scharf, Berlin, November 5, 1981.

92. Ibid.

93. EZA, KKA, Nr. 385/51–54.

Chapter 6. The Murder of the Institutionalized Patients

1. Hilgemann, *Atlas*, 69.

2. Ibid., 113.

3. Ernst Klee, *"Euthanasie" im NS-Staat: Die "Vernichtung lebensunwerten Lebens"* (Frankfurt, 1985), 20.

4. Ibid., 32.

5. Ibid., 28.

6. Friedrich von Bodelschwingh, "Die Frage des 'lebensunwerten Lebens' und das Erste Gebot," in Hans Christoph von Hase, ed., *Evangelische Dokumente zur Ermordung der "unheilbar Kranken" unter der nationalsozialistischen Herrschaft in den Jahren 1939–1945* (Stuttgart, 1964), 120.

7. Paul Braune, "Der Kampf der Innere Mission gegen die Euthanasie," in *Evangelische Dokumente*, 114–15.

8. Klee, *"Euthanasie" im NS-Staat*, 78ff.

9. Klee, *"Euthanasie" im NS-Staat*, 31.

10. Anneliese Hochmuth, "Bethel in den Jahren 1939–1943: Eine Dokumentation zur Vernichtung lebensunwerten Lebens," *Bethel Arbeitsheft* 1, 1970, 6.

11. Klee, *"Euthanasie" im NS-Staat*, 100.

12. Ibid., 89.

13. Eugen Kogon, *Der SS-Staat: Das System der deutschen Konzentrationslager* (Frankfurt, 1983), 46–47.

14. Klee, *"Euthanasie" im NS-Staat*, 148.

15. Ibid., 130–41.

16. Ibid.; see 163–65, also 226–32.

17. Ludwig Schlaich, "Lebensunwert? Kirche und Innere Mission Württembergs im Kampf gegen die 'Vernichtung lebensunwerten Lebens,'" in *Evangelische Dokumente*, 73. This is an excerpt from Schlaich's book of the same title, written in 1947.

18. Ibid., 69–70.

19. Ibid.

20. Ibid., 71

21. Ibid., 91.

22. Ibid.

23. Interview, Annemarie Grosch. She may be in error on the date; the fall of 1939 would have been very early for Confessing Church parishes to have received this information.

24. Schlaich, "Lebensunwert?" in *Evangelische Dokumente*, 102.

25. Ibid., 104.

26. Ibid., 105.

27. Ibid., 103.

28. Klee, *"Euthanasie" im NS-Staat* 210, 325.

29. EZA, KKA, Nr. 11, letter dated 11.2.41.

30. Schlaich, "Lebensunwert?" in *Evangelische Dokumente*, 76.

31. Interview, Berta Braune, Bielefeld, February 12, 1986.

32. Reprinted in Berta Braune, *Hoffnung gegen die Not: Mein Leben mit Paul Braune* (Wuppertal, 1983), 140.

33. Interview, Berta Braune.

34. Klee, *"Euthanasie" im NS-Staat* 270, Note 164.

35. Berta Braune, *Hoffnung*, 66.

36. Paul Braune, "Der Kampf der Innere Mission," in *Evangelische Dokumente*, 108.

37. As justice minister, Gürtner was instrumental in trying to preserve the independence of the civil courts as long as possible (see Broszat, *Staat Hitlers*, 154ff.). A number of Confessing Church leaders trusted him and turned to him on various occasions. Gürtner apparently thwarted an early arrest of Martin Niemöller (see Helmreich, *German Churches*, 511, Note 38), and Dietrich Bonhoeffer met with him in the hope that Gürtner could block the wholesale mobilization of Confessing Church Illegals by the Wehrmacht (see Bethge, *Bonhoeffer*, 776). Gürtner died several weeks after his meeting with Bonhoeffer. Gürtner's assistant at the justice ministry was Hans von Dohnanyi, Bonhoeffer's brother-in-law, who was executed by the Nazis in April 1945.

38. Paul Braune, "Der Kampf der Innere Mission," in *Evangelische Dokumente*, 111.

39. Ibid.

40. Interview, Berta Braune.

41. Ibid.

42. Interview, Ernst Wilm.

43. Klee, *"Euthanasie" im NS-Staat*, 281.

44. Interview, Ernst Wilm. See, too, *Evangelische Dokumente*, 24ff.

45. Hochmuth, "Pastor von Bodelschwinghs Verhaltensweise," *Bethel Arbeitsheft* 1, 1970, 31ff.

46. Interview, Berta Braune.

47. Ibid.

48. Schlaich, "Lebensunwert?" in *Evangelische Dokumente*, 93.

49. Ibid., 80.

50. Klee, *"Euthanasie" im NS-Staat*, 209.

51. Helmreich, *German Churches*, 312.

52. Paul Braune, "Der Kampf der Innere Mission," in *Evangelische Dokumente*, 112.

53. Hochmuth, "Bethel in den Jahren 1939–1943," *Bethel Arbeitsheft* 1, 1970, 29.

54. Ibid., 34–35.

55. Hauptarchiv der von Bodelschwingschen Anstalten Bethel, Best. 2/18-2. Letter dated 13.4.42.

56. Schlaich, "Lebensunwert?" in *Evangelische Dokumente*, 99.

57. Interview, Ernst Wilm.

58. Ibid.

59. Klee, *"Euthanasie" im NS-Staat*, 284.

60. *Evangelische Dokumente*, 25–26.

61. Interview, Berta Braune.

62. Klee, *"Euthanasie" im NS-Staat*, 338–39.

63. Julius Schniewind, a New Testament scholar in the Confessing Church.

64. Interview, Ernst Wilm.

65. Schlaich, "Lebensunwert?" in *Evangelische Dokumente*, 102. This was true of other institutions, too (see Kogon, *SS-Staat*, 45).

66. Hochmuth, *Bethel Arbeitsheft* 1, 24.

67. Klee, *"Euthanasie" im NS-Staat*, 336.

68. Quoted in Annedore Leber, ed., *Das Gewissen Entscheidet* (Frankfurt, 1960), 181.

69. Hilgemann, *Atlas*, 113.

70. Klee, *"Euthanasie" im NS-Staat*, 336.

71. Ibid., 429.

72. Ibid., 166, 171.

73. Ibid., 422.

74. Interview, Anneliese Hochmuth, Bethel, May 6, 1991.

75. Interview, Ernst Wilm.

76. Paul Braune, "Der Kampf der Innere Mission," in *Evangelische Dokumente*, 115.

77. Schlaich, "Lebensunwert?" in *Evangelische Dokumente*, 80.

78. Ibid., 74.

79. Ibid., 98.

80. *Evangelische Dokumente*, 27–28.

81. Interview, Berta Braune.

82. Interview, Ernst Wilm.

83. Interview, Berta Braune.

84. Reinhard Heydrich, head of the SS Security Service (*Reichssicherheitsamt*) until his assassination in Prague in 1942.

85. Interview, Ernst Wilm.

Chapter 7. The Confessing Church and the Jews

1. Interview, "Matthias K."

2. Hermann Kinder and Werner Hilgemann, *Atlas zur Weltgeschichte* (Munich, 1982), 62. The percentage of Jews in urban areas like Berlin and Frankfurt was higher, but had remained fairly stable between the late nineteenth century and the Weimar years, even dropping in Frankfurt by almost half during that period (*Vierteljahrshefte zur Statistik des Deutschen Reiches*, Vol. I, Nr. 2 (1873); Kreppel, *Juden und Judentum von Heute*).

3. Gerlach, *Als die Zeugen schwiegen*, 26.

4. Cited in ibid, 40.

5. Ibid., 23.

6. Institute Kirche und Judentum, *Judenfeindschaft im 19. Jahrhundert*, (Berlin, 1977), 12–13.

7. Ibid., 13.

8. Adolf Hitler, *Mein Kampf* (Munich, 1941), 70.

9. Interview, Helmut Gollwitzer.

10. For an analysis of this, see Eberhard Bethge's essays, "Kirchenkampf und Antisemitismus" and "Adolf Stoecker," in Bethge, *Am gegebener Ort.*

11. Gerlach, *Als die Zeugen schwiegen*, 120.

12. Letter, Ilse Härter to author, 25.10.89.

13. Bethge, "Adolf Stoecker," in *Am gegebener Ort*, 207.

14. Ibid.

15. See *Judenfeindschaft im 19. Jahrhundert*, 11–17; and, in the same volume, Hermann Müntingen, "Das Bild vom Judentum im deutschen Protestantismus," 21–51.

16. Ibid., 13 and 17.

17. Müntigen, "Das Bild vom Judentum," in *Judenfeindschaft*, 23.

18. Ibid., 27.

19. Hartmut Ludwig, "Die Opfer unter dem Rad verbinden," Ph.D. dissertation, Humboldt University, East Berlin, 1988, 44.

20. Interview, Dietrich Goldschmidt, Berlin, November 1, 1988.

21. See Marlies Flesch-Thebesius, *Hauptsache Schweigen: Ein Leben unterm Hakenkreuz* (Stuttgart, 1988), for a moving account of her own family's attitudes.

22. Gerlach, *Als die Zeugen schwiegen*, 147.

23. Ludwig, "Die Opfer," 221, note 101.

24. Klepper, *Unter dem Schatten*, 80.

25. Interview, Heinrich Schmidt.

26. World Council of Churches, *Die Evangelische Kirche in Deutschland und die Judenfrage* (Geneva, 1945), 27.

27. Ludwig, "Die Opfer," 12; see, too, 219, note 38

28. Ibid.

29. EZA, KKA, Nr. B19, 123–25

30. Ibid.

31. Interview, Dietrich Goldschmidt.

32. Craig, *Germany*, 579.

33. Bethge, "Kirchenkampf und Antisemitismus," in *Am gegebenen Ort*, 231.

34. EZA, KKA, Nr. 463/16

35. Ludwig, "Die Opfer," 27; see, too, 194, note 6 in Ludwig.

36. Helmreich, *German Churches*, 145–46.

37. Ilse Härter, letter to author, 25.10.89.

38. Interview, Ilse Härter. According to Härter, the Wannsee Presbytery did plan to pursue the matter. Before that happened, she was fired from the parish because she refused to take the Nazi loyalty oath.

39. *Kirche und die Judenfrage* (WCC), 44.

40. Ludwig, "Die Opfer," 47–48.

41. See Gerlach, *Als die Zeugen schwiegen*, 85–86.

42. Ilse Härter, "Ina Gschlössl," in *Junge Kirche*, Heft 11/1988, 609–13.

43. EZA, KKA 636, Marga Meusel, "Denkschrift über die Aufgaben der BK an den evangelische Nichtariern," 4.

44. Ibid., 7.

45. Ludwig, "Die Opfer," 36.

46. Ibid., 34–35.

47. Information from Ilse Härter. See, too, Bethge, *Bonhoeffer*, 838ff.

48. Gerlach, *Als die Zeugen schwiegen*, 61.

49. In his book, Gerlach analyzed the ambivalence in both men's statements. He concluded that a decisive difference between the two was that Bonhoeffer, after his initial uncertainty, opted to try to rescue the Jews first and use this practical step as the point of departure for his theological existence. Gerlach believed Barth did the reverse: He tried to develop a theological foundation as the basis for Christian advocacy for the Jews. See Gerlach, 61, 139ff., and 420.

50. Interview, Eberhard Bethge.

51. Interview, Helmut Gollwitzer.

52. Gerlach, *Als die Zeugen schwiegen*, 200.

53. Ibid., 97 and 101.

54. Wilhelm Niemöller, "Die Synode zu Steglitz," in *Arbeiten zur Geschichte des Kirchenkampfes* (Göttingen, 1972), 83ff.

55. Gerlach, *Als die Zeugen schwiegen*, 157.

56. Ludwig, "Die Opfer," 51.

57. Klepper, *Unter dem Schatten*, 309.

58. Gerlach, *Als die Zeugen schwiegen*, 157.

59. Interview, Dietrich Goldschmidt.

60. Gerlach, *Als die Zeugen schwiegen*, 254–55; see, too, 253, note 20. Higher estimates include "Aryan" pastors with "non-Aryan" wives. Gerlach counts 33 "non-Aryan" pastors.

61. Helmreich, *German Churches*, 148.

62. Gerlach, *Als die Zeugen schwiegen*, 61.

63. Ibid., 68.

64. Klügel, *Landeskirche Hannovers*, 491.

65. LKA, EKvW, 5,1:328:Fasc. 1.

66. LKA, EKvW, 5,1:329:1, letter, 12.9.37.

67. Ibid., letter, 7.5.37.

68. Ehrenberg was arrested on November 1, 1938 — one week before the *Kristallnacht*. In Buchenwald, he had to carry corpses to the crematorium.

69. Interview, "Anton L."

70. Interview, "Gertrud S.," Karlsruhe, January 25, 1984. Speaker wished to remain anonymous.

71. Klepper, *Unter dem Schatten*, 1,032.

72. The Cimada, a French Christian group, helped camp inmates wherever they could. They were able to do this until 1942; after that, they joined the French Resistance and worked to help Jews over the Swiss border.

73. Interview, "Gertrud S."

74. Ibid.

75. Klepper, *Unter dem Schatten*, 330–31.

76. Interview, Dietrich Goldschmidt.

77. Ibid.

78. Gerlach, *Als die Zeugen schwiegen*, 234.

79. Ludwig, "Die Opfer," 82.

80. Gerlach, *Als die Zeugen schwiegen*, 234–35. Other estimates go as high as 35,000.

81. Interview, "Anton L."

82. Interview, "Matthias K."

83. Interview, Helmut Gollwitzer.

84. Interview, Dietrich Goldschmidt.

85. Ibid.

86. Ibid.

87. Ilse Härter, letter to author, 25.10.89.

88. Laura Livingstone, writing in Rudolf Weckerling, ed., *Durchkreuzter Haß* (Berlin, 1961), 43–44.

89. Interview, Dietrich Goldschmidt.

90. Gerlach, *Als die Zeugen schwiegen*, 237.

91. Ibid., 242.

92. Ibid.

93. Interview, Albrecht Schönherr, Bünde, May 29, 1986.

94. Interview, Berta Braune. See, too, Ludwig, "Die Opfer," 84–85 and 213, note 39.

95. Gerlach, *Als die Zeugen schwiegen*, 271ff.

96. The actress Eva Bildt was his fiancée; they did not marry.

97. Interview, Helmut Gollwitzer.

98. Ludwig, "Die Opfer," 107.

99. Ibid., 223, note 116.

100 Ibid., 77.

101. Ibid., 106ff., 119ff.

102. Ibid., 77.

103. Ibid., 102–3.

104. Ibid., 145.

105. Ibid., 127ff.

106. Ibid., 106ff. Ludwig cites East German historian Kurt Pätzold as one proponent of this view; Pätzold argues that Nazi policies toward Jewish emigration cannot be explained otherwise. The contention that the genocide of the Jews was not planned, and evolved under wartime pressure, was a prominent thesis of "revisionist" German historians like Ernst Nolte during the 1980s.

107. Gerlach, *Als die Zeugen schwiegen*, 232.

108. Ibid., 222.

109. Ludwig, "Die Opfer," 112.

110. Ibid. Adolf Freudenberg's estimate (in Weckerling, *Durchgekreuzter Haß*, 72) is 5,000.

111. Interview, Helene Jacobs.

112. Ludwig, "Die Opfer," 147.

113. Interview, Helga Weckerling.

114. Ibid.

115. Interview, Elsie Steck.

116. Interview, Helga Weckerling.

117. Interview, Elsie Steck.

118. Interview, Annemarie Grosch.

119. Interview, Helmut Gollwitzer.

120. Max Krakauer, *Licht im Dunkel* (Stuttgart, 1959).

121. Interview, "Marta S."

122. Interview, Ilse Härter.

123. In the long run, Kaufmann would not have remained unscathed; at the time he began his underground activities, however, many Jews in "privileged" marriages with "Aryans" believed they would escape the worst.

124. Interview, Helene Jacobs.

125. Interview, Gertrud Staewen.

126. Ibid.

127. Interview, Helene Jacobs.

128. Interview, Gertrud Staewen.

129. Ludwig, "Die Opfer," 238, note 231.

130. Heinz Brunotte, "Die Kirchenmitgliedschaft der nichtarischen Christen im Kirchenkampf," in *Zeitschrift für evangelisches Kirchenrecht* (Tübingen, 1968), 159.

131. Ibid.

132. Gerlach, *Als die Zeugen schwiegen*, 327.

133. Ilse Härter, letter to author, 25.10.89

134. Brunotte, "Kirchenmitgliedschaft," 165.

135. EZA, 155b — 71, 22.12.41.

136. Ibid., 172.

137. Ibid., 174.

138. EZA, KKA N. 155b/71, 22.12.41.

139. Ilse Härter, letter to author, 26.4.89.

140. Helene Jacobs, "Als wenn nichts geschehen wäre . . . ," in *Widerstand zur rechten Zeit* (Gesellschaft für christlich-jüdische Zusammenarbeit e.V., Frankfurt, Arbeitshilfe, 1983), 42–48.

141. Interview, Dietrich Goldschmidt.

142. Ibid.

Chapter 8. The War

1. Peter Steinbach, "Der Widerstand als Thema der politischen Zeitgeschichte," in G. Besier and G. Ringshausen, eds., *Bekenntnis, Widerstand Martyrium* (Göttingen, 1986), 69.

2. Gerhard Ringshausen, "Der 20. Juli als Thema des evangelischen Religionsunterrichts im Sekundarstufe I und II," in Besier and Ringshausen, *Bekenntnis*, 364.

3. See Bethge, *Bonhoeffer*, 747ff. See, too, Wilhelm Niemöller's interpretation of his brother's behavior, in his introduction to Martin Niemöller, *Briefe aus der Gefangenschaft* (Frankfurt, 1975), 13–14.

4. Interview, Martin Niemöller.

5. Ibid.

6. Dietrich Bonhoeffer, in E. Bethge, ed., *Gesammelte Schriften*, (Munich, 1958), Band II, 430.

7. Helmreich, *German Churches*, 306–7.

8. Karl Barth said he would be willing to take the oath with this interpretation of it, but he had already been dismissed from the university in Bonn; Helmreich, *German Churches*, 178.

9. Klügel, *Landeskirche Hannovers*, 324.

10. Wilhelm Niemöller, *Kampf und Zeugnis der Bekennende Kirche* (Bielefeld, 1948), 438.

11. Interview, Ilse Härter.

12. Ibid.

13. Klügel, *Landeskirche Hannovers*, 322.

14. Interview, Helmut Gollwitzer.

15. Broszat, *Staat Hitlers*, 432. For more descriptions of the German mood in 1939, see Craig, *Germany*, 732–736, and William Shirer, *The Nightmare Years*, Boston, 1984), 441 and 454.

16. Dibelius, *Ein Christ*, 200.

17. Helmreich, *German Churches*, 307.

18. Ibid.

19. EZA, Best. KKA, Nr. 588.

20. Martin Niemöller, *Briefe aus der Gefangenschaft*, 13–14.

21. Interview, Eberhard Bethge.

22. Ibid.

23. Interview, Albrecht Schönherr.

24. Interview, Heinrich Albertz, Berlin, November 6, 1980.

25. A detailed account of these pressures is given in a Westphalian Confessing Church document, "Der Weg der 'renitenten' Brüder," particularly page 4, LKA, EKvW, 5, 1: 238:1ff.

26. Dibelius, *Ein Christ*, 202–203.

27. Interview, Helmut Gollwitzer.

28. Ibid.

29. Interview, Karl Steck, Bad Homburg, December 8, 1981.

30. Interview, Rudolf Weckerling.

31. Ibid.

32. Interview, Elisabeth Schwarzhaupt.

33. Gerlach, *Als die Zeugen schwiegen*, 283.

34. Interview, Helmut Gollwitzer.

35. Interview, Martin Schröter.

36. The Sunday after the Germans invaded Poland, Poles in the town of Bromberg attacked and killed several German townspeople there. (Bromberg was in the region ceded to Poland after World War I and included residents of both Polish and German ancestry.) The Nazi press inflated the incident as a Polish "massacre" of innocent Germans and used it to justify German behavior in Poland.

37. Interview, Helmut Gollwitzer.

38. Craig, *Germany*, 746.

39. Annedore Leber, *Das Gewissen Entscheidet* (Frankfurt a. M., 1960), 248.

40. Interview, Helmut Gollwitzer.

41. Interview, Herbert Mochalski.

42. Ibid.

43. Interview, Martin Schröter.

44. Ibid.

45. Bethge elaborates on this incident in *Bonhoeffer*, 755. For a deeper study of both the distinctions and the ties between the Waffen-SS and the Wehrmacht, see George Stein, *The Waffen SS* (Ithaca, NY, 1966), 282ff.

46. Bethge, *Bonhoeffer*, 813.

47. Hitler's critics in the Wehrmacht had approached von Brauchitsch several times to convince him to remain as *Oberbefehlshaber* in the event of a coup, and he had finally agreed. When, in December 1942, Hitler dismissed von Brauchitsch and other leading officers after the heavy German losses in Russia, it was a blow to the July 20 conspirators (see Bethge, *Bonhoeffer*, 842ff.). After this, Hitler was commander-in-chief of all the armed forces.

48. Interview, Eberhard Bethge.

49. In Walter and Hans Bähr eds., *Kriegsbriefe gefallener Studenten* (Stuttgart, 1952), 381–82.

50. Hans Dollingers, ed., *Weltgeschichte 1939–1945* (Freiburg, 1989), 111 and 151.

51. It is impossible to get exact figures here for the Confessing Church, particularly because many Confessing pastors who were not Illegals are included in the overall casualty lists of German Protestant pastors. The claim that Confessing Church losses, particularly of Illegals, were proportionately greater remains a logical deduction for which we lack statistics. It is supported by the political realities of the time (see, too, p. 159, note 19, this chapter). When one goes through lists of Illegals, the number killed on the front is striking.

52. Interview, Helmut Gollwitzer.

53. EZA, KKA, Nr. 474/263: letter, 1.9.43; Nr. 474/267: letter, 24.7.43.

54. Interview, Doris Faulhaber.

55. EZA, KKA, Nr. 615/424, 19.12.39.

56. EZA, KKA, Nr. 503/81, "Eingabe," 2.

57. Ibid.

58. Ibid.

59. Interview, Doris Faulhaber.

60. Interview, Helmut Gollwitzer.

61. Interview, Annemarie Grosch.

62. Ibid.

63. Ibid.

64. Ibid.

65. Ibid.

66. Ibid.

67. Telephone conversation with Sieghild Jungklaus, April 1, 1981.

68. Interview, Sieghild Jungklaus, Berlin, February 6, 1986.

69. Interview, Ilse Härter.

70. Interview, Heinrich Vogel.

71. Interview, Ilse Härter.

72. Gerlach, *Als die Zeugen schwiegen*, 349.

73. See Leber, *Das Gewissen Steht Auf*, 174–77.

74. Gerlach, *Als die Zeugen schwiegen*, 349.

75. Ibid.

76. Interview, Christian Berg.

77. Ibid.

78. Interview, Tüsnelda Schröter, Warburg, February 8, 1982.

79. Steck's spontaneous impulse was risky. In 1937, Bavarian Pastor Karl Steinbauer, after removing a Nazi poster in a church room and criticizing the Nazis to his church youth group, was arrested and tried by a Gestapo court. (EZA, Nr. 92; see, too, Hans Prolingheuer's account of Steinbauer's resistance, in *Kleine politische Kirchengeschichte* (Cologne, 1984).

80. Interview, Elsie Steck.

81. Interview, "Luise M."

82. Ibid.

83. Ibid.

84. Interview, Kurt Scharf.

85. Interview, "Marta S."

86. Ibid.

87. Interview, Gerda Keller.

88. Interview, Dietrich Goldschmidt.

89. Hilgemann, *Atlas*, 99.

90. Ibid., 115. After 1945, the International Military Tribunal listed 1,500 concentration and detention camps and institutions. (LKA, EKvW, 5,1: 32: 1 and 2, "Widerstand.")

91. Hilgemann, *Atlas*, 115.

92. Ibid., 119.

93. That is, "privileged" marriages with "Aryans."

94. Interview, Dietrich Goldschmidt.

95. Ibid.

96. Interview, Hebe Kohlbrugge.

97. Ibid.

98. See Stein, *The Waffen-SS*. After the SS's heavy losses in Russia, it began to draft (and, eventually, force) men in the occupied countries into duty. The "Prince Eugene" division (the 7th Waffen-SS division) consisted of Serbian "folk Germans." The SS capitalized on internal tensions in the occupied regions, drafting, for example, thousands of Yugoslavian Moslems who hated Tito's Christian partisans (Stein, 179ff.). By 1945, writes Stein, none of the SS divisions "was exclusively German and at least nineteen consisted largely of foreign personnel" (Stein, 287). As the war proceeded, the Germans transferred more and more able-bodied guards from the concentration camps to the front and replaced them with older SA members, wounded soldiers, and ethnic Germans from occupied territories.

99. Interview, Ernst Wilm. The first SS "Death's Head" unit was formed in 1933 in Dachau by Theodor Eicke, who at that time was simultaneously the head of Dachau and the SS. Part of the SS bureaucracy remained in Dachau until 1945, including, as Wilm recalled, the payments' office.

100. Interview, Emmi Bonhoeffer.

101. From Dietrich Bonhoeffer, *Ethics* (New York, 1965), 242–43.

102. The legacy of Steil and Schneider's work is discussed in Helmut Gollwitzer, *Du has mich heimgesucht bei Nacht* (Munich, 1959). Gusti Steil wrote a memoir about her husband, *Ludwig Steil: Ein Leben in der Nachfolge Jesu* (Bielefeld, undated).

103. Interview, Emmi Bonhoeffer.

104. Interview, Marion Yorck von Wartenburg.

105. All three men were legation counselors in the foreign ministry. According to *The Berlin Diaries of Marie Vassiltschikov* (London, 1985), von Haeften was never in the Nazi party.

106. Interview, Marion Yorck von Wartenburg.

107. Interview, Emmi Bonhoeffer. The Gedenkstätte Deutscher Widerstand Berlin (Stauffenbergstr. 13/14, Berlin) has published a series of booklets about this and other aspects of the resistance. Particularly helpful is booklet number 29, Klaus-Jürgen Muller's "Der deutsche Widerstand und das Ausland." Peter Hoffmann, in *The History of the German Resistance* (Cambridge, MA, 1979), also discusses this.

108. Philosophy Professor Adolf Reichwein's political activities began after 1933 when he became a Social Democrat to protest against Nazism. Theodor Haubach, also a philosopher, had worked in the government press office during the Weimar Republic and spent much of the 1930s in Nazi prisons. Carlo Mierendorff, an active Social Democrat during the Weimar Republic, spent the years between 1933 and 1937 in a concentration camp and joined the German resistance upon his release.

109. In March 1943, Lieutenant Fabian von Schlabrendorff, in a plan developed with several other military leaders, put a bomb on a plane carrying Hitler and several others to the eastern front. The bomb failed to go off. For an account of this and several other failed assassination attempts, see Hoffmann, *History of the German Resistance*.

110. Interview, Eberhard Bethge.

111. See Hoffmann, *History of the German Resistance*, for a detailed account of this.
112. Ibid.
113. Hoffmann, *History of the German Resistance*, 512.
114. Ibid., 516.
115. Marie Vassiltschikov, *The Berlin Diaries*, 234.
116. Interview, Emmi Bonhoeffer.
117. Ibid.
118. Interview, Gertrud Staewen.
119. Interview, Helene Jacobs.
120. Ibid.
121. Ibid.
122. Interview, Annemarie Grosch.
123. Interview, Rudolf Weckerling.
124. Hilgemann, *Atlas*, 171.
125. Interview, Sieghild Jungklaus.
126. Interview, "Marta S."
127. Ibid.
128. Interview, Gerda Keller.
129. Interview, "Friedemann M."
130. Interview, Gertrud Staewen.
131. Interview, Helene Jacobs.
132. Ibid.
133. Interview, Dietrich Goldschmidt.
134. Ibid.
135. Interview, Marion Yorck von Wartenburg.
136. Von Sell became Martin Niemöller's second wife.
137. Interview, Emmi Bonhoeffer.

Chapter 9. Reflections on Resistance

1. Interview, Annemarie Grosch.
2. Interview, Marion Yorck von Wartenburg.
3. Cited in Gerlach, *Als die Zeugen schwiegen*, 378.
4. Ibid.
5. *Die Evangelische Kirche in Deutschland and die Judenfrage: Ausgewählte Dokumente aus den Jahren des Kirchenkampfes 1933 bis 1943* (Geneva, 1945), 196ff.
6. Meiser's words were noted in 1943 by Emil Höchstädter, a member of the Lempsschen group. His son later reconstructed the incident from these notes. Meiser himself apparently kept no record of the meeting or the group's letter to him. Gerlach, *Als die Zeugen schwiegen*, 370.
7. Bonhoeffer, "Die Kirche vor der Judenfrage" (1933), in *Gesammelte Schriften*, Band 2, 45ff.
8. Frederich Spotts, *The Church and Politics in Germany* (Middletown, CT, 1973), 8, note 6.
9. See Hoffmann, *History of the German Resistance*, 371.
10. Interview, Hebe Kohlbrugge.
11. Ibid.
12. Ibid.
13. Bethge, *Bonhoeffer*, 843.

14. Ringshausen, "Der 20. Juli," in Besier and Ringshausen, *Bekenntnis*, 377–79.

15. Interview, Emmi Bonhoeffer.

16. Interview, Marion Yorck von Wartenburg.

17. Ringshausen, "Der 20. Juli," in Besier and Ringshausen, *Bekenntnis*, 367

18. Interview, Elsie Steck.

19. Ibid.

20. Leber, *Das Gewissen Steht Auf*, 202.

21. Dr. Karl Strölin, "Der 20. Juli: Verräter oder Patrioten?" (Stuttgart, 1952), 45.

22. Interview, Hebe Kohlbrugge.

23. Dietrich Bonhoeffer, "Was heißt: Die Wahrheit sagen?" in *Unterwegs*, Heft 6, 1947, 11–15. (Bonhoeffer wrote the essay during his imprisonment in Tegel.)

24. Interview, Annemarie Grosch.

25. Interview, Heinrich Schmidt.

26. EZA, Nachlaß Harder, Nr. 42, "Kirchliche Ereignisse, Nov. 1942–Aug. 1946."

27. Strölin, "Der 20. Juli."

28. Quoted in Besier, "Bekenntnis-Widerstand-Martyrium als historisch Theologische Kategorien," in Besier and Ringshausen, *Bekenntnis,* 138.

29. The differences between the Kreisau Circle and Goerdeler's group are analyzed by Hoffmann, *History of the German Resistance*, 360ff. Adenauer's distrust of Goerdeler and his attitude toward the July 20 conspiracy is mentioned in Terence Prittie, *Konrad Adenauer* (Stuttgart, 1971), 128.

30. Interview, Emmi Bonhoeffer.

31. Leber, *Das Gewissen Steht Auf*, 202. See, too, Gollwitzer, *Du hast mich heimgesucht bei Nacht.*

32. Leber, *Das Gewissen Steht Auf*, 202.

33. Margaret Boveri, *Verzweigungen*, ed. Uwe Johnson (Zurich, 1977).

34. Interview, Emmi Bonhoeffer.

35. Dietrich Bonhoeffer, *Letters and Papers from Prison* (New York, 1972), 3–4.

36. Leber, *Das Gewissen Steht Auf,* 148.

37. Ringshausen, "Der 20. Juli," in Besier and Ringshausen, *Bekenntnis,* 370–71.

Chapter 10. The Guilt of Others

1. Martin Geschat, ed., *Die Schuld der Kirche* (Munich, 1982), 91.

2. Ibid., 100.

3. Ibid., 101.

4. Ibid., 94, 100–101.

5. Ibid., 94.

6. Ibid., 226.

7. Ibid., 243.

8. Ibid., 225–26.

9. Ibid., 136.

10. Dibelius, *Ein Christ*, 311.

11. LKA, EKvW, 5,1:655:1, "Diem, Kirchlichetheologische Sozietät," letter 18.9.46.

12. Greschat, *Schuld der Kirche*, 186.

13. Konrad Adenauer, *Erinnerungen 1945–1953* (Stuttgart, 1965), 32.

14. Helmut Thielicke and Hermann Diem, *Die Schuld der Anderen: Ein Briefwechsel* (Göttingen, 1948), 7.

15. Interview, Helmut Gollwitzer.

16. Interview, "Marta S."

17. Interview, "E.P.," Bremen, March 18, 1982. Speaker wished to remain anonymous.

18. Interview, "Anton L."

19. Interview, Kurt Scharf.

20. Interview, "Matthias K."

21. Interview, Hebe Kohlbrugge.

22. Ibid.

23. Interview, Martin Schröter.

24. Spotts, *Churches and Politics*, 75.

25. Ibid., 53–54.

26. Ibid., 63.

27. Ibid., 59.

28. Ibid., 80.

29. Armin Boyens, "Die Kirchenpolitik der amerikanischen Besatzungsmacht in Deutschland von 1944 bis 1946," in Boyens, A., M. Greschat, R. von Thadden, and P. Pombeni, eds., *Kirchen in der Nachkriegszeit* (Göttingen, 1979), 88.

30. This was true of Catholic and Protestant church leaders. See Spotts, *Churches and Politics*, 62–69, 76ff., and 101ff.

31. Boyens, "Kirchenpolitik," in *Kirchen in der Nachkriegszeit*, 88–89.

32. See Spotts, *Churches and Politics*, Chapters 3 and 4. See, too, Justus Fürstenau, *Entnazifizierung: Ein Kapitel deutscher Nachkriegspolitik* (Berlin, 1969), Chap. 3.

33. Spotts, *Churches and Politics*, 96.

34. Ibid., 99.

35. Interview, Elisabeth Schwarzhaupt.

36. Spotts, *Churches and Politics*, 109.

37. Ibid.

38. Ibid., 111–12.

39. EKD letter to U.S. military government, 26.4.46, in Hermann Diem, ed., *Kirche für die Welt: Kirche und Entnazifizierung* (Stuttgart, 1946), 74.

40. "Denkschrift der kirchlich — theologische Sozietät in Württemberg," in Diem, *Kirche für die Welt*, 37.

41. Ibid., 40.

42. Eberhard Röhm and Jorg Thierfelder, *Evangelische Kirche zwischen Kreuz und Hakenkreuz* (Stuttgart, 1981), 125.

43. "Denkschrift" in Diem, *Kirche für die Welt*, 37–38.

44. EKD letter in Diem, *Kirche für die Welt*, 78–79.

45. Ibid.

46. Spotts, *Churches and Politics*, 61.

47. EKD letter, in Diem, *Kirche für die Welt*, 74.

48. "Denkschrift," in Diem, *Kirche für die Welt*, 26.

49. Spotts, *Churches and Politics*, 97.

50. T. Wurm, M. Niemöller, and Prelate Dr. Hartenstein, eds., "Memorandum by the Evangelical Church of Germany on the Question of War Crimes Trials before American Military Courts," printed and numbered as manuscript, 1949.

51. See Hans Prolingheuer, *Kleine politische Kirchengeschichte* (Cologne, 1984), Chaps. 17 and 18.

52. Wilhelm Niemöller, *Die Evangelische Kirche im Dritten Reich: Handbuch des Kirchenkampfes* (Bielefeld, 1956), 396.

53. Interview, Berta Braune.
54. Interview, Dietrich Goldschmidt.
55. Interview, Helene Jacobs.
56. "Denkschrift," in Diem, *Kirche für die. Welt*, 36.
57. Ibid., 43.
58. Diem and Thielicke, in *Schuld der Anderen*, 17.
59. Interview, Rudolf and Helga Weckerling.
60. In Spotts, *Churches and Politics*, 95.
61. Interview, Wilhelm Niemöller.
62. Fürstenau, *Entnazifizierung*, 227–28.
63. Spotts, *Churches and Politics*, 107.
64. Interview, Helmut Gollwitzer.
65. Spotts, *Churches and Politics*, 304–8.
66. In Diem and Thielicke, *Schuld der Anderen*, 10–11.
67. Ibid., 39.
68. Ibid., 39–41.
69. Ibid., 19.
70. Ibid., 21, 22.
71. The political uses to which this was put are revealed by a letter written to Helmut Thielicke by a former Nazi, who condemned the Evangelical Church for not clarifying the fronts between "God and Satan," both before and after 1945 (when, in this man's opinion, Allied "revanchist" policies revealed Satanic intentions): "the well-intentioned mass of Germans was left to the retinue of satanic powers; that is due to the silence of the church at the time. The confession of this guilt today by the church must lose credibility . . . if the church today continues the cursed silence of those days and doesn't contribute to a current clarification of the fronts between the kingdom of God and the dominion of Satan." From Diem and Thielicke, *Schuld der Anderen*, 34.
72. Interview, Hans Thimme.
73. For the regulations and statutes of limitation declared by the individual German states, see Fürstenau, *Entnazifizierung*, 233–59.
74. Interview, Emmi Bonhoeffer.
75. Interview, Martin and Tüsnelda Schröter.
76. Ralph Giordano, *Die zweite Schuld oder von der Last, Deutscher zu sein* (Hamburg, 1986).
77. Interview, Dietrich Goldschmidt.
78. Quoted in Spotts, *Churches and Politics*, 94.
79. Interview, Helga Weckerling.
80. Interview, "Gertrud S."
81. Incredible as this seems, it is true. Some Polish Jews who subsequently became Israeli citizens have received reparations, but, in general, Jews from Poland and the Soviet Union, as well as forced laborers who were deported to Nazi concentration camps from those countries, did not receive reparations. The Polish and Soviet governments renounced national reparations in the 1950s, and the West German government subsequently rejected individual reparations for citizens of those countries. In the 1953 London treaty, all reparations not provided for by the treaty (such as those described above) were put off until the two German governments could agree on the final postwar Polish-German border—practically, that is, until a reunified greater Germany signed a treaty with Poland declaring the Oder-Neisse border permanent. When that day finally came, it was naturally too late for many of those who suffered in the Nazi camps and never received reparations.

82. Interview, Dietrich Goldschmidt.
83. Interview, Helene Jacobs.
84. Interview, Eberhard Bethge.
85. Interview, Heinrich Vogel.
86. Ibid.
87. Prolingheuer, *Kleine politische Kirchengeschichte*, 114.
88. Ibid., 110–11.
89. *Berlin-Weissensee Synod 1950* (Berlin, 1950), 335.
90. Ibid., 339.
91. Ibid., 357–58.

Chapter 11. Postwar Germans and Their Church

1. New York: Grove Press, 1975.
2. Hannah Arendt, "The Aftermath of Nazi Rule," *Commentary*, October 1950, 10(4):342, 345.
3. This statement has often been attributed to Dibelius; the occasion on which he said it is unclear. It was Dibelius' belief, as he explained in his memoirs, that the threat of Soviet control of Berlin church affairs made it imperative that the postwar EKD be re-established on "existent legal structures," that is, those that had existed up to 1933. (In *Ein Christ*, 207ff.)
4. EZA, KKA, Nr. 588, "Zum Stand des kirchlichen Lebens," Dezember 1944.
5. Bodo Heyne, "Die Innere Mission 1933–1952," in *Kirchliches Jahrbuch 1952*, 377–432.
6. Karl Silex, "Das Hilfswerk der evangelische Kirche in Deutschland," in *Kirchliches Jahrbuch 1945–1948*, 403.
7. Ibid., 411.
8. Interview, Brigitte Möckel, Berlin, January 26, 1982.
9. Ibid.
10. Interview, Emmi Bonhoeffer.
11. Ibid.
12. Ibid.
13. Ibid.
14. Silex, "Das Hilfswerk," 400.
15. Interview, Hans Thimme.
16. Interview, Gerda Keller.
17. Interview, "Anton L."
18. Interview, Annemarie Grosch.
19. Interview, Rudolf Weckerling.
20. *Unterwegs*, Nr. 1, 1947.
21. Spotts, *Churches and Politics*, 120.
22. In *Kirchliches Jahrbuch 1945–1948*, 12.
23. Interview, "E. P."
24. Interview, Rudolf Weckerling.
25. Interview, Heinrich Albertz.
26. Interview, Albrecht Schönherr.
27. Interview, Elsie Steck.
28. Interview, Hans Thimme.

29. See Prolingheuer, *Kleine politische Kirchengeschichte*, Chapter 15, for a description of what Karl Barth sarcastically termed "the hour of the great unrecognized anti-Nazis, confessors, heroes and almost-martyrs."

30. "Der Bruderrat der EKD," in *Kirchliches Jahrbuch 1949*, 76–77.

31. Church president Koch was succeeded by 1948 by Ernst Wilm, the pastor whose protests against euthanasia had put him in Dachau. Wilm's successor in 1969 was Hans Thimme, who was followed in 1977 by Heinrich Reiß, who had been an illegal vicar in the Confessing Church.

32. Hey, *Kirchenprovinz Westfalen*, 189ff.

33. Interview, Hans Thimme.

34. Ibid.

35. Spotts, *Churches and Politics*, 109–16.

36. Reinhard Scheerer, *Evangelische Kirche und Politik 1945–1949* (Cologne, 1981), 323, note 84.

37. Ibid., 143. Iwand charged that, in some instances, these "German Christians" even tried "old style" methods of censoring the sermons of Confessing Christians under their jurisdiction. "Everyone who attempts to work here on the inner transformation of the church," complained Iwand, "is being hampered in his effectiveness."

38. Interview, Martin Fischer.

39. Interview, Wilhelm Niemöller.

40. Interview, Kurt Scharf.

41. Interview, Doris Faulhaber.

42. Interview, Annemarie Grosch.

43. Interview, Doris Faulhaber.

44. Interview, Marion Yorck von Wartenburg.

45. Interview, Gertrud Staewen.

Chapter 12. Political Developments and the East German Church

1. Interview, "Luise M."

2. Ibid.

3. Interview, "E. P."

4. Interview, Albrecht Schönherr.

5. Gustav Heinemann, *Glaubensfreiheit-Bürgerfreiheit: Reden and Aufsätze zu Kirche-Staat-Gesellschaft 1945–1975* (Frankfurt, 1976), 72.

6. Ibid., 72–73.

7. Interview, Kurt Scharf.

8. Ibid.

9. Ibid.

10. Ibid.

11. Ibid.

12. Interview, Sieghild Jungklaus.

13. Interview, Kurt Scharf.

14. Heinemann, *Glaubensfreiheit*, 211.

15. Press Release, Evangelische Pressedienst, May 1977.

16. Interview, Martin Fischer.

17. Kinder and Hilgemann, *Atlas zur Weltgeschichte*, 250.

18. Interview, Albrecht Schönherr.

19. Interview, "Friedemann M." This interview, like all others, was conducted before the changes after the autumn of 1989.

20. Interview, "Luise M."

21. Interview, Martin Fischer.

22. Interview, Kurt Scharf.

23. Kinder and Hilgemann, *Atlas zur Weltgeschichte*, 255.

24. Interview, Kurt Scharf.

25. Interview, Martin Fischer.

26. Interview, Liselotte Lawerenz, Berlin, November 4, 1981.

27. Interview, Kurt Scharf.

28. Interview, Albrecht Schönherr.

29. Ibid.

30. Fred Mahlburg, "Die Rolle der Kirche im Aufbruch der DDR," in *Junge Kirche*, 4/90, 229.

31. Ibid., 229.

32. Ibid., 230.

Chapter 13. Political Issues and the West German Church

1. LKA, EKvW, Best. 5,1, Nr. 685: Fasc. 1, Memorandum, 31.1.50.

2. Interview, Martin Schröter.

3. Karl Barth, *Die Kirche zwischen Ost und West* (Zurich, 1949).

4. Spotts, *Churches and Politics*, 240.

5. Prolingheuer, *Kleine politische Kirchengeschichte*, 112.

6. Interview, Herbert Mochalski.

7. Interview, Elisabeth Schwarzhaupt.

8. Interview, "Luise M."

9. Ibid.

10. Interview, Helmut Gollwitzer.

11. Interview, Eberhard Bethge.

12. Spotts, *Churches and Politics*, 245. Niemöller was no less vituperative, describing the Federal Republic as "conceived in the Vatican and born in Washington." This remark illustrates Niemöller's resentment of U.S. influence and what he perceived as conservative Catholic control (Adenauer was Catholic) of German affairs. Niemöller was not entirely anti-Catholic; at one point in Dachau, he had even considered converting. His attitude toward "Catholic politics" reflects the fact that voting patterns in Germany, even today, often follow sectarian lines, with Catholics tending to vote CDU and Protestants SPD. See Spotts, Chapters 11 and 12.

13. The political position of the more radical members of the Confessing Church kept them out of the Social Democrats (SPD) as well, or on its left wing. Very few Confessing Church radicals actually joined either party; one exception was Ernst Wilm, who joined the SPD at the height of the peace movement in the 1980s.

14. Rudolf von Thadden, "Bonhoeffer und der Nachkriegsprotestantismus," in Boyens, A., M. Groschat, R. von Thadden, and P. Pomberi, *Kirchen in der Nachkriegszeit. Vier zeit-geochichtliche Beiträge* (Göttingen, 1979), 127.

15. Spotts, *Churches and Politics*, 126.

16. Interview, "Marta S."

17. Interview, Stefanie von Mackensen.

18. Heinemann, *Glaubensfreiheit*, 153–58.

19. Interview, Heinrich Albertz.

20. Interview, Elisabeth Schwarzhaupt.

21. Eugen Gerstenmaier, *Neuer Nationalismus*? (Stuttgart, 1965), 87–88.

22. Andreas Lindt, "Kirchenkampf und Widerstand als Themen der kirchliche Zeit-geschichte," in Besier and Ringshausen, *Bekenntnis*, 75–76.

23. Ibid.

24. See Lindt's essay; also Prolingheuer, *Kleine politische Kirchengeschichte*.

25. Interview, Hebe Kohlbrugge.

26. Interview, Heinrich Vogel.

27. Interview, Marion Yorck von Wartenburg.

Chapter 14. Christian Faith and Political Vision in Germany

1. Interview, Martin Fischer.

2. Interview, Brigitte Möckel.

3. Interview, Martin Schröter.

4. Interview, Helmut Gollwitzer.

5. LKA, EKvW, 5,1: 685:1, "Diem, Kirchliche-theologische Sozietät, 1946."

6. Interview, Erika Dalichow, Berlin, January 15, 1982.

7. Dibelius, *Reden-Briefe 1953–1967* (Zurich, 1970), 155–56.

8. Interview, Elisabeth Schwarzhaupt.

9. Ibid.

10. Cited in *Junge Kirche*, 1968, 364.

11. Martin Greschat, "Kirche und Öffentlichkeit," in Boyens et al., *Kirchen in der Nachkriegszeit*, 124. The Mitscherlichs also discussed this issue in their book, *Die Unfähigkeit zu Trauern*.

12. Cited in *Junge Kirche*, 1976, 320–21.

13. Ibid.

14. Interview, Eberhard Bethge.

15. Interview, Heinrich Albertz.

16. Interview, Helmut Gollwitzer.

17. Gollwitzer, "Die Weltbedeutung des Judentums," in *Juden-Christen-Deutsche* (Stuttgart, 1961), 77.

18. Moltmann, *The Way of Jesus Christ* (San Francisco, CA, 1990), 31.

19. Ibid.

20. Radford Reuther, *Faith and Fratricide* (New York, 1979), 257.

21. See the collection of essays by Jewish and Christian thinkers in *Juden-Christen-Deutsche* for the early examples of Germans who wrestled with this issue. But the real break comes in Friedrich-Wilhelm Marquardt's work.

22. Albrecht Goes, "Schmerzhafte Liebe," in *Das Judentum lebt: Ich bin ihm begegnet* (Freiburg, 1985), 62.

23. Interview, Annemarie Grosch.

24. Gerlach, *Als die Zeugen schwiegan*, 376.

25. The political "symptoms" of this were fairly widespread in postwar Germany: the denial of anti-Semitism, the denial of individual responsibility for what had happened under Nazism, the "we did what we could" rationalizations, even the surprising number of Germans who contended that the sufferings of ethnic Germans under the Soviet occupation had equaled,

or even surpassed, those of the Jews under Hitler. These attitudes relegated the significance of the concentration camps to being an almost accidental injustice of wartime, and fueled the historians' debate in the 1980s.

26. Judith Miller's book, *One by One by One* (New York, 1990) examines this some. Henryk Broder's work, particularly *Der ewige Antisemit* (Frankfurt, 1986), is a polemical example of this.

27. Interview, Helene Jacobs.

Chapter 15. Faith and the Fatherland

1. Dibelius, *Ein Christ*, 7.
2. Interview, "Marta S."
3. Interview, Stefanie von Mackensen.
4. Interview, Elisabeth Grauer.
5. Interview, Hans Thimme.
6. Telephone interview with author, February 1990.
7. Richard von Weiszäcker, speech given in Jerusalem, 1985.
8. Interview, Ernst Wilm.
9. Interview, Dietrich Goldschmidt.
10. Interview, Eberhard Bethge.
11. Interview, Marion Yorck von Wartenburg.
12. Interview, Elisabeth Schwarzhaupt.
13. Interview, Rudolf and Helga Weckerling.
14. Interview, Herbert Mochalski.
15. Interview, Martin and Tüsnelda Schröter.
16. Ibid.
17. Ibid.
18. Interview, Emmi Bonhoeffer.
19. Interview, Berta Braune.
20. Interview, Helene Jacobs.
21. Interview, Stefanie von Mackensen.
22. Interview, Marion Yorck von Wartenburg.
23. Ibid.
24. Interview, Heinrich Vogel.
25. Ibid.
26. Interview, Martin Niemöller.
27. Ibid.
28. Interview, Eberhard Bethge.

Sources and Bibliography

Archival material cited in the text appears in the Notes. Other archival material, although helpful in deepening my understanding of the era, is too numerous to list here. In addition, many persons interviewed for this book furnished me with letters and documents from the era of the Third Reich. These were helpful in reconstructing some incidents and giving a general impression of the atmosphere of those times, but they are not listed here. This bibliography includes only works actually cited in the book or works that were particularly valuable in deepening my insight into this history.

I. Interviews Conducted by Author

Albertz, Heinrich. Berlin, November 6, 1980
"R. A." Hamburg, August 27, 1980
Barutzky, Helmut. Dortmund, July 1979
Berg, Christian. Berlin, January 13, 1982
Berli, Liselotte. Berlin, January 26, 1982
Bethge, Eberhard. Bad Godesberg, November 12, 1985
Bonhoeffer, Emmi. Düsseldorf, May 16, 1986
Braune, Berta. Bielefeld, February 13, 1986
Dalichow, Erika. Berlin, January 15, 1982
Döring, Lotte. Göttingen, February 10, 1986
Faulhaber, Doris. Mannheim, January 25, 1984
Fischer, Martin. Berlin, November 5, 1980
Flender, Wilhelm. Wuppertal, April 13, 1981
Goldschmidt, Dietrich. Berlin, November 1, 1988
Gollwitzer, Helmut. Berlin, November 6, 1980
Grauer, Elisabeth. Göttingen, February 9, 1982
Grosch, Annemarie. Neumünster, December 31, 1980
Härter, Ilse. Goch, December 3, 1981
Jacobs, Helene. Berlin, February 3, 1986
Jungklaus, Sieghild. Berlin, April 1, 1981 (telephone) and February 6, 1986 (in person)
Keller, Gerda. Dortmund, February 20, 1980
Koch, Werner. Emlichheim, May 15–16, 1981
Kohlbrugge, Hebe. Utrecht, February 24, 1982

"Matthias K." Frankfurt, December 6, 1981
"Anton L." Berlin, January 15, 1982
Lawerenz, Liselotte. Berlin, November 4, 1981 and January 25, 1984
von Mackensen, Stefanie. Iserlohn, April 2, 1984
Mochalski, Herbert. Kronberg-Oberhöchstadt, December 10, 1981
Möckel, Brigitte. Berlin, January 26, 1982
"Friedemann M." East Berlin, August 1980
"L. M." (Luise M.) Bremerhaven, March 5, 1982
Niemöller, Martin. Wiesbaden, December 9, 1981
Niemöller, Wilhelm. Bielefeld, March 9, 1982
Perels, Otto. Berlin, November 4, 1980
"E. P." Bremen, March 18, 1982
Rutenborn, Angelika. Berlin, January 24, 1982
Scharf, Kurt. Berlin, August 6, 1981 and November 5, 1981
Schmidt, Heinrich. Dortmund, July 18, 1979
Schönherr, Albrecht. Bünde, May 29, 1986
Schröter, Martin and Tüsnelda. Warburg, February 8, 1982
Schwarzhaupt, Elisabeth. Frankfurt, June 6, 1986
Staewen, Gertrud. Berlin, January 27, 1982
Steck, Elsie and Karl. Bad Homburg, December 8, 1981
"Marta S." Bremen, March 18, 1982
"Gertrud S." Karlsruhe, January 25, 1984
Thimme, Hans. Babenhausen, May 26, 1988
Vogel, Heinrich. Berlin, January 25, 1982
Weckerling, Helga and Rudolf. Berlin, January 21, 1982 and February 5, 1986
Wilm, Ernst. Espelkamp, March 11, 1982
Yorck von Wartenburg, Marion. Berlin, February 5, 1982.

Books and Articles

Adenauer, Konrad. *Erinnerungen 1945–1952*. Stuttgart: Deutsche-Verlags-Anstalt, 1965.
Arendt, Hannah. "Aftermath of Nazi Rule, The" *Commentary*, October 1950, 10(4):342–53.
Bähr, Walter, and Hans Bähr. *Kriegsbriefe gefallener Studenten*. Tübingen: Rainer Wunderlich Verlag, 1952.
Barth, Karl. *Die Kirche zwischen Ost und West*. Zurich: Evangelisches Verlagshaus, 1949.
Bentley, James. *Martin Niemöller: Eine Biographie*. Karl Heinz Siber, trans. Munich: Beck, 1985. Originally published as *Martin Niemöller* (Oxford: Oxford University Press, 1984).
Bergschicker, Heinz, ed. *Deutsche Chronik 1933–1945: Alltag im Faschismus*. Berlin: Elefanten Press, 1983.
Besier, Gerhard, and Gerhard Ringshausen, eds. *Bekenntnis, Widerstand, Martyrium: Vom Barmen 1934 bis Plötzensee 1944*. Göttingen: Vandenhoeck & Ruprecht, 1986
Bethel Arbeitsheft 1. "Bethel in den Jahren 1939–1943: Eine Dokumentation zur Vernichtung lebensunwerten Lebens." Anneliese Hochmuth, ed. Bethel, 1970.
Bethel Arbeitsheft 2. "Bethel 1867–1972: Werden und Wachsen." Bethel, 1973.
Bethge, Eberhard. *Dietrich Bonhoeffer. Theologe-Christ-Zeitgenosse*. Munich: Christian Kaiser Verlag, 1967.
———. *Dietrich Bonhoeffer: Man of Vision, Man of Courage*. Translated from the German by

Eric Mosbacher (and others) under the editorship of Edwin Robertson. New York: Harper & Row, 1970.

———. *Bonhoeffer: Exile and Martyr*. New York: Seaburg Press, 1975.

———. *Am gegebenen Ort: Aufsätze und Reden*. Munich: Christian Kaiser Verlag, 1979.

Bielenberg, Christabel. *The Past Is Myself*. London: Chatto & Windus, 1968.

Boberach, Heinz, ed. *Berichte des SD und der Gestapo über Kirchen und Kirchenvolk in Deutschland, 1934–1944*. Mainz: Matthias-Grünewald Verlag, 1971.

Bonhoeffer, Dietrich. *Gesammelte Schriften*. Eberhard Bethge, ed. 4 vols. Munich: Christian Kaiser Verlag, 1958–1961.

———. *Ethics*. Neville Horton Smith, trans. New York: Macmillan, 1965.

———. *Letters and Papers from Prison*. R. Fuller, F. Clark, and J. Bowden, trans. New York: Macmillan, 1972.

Boyens, A., M. Greschat, R. von Thadden, and P. Pombeni. *Kirchen in der Nachkriegszeit. Vier zeitgeschichtliche Beiträge*. Arbeiten zur kirchlichen Zeitgeschichte, Reihe B: Band 8. Göttingen: Vandenhoeck & Ruprecht, 1979.

Braune, Berta. *Hoffnung gegen die Not. Mein Leben mit Paul Braune 1932–1954*. Wuppertal: Brockhaus Verlag, 1983.

Broch, Hermann. "The Atonement." In George E. Wellwarth, ed. *German Drama between the Wars*. New York: Dutton, 1974.

Broszat, Martin. *Der Staat Hitlers*. Munich: Deutscher Taschenbuch Verlag, 1969.

Brunotte, Heinz. "Die Kirchenmitgliedschaft der nichtarischen Christen im Kirchenkampf." In *Zeitschrift für evangelisches Kirchenrecht*, 13. Band 1967/68. Tübingen: 1968, 140–74.

Conway, John. *The Nazi Persecution of the Churches*. New York: Basic Books, 1968.

Craig, Gordon A. *Germany 1866–1945*. New York: Oxford University Press, 1978.

Dahm, Karl-Wilhelm. *Pfarrer und Politik: Soziale Position und politische Mentalität des deutschen evangelischen Pfarrerstandes zwischen 1918 und 1933*. Cologne: Westdeutscher Verlag, 1965.

Dibelius, Otto. *Ein Christ ist immer in Dienst*. Stuttgart: Kreuz-Verlag, 1961.

Diem, Hermann, ed. *Kirche für die Welt: Kirche und Entnazifizierung*. Stuttgart: W. Kohlhammer Verlag, 1946.

———, and Helmut Thielicke. *Die Schuld der Anderen: Ein Briefwechsel zwischen Helmut Thielicke und Hermann Diem*. Göttingen: Vandenhoeck & Ruprecht, 1948.

Drobisch, Klaus, and Gerhard Fischer. *Widerstand aus Glauben: Christen in der Auseinandersetzung mit dem Hitlerfaschismus*. East Berlin: Union Verlag, 1985.

Duncan-Jones, A. S. *The Struggle for Religious Freedom in Germany*. London: Victor Gollancz, 1938.

Ericksen, Robert P. *Theologians under Hitler*. New Haven, CT: Yale University Press, 1985.

Evangelischer Pressedienst. "Als die Synagogen brannten. . . ." EPD Dokumentation, Nr. 45–46/78, Frankfurt am Main, 23 Oktober 1978.

EKD, Council of. *Memorandum by the Evangelical Church in Germany on the Question of War Crimes Trials before American Military Courts*. Printed and numbered as manscript, 1949. Copy available in the Landeskirchliche Bibliothek, Bielefeld.

EKD, Innere Mission und Hilfswerk. *Evangelische Dokumente zur Ermordung der "unheilbar Kranken" unter der nationalsozialistischen Herrschaft in den Jahren 1939–1945*. Hans Christoph von Hase, ed. Stuttgart: 1964.

EKD Kirchenkanzlei, Berlin. *Berlin-Weissensee Synod 1950*. (Report and minutes of the synod.)

Fischer, Martin. *Geschichte in Gestalten*. Stuttgart: J. F. Steinkopf Verlag, 1975.

Fleischhauer, Ingeborg. *Der Widerstand gegen den Rußlandfeldzug.* Berlin: Gedenkstätte Deutscher Widerstand, 1987.

Flesch-Thebesius, Marlies. *Hauptsache Schweigen: Ein Leben unterm Hakenkreuz.* Stuttgart: Radius Verlag, 1988.

Fried, Erich. *Um Klarheit: Gedichte gegen das Vergessen.* Berlin: Verlag Klaus Wagenbach, 1985.

Fürstenau, Justus. *Entnazifizierung. Ein Kapitel deutscher Nachkriegspolitik.* Berlin: Luchterhand, 1969.

Gerlach, Wolfgang. *Als die Zeugen schwiegen: Bekennende Kirche und die Juden.* Berlin: Institut Kirche und Judentum, 1987.

Gerstenmaier, Eugen, ed. *Kirche, Volk und Staat.* Berlin: Furche Verlag, 1937.

——. *Neuer Nationalismus?* Stuttgart: Deutsche Verlags-Anstalt, 1965.

Gollwitzer, Helmut. *Du hast mich heimgesucht bei Nacht. Abschiedsbriefe und Aufzeichnungen des Widerstandes 1933–1945.* Munich: Christian Kaiser Verlag, 1954.

Greiffenhagen, Martin. *Pfarrerskinder. Autobiographisches zu einem protestantischen Thema.* Stuttgart: Kreuz Verlag, 1982.

Greschat, Martin, ed. *Die Schuld der Kirche. Dokumente und Reflexionen zur Stuttgarter Schulderklärung vom 18./19. Oktober 1945.* Munich: Christian Kaiser Verlag, 1982.

Haffner, Sebastian. *Anmerkungen zu Hitler.* Munich: Kindler Verlag, 1978.

Harder, Günther, and Wilhelm Niemöller. *Die Stunde der Versuchung. Gemeinden im Kirchenkampf 1933–1945.* Munich: Kaiser Verlag, 1963.

Harenberg, Bodo, ed. *Chronik des 20. Jahrhunderts.* Dortmund: Chronik, 1990.

Heinemann, Gustav. *Glaubensfreiheit-Bürgerfreiheit. Reden und Aufsätze zu Kirche-Staat-Gesellschaft 1945–1975.* Frankfurt: Suhrkamp Verlag, 1976.

Helmreich, Ernst Christian. *The German Churches under Hitler. Background, Struggle and Epilogue.* Detroit, MI: Wayne State University Press, 1979.

Henkys, Reinhard. *Bund der Evangelischen Kirchen in der DDR. Dokumente zu seiner Entstehung.* Witten/Frankfurt: 1970.

Hey, Bernd. *Die Kirchenprovinz Westfalen 1933–1945. Beiträge zur Westfälischen Kirchengeschichte*, Band 2. Bielefeld: Luther Verlag, 1974.

Hilgemann, Werner. *Atlas zur deutschen Zeitgschichte 1918–1968.* Munich: Piper Verlag, 1984.

Hoffman, Peter. *The History of the German Resistance 1933–1945.* Richard Barry, trans. Cambridge, MA: MIT Press, 1979 (reprint). Originally published as *Widerstand, Staatsstreich, Attentat* (Munich, Piper Verlag, 1969).

Institut Kirche und Judentum. *Juden in Deutschland. Zur Geschichte einer Hoffnung.* Berlin, 1980.

Jacobs, Helene. "Als wenn nichts geschehen wäre. . . ." In *Widerstehen zur rechten Zeit.* Frankfurt: Gesellschaften für christlich-jüdische Zusammenarbeit, 1983.

Just-Dahlmann, Barbara. *Simon.* Stuttgart: Radius Verlag, 1980.

Kinder, Hermann, and Werner Hilgemann, *Atlas zur Weltgeschichte.* Munich: Piper Verlag, 1982.

Kirchliches Jahrbuch, 1945–. Gütersloh: Bertelsmann Verlag.

Klee, Ernst. *"Euthanasie" im NS-Staat. Die "Vernichtung lebensunwerten Lebens."* Frankfurt am Main: Fischer Taschenbuch Verlag, 1985.

Klepper, Jochen. *Unter dem Schatten Deiner Flügel. Aus den Tagebüchern 1932–1942.* Stuttgart: Deutsche Verlags-Anstalt, 1956.

Klotz, Leopold, ed. *Die Kirche und das Dritte Reich, Fragen und Forderungen deutscher Theologen.* Gotha: Leopold Klotz Verlag, 1932.

Klügel, Eberhard. *Die lutherische Landeskirche Hannovers und ihr Bischof 1933–1945.* Berlin and Hamburg: Lutherisches Verlagshaus, 1965.

Koch, Hans-Gerhard. *Staat und Kirche in der DDR. Zur Entwicklung ihrer Beziehungen 1945–1974.* Stuttgart: Quell Verlag, 1975.

Koch, Werner. *Heinemann im Dritten Reich. Ein Christ lebt für Morgen.* Wuppertal: Aussaat Verlag, 1972.

———. *Der Kampf der Bekennenden Kirche im Dritten Reich.* Berlin: Gedenkstätte Deutscher Widerstand, 1974.

Kogon, Eugen. *Der SS-Staat: Das System der deutschen Konzentrationslager.* Frankfurt am Main: S. Fischer Verlag, 1983.

Krusche, Werner. *Schuld und Vergebung. Der Grund christlichen Friedenshandelns.* Berlin: Aktion Sühnezeichen, 1984.

Laquer, Walter. *The Terrible Secret. Suppression of the Truth about Hitler's "Final Solution."* 1981. New York: Penguin Books, 1982 (reprint).

Leber, Annedore. *Das Gewissen Entscheidet.* Frankfurt am Main: Büchergilde Gutenberg, 1960.

———. *Das Gewissen Steht Auf. 64 Lebensbilder aus dem deutschen Widerstand 1933–1945.* Frankfurt am Main: Büchergilde Gutenberg, 1960.

Lilje, Hanns. *Memorabilia. Schwerpunkt eines Lebens.* Nuremberg: Laetare Verlag, 1973.

Littell, Franklin Hamlin. *The German Phoenix. Men and Movement in the Church in Germany.* New York: Doubleday, 1960.

Ludwig, Hartmut. "Die Opfer unter dem Rad verbinden. Vor- und Entstehungsgeschichte, Arbeit und Mitarbeiter des 'Büro Pfarrer Grüber.'" Ph.D. dissertation, Humboldt University, East Berlin, 1988.

Mahlberg, Fred. "Die Rolle der Kirche im Aufbruch der DDR," *Junge Kirche,* 4/90, 228–31.

Mann, Golo. *Deutsche Geschichte des XX. Jahrhunderts.* Frankfurt am Main: Büchergilde Gutenberg, 1958.

Meier, Kurt. *Die Deutsche Christen, Das Bild einer Bewegung im Kirchenkampf des Dritten Reiches.* Göttingen: Vandenhoeck & Ruprecht, 1964.

Mitscherlich, Alexander and Margarete. *Die Unfähigkeit zu trauern.* Munich: Piper Verlag, 1967.

Moltmann, Jürgen. *The Way of Jesus Christ: Christology in Messianic Dimensions.* San Francisco, CA: HarperCollins, 1990.

Mommsen, Hans. "Der 20. Juli und die deutsche Arbeiterbewegung." Berlin: Gedenkstätte Deutscher Widerstand, 1985.

Müller, Klaus-Jürgen. *Der deutsche Widerstand und das Ausland.* Berlin: Gedenkstätte Deutscher Widerstand, 1986.

Niemöller, Martin. *Vom U-Boot zur Kanzel.* Berlin: Martin Warneck Verlag, 1934.

———. *Briefe aus der Gefangenschaft.* Wilhelm Niemöller, ed. Frankfurt am Main: Lembeck Verlag, 1975.

———. *Dahlemer Predigten 1936/1937.* Munich: Kaiser Verlag, 1981.

Niemöller, Wilhelm. *Kampf und Zeugnis der Bekennenden Kirche.* Bielefeld: Ludwig Bechauf Verlag, 1948.

———. *Der Pfarrernotbund: Geschichte einer kämpfenden Bruderschaft.* Hamburg, 1973.

———. *Die Synode zu Steglitz.* Göttingen: Vandenhoeck & Ruprecht, 1970.

van Norden, Günther. *Der deutsche Protestantismus im Jahr der nationalsozialistische Machtergreifung.* Gütersloh: Gerd Mohn, 1979.

Palmer, Alan. *The Kaiser.* London: Weidenfeld & Nicolson, 1978.

Paulsen, Anna. *Amt und Auftrag der Theologin.* Gelnhausen: Burckhardthaus Verlag, 1963.

Poelchau, Harald. *Die Ordnung der Bedrängten*. Berlin: Käthe Vogt, 1963.

Prittie, Terence. *Konrad Adenauer: Vier Epoche deutscher Geschichte*. Stuttgart: Goverts Krüger Stahlberg, 1971. Helmut Jaesrich, trans. Originally published as *Adenauer* (London: Tom Stacey Ltd., 1970).

Prolingheuer, Hans. *Kleine politische Kirchengeschichte. 50 Jahre evangelischer Kirchenkampf*. Cologne: Pahl-Rugenstein, 1985.

Röhm, Eberhard, and Jörg Thierfelder. *Evangelische Kirche zwischen Kreuz and Hakenkreuz*. (Documentation and commentary for an exhibit of the same title, sponsored by the EKD.) Stuttgart: Calwer Verlag, 1981.

Rosenberg, Alfred. *Der Mythus des 20. Jahrhunderts: Eine Wertung der seelisch-geistigen Gestaltenkämpfe unserer Zeit*. Munich, 1930.

Rürup, Reinhard. *Topographie des Terrors. Gestapo, SS und Reichssicherheitshauptamt auf dem "Prinz-Albrecht-Gelände."* (Documentation for the exhibition of the same title at the Martin-Gropius-Bau, Berlin). Berlin: Willmuth Arenhövel, 1987.

Scharf, Kurt. *Für ein politisches Gewissen der Kirche. Aus Reden and Schriften 1932–1972*. Stuttgart: J. F. Steinkopf Verlag, 1972.

Scheerer, Reinhard. *Evangelische Kirche and Politik 1945 bis 1949*. Cologne: Pahl-Rugenstein Verlag, 1981.

Schoeps, Hans Joachim. *Wir Deutschen Juden*. Berlin: Vortrupp Verlag, 1934.

Scholder, Klaus. *Die Kirche und das Dritte Reich*. Vol. 1, *Vorgeschichte und Zeit der Illusionen, 1918–1934* . Stuttgart, 1972. Vol. 2, *Das Jahr der Ernüchterung. 1934: Barmen and Rom*. Berlin: Siedler Verlag, 1985.

Schultz, Hans-Jürgen, ed. *Juden-Christen-Deutsche*. Stuttgart: Kreuz Verlag, 1961.

See, Wolfgang, and Rudolf Weckerling. *Frauen im Kirchenkampf. Beispiele aus der Bekennenden Kirche Berlin-Brandenburg 1933 bis 1945*. Berlin: Wichern-Verlag, 1984.

Shirer, William L. *The Nightmare Years: 1930–1940*. Boston, MA: Little, Brown, 1984.

Siegele-Wenschkewitz, Leonore. *Nationalsozialismus und Kirchen: Religionspolitik von Partei and Staat bis 1935*. Düsseldorf: Droste Verlag, 1974.

Spotts, Frederic. *The Churches and Politics in Germany*. Middletown, CT: Wesleyan University Press, 1973.

Steil, Gusti. *Ludwig Steil. Ein Leben in der Nachfolge Jesu*. Bielefeld: Ludwig Bechauf Verlag, undated.

Stein, George. *The Waffen SS*. Ithaca, NY: Cornell University Press, 1966.

Ueberschär, Gerd R. *Das Dilemma der deutschen Militäropposition*. Berlin: Gedenkstätte Deutscher Widerstand, 1988.

Unterwegs. Berlin, monthly, 1947–1949.

Vassiltchikov, Marie. *The Berlin Diaries 1940–1945 of Marie "Missie" Vassiltchikov*. 1985. London: Methuen London Ltd., 1987 (reprint).

Vogel, Rolf, ed. *Deutschlands Weg nach Israel. Eine Dokumentation*. Stuttgart: Seewald Verlag, 1967.

Walter, Rudolf, ed. *Das Judentum lebt: Ich bin ihm begegnet*. Freiburg: Herder, 1985.

Weckerling, Rudolf, ed. *Durchkreuzter Haß*. Berlin: Käthe Vogt Verlag, 1961.

Wilm, Ernst. "Dachau. Bericht auf der Gemeindeversammlung Sonntag, den 28. Oktober 1945 in der evangelischen Kirche zu Mennighüffen." Dortmund-Hombruch: Evangelischen Vortragsdienst.

——. *So sind wir nun Botschafter*. Witten: Luther Verlag, 1953.

——. *Die Bekennende Gemeinde in Mennighüffen*. Bielefeld/Bethel: Verlagshandlung der Anstalt Bethel, 1957.

World Council of Churches. *Die Evangelische Kirche in Deutschland und die Judenfrage: Ausgewählte Dokumente aus den Jahren des Kirchenkampfes 1933 bis 1943.* Geneva: Oikumene Verlag, 1945.

Wurm, D. Theophil. *Erinnerungen aus meinem Leben.* Stuttgart: Quell-Verlag, 1953.

Yorck von Wartenburg, Marion. *Die Stärke der Stille. Erzählung eines Lebens aus dem deutschen Widerstand.* Cologne: Eugen Diederichs Verlag, 1984.

Zilleßen, Horst. *Volk-Nation-Vaterland, Der deutsche Protestantismus und der Nationalsozialismus.* Gütersloh: Gerd Möhn, 1970.

Index